Invisible Labor

University of California Press, one of the most
distinguished university presses in the United States,
enriches lives around the world by advancing scholarship
in the humanities, social sciences, and natural sciences. Its
activities are supported by the UC Press Foundation and
by philanthropic contributions from individuals and
institutions. For more information, visit www.ucpress.edu.

University of California Press
Oakland, California

Library of Congress Cataloging-in-Publication Data

Names: Crain, Marion G., editor. | Poster, Winifred R.,
editor. | Cherry, Miriam A., editor.
Title: Invisible labor : hidden work in the
contemporary world / edited by Marion G. Crain,
Winifred R. Poster, Miriam A. Cherry.
Description: Oakland, California : University of
California Press, [2016] | Includes bibliographical
references and index.
Identifiers: LCCN 2015039590| ISBN 9780520286405
(cloth : alk. paper) | ISBN 9780520287174 (pbk. : alk.
paper) | ISBN 9780520961630 (ebook)
Subjects: LCSH: Work. | Labor. | Work environment.
Classification: LCC HD4855 .I58 2016 | DDC 331—dc23
LC record available at http://lccn.loc.gov/2015039590

Manufactured in the United States of America

25 24 23 22 21 20 19 18 17 16
10 9 8 7 6 5 4 3 2 1

In keeping with a commitment to support
environmentally responsible and sustainable printing
practices, UC Press has printed this book on Natures
Natural, a fiber that contains 30% post-consumer waste
and meets the minimum requirements of ANSI/NISO
Z39.48–1992 (R 1997) (Permanence of Paper).

Contents

Acknowledgments

In February of 2013, the editors organized a colloquium entitled "Invisible Labor" at Washington University School of Law in St. Louis, sponsored by the School of Law's Center for the Interdisciplinary Study of Work and Social Capital. Professor Arlie Russell Hochschild led off with a public lecture, "The Outsourced Self: Intimate Life in Market Times," delivered as part of Washington University School of Law's Public Interest Law and Policy Speakers Series. A group of scholars then gathered to explore the shifting boundaries between market work and leisure, economic coercion and choice, embodied and disembodied labor, and the commercial and the social. The ensuing dialogue traced the process of the marketization of traditionally unpaid activities and the opposing process of the transfer of work from paid to unpaid workers. The colloquium was generative; in bringing together a group of scholars from the fields of law, sociology, media studies, and gender studies, we realized that there was much more territory to explore.

This book—a collective work in the truest sense—is the result. It would not have been possible without the generous support of Washington University School of Law and Dean Nancy Staudt. At the Center for the Interdisciplinary Study of Work and Social Capital, Shelly Henderson and Bev Owens offered valuable administrative support. The Center also provided funding for copyediting during the manuscript preparation stages, performed by Robert L. Rogers and Vici Casana, to whom we are thankful.

We are indebted to our authors, without whom the book would not exist. We encourage you to learn more about them and their impressive bodies of work by reading "About the Editors and Contributors." In addition, we thank our colleagues who contributed to the dialogue at the colloquium by presenting papers and moderating panels: Matthew Bodie, Devon Carbado, Adrienne Davis, Susan "Tonie" Fitzgibbon, Rafael Gely, Erin Hatton, Pauline Kim, Marcia McCormick, Lisa Nakamura, Laura Rosenbury, Trebor Scholz, Peggie Smith, and Karen Tokarz.

No work finds its way into print without an enthusiastic editor and a supportive press. We are especially grateful to Naomi Schneider and University of California Press for embracing this project. We received a number of thoughtful academic critiques that undeniably enhanced and deepened our analysis: one from an anonymous reviewer, one from Jennifer Pierce, and another from Eric Avila on the Board of Directors. At UC Press, we also thank Francisco Reinking and Elizabeth Berg for copyediting expertise.

Saint Louis University was a formative site of ideas and support along the way. At the Law School, Chad Flanders and Doug Williams were gracious enough to put us on the schedule of the Faculty Workshop Series. At that session, we gained invaluable feedback from scholars like Elizabeth Chiarello, Monica Eppinger, Marcia McCormick, and Carol Needham. In addition, we were fortunate to have assistance from several staff members at Saint Louis University. David Kullman, research librarian at the Law School, provided research services, as did Umo Ironbar as a faculty fellow. Sharon "Shari" Baird provided outstanding clerical and administrative support in the final stages of the project.

The growing relevance of invisible labor is evident in that the Eastern Sociological Society (ESS) organized a similarly themed conference shortly after we began this project. We thank ESS president Marjorie DeVault for supporting our project and allowing us to organize three panels at "Invisible Work," 2014. Several scholars, along with many of our own, participated in those sessions, and we enjoyed and benefited from their lively debates: Christopher Andrews, Aneesh Aneesh, Michel Anteby, Curtis Chan, Alexandre Frenette, and Christian Zlolniski.

On a more personal level, the authors also wish to thank others for their help and assistance. Marion Crain wishes to thank Dean Nancy Staudt for summer research support, Shelly Henderson for grace under pressure, and Tom English for understanding and supporting the time and energy that goes into a project of this duration. Winifred Poster wishes to thank Jamie Poster, who came to the rescue (on a moment's notice, no less) with much-needed references. Sanjay Jain, Ketan Jain-Poster, and Natasha Jain-Poster helped to formulate ideas at our dinner table and to circulate (unprompted) discussions of invisible labor within their schools and workplaces. Miriam A. Cherry wishes to thank her former dean, Annette Clark (present dean at the University of Seattle School of Law), for supporting the writing sabbatical that made this book, among other projects, possible. Continued support from her present dean, Michael Wolff, has been appreciated. Special thanks to Lucas Amodio, who was very patient and understanding of the time and effort that the volume required.

Foreword

Invisible Labor, Inaudible Voice

ARLIE HOCHSCHILD

Imagine you are walking into an American department store to buy a dress. A saleswoman in a dress remarkably similar to that on a nearby mannequin asks in a friendly voice about the fashion, color, brand, and size you have in mind and directs you to the right rack. She might tell you what other shoppers have bought or what she herself favors. The saleswoman herself is visible, of course, but harder to discern are the company strategies that bring her to you in this way.

A recruitment strategy, for starters: She should fit the age, beauty, class, and racial ideals of those customers whom the store wishes to attract. She might also reflect the store's marketing strategy: by compensating her through discounts on merchandise, the store makes her into its customer and a model for its garments (chapter 13, chapter 10). Stores train their sales staff to encourage the customer—by commenting on the flattering colors, nice fit, good durability, or popularity of a garment—to buy clothing ("Oh, that's a great fit . . . and you could wear it with our . . ."). Such remarks are likely to reflect company training.

The dress is sewn of cotton grown on the western plains of India, let us say, and harvested by underpaid laborers who are exposed to pesticides. (Conventionally grown cotton uses more insecticides than any other single crop, accounting for over 10 percent of all pesticide use and nearly 25 percent of insecticides used worldwide.) Invisible are the workers who plant, irrigate, pick, clean, compress, tag, store, and bale the cotton and truck it to factories where it is spun, woven, dyed, and shipped as bolts of cloth to be then cut and sewn into dresses by workers in overcrowded backstage factories in Bangladesh. It is then tagged, wrapped, and shipped to stores where dresses are unpacked, priced, shelved, hung, and sold. (Otis and Zhao, chapter 8, take us to a similar backstage for food.) The faces of such workers are hidden behind the labels of garments (Ann Taylor, Ralph Lauren, Urban Outfitters, and others) and the models we see wearing these garments in women's magazines or on company Web sites. We focus on the blonde model or the brunette, the one in the red dress and the blue. The model becomes a stand-in for what we don't see—the hundreds of people around the globe who produced the dress (chapter 7).

Some workers disappear from view due to outsourcing. An American store may outsource its payroll and billing to an office in Bangalore, for example, or call a company based in Canada or Ukraine for help with a computer glitch. Eighty percent of Fortune 500 companies now send work aboard, lost to the view of the American consumer (chapter 5, chapter 10).

Other workers disappear from view due to automation. Engineers have devised whole living room "entertainment systems" to occupy a family, for example. Fictive characters in online games such as *Second Life* or *World of Warcraft* are made visible by programmers hunched over their computers in gaming workshops in cities such as Nanjing, China, where, for $1.25 an hour, they buy and sell virtual items in a virtual currency used by other players in an online game. Automation gets rid of workers. But it also calls for an invisible workforce that keeps it going.

Through robotics, engineers are also automating care. Carnegie Mellon has now produced robotic nurses (called NurseBots), such as "Pearl," fitted with eyelashes and lipstick and designed for eventual use on floors in Alzheimer's wards and nursing homes. As the Web site of Jetspark Robotics (2014) notes, "Say hello to the new world of nursing care. . . . Soon patients will be relying on machines to do bedside care. . . . With the aging population increasing, there will not be enough people to take care of the sick. Researchers from HStar Technologies have already predicted this imbalance in the nurse–patient ratio in the future. Now they are taking in more orders for their invention of a nurse assistant named RoNA. . . . This humanoid nurse is very stable, bi-manual and able to do the job of a nurse assist." Some companies have also created life-size images of receptionists in the form of holograms, which, as their producers note, "never cost overtime, need lunch breaks, . . . get sick," or ask for better hours and pay (chapter 5). While such machines employ engineers, they put nurses and receptionists out of work—and remove a human concern for service.

Still, the living, breathing American service sector is also growing and now makes up 80 percent of the American workforce. Many are care workers who, as a manager of hotel housekeepers told Chris Warhurst, remain out of view "like the elves in Harry Potter" (chapter 11, p. 215). We see people, and we also *see through* them. I am reminded of a nanny who told me, in an interview for *The Outsourced Self*, of a compliment her employer had once given her: "When you're with us, it's as if you're invisible." "He thought he was complimenting me," she reflected, adding, "at the time, so did I" (Hochschild 2012: 161). At the other extreme, waitresses at Hooters and other "breastaurants" are asked to make themselves as obvious as possible, creating a form of entertainment, as the employers see it, free to company and customers alike (chapter 9, p. 171). (A rival chain called Twin Peaks is the fastest growing restaurant chain in the United States [Leonard 2014].)

Sometimes it is not the person who is invisible but rather the work he or she is asked to do. For example, ten thousand college students were hired in 2011 in the United States as brand ambassadors to approach friends, fellow students, and store browsers pretending to be friendly coconsumers and to encourage unsuspecting people to buy such things as computers, clothing, and school supplies (chapter 13).

For each form of invisibility, there is a corresponding form of hidden emotional labor. The front-stage saleswoman is asking us if we are having a good day, but may be suppressing the anxieties of a bad day. The maid may feel isolated and confined as a Harry Potter elf. The brand ambassadors may feel ashamed about misleading people. Working-class or nonwhite employees may be tacitly trained to enact a more white or middle-class self for the job, just as women in male-dominated workplaces may feel called to enact a more male self. In each case the worker may disguise or manage an inner sense of loss, discomfort, or alienation from an earlier, more essential inner self. In addition, many now work shifting or irregular hours that prevent them from enjoying the happy, cohesive family to which they aspire. They are often obliged to mask discontent about those crazy hours under a customer-friendly attitude of "have a nice day."

Why do all these forms of invisibility matter? Because unless we look, see, and think about them, we are likely to miss the big picture of a vast global workshop. And we are likely to miss the very idea of coercion. That's because we imagine that coercion requires personal contact. We think back to Ebenezer Scrooge in Charles Dickens's 1843 *A Christmas*

Carol: the heartless boss who oversees the daily labors of the hapless Bob Cratchit from a nearby desk in the same dingy London office. Today, the watchful boss may keep a close eye on child-care or elder-care workers via video monitoring while call-center supervisors listen in on their workers' voices and conversations, and supervisors monitor electronically recorded workers in the cavernous warehouses of Amazon.com.

But while bosses can monitor workers, workers cannot so easily see or hear their bosses or get to know other workers on the same cross-national assembly line. In *White Collar,* sociologist C. Wright Mills (1951: ix) described the American middle class of the 1950s as "internally . . . split, fragmented; externally . . . dependent on larger forces" (quoted in chapter 12), words that also apply to much of the American workforce today. These workers are "fragmented" because they cannot see each other or see the entire system of production and consumption of which they are one small part. What becomes inaudible is the collective voice of the workers.

We are continually invited to get our minds off the big questions. Television game shows, shoot-'em-up adventure films, and the Internet can distract us from asking what world we want to live in. When we do ask that question, our attention is often directed to "free choice" in the restricted sense of "freedom to buy." We are free to choose between this dress and that one, the red or the green, the large or the small, at this price or that. We are told that it is enough in a democracy to "vote with your dollar." But let us not be fooled. Instead, let us turn the pages of this timely, probing, ethnographically rich, brilliant book as it takes us backstage around the world and puts the big questions front and center.

REFERENCES

Hochschild, Arlie. 2012. Chapter 10: "I Was Invisible to Myself." Pp. 157–71 in *The Outsourced Self: Intimate Life in Market Times.* New York: Metropolitan Press.

Jetspark Robotics. 2014. "Will Serbot, Rona and Pearl Robots Be the Future of Assistive Nursing?" Retrieved December 29, 2014 (http://jetsparkrobotics.com/).

Leonard, Devin. 2014. "Twin Peaks: 'Hooters Just Wasn't Racy Enough,'" *Bloomberg Businessweek,* September 25. Retrieved September 25, 2014 (www.businessweek.com/articles/2014–09–25/inside-twin-peaks-americas-fastest-growing-restaurant-chain).

Mills, C. Wright. 1951. *White Collar.* Oxford: Oxford University Press.

PART ONE

Exposing Invisible Labor

CHAPTER I

Introduction

Conceptualizing Invisible Labor

WINIFRED R. POSTER, MARION CRAIN, AND MIRIAM A. CHERRY

This volume brings together an interdisciplinary group of scholars to pose two fundamental questions: what counts as work, and why are some forms of work invisible? We focus on labor that occurs within formal employment relationships but is not conceptualized as work and so remains hidden from view—sometimes in the public imagination, sometimes from consumers, and sometimes from the workers themselves. When their work is erased, the workers themselves are sometimes rendered invisible as well. We ask what forces and trends are preventing employers, consumers, and employees from "seeing" the work that is done and blocking regulators and policy makers from addressing its impacts.

Visible labor has traditionally been defined as work that is readily identifiable and overt. It is located in a physical "workplace" and is self-recognized as work by management, employees, and consumers. It is typically paid, occurs in the public sphere, is directly profit generating, and has historically been full-time, long-term, and state regulated.

Starting in the 1980s, however, sociologists began to write about work that falls outside that domain. Arlene Daniels's (1987) article "Invisible Work" solidified and propelled the field, becoming a reference point for the social science literature. Centering on the household and voluntary work performed within it, Daniels's article noted the gendered character of this invisible work, observing that women are often associated with kinds of labor that are widespread throughout society and yet not conceived as work and, moreover, not valued.

Subsequently, Marjorie DeVault's (1994) research on *Feeding the Family* showed how activities like preparing meals have been considered "act[s] of love" or "expression of a natural role" (Star and Strauss 1999: 10) rather than work activities. Other scholars expanded the analysis to women's work performed inside the home but more clearly associated with income-generating and productive capacities such as piece-rate electronics assembly, auto parts assembly, seamstress work, and snack food production (Boris and Prugl 1996). As DeVault (2014) outlined in her recent Presidential Address to the Eastern Sociological Society meeting on "Invisible Work," many of these early writings (Kanter 1993; Rollins 1987; Smith 1988) were crucial academically, enabling scholars to "see" the work and visualize workers in places previously invisible to conventional sociology.

Our analysis considers how the concept of *invisibility* applies to a larger range of labor performed inside formal employment relationships. We take our inspiration from Arlie Hochschild, one of the most influential theorists on the dynamics of invisible labor within the context of paid employment. Her early work uncovered how emotions become commodities for employers in the service economy, who compel workers to undergo "feeling management" and present genuine care for their clienteles (Hochschild 1983). The emotion work done by flight attendants, she explained, was a form of labor that generated significant profits for the airlines and represented a core part of the brand marketed to consumers.

In other scholarship addressing the concept of *hidden labor* within the context of paid employment, invisibility has typically been associated with minimum-wage jobs or the underground economy. This implicit pairing is particularly apparent given scholarly attention to recent expansions of low-wage sectors of the labor force such as low-end service work (Ehrenreich 2010), seasonal farmwork (Griffith and Kissam 1995), and inner-city retail and fast-food work (Newman 2000). The notion of *invisibility* has also been widely discussed in relation to the Global South, where the marginalized workforce is connected to other dynamics like child labor, urban slums, and the poverty of rural households.

Expanding this focus, our analysis considers the meaning and significance of visibility *across* class and social hierarchies. Our authors examine jobs that span a range of pay scales and workers who hail from diverse social classes, including retail workers, computer workers on crowdsourcing Web sites, sexualized servers, virtual receptionists, college students functioning as brand ambassadors on campus, white-collar workers in organizations, and engineers. We balance our perspective to account for a range of occupational positions that include the middle and professional strata of the workforce. Our authors consider the role of affluent or middle-class workers in retail; the increasing use of unpaid internships that are disproportionately available to college-educated, economically privileged students; and the status of skilled knowledge workers on the Internet.

Broadening the category of invisible labor matters for several reasons. First, work that is not seen is not valued, either symbolically or materially. Second, if workers themselves do not see their efforts as valuable work, they are less likely to organize, appeal for public support, or challenge their working conditions through the legal system. Even if they want to mobilize, the invisibility of their work—and in many cases, of the workers themselves—may make it difficult for them to gain political traction or support from consumers. Finally, and most crucially, if the state and legal systems do not acknowledge the labor, it will not be addressed in policy and law. A prominent theme running throughout this book is how invisible labor is often unregulated.

This book adopts an interdisciplinary approach that integrates perspectives from law, sociology, industrial relations, critical race and feminist theory, science and technology studies, and global and international relations. These varied intellectual traditions offer complementary approaches to provide a wide-ranging (but by no means complete) picture of contemporary invisible labor. Nuanced social science analysis enables us to mark and track subtle dynamics of the labor process that have been overlooked. Structural, policy, and legal approaches facilitate our inquiry into how these uncovered dynamics could fit within the regulatory system. In so doing, they allow us to bring two major fields—sociology and law—into conversation with one another. While the sociology chapters provide ethnographic detail and new conceptualizations of invisible labor, the legal chapters explore the limits of regulation in protecting invisible workers. Together they deepen and complicate the social and legal implications of such labor.

This introduction begins by defining *invisible labor,* contemplating and mapping its forms along a spectrum. Next, we chart the trends that have spurred the proliferation of invisible labor. Then we outline the chapters in the volume, organizing them around several themes for conceptualizing labor and invisibility: "Exposing Invisible Labor,"

"Virtually Invisible," "Pushed out of Sight," "Looking Good at Work," and "Branded and Consumed." Finally, we consider the implications of revealing invisible labor for the intersections of gender, race, class, nationality, and disability.

DEFINING INVISIBLE LABOR

The word *labor* has multiple meanings, and we use the word intentionally here. *Labor* may refer to work itself or to tasks that are performed ("She labored at the construction site all day"). Within critical social theory, the labor process has referred to the larger context of work, like the sequence of tasks in a production process, the role of a job within an organization, and especially the relations between employees and managers. At the same time, *labor* may refer to a collective group of workers themselves (the "labor force" or "labor movement").

We define *invisible labor* as activities that occur within the context of paid employment that workers perform in response to requirements (either implicit or explicit) from employers and that are crucial for workers to generate income, to obtain or retain their jobs, and to further their careers, yet are often overlooked, ignored, and/or devalued by employers, consumers, workers, and ultimately the legal system itself.

We also seek to highlight ambiguous work that lies at the intersection between paid and unpaid labor. For instance, some work within the context of formal labor is *un*paid, such as the time spent preparing for the performance of aesthetic labor (which we discuss in more detail below). Some work is *under*paid either because employers (as well as others) do not see the full range of tasks that the worker is performing and from which employers benefit, or because the law lacks rigorous regulation in the area, such as tipped service work.

Sometimes invisibility is not strictly related to "seeing" or to a visual act. As our authors discuss, there are many instances when invisibility is a *symbolic concept*. In this sense, it may refer to market devaluation or to a social judgment that labels some tasks as "not work." Invisibility happens because these tasks are associated (and confused) with leisure, are considered to be part of consumption, are seen as voluntary, and fall outside the legal structure. Of course, the term *invisible* may also refer to the *visual act* of not seeing the workers or not understanding that they are performing work. An example is when an Internet platform obscures which tasks are performed by humans and which are performed by computers (Cherry 2009).

This analysis attempts to complicate our understandings of the interplay between the work and the worker as center points of invisibility. Even though these two factors are tied together within the labor process, their visibility may vary independently of each other. Critical in this regard is uncovering the complex and multilayered process of foregrounding and backgrounding labor. Many useful typologies have revealed how this process operates (Nardi and Engeström 1999; Star and Strauss 1999): visible work done by invisible people (domestic workers, librarians); visible people whose labor is relegated to the background (the care work of nurses); or the hidden tasks of visible labor (like informal conversations, storytelling, and humor that may aid the work environment). Along these lines, we show many cases of this foregrounding and backgrounding process. An example is when the work is visible, but the worker is invisible (like when a nonperson—a robot or a hologram—performs the work or when a campus brand ambassador markets a brand, appearing in the guise of a voluntary consumer). An opposite case occurs when visible workers perform work that is invisible (like the emotion work performed by Hochschild's flight attendants). We seek here to situate the concept of invisibility in deeper contexts of the political economy of labor.

We also aim to highlight the range of participants in the employment relation who have significant roles in viewing labor. To each, labor may be invisible in unique and consequential ways. *Consumers* may be unaware of the conditions of the labor for the products they buy or the services they contract. *Managers,* for instance, may not witness or recognize the range of preparations that workers do for their jobs, sometimes at their own cost (like taking accent lessons to improve diction for sales work). Or consider the example of *the worker* as viewer. Work may be hidden from the worker himself, as we will show. For example, retail store clerks desire jobs in prestigious brand stores because buying and wearing the company's clothes is to them a form of leisure (notwithstanding that these activities may also be a condition of their employment). These clerks perform such activities without realizing that they are also doing work in promoting the brand. Crucially, some work is invisible as a policy matter: regulatory authorities may be aware of the work, but a choice has been made to underregulate it, as is the case with tipped labor.

But not everything qualifies as "invisible labor" for our purposes. Our authors are concerned with activities that are *tied to a job and its rewards,* often as required by the employer. Among the range of formal and informal work activities, we focus on those that are performed for the benefit of the employer and from which the employer reaps profits.

Likewise, we do not suggest that invisibility and devaluation are synonymous. To be sure, there are many counterexamples. Some forms of devalued labor are readily visible, such as that of fast-food worker (Leidner 1996) and nail technician (Kang 2010). Alternatively, some kinds of labor that are valued by the market economy may be well hidden from the public, like the shift of stock market traders from open-floor styles of buying and selling futures contracts to trading on electronic platforms (Levin 2005). A critical point, however, is that by "devalued" we do not necessarily mean "lowly paid." Certainly, the value of a task may be signified by remuneration, but that is not the only criterion for invisibility. Instead, we focus as well on a more basic principle of value in labor: whether the task is recognized as worthy of inclusion in the category of "work"—and regulated as such.

SOCIALLY CONSTRUCTING THE INVISIBLE

Conventional approaches would say that the invisible and the visible are manifest in themselves (that is, neutral, or uniformly viewed the same way). The premise of this view, as summarized by Hall, Evans, and Nixon (2013), is that "'things' exist in the material and natural world; that their material or natural characteristics are what determines or constitutes them; and that they have a perfectly clear meaning" therein (p. xix).

Yet sociologists and cultural studies theorists have urged us to understand these categories as *socially constructed*. This is the idea that social phenomena are products of interactions among individuals, groups, and communities. The related concept of *representation* explains that meaning is not conferred on objects themselves, but rather created in the way we incorporate cultural objects into our daily lives, the way they come to represent or symbolize ideas and feelings, and in turn, the way those meanings regulate and set norms for subsequent action (Hall, Evans, and Nixon 2013).

Accordingly, we argue that many social actors are involved (directly or indirectly) in the generation and promotion of labor as visible or invisible. For instance, authors in this volume examine how the act of seeing and the visible are socially constructed. Chapter 7 discusses Berger's seminal writing on this topic in his book *Ways of Seeing* (1972), noting how artists have historically represented smiling laborers in their paintings for the wealthy. Several of our chapters (9 and 10) examine the labor of frontline service workers and the role of stylists, cosmeticians, breast enhancement surgeons, and others in cultivating the "right look" for women employees. This exploration echoes the writings of feminist media scholars such as Walters (1995) on the way that women's appearance is crafted for viewing by men.

Dynamics of visibility, therefore, may serve to obscure and even *misrepresent* those being viewed. This is especially common when marginalized groups are objects of the visible. The field of cultural studies has been important in exposing patterns of inequality within representation and demonstrating how systems of patriarchy, classism, heterosexism, and imperialism (Said 2014) shape what appears in the media, culture, and society. Visibility, in this sense, is problematic because it can be a tool of power. The act of putting people (like workers) on display can be harmful to them in certain situations. Foucault's (1979) theory of visibility provides an example of how this is carried out through the dominating practices of observation and surveillance.

Yet our interest is in the reverse analysis as well. Instead of only asking who is *seen* and why, we also ask who and what are *not seen*, and with what implications for the labor process. Invisibility is socially constructed, just like visibility. Ironically, in fact, there are many overt tasks that go into making particular kinds of work invisible. Evidence is in the labor of editors and photographers who, in their daily routines, decide, shape, and subtly manipulate what is not seen by the public. Along these lines, chapter 4 begins with a discussion of virtual content editors, who delete and moderate comments and disturbing images on social media. Described more below, these are workers who "do" (that is, create) invisibility within labor.

Toward this end, we focus on how people and things disappear in the employment context. Disempowerment is embedded in this dynamic, given that the rewards and compensation for labor are typically dependent upon the visibility of the worker, the work process, or the worker's visible output.

A SPECTRUM OF VISIBILITIES

In short, invisibility is a multivalent concept. We depart in our conceptualization from many previous accounts by exploring the range of permutations of invisible labor—including the ways these forms may seemingly contradict each other. Toward this end, we map invisibility along a spectrum.

On one end of the scale are the *absent and disappeared* workers. An example is the job of "content moderator," which Miriam A. Cherry discusses (chapter 4). These online laborers who monitor social media for unethical or objectionable material illustrate a case in which everything about the labor process is invisible. The worker is invisible to the user, as there is no sign or trace of her presence on the Web site (e.g., Facebook). Users may even presume that the work is done by a computer. The job is invisible, often outsourced overseas to places like the Philippines or India. Finally, the work is invisible because there is no tangible product. In fact, the purpose of the job is literally to erase content.

Near this "invisible" side of the scale (but not quite at the very end) are several other cases in our volume: crowdsourced coding engineers, internationally outsourced clerical workers, migrant farmworkers, and disabled workers in sheltered workshops. Here, the workers are not visible to the consumer and sometimes are not even visible to the employer. Moreover, some are physically confined and shielded from the formal labor market. Some are digitally wiped from corporate images and advertising (like Mexican American fruit pickers) and from existence (like video secretaries in organizational front offices).

At the other end, some workers are *hypervisible* and almost serve as a foil to the disappeared workers mentioned above. Groups like Abercrombie & Fitch salesworkers, college campus brand ambassadors, and Hooters waitresses are not only well apparent to most parties; they are in fact deliberately spotlighted by employers as part of the service relationship. This trend reflects a growing employment sector with requirements to represent the firm's brand as well as to serve as its interface with consumers. Ironically, visibility marks these employees as appropriate candidates for that product or service, and brand-friendly aesthetics are often a central qualification for the job.

This situation is perhaps most apparent in the example of "breastaurant" workers (as Dianne Avery, chapter 9, shows), whose physiques as well as labor in serving food and drink are both highly visible to the consumer. What is hidden in this case is not the worker herself but rather the unstated or stated requirements to achieve visibility *in the right way* and the labor those requirements entail. This labor may include, for instance, enduring breast augmentation surgery, donning makeup, and accessorizing oneself so as to attract sexual attention.

These are the invisible efforts required both to obtain the job and then to earn sufficient tips to garner a living wage, given the subminimum wage paid to these employees.

Another example of the hypervisible is labor trafficking. Workers in forced or coerced employment situations are common around the world, with estimates of 20.9 million (Owens et al. 2014). Some cross national borders, responding to fraudulent promises by recruiters or becoming captive to traffickers who withhold their passports. Yet many are hidden in plain sight. They may work in frontline service jobs and interact with the public (Owens et al. 2014) in industries like restaurants (busboys, waiters), hospitality (hotel bell clerks, room cleaners), and hair salons (braiding hair, sweeping floors). Invisible in this case is neither the worker nor the work, but rather the system of egregious exploitation, which brought these workers here, which they live under, and which they cannot reveal to anyone.

The majority of our cases, however, fall between these two poles. One might consider these *semivisible* types of labor. Either the worker or the work is unrecognized. The invisible labor may be central or peripheral to the occupation, and the number of viewers may vary from a few to many. These jobs may have some commonalities with visible labor in that they are located in the public sphere, physically identifiable, and formalized on the books. However, they are devalued socially, politically, and economically in ways that subordinate them relative to visible labor. It is this contradictory nature of invisibility within visibility that we seek to tease out.

TRENDS PROPELLING THE INVISIBILITY OF LABOR

In accounting for the rise of invisible labor, we locate several trends that have emerged in recent decades to make certain types of work and/or workers less visible.

First, we have seen a *rise in precarious work* (Ross 2009; Vosko 2006), "employment that is uncertain, unpredictable, and risky" (Kalleberg 2009: 2). This expanding group of workers is experiencing an increased likelihood of unemployment, job insecurity, contingent and nonstandard work, and shouldering expenses like health insurance and pensions. This degradation of labor is felt by a range of workers, from fast-food servers (Ehrenreich 2010; Newman 2000) to engineering consultants (Barley and Kunda 2004). Significantly for our purposes, precarious work often contributes to the invisibility of labor. As jobs become fragmented, their parts become increasingly dispersed and hard to see. Nevertheless, while precariousness is a driver of invisible labor, not all precarious work is invisible. In this volume, we focus on the point where these two dynamics meet: when the undercutting of stable, permanent employment also involves, or even leads to, the hiding of those jobs from view (see chapters by Evan Stewart [7] and Adam Arvidsson, Alessandro Gandini, and Carolina Bandinelli [12]).

Second is the *expansion of the service sector.* The basic foundations of the economy have shifted as most of the new jobs are in service work; that is, they are jobs that involve performing a function for customers rather than producing goods. This transition to a service economy has vastly increased the share of workers who are interacting with the public and who are evaluated according to the quality of that interaction. The provision of the service is often defined precisely by the employee's ability to be invisible—to blend in and do the job fluidly without being noticed (Suchman 1995).

Third is the *rise of consumerism,* which has intersected in significant ways with the expansion of the service economy. Consumerism involves the growing social pressure to buy goods and services even when they are not needed. It also involves a changed understanding of the self for the everyday citizen. The rise of large shopping malls has coincided with a loss of public space for politics (Cohen 2008). Accordingly, one's consumer identity has come to take precedence over other social roles, particularly the role of worker or citizen.

Closely related to the rise of consumerism is an *increased reliance on corporate brands* to create value. When service businesses rely heavily on branding, they depend upon frontline workers to convey the brand's meaning (including associated immaterial, subjective, and affective meanings). Employers must more aggressively manage the consumer–worker interaction. Ultimately, the lines between consumption and work are blurred for both employees and consumers. Brand culture makes and remakes the relationship between consumer and worker through interactive engagement online (Banet-Weiser 2012).

A fourth trend is the *growth of technology, communication, and networks.* In what Cherry (2011) calls "virtual work" and Scholz (2013) calls "digital labor," current technology is restructuring previous jobs and generating new types of employment. We examine how the Internet, networks, and mobile devices are transforming the foundations of where, when, and how work is performed. Technology has created entirely distinct categories of work such as crowdsourcing, social media blogging, and even virtual assistants. In the process, technology obscures the worker from the view of the Web site user or ultimate consumer and, in addition, elides the line between leisure and work.

Advancing technology also leads to trends of surveillance in the workplace, which shape new patterns of invisibility and visibility of employees through the collection of big data on worker practices and the visual monitoring of worker movements (Poster 2011). Our chapters also consider the rise of new media (like the transfer of content from television to Web platforms like YouTube) and its role in hiding (or revealing) workers who are behind products and services offered in the market. A critical factor in the expansion of such platforms is the growth of labor market intermediaries—that is, new kinds of online actors and businesses that intervene in the matching between labor supply and demand. Indeed, many of the virtual jobs that we discuss in this volume are provided not directly by an employer but rather through an organization on the Internet that acts as a go-between for the employer and the worker. The role of such networked organizations is becoming paramount in reshaping the conditions of employment, the structuring of job rewards, and the means of directing grievances for workers.

A fifth trend is *globalization*. Our authors consider several transnational dynamics that are reshaping invisible labor. One is *the rise of large multinational firms*. The geographic dispersion of business is altering the nature of everyday work. Global firms are setting up subsidiaries abroad and gaining massive influence on employment systems. Wal-Mart, as Eileen Otis and Zheng Zhao discuss in chapter 8, is the largest private sector employer in the world and ranks second in the *Fortune* Global 500. This development has significant implications for the visibility of labor both in the hosting country (for workers on the shop floor) and in the home country (for the production process more broadly).

Globalization of labor also includes trends of subcontracting and outsourcing. Rather than sending a whole organization abroad (as described above), firms in the United States are increasingly sending parts or divisions of their operations to third-party firms in other countries in the Global South (Poster and Yolmo 2016). While firms have traditionally offshored their lower-level work in manufacturing (to places like Mexico and Southeast Asia), they have recently expanded to offshoring many kinds of professional and office work (to places like India and the Philippines). Such labor includes both pink-collar work (in clerical and customer services) and white-collar work (in engineering, medical, and legal services), as Winifred R. Poster discusses in chapter 5. Thus labor is submerged from view on a transnational scale.

Finally, a key feature of globalization is *the migration of labor.* The movement of workers across borders is reshaping the labor process and which types of labor are visible within it. Citizenship has historically been tied to labor in the United States through the making of the ideal "worker-citizen" by national founders (Glenn 2009). Denial of citizenship is therefore integrally linked with the control of labor, as many migrant groups have been incorporated into types of work only ephemerally and temporally based on the employment needs of particular industrial sectors (Lowe 1996). Maintaining the status of the noncitizen worker serves to restrict wages, mobility, and capability to organize. We see the impact of this phenomenon today in the experiences of undocumented workers, of which there are 9 million in the United States (Gordon 2009). Many work in underground businesses that are "structured to avoid detection" (p. 24) and live in fear of deportation.

INEQUALITIES AND INTERSECTIONALITY

Our analysis is informed by critical sociology and legal studies and by frameworks of race, class, gender, sexuality, nationality, and disability. These frameworks operate as systems of inequality that structure the labor process and create unique dimensions of invisibility for particular groups of workers.

An important contribution of this volume is recognizing disability as a factor structuring invisibility. Although rarely discussed in the literature on work in the contemporary economy, disability is a powerful axis of stratification (DeVault 2008; DeVault 2014). Despite advances in medical technology, the number of people categorized as disabled in the United States (meaning those receiving disability payments) has shot up over the last few decade—now reaching 14 million (Joffe-Walt 2013). This result is due partially to an aging population, but also to the way that the government has been handling people who cannot find work. In fact, some states have been hiring private firms to identify and push people off welfare and onto disability programs so that the federal government will foot the bill instead.

Our analysis considers the disabled through a prism of agency, that is, as active participants in society through their labor rather than as objects to be cared for or those upon whom work is done. Pendo's chapter (6) shows how the majority of disabled people express a desire to participate in the formal workforce. Yet, ironically, the United States government has defined the disabled precisely by an inability to work. Pendo illustrates how this issue continues to operate in the labor market, given that both state programs and private benefits systems funnel the disabled away from full employment even when accommodations could be made for them to participate in meaningful ways.

Our project also explores *race* as an element of invisibility. The existing literature has insightfully outlined how managerial and other informal practices produce racial inequality in the workplace. It is important to recognize, however, how the visibility of those dynamics has changed over time. In the pre–civil rights era, these racialized practices were often explicit. Yet in the post–civil rights era, these practices can be much more subtle. As our authors Wingfield and Skeete (chapter 3) examine, "racial tasks" at work are now seemingly neutral—and hence invisible to outsiders—while still producing racial inequality.

Using different terminology, Eduardo Bonilla-Silva (2006) calls this "color-blind racism." David Roediger and Elizabeth Esch (2012) call it "whiteness as management" (p. 14). Jennifer Pierce (2012) illuminates a process of "racing for innocence," as the white lawyers she interviewed would explicitly deny racism while simultaneously practicing exclusionary behavior against African American employees. Significantly, rendering these practices visible not only illuminates how racism operates but also facilitates our understanding of practices and policies that may bring about change. A critical race view of invisibility, therefore, helps us recognize how everyday labor practices produce structural racial inequalities.

Of particular importance for racialized invisible labor is the gap in research on Latinos. In a sociopolitical context that has tended to define race/ethnicity in terms of a black–white binary, Latinos have been underrepresented in the scholarly literature (for discussion of that gap in labor studies, see Romero, Hondagneu-Sotelo, and Ortiz 1997; and in sociology, see Saenz, Douglas, and Morales 2013). Excellent studies on Latino labor have emerged in the last few decades across the occupational scale, from meat packers (Miraftab 2016), to secretaries and garment workers (Segura 1994), to attorneys (García-López 2008). This field can hardly keep up with the growing presence of Latinos in the current employment landscape of the United States. Latinos are already the *largest* ethnic group in two U.S. states (surpassing whites) and the fastest growing ethnic group nationwide. They comprise a highly diverse group from many different national origins, languages, and ethnicities, yet their common experiences represent significant dimensions of immigration and citizenship that structure invisibility.

An emerging theme in this literature is overrepresentation of Latinos in lower-paying service occupations of invisible labor. These include janitors and street vendors (Zlolniski 2006); housecleaners and home child-care workers (Hondagneu-Sotelo 2001); day laborers, car wash attendants, and car valets (Cleaveland and Pierson 2009; Valenzuela 2003); and gardeners (Huerta 2007). Focusing on Latino workers, and the racialized construction of these jobs, yields valuable insights on invisibility. Space and sound can be critical markers of tensions in their work. Latinos are often under contradictory pressures to be visible and invisible at the same time, or to reduce their visibility in situations where they are hypervisible. Gardeners, for instance, face legal ordinances banning leaf-blowing machines in favor of quieter, back-bending labor by hand (Cameron 2000). Day laborers face challenges in hiding from police within the public spaces of parking lot employment queues (Cleaveland and Pierson 2009).

Our volume considers several additional sectors where Latinos are increasingly employed: farmwork, retail sales, and security guards. Geographically, chapters examine regions of the United States where immigration has been especially high. Stewart (chapter 7), by focusing on Florida, sheds light on the integral role of Latinos in farmwork. Two-thirds of the workforce in U.S. agriculture is Mexican born, and one-half is undocumented. Yet rather than showcasing these Latino workers in television and Internet commercials for fruit products, companies represent the workers as talking and dancing oranges or else as white male farm owners. In this way, the ads "racially code the farmworkers as white and conflate ownership with labor" (p. 141). To counter this, Stewart offers statistics on Latino immigration as well as descriptions and images of the conditions of picking fruit and their impact on workers' health.

Williams and Connell (chapter 10) base their study in Texas, where one can see the effects of ethnically mixed workforces on upscale retail work. Latino workers report discrimination on the basis of language since employers favor accents from Austin (located near the center of the state) over those from El Paso (closer to the Mexican border). Employers also segregate workers spatially, initially assigning Latino workers to the stockroom instead of the showroom floor. Similar policies of racialized job channeling are also implicated in the "backstage" work that Otis and Zheng discuss (chapter 8).

Finally, Wingfield and Skeete illuminate the experience of blacks and Latinos as security guards (as well as janitors and maintenance workers) in chapter 3. Their discussion provides a vivid account of contradictory roles in these jobs: using the *visibility* of their bodies for gatekeeping functions vis-à-vis the public, while using the *invisibility* of their bodies to appear inconspicuous to higher-level coworkers.

In short, our chapters illustrate a standard of whiteness deployed by employers that operates at both affluent and low-wage levels. Stewart describes an explicit case of "whitewashing," as the bodies of farmworkers are changed from Latino to Caucasian through representations of the brand in the media. Williams and Connell's study reveals an implicit standard of whiteness as salesworkers, whose bodies and voices fail to conform to the mainstream Euro/Anglo model, are channeled into nonvisible jobs or not hired.

These examples, moreover, signal a deeper, racialized dynamic that pervades other chapters: the erasing of workers' identities (ethnic as well as national) for the purpose of masking covert employer practices that consumers and the public in general may find objectionable. Poster (2007b) explains how firms hide the process of outsourcing and the transfer of white-collar work overseas to India by attempting to Americanize the accents, names, and settings of the workers. In Stewart's analysis, firms hide the "underlying racial power structure that keeps their workers in a profitable, but highly precarious, state" (p. 130).

Still, the analytical strategy in the book is not merely to note the *misrepresentation* of labor by Latinos and other peoples of color in the media and digital world, but also to detail *the lived experiences, practices, and images of that racialized labor.* Our aim is twofold: to uncover the process of labor masking, while also to reveal the actual workers and the work that they do.

Our authors give renewed attention to *class* by charting burgeoning sectors of both low-wage and high-wage (or class-privileged) invisible labor. Starting at the bottom end, scholars have noted how the working poor are "Invisible in America" (Shipler 2008). At a time of unprecedented prosperity, millions of Americans live in the shadows as employees who earn poverty-level wages. Updating and expanding this analysis, Warhurst (chapter 11) documents how working-class employees in the United Kingdom are excluded from the labor of the service economy because they lack the right look and sound for middle-class interactions.

Alternatively, Crain (chapter 13) shows how educated, wealthy youth are persuaded to work for nothing in prestigious internships, learning to see work as a privilege rather than an economic exchange. Firms appeal to this demographic to exploit their social connections, simultaneously playing on their desperation for work in an ever-shrinking market of professional jobs. Williams and Connell show how class itself is manipulated by upscale retail employers. They deliberately select affluent employees, counting on the fact that those workers will be motivated by the status of the brand rather than the need for remuneration, and thus will be less likely to agitate for higher wages.

Several authors look at the downgrading of office and professional jobs, and what may have been formerly well-remunerated work. Arvidsson, Gandini, and Bandinelli (chapter 12) consider how skilled knowledge work is degraded through organizational transitions to flexibility, project-based work, and deployment of freelancers. Cherry and Poster (chapters 4 and 5, respectively) expose the undermining effects of invisible labor for the middle class, from the transformation of engineering, data coding, and call centers into micro tasks, crowdsourced labor, and virtual receptionist work, some of which earns cents on the dollar.

Finally, *gender* is central to many of our chapters. While previous discussions have laid a solid foundation on the connection of women to the invisible labor of housework, volunteer work, and emotion work, our project explores how gender is interwoven with contemporary patterns of the globalized, technologized, and consumerized labor market. Firms exploit women's sexuality through the disembodied process of digitizing them into software programs (chapter 5) and through the embodied process of selling their sexuality through niche restaurants and retail outlets (chapters 9 and 10).

As critical race and feminist scholars have demonstrated, systems of inequality are interlocking and indivisible (Collins 2000; Crenshaw 1989; Poster 2002). Groups may experience contradictory locations of privilege and subordination on different axes of inequality. For women of color, this phenomenon results in particularly troublesome experiences of double or triple discrimination and opposing demands among the multiple subordinate groups with which they are affiliated. With intersectionality in mind, we do not structure our analysis by separating sections according to these axes of discrimination. Rather, we intersperse and connect race, class, gender, and nationality throughout the book.

ORGANIZING THEMES

The chapters in this book are organized around five broad themes emphasizing the role of invisibility in the labor process. These themes are neither exclusive nor independent. A given type of labor may involve several intersecting and crossover processes at one time. We separate them here for the purpose of outlining the range of ways that work or workers may be erased in the workplace.

Exposing Invisible Labor. We begin by theorizing what counts as work and what makes work invisible, laying out some of the costs of invisibility. This introduction initiates that process by conceptualizing invisible labor. John W. Budd (chapter 2) then explains how relatively narrow conceptualizations of work in conventional thinking dictate how we recognize, remunerate, and treat work. This explanation is helpful in understanding how particular forms of work are valued and why. He argues for training the mind to think more broadly about the forms that work takes in order to enable the eye to see it. Adia Harvey Wingfield and Renée Skeete (chapter 3) provide a much-needed critique and understanding of invisible labor from a racial perspective. Their concept of *racial tasks* pinpoints the wide range of activities (often informal and unstated) that employees of color must do "to preserve and uphold whites' advantage in work settings" (p. 48). With their broad framework that crosses organizational hierarchies (from elites and CEOs, to middle-level management, to lower-level custodial staff), Wingfield and Skeete reveal how invisible labor is structurally distinct for minority versus majority employees in predominantly white workplaces.

Virtually Invisible. This section of the book considers managerial strategies to erase, transform, or digitize the worker's body. The disembodiment of labor is carried out through the aid of technology and outsourcing.

Miriam A. Cherry (chapter 4) outlines several types of "virtual work," in which new technologies are mediating where, when, and how labor is done. Employers are using digital tools like algorithms, robots, and Internet platforms to make workers invisible to consumers or other end users of Web sites or services. Focusing on what goes on "behind the Web site," Cherry illuminates the hidden labor of warehouse workers processing orders for Internet giant Amazon.com, crowdsourcing workers for Web sites like Amazon Mechanical Turk, avatar representations of employees in virtual worlds like *Second Life,* and Internet users who may not even realize they are doing work for corporations as they play online games. Cherry's analysis raises fascinating questions: Should virtual work count as "real" work? What should be the boundaries between work and play online? When is an Internet user deliberately or unknowingly also a worker? In the world of virtual work, playing a game might actually function to assist a computer network in improving its image-searching process. Thus the boundaries among workspace, work, and leisure are blurred.

Boundaries are further deconstructed when globalization interacts with virtualization. Winifred R. Poster (chapter 5) considers how outsourcing and automation allow employers to avoid the expenses of hiring a live on-site employee such as a receptionist, traditionally the "human face" of the company. Her analysis takes us to South Asia, where a $16 billion industry has developed in back-office work by incorporating 2.8 million cheap, educated, English-speaking employees. Through outsourcing, employers transfer customer-service phone work and data processing from the United States to "virtual teams" of workers in India whom they may never see or with whom they may have only minimal interaction. Through automation, on the other hand, employers replace the receptionist with various kinds of computer programs (avatar assistants, interactive screens, and holographic kiosks), bringing the issue of "disembodied" labor into sharp relief. These examples illustrate how workers are deconstructed into the component parts of their humanity and employed selectively—for their voice and relational capacity, for the body they display to customers, and for their words delivered electronically through texting and chatting. In the process, gender, sexuality, race, and nationality are manipulated to emphasize those qualities that employers believe will appeal to their customer base in the United States.

Pushed out of Sight. Alternatively, labor may be hidden from public view when it is separated architecturally, institutionally, or socially. Recent trends have expanded the spatial segregation of workers. Physical labor becomes invisible through dynamics of the service sector and globalization that submerge work needed to sustain the consumer economy. Much of this work occurs behind the scenes, geographically and/or temporally (Poster 2007a; Zlolniski 2006): workers telecommute from home, warehouse workers perform manual labor at Amazon.com, cooks and caterers prepare packaged food, and nighttime janitors clean offices while those who work in them sleep.

Our first example of "out of sight, out of mind" labor involves marginalized disabled workers. Elizabeth Pendo (chapter 6) explores how persons with disabilities are spatially segregated into "sheltered workshops," where they are invisible to consumers and outside the formal labor process altogether. A sheltered workshop is a state program of supervised, exclusive workplaces for physically disabled or mentally handicapped adults. Conceptualized either as job-training programs or as alternatives to competitive employment, many sheltered workshops nonetheless lack meaningful opportunities for education and training, fail to provide meaningful "work" experience, confine persons with disabilities away from other workers, and pay a subminimum wage.

Evan Stewart (chapter 7) explores the submerging of one of the most arduous types of physical labor—farmwork. He reveals how both the work and the workers are erased in the marketing representations of the product. Using the methodology of visual sociology, Stewart examines television commercials for major orange juice companies and their distribution on Internet channels like YouTube. Strikingly, while these commercials foreground the *production* of the juice, they simultaneously remove the *worker* and the *act of growing and picking* the fruit from the images. Stewart argues that this seeming contradiction serves a deliberate purpose: to mask the racial and immigration status of the employees, the egregious conditions under which they work, and the ultimate source from which consumers receive food.

This section also explores the embodied manual labor hidden in retail settings. Eileen Otis and Zheng Zhao (chapter 8) explain how Wal-Mart produce workers, who perform heavy lifting and other kinds of physically demanding labor, are hidden from customers when in the "backstage" area of the warehouse and ignored when they are in the "front stage" stocking the shelves. While "directly under the nose of customers" (p. 156), they are socially invisible. The authors also reveal how the transnational nature of retail submerges this process even further as Wal-Mart traverses the globe into countries like China. Otis and Zhao note how globalization not only renders the worker invisible but also hides the fundamental tasks of food production. Activities that used to be done in public markets in full view of consumers (like "cleaning, ordering, packaging" [p. 149]) are now done behind the scenes in Wal-Mart storerooms. In the process, global retail has co-opted the food sales chain between farm and customer and steamrolled local street vendors.

Looking Good at Work. The chapters in this part of the book explore situations in which workers are deliberately put on a stage in order to showcase products and services for the benefit of the employer. These are the "hypervisible" workers described above, for whom what is hidden is not the worker or her work but rather the labor that occurs behind the scenes and the employer policies that incentivize it. Many of the jobs discussed in this section fall under the category of "aesthetic labor." Employers may mandate or suggest that workers look and act a certain way, display a particular habitus, adopt a particular way of speaking, and purchase and model the brands they sell. These dynamics have become particularly salient with the rise of the service economy. Because the work is interactive with consumers, employers emphasize and encourage this aesthetic quality as the primary function of the job.

Dianne Avery (chapter 9) explores these issues in the context of the "breastaurant" industry, which requires its food servers to conform their bodies to the company image. Highly sexualized waitresses are required to follow dress and appearance standards designed to generate corporate profits. Paid a subminimum wage for the traditional labor they perform—restaurant service work—the real allure of the job lies in the high tips, eroticized glamorous image, and semicelebrity status that Hooters Girls can achieve only by investing in expensive undergarments, cosmetics and beauty treatments, plastic surgery, and breast implants (as well as by tolerating sexual harassment). Weak minimum-wage laws and unregulated tipping economies conceal the costs to workers and the benefits to employers of this business model.

While the workers in aesthetic jobs are highly visible to consumers, the management practices that shape the workers' visible identities are not. As Christine Williams and Catherine Connell (chapter 10) illustrate through their study of upscale retail sales work in stores like Express and Victoria's Secret, employers utilize a selection process that privileges certain types of workers. These workers have a social class habitus that makes them likely to shop at the store and to regard the job as a form of leisure rather than as a way to make a living. Seduced into the jobs by the allure of a prestigious brand, retail workers miss the implications of these practices and unquestioningly accept unpleasant and onerous working conditions and low wages.

Chris Warhurst (chapter 11) describes similar dynamics in his research on hospitality, call center, and retail work. He emphasizes the vocal aspects of aesthetic labor and the search for workers who "sound right," using the case of the UK service sector. He explains how employers that depend on aesthetics mandate that workers assume particular appearances, present a certain habitus, and adopt a particular way of speaking. These employers are willing to invest in a workforce that "sounds right," to the point of offering workers training in proper ways of speaking and presenting themselves.

Branded and Consumed. Branding is a theme that pervades this volume. Many of the chapters discussed above address the invisible requirements of the job to embody, integrate, or transmit a corporate image. Otis and Zhao recount how stockroom employees at Wal-Mart perform physical acts of branding (i.e., literally sticking the label on the fruit). Avery and Williams and Connell show how restaurant and sales workers transform their bodies to represent the corporate brand, either directly by wearing the name of the company or else more subtly through their dress, makeup, and style. Some of these workers even have this process laid bare in their job titles: "brand representatives." Poster shows how branding extends to the realm of digital work, as the "bodies" of virtual secretaries (i.e., the kiosks on which their video screens stand) are labeled with corporate sponsors. Alternatively, Stewart's case shows how branding may involve removing the worker (or certain kinds of workers according to race, class, nationality, and citizenship) from the corporate image altogether. In this section, we continue this discussion by considering two forms: self-branding versus employer-mandated branding.

This section is also concerned with the invisibility of the new category of "consumer-worker" (chapter 10, p. 212). The contemporary labor process turns consumers into workers and workers into consumers. On one hand, employers capitalize on prospective workers' desire to affiliate with the brand by hiring them off the floor while they are present as consumers. On the other hand, employers encourage or mandate consumption as a part of the job and fool employees into believing they are not "working." These hiring and employment practices blur the lines of labor agency for workers themselves: are workers consuming items on their own initiative or because they have to do so to survive in the current market? These analyses raise deeper questions about whether such consumptive labor is consensual or coercive and whether the work performed is labor or leisure.

Adam Arvidsson, Alessandro Gandini, and Carolina Bandinelli (chapter 12) describe the recent pressures for "self-branding" among knowledge workers. Against a backdrop of intense competition for jobs and an increasingly precarious standing, knowledge workers must construct themselves as entrepreneurial subjects responsible for their own market success. Yet these personal brands have evolved into public entities that are negotiated in competition with others, and they ultimately structure our social relations both within and beyond the workplace. This development should concern us, Arvidsson and his colleagues explain, because we are witnessing the construction of a new form of sociality imbued with a different conception of value and ethics. Uncovering this process is vital to the health of our democracy.

Combining an analysis of branding and consumption, Marion Crain (chapter 13) focuses on explicit practices firms use to brand employees, exploring how these practices alter the conception of work. She offers accounts of workers who are paid to represent the brand in retail jobs at Abercrombie & Fitch, Starbucks, and Apple as well as accounts of "brand ambassadors" who live the brand on college campuses. Employers may require employees to purchase and model the brands they sell, offering (in lieu of compensation) discounts on merchandise, the promise of marketing experience, and the lure of affinity with a prestigious brand. The rise of unpaid or lowly paid internships for college students offers another example of substituting brand allure (with résumé value) for wages, rendering student interns consumers of the firm's brand. By converting workers into consumers, Crain suggests, communication between workers is constrained by the brand itself, limiting the forms that resistance might assume. She asks what the ramifications are for democracy when citizens learn to quit rather than speak up when responding to unacceptable workplace conditions that structure their lives.

We close the volume with a concluding chapter outlining future directions for research and considering the larger policy implications of the continuing invisibility of labor.

We invite readers now to journey with our authors over terrain that spans the globe and covers many different types of occupations and settings. We hope that through that journey, some of the invisible will become visible.

REFERENCES

Banet-Weiser, Sarah. 2012. Authentic™: The Politics of Ambivalence in a Brand Culture. New York: New York University Press.
Barley, Stephen R., and Gideon Kunda. 2004. Gurus, Hired Guns, and Warm Bodies. Princeton, NJ: Princeton University Press.
Berger, John. 1972. Ways of Seeing. New York: Viking Press.
Bonilla-Silva, Eduardo. 2006. Racism without Racists: Color-Blind Racism and the Persistence of Racial Inequality in the United States. Lanham, MD: Rowman & Littlefield.
Boris, Eileen, and Elisabeth Prugl, eds. 1996. Homeworkers in Global Perspective: Invisible No More. New York: Routledge.
Cameron, Christopher David Ruiz. 2000. "The Rakes of Wrath: Urban Agricultural Workers and the Struggle against Los Angeles's Ban on Gas-Powered Leaf Blowers." UC Davis Law Review 33: 1087–1104.

Cherry, Miriam A. 2009. "Working for Virtually Minimum Wage." *Alabama Law Review* 60: 1095–1102.

———. 2011. "A Taxonomy of Virtual Work." *Georgia Law Review* 45 (4): 951–91.

Cleaveland, Carol, and Leo Pierson. 2009. "Parking Lots and Police: Undocumented Latinos' Tactics for Finding Day Labor Jobs." *Ethnography* 10 (4): 515–33.

Cohen, Lizabeth. 2008. *A Consumers' Republic: The Politics of Mass Consumption in Postwar America*. New York: Vintage Books.

Collins, Patricia Hill. 2000. *Black Feminist Thought: Knowledge, Consciousness, and the Politics of Empowerment*. 2nd ed. New York: Routledge.

Crenshaw, Kimberlé. 1989. "Demarginalizing the Intersection of Race and Sex: A Black Feminist Critique of Antidiscrimination Doctrine, Feminist Theory, and Antiracist Politics." *University of Chicago Legal Forum*, 139–67.

Daniels, Arlene. 1987. "Invisible Work." *Social Problems* 34 (5): 403–15.

DeVault, Marjorie L. 1994. *Feeding the Family: The Social Organization of Caring as Gendered Work*. Chicago: University of Chicago Press.

———, ed. 2008. *People at Work: Life, Power, and Social Inclusion in the New Economy*. New York: New York University Press.

———. 2014. "Mapping Invisible Work: Conceptual Tools for Social Justice Projects." *Sociological Forum* 29 (4): 775–90.

Ehrenreich, Barbara. 2010. *Nickel and Dimed: On (Not) Getting By in America*. New York: Henry Holt.

Foucault, Michel. 1979. *Discipline and Punish*. New York: Vintage Books.

García-López, Gladys. 2008. "'Nunca Te Toman En Cuenta [They Never Take You into Account]': The Challenges of Inclusion and Strategies for Success of Chicana Attorneys." *Gender & Society* 22 (5): 590–612.

Glenn, Evelyn Nakano. 2009. *Unequal Freedom: How Race and Gender Shaped American Citizenship and Labor*. Cambridge, MA: Harvard University Press.

Gordon, Jennifer. 2009. *Suburban Sweatshops: The Fight for Immigrant Rights*. Cambridge, MA: Harvard University Press.

Griffith, David Craig, and Edward Kissam. 1995. *Working Poor: Farmworkers in the United States*. Philadelphia: Temple University Press.

Hall, Stuart, Jessica Evans, and Sean Nixon, eds. 2013. *Representation*. 2nd ed. Los Angeles: Sage Publications.

Hochschild, Arlie Russell. 1983. *The Managed Heart: Commercialization of Human Feeling*. Berkeley: University of California Press.

Hondagneu-Sotelo, Pierrette. 2001. *Doméstica: Immigrant Workers Cleaning and Caring in the Shadows of Affluence*. Berkeley: University of California Press.

Huerta, Alvaro. 2007. "Looking Beyond 'Mow, Blow and Go': A Case Study of Mexican Immigrant Gardeners in Los Angeles." *Berkeley Planning Journal* 20 (1): 1–23.

Joffe-Walt, Chana. 2013. "Unfit for Work." *All Things Considered*, National Public Radio, March 22, 2013. Retrieved March 24, 2013 (www.npr.org).

Kalleberg, Arne L. 2009. "Precarious Work, Insecure Workers : Employment Relations in Transition." *American Sociological Review* 74 (February): 1–22.

Kang, Miliann. 2010. *The Managed Hand: Race, Gender, and the Body in Beauty Service Work*. Berkeley: University of California Press.

Kanter, Rosabeth Moss. 1993. *Men and Women of the Corporation*. New York: Basic Books.

Leidner, Robin. 1996. "Rethinking Questions of Control: Lessons from McDonald's." Pp. 29–49 in *Working in the Service Society*, edited by Cameron Lynne MacDonald and Carmen Sirianni. Philadelphia: Temple University Press.

Levin, Peter. 2005. "Information, Prices, and Sensemaking in Financial Futures Trading." *Academy of Management Proceedings* (August): L1–6.

Lowe, Lisa. 1996. *Immigrant Acts*. Durham, NC: Duke University Press.

Miraftab, Faranak. 2016. *Global Heartland: Displaced Labor, Transnational Lives, and Local Placemaking*. Indianapolis: Indiana University Press.

Nardi, Bonnie A., and Yrjö Engeström. 1999. "A Web on the Wind: The Structure of Invisible Work." *Computer Supported Cooperative Work* 8: 1–8.

Newman, Katherine S. 2000. *No Shame in My Game: The Working Poor in the Inner City*. New York: Random House.

Owens, Colleen, et al. 2014. *Understanding the Organization, Operation, and Victimization Process of Labor Trafficking in the United States*. Boston: Urban Institute, Northeastern University.

Pierce, Jennifer. 2012. *Racing for Innocence*. Palo Alto, CA: Stanford University Press.

Poster, Winifred R. 2002. "Racialism, Sexuality, and Masculinity: Gendering 'Global Ethnography' of the Workplace." *Social Politics* 9 (1): 126–58.

———. 2007a. "Saying 'Good Morning' in the Night: The Reversal of Work Time in Global ICT Service Work." Pp. 55–112 in *Research in the Sociology of Work*. Vol. 17, edited by Beth Rubin. Amsterdam: Elsevier.

———. 2007b. "Who's on the Line? Indian Call Center Agents Pose as Americans for U.S.–Outsourced Firms." *Industrial Relations* 46 (2): 271–304.

———. 2011. "Emotion Detectors, Answering Machines and E-Unions: Multi-surveillances in the Global Interactive Services Industry." *American Behavioral Scientist* 55 (7): 868–901.

Poster, Winifred R., and Nima Lamu Yolmo. 2016. "Globalization and Outsourcing." In *The Sage Handbook of the Sociology of Work and Employment*, edited by Stephen Edgell, Heidi Gottfried, and Edward Granter. London: Sage.

Roediger, David R., and Elizabeth D. Esch. 2012. *The Production of Difference: Race and the Management of Labor in U.S. History*. New York: Oxford University Press.

Rollins, Judith. 1987. *Between Women: Domestics and Their Employers*. Philadelphia: Temple University Press.

Romero, Mary, Pierrette Hondagneu-Sotelo, and Vilma Ortiz, eds. 1997. *Challenging Fronteras: Structuring Latina and Latino Lives in the U.S.* New York: Routledge.

Ross, Andrew. 2009. *Nice Work If You Can Get It: Life and Labor in Precarious Times*. New York: New York University Press.

Saenz, Rogelio, Karen Manges Douglas, and Maria Cristina Morales. 2013. "Latina/o Sociology." Pp. 59–68 in *The Handbook of Sociology and Human Rights,* edited by David L. Brunsma, Keri E. Iyall Smith, and Brian K. Bran. Boulder, CO: Penguin.

Said, Edward W. 2014. *Culture and Imperialism.* New York: Random House.

Scholz, Trebor, ed. 2013. *Digital Labor: The Internet as Playground and Factory.* New York: Routledge.

Segura, Denisa A. 1994. "Inside the Work Worlds of Chicana and Mexican Immigrant Women." Pp. 95–112 in *Women of Color in U.S. Society,* edited by Maxine Baca Zinn and Bonnie Thornton Dill. Philadelphia: Temple University Press.

Shipler, David K. 2008. *The Working Poor: Invisible in America.* New York: Random House.

Smith, Dorothy. 1988. *The Everyday World as Problematic.* Toronto: University of Toronto Press.

Star, Susan Leigh, and Anselm Strauss. 1999. "Layers of Silence, Arenas of Voice: The Ecology of Visible and Invisible Work." *Computer Supported Cooperative Work* 8: 9–30.

Suchman, Lucy. 1995. "Making Work Visible." *Communications of the ACM* 38 (9): 56–64.

Valenzuela, Abel. 2003. "Day Labor Work." *Annual Review of Sociology* 29 (1): 307–33.

Vosko, Leah F. 2006. *Precarious Employment: Understanding Labour Market Insecurity in Canada.* New York: McGill-Queen's University Press.

Walters, Suzanna Danuta. 1995. *Material Girls: Making Sense of Feminist Cultural Theory.* Berkeley: University of California Press.

Zlolniski, Christian. 2006. *Janitors, Street Vendors, and Activists: The Lives of Mexican Immigrants in Silicon Valley.* Berkeley: University of California Press.

CHAPTER 2

The Eye Sees What the Mind Knows

The Conceptual Foundations of Invisible Work

JOHN W. BUDD

Work can be invisible in two broad ways. First, within the domain of work, some forms of work are celebrated and highly valued while other forms are marginalized or not even socially recognized as work. In this way, undervalued and overlooked forms of work are "invisible labor." The classic example is unpaid household work, but the chapters in this volume illustrate that invisible labor can take many forms. Second, within the broader sociopolitical/socioeconomic realm, other issues and interests are commonly prioritized over those pertaining to work and workers. For example, labor standards are seldom at the top of the international, national, or local political agenda; employees are typically invisible in corporate governance in Anglosphere countries; and individual members of capitalist societies are seen more as consumers than as workers. In this way, work itself generally is undervalued and overlooked and therefore also warrants an *invisible* label.

The different forms of the invisibility of work undoubtedly reflect complex sets of factors, including power relations, gender norms, and labor market dynamics. This chapter focuses on the conceptual foundations of invisible work. The premise of this chapter is reflected in an adage that states that the eye sees what the mind knows. We see and value work only when it conforms to our mental models of what work is. In the public imagination, why is work less visible than other key aspects of human life? It is so because dominant ways of thinking about work reduce it to a curse or a commodified, instrumental activity that supports consumption. So we do not think of work as having deeper value; therefore, we overlook work in favor of other human activities. Similarly, why are certain forms of work invisible? They are because when we think of work in certain ways—especially as a commodified, instrumental activity—forms of work that are considered different from or only weakly fulfilling these dominant conceptualizations of work are devalued and rendered invisible.

In these ways, then, how we think about and how we conceptualize work have real consequences for what is seen and valued as work. Unfortunately, conceptualizations of work are frequently narrowly conceived and are typically unstated. To better understand issues of invisible work and questions about what forms of work are valued and why, it is important to *explicitly* consider the diverse ways in which work can be conceptualized. This chapter therefore draws on my 2011 book, *The Thought of Work*, to present a framework of ten conceptualizations of work that synthesize contemporary and historical thinking about work—and invisibility.

By making these conceptualizations explicit, this chapter provides a foundation for thinking more clearly about how we define work and for gaining a deeper understanding of why (some) work is invisible. By broadening our thinking on work, this framework can further provide a foundation for crafting inclusive definitions of work that recognize not only the deep importance of work for individuals and society but also the value of diverse forms of human activity that should be fully embraced as work rather than overlooked or marginalized. In short, in order for the eye to recognize wider forms of work, we need to train the mind to think more broadly and deeply about work.

BROADENING THE CONCEPTUALIZATION OF WORK

Work can be a challenge to define. It is defined here as purposeful human activity involving physical or mental exertion that is not undertaken solely for pleasure and that has economic or symbolic value. The first part of this definition ("purposeful human activity") distinguishes work from the broader realm of all human effort. The second part ("not undertaken solely for pleasure") separates work from leisure while allowing for work to be pleasurable and thereby recognizing that there can sometimes be a nebulous boundary between work and leisure. The final part ("that has economic or symbolic value") allows work to be more encompassing than paid employment by also including unpaid caring for others, self-employment, subsistence farming, casual work in the informal sector, and other activities outside the standard Western boundaries of paid jobs and career aspirations. The purpose of this broad definition of work is to encompass the diverse conceptualizations of work found across the spectrum of work-related theorizing and analyses, not to precisely delimit what is and is not considered work (Glucksmann 1995).

From this broad definition of *work*, I identify ten conceptualizations of work that capture the rich ways in which work has been modeled in the behavioral, social, and philosophical sciences; these conceptualizations provide the range of possible individual and social meanings of work: work as curse, freedom, commodity, occupational citizenship, disutility, personal fulfillment, social relation, caring for others, identity, and service. These conceptualizations are summarized in the middle column of table 2.1 (on page 31) and presented in the remainder of this section. For the rich bodies of scholarship that lie behind each conceptualization, see Budd (2011). The connections to invisible work are briefly noted in this section and then described more fully in the following section after the entire framework of conceptualizations has been presented.

Work as a Curse

For thousands of years, work has been seen as painful toil necessary for survival that conflicts with life's more virtuous or pleasurable pursuits. When it is assumed that God or nature requires all or some to engage in arduous or dirty work, then work is conceptualized as a curse. Seeing hard work as a God-given curse has deep roots in Western thought. The Judeo-Christian tradition and Greco-Roman mythology share a common story in which humans originally did not have to work (at least not very hard), but a displeased god (for example, the Judeo-Christian God punishing Adam for his disobedience in the Garden of Eden or Zeus punishing humankind because Prometheus stole fire for it) punishes humans with toil. Hard work is thereby seen as a necessary part of the human experience but not as one of the higher purposes of the human experience. So by emphasizing the importance of other human activities, seeing work as a necessary evil contributes to the invisibility of work.

Elite segments of societies also tend to see the lower classes as occupying their natural place in the social and occupational hierarchy. Perhaps most famously, Aristotle reasoned that nature creates humans of varying intellectual abilities and that the intellectually inferior are naturally

Work as . . .	Definition	Implications for Invisible Labor
1. A Curse	An unquestioned burden necessary for human survival or maintenance of the social order	Devaluing of work is preordained by the natural order; other human activities are more important.
2. Freedom	A way to achieve independence from nature or other humans and to express human creativity	Work that fails to achieve economic independence or lacks creativity is less likely to be valued and visible.
3. A Commodity	An abstract quantity of productive effort that has tradable economic value	Visible work is exchanged in primary labor markets; high pay is required to indicate economic value.
4. Occupational Citizenship	An activity pursued by human members of a community entitled to certain rights	All forms of work should be valued more highly, with rights provided to all types of workers.
5. Disutility	An unpleasant activity tolerated to obtain goods and services that provide pleasure	Work that does not support high levels of consumption is less likely to be valued and visible.
6. Personal Fulfillment	Physical and psychological functioning that (ideally) satisfies individual needs	Work that does not provide intrinsic rewards is less likely to be valued and visible.
7. A Social Relation	Human interaction embedded in social norms, institutions, and power structures	The invisibility of work reflects socially created institutions and power structures.
8. Caring for Others	The physical, cognitive, and emotional effort required to attend to and maintain others	Though frequently invisible, caring work should be valued as real work.
9. Identity	A method for understanding who you are and where you stand in the social structure	All forms of work should be valued more highly and be more visible.
10. Service	The devotion of effort to others, such as God, household, community, or country	Though frequently invisible, service toward others should be valued as real work.

NOTE: Table by John W. Budd.

suited to be slaves. More recently, the belief in a natural ordering of work is reflected in Herrnstein and Murray's (1994) claims in *The Bell Curve* that contemporary America is stratified by genetically determined intellectual ability. The marginalization in contemporary Western societies of some occupations as "women's work" or as fit only for minorities or immigrants can similarly reflect a belief in a natural social hierarchy. In this way, less desirable forms of work are conceptualized as a curse of the lower classes, a view that in turn renders this work invisible to elite segments of society, who see themselves as engaged in more valuable forms of labor.

Work as Freedom

For much of human history, work was typically seen as forced by God, nature, custom, law, or physical violence. The centrality of the individual and freedom in modern Western thought, however, provides the basis for conceptualizing work as a source of freedom in several ways. One strain of this thinking is freedom from nature. This line of thought emphasizes the creative nature of work that is done independently of the daily necessities of nature. In this way, a worker is a creator—someone who "rebels against nature's dictates" (Mokyr 1990: viii) and is able "to impose culture" on the natural world (Wallman 1979: 1). Ideally, creative work allows us "to be ourselves, set our own schedules, do challenging work[,] and live in communities that reflect our values and priorities" (Florida 2002: 10).

Other ways of thinking about work as freedom pertain to individual liberty from the coercion of other people. John Locke famously argued in the seventeenth century that labor is the foundation for political freedom because it establishes ownership of private property. In other words, by being able to control the fruits of your own labor, work can be a classical source of liberty not from nature but from other humans and human institutions. This theorizing on the roots of political freedom also has important implications for economic liberalism (Macpherson 1962). When work is conceptualized as one's own property, workers become free to sell their labor for pay if they so choose. Moreover, when a person's work is hers and hers alone, there are no social obligations or limitations on how much she can accumulate through her work. Wage work and unchecked capitalist accumulation are therefore given moral approval, and the foundation is laid for seeing work as an economic commodity to be bought and sold in free markets. Such perspectives are reinforced by the legal systems of capitalist economies in which work is seen as an activity undertaken by individuals who are free to pursue occupations of their choosing and to quit at will. From this standpoint, employment is a contractual relation between legal equals, albeit with continuing tensions between the unrestricted freedom derived from legal principles of free contracting and the lingering influence of status-based standards (Deakin and Wilkinson 2005). Seeing work as freedom is important for the invisibility of work because work that fails to fulfill the standards created by various perspectives on freedom—such as work that lacks creativity or fails to provide economic independence—is devalued relative to work that meets these standards.

Work as a Commodity

The emergence of Western liberalism created a new conceptualization of work: "What could be more natural in a social universe composed of separate and autonomous individuals whose chief occupation was trading commodities back and forth than that some individuals should sell the property in their labor to other individuals, to whom thereafter it would belong?" (Steinfeld 1991: 92). In this way work comes to be seen as a commodity in which an individual's capacity to work—what Marx called "labor power"—is viewed as an abstract quantity that can be bought and sold. Diverse forms of concrete labor are all reduced to sources of economic value that can be made equivalent by exchanging them at an appropriate set of relative prices. Work is thought of as a generic input into a production function, and employers and workers buy and sell generic units of this commodity called *work* or *labor* (or *labor power* in Marxist terminology).

Mainstream (neoclassical) economic thought embraces the commodity conceptualization of work. Employers are assumed to maximize their profits by utilizing the optimum amounts of labor, capital, and other inputs to produce goods and services for sale. Work and workers are thus treated like any other factor of production. On the supply side, work is something that individuals choose to sell in varying quantities in order to earn income and maximize their individual or household utility. Employers and employees are therefore both modeled as treating hours of labor as one of a number of quantities to factor into the relevant optimization problem; marginal analysis determines the optimum amount of labor to buy or sell in the labor market no differently than it determines the exchange of other commodities. Moreover, when one sees work as a commodity, its allocation is seen as governed by the impersonal "laws" of supply and demand. The intersection of labor supply and labor demand determines the terms and conditions of employment, and work is analyzed like all other economic commodities—"the theory of the determination of wages in a free market is simply a special case of the general theory of value" (Hicks 1963: 1). The commodity perspective is instructive for considerations of the invisibility of labor because it reveals why paid work, and especially highly paid work, is privileged over other forms.

Work as Occupational Citizenship

Work can also be conceptualized not as an activity undertaken by autonomous individuals but as one undertaken by citizens who are part of human communities. To see workers as citizens is to decommodify them, to give them a status as more than just factors of production or individuals seeking personal fulfillment or identities (Standing 2009). Specifically, citizens should be seen as having inherent equal worth and thus being entitled to certain rights and standards of dignity and self-determination irrespective of what the market provides. Work, then, is conceptualized as occupational citizenship when we think of what it means for workers to be citizens of a human community.

Industrial relations research (e.g., Budd 2004) and legal scholarship (e.g., Crain 2010) frequently argue that citizen-workers are entitled to minimum working and living conditions that are determined by standards of human dignity, not by supply and demand, and to meaningful forms of self-determination in the workplace that go beyond the freedom to quit. Closely related approaches include conceptualizations of workers' rights as human rights, the International Labour Organization's campaign for decent work, and various theological and ethical approaches that emphasize that work should respect standards of human dignity. From these perspectives, the invisibility of work is a significant concern because all forms of work should be valued, and all workers should enjoy decent conditions, although there tends to be a bias toward traditional views that equate work with paid employment.

Work as Disutility

In mainstream economic theorizing, individuals are modeled as rational agents seeking to maximize a utility function that is increasing in the consumption of goods, services, and leisure. Work is a central element of an individual's maximization problem because work yields goods and services directly through self-production or indirectly through earned income. However, the physical and mental activity of working is seen as *reducing* one's utility. This perspective on work has two roots: seeing it as a painful or stressful activity and seeing it as something that is less pleasurable than leisure since work involves the opportunity cost of reduced time for pleasurable leisure (Spencer 2009). In either case, work is conceptualized as *disutility*—an unpleasant activity tolerated only to obtain goods, services, and leisure that provide pleasure. This conceptualization further perpetuates the negative views of work that originally arose from seeing work as a curse and therefore has similar implications for the invisibility of labor.

When imperfect information makes employment contracts incomplete, economists frequently assume that employers face a principal–agent problem—how to get the agent (in this case, a worker) to act in the interests of the principal (in this case, the owners of the organization). This assumption is made because work is being conceptualized as disutility, so workers are presumed to want to exert minimal levels of effort ("shirking"). By assuming that monitoring workers is typically difficult or imperfect, theorizing in personnel and organizational economics thereby focuses on solving these principal–agent problems by using optimal monetary incentives to combat disutility by making additional worker effort utility-enhancing (Lazear 1995). This monetary emphasis parallels the materialistic focus of the work-as-a-commodity perspective and similarly privileges highly compensated jobs, an effect that renders other forms of work invisible.

Work as Personal Fulfillment

A focus on the positive and negative physical and especially on the psychological outcomes that are inherent in work creates a conceptualization of work as personal fulfillment. In this way of thinking, work is cognitively and emotionally directed by the brain. Mental states such as attitudes, moods, and emotions can affect individuals' work behaviors; the nature of one's work—such as the job tasks, rewards, relations with coworkers, and supervision—can affect one's mental state. As such, work is viewed as an activity that arouses cognitive and affective functioning. Ideally, work should be a source of personal fulfillment and psychological well-being that satisfies needs for achievement, mastery, self-esteem, and self-worth (Turner, Barling, and Zacharatos 2002). But work with mindless repetition, abusive coworkers or bosses, excessive physical or mental demands, or other factors that comprise unpleasant work can have negative psychological consequences.

The centrality of cognitive and affective mental processes for conceptualizing work is emphasized most strongly by scholars in industrial-organizational psychology, organizational behavior, and human resource management. Some key foundational research topics that result from conceptualizing work in this way are individual psychological differences such as cognitive ability or personality, job satisfaction, organizational justice, and intrinsic work motivation. Human resource management scholarship builds on the conceptualization of work as personal fulfillment by assuming that to be effective, human resource management practices must satisfy workers' psychological needs by managing their cognitive and affective functioning. This is typically seen as a win-win situation by embracing a unitarist vision of the employment relationship that assumes that the interests of workers and their organizations can be aligned: Psychological needs can be fulfilled through fair treatment, intrinsic rewards, and placement of workers into appropriate jobs; employees will reciprocate by being hardworking and loyal; and high levels of organizational performance, including profitability and shareholder returns, will result. An important implication for the invisibility of labor is that work that fails to conform to these norms is seen as anomalous and therefore receives less attention and respect.

Work as a Social Relation

The extrinsic rewards of work emphasized in mainstream economics or the intrinsic rewards emphasized in psychology underappreciate the extent to which work is embedded in complex social phenomena such that individuals seek approval, status, sociability, and power. The social context also provides constraints such as (a) social norms that define the boundaries of acceptable behaviors or work roles or (b) power relations that define access to resources. To regard work as consisting of human interactions that are experienced within and shaped by social networks, social norms, and institutions and that are socially constructed power relations is to conceptualize work as social relation. The invisibility of work is therefore seen as constructed by these social forces, and the path to combatting problems of invisible labor is to change these social forces.

Three major approaches to thinking about work occurring within a rich social context are instructive. First, the social dynamics of interpersonal work interactions are highlighted by theories of social exchange and social networks (Cropanzano and Mitchell 2005; Portes 1998). Work is thus seen as a social exchange consisting of open-ended, ongoing relationships occurring within networks of social ties based on trust and reciprocity that have imperfectly specified obligations and a multiplicity of objectives. A second approach to conceptualizing work as a social relation focuses on the importance of social norms for how work is experienced and structured. These norms can stem from direct, interpersonal contact—such as norms in work groups to limit output or work effort—while other norms are organizational in nature, and still other work norms are societal-level constructions.

A third social relations approach emphasizes socially constructed hierarchies and power relations. For example, Marxist-inspired theorizing on work embraces a social relations conceptualization of work by seeing capital–labor or employer–employee power dynamics as socially constructed. Work, then, is viewed as contested terrain in which employers and employees continuously seek control and make accommodations. This dialectic of control and accommodation can occur through formal policies, rules, and other structural features of the employment relationship (Thompson and Newsome 2004) as well as through an organization's culture and other discursive elements (Knights and Willmott 1989). Another approach that emphasizes socially constructed hierarchies consists of feminist theories of patriarchy and gender (Gottfried 2006).

Work Caring for Others

The traditional conceptualizations of work in the social and behavioral sciences and in the accompanying research that primarily focuses on paid employment to the exclusion of unpaid household work and other caring activities that do not produce economic commodities are criticized by feminist scholarship for ignoring gender issues (Gottfried 2006). Feminist thought rejects the resulting devaluing of "woman's work" and asserts that it should be seen as real work. Specifically, it is work as caring for others—the physical, cognitive, and emotional effort required to attend to and maintain others.

While caring for others is not limited to unpaid household work and is not the exclusive domain of women, it powerfully affects the gendered work experiences of women. Housewives are frequently seen as unproductive, working women are often saddled with a majority of the burdens of household work, and women in the workplace face gendered expectations about appropriate occupations and work behaviors that are frequently rooted in idealized visions of caring, domesticity, and femininity. In feminist theorizing, this gendered nature of work—and thus the invisibility of "woman's work"—is the result of socially constructed norms and power dynamics, not maternal instincts or other biological features (Jackson 1998).

Work as Identity

To help understand who they are, individuals create identities that enhance their comprehension of where they fit into the broader world. Given that work is a significant part of many people's lives, work can be conceptualized as identity—that is, as a source of understanding and meaning (Leidner 2006). Work can be a source of meaning on several levels. The personal identity dimension consists of stable attributes and traits that an individual sees as making him unique, including descriptors related to his work. The social identity approach highlights identity construction via categorizing oneself into various groups, such as one's occupation and employer. The interactionist approach focuses on the role of social interactions in creating individual identities. From this perspective, the social roles attached to occupations and careers are a major source of one's self-presentation and identity. Identity related to class and class consciousness is also rooted in work.

At a more fundamental level, work can be viewed as a central element of creating a species identity for humans. The importance of work for humanness was most famously advanced by Marx's ([1844] 1988) argument that "in creating an objective world by his practical activity, in working-up inorganic nature, man proves himself a conscious species being, i.e., as a being that treats the species as its own essential being" (pp. 76–77). It is from this belief that self-directed work is the essential quality of being human that Marx further argued that the commodification of work causes alienation—the loss of humanness experienced when workers are forced to sell an inherent part of themselves. In the 1981 papal encyclical *Laborem exercens* (On human work), Pope John Paul II articulated the importance of work in terms strikingly similar to those presented by Marx: "Work is one of the characteristics that distinguish man from the rest of creatures, whose activity for sustaining their lives cannot be called work. Only man is capable of work, and only man works, at the same time by work occupying his existence on earth. Thus work bears a particular mark of man and of humanity, the mark of a person operating within a community of persons. And this mark decides its interior characteristics; in a sense it constitutes its very nature" (Preface, emphasis omitted).

While the differing views on work as identify differ as to the depth of work's contributions to an individual's identity, they all share a concern with the invisibility of work because work should be valued and respected, not invisible, in order to contribute to a positive self-identity.

Work as Service

Since the early years of the Christian church, work has been seen as a way to serve God's kingdom by preventing idleness (leading to sin), providing for one's family, and generating surpluses for charitable giving. Later, Martin Luther and John Calvin further enhanced the status of daily work by believing that everyone's (nonsinful) occupation represents something that God summons us to do by providing special gifts or talents—that is, a calling: "something that fits how we were made, so that doing it will enable us to glorify God, serve others, and be most richly ourselves" (Placher 2005: 3). Furthermore, today's Christian theology of work is frequently complemented by a conceptualization of work as an act of cocreation with God, as captured here by Pope John Paul II (1981) in *Laborem exercens*: "Awareness that man's work is a participation in God's activity ought to permeate . . . even the most ordinary everyday activities. For, while providing the substance of life for themselves and their families, men and women are performing their activities in a way which appropriately benefits society. They can justly consider that by their labor they are unfolding the Creator's work, consulting the advantages of their brothers and sisters, and contributing by their personal industry to the realization in history of the divine plan" (sec. 25).

Whether for religious or secular reasons, a popular way of serving a community is through volunteering. Even though volunteering is typically unpaid or minimally paid, it should be seen as work because it involves effort, produces value, and is structured by the same factors that shape paid work, such as labor market opportunities, individual motivation, social norms, and gender (Taylor 2005). There are diverse reasons why individuals pursue or are encouraged to pursue volunteer work, civic service, and community building. Helping others who are impoverished frequently stems from humanitarian concerns motivated by religious and/or ethical principles. In a very different vein, the classical republicanism school of thought in political philosophy emphasizes civic virtue in order to hold a community or a nation together. Serving others is also advocated as a way of repaying one's debt to society, while military service is frequently seen as patriotic service for one's country.

Confucianism provides another foundation for seeing work as service. Specifically, the centrality of the family in Confucian thought means that in East Asia work is frequently seen as serving the multigenerational family and the common good, not the individual. As the East Asian countries have become industrialized, Confucian values have also carried over into the employment relationship for wage and salary workers. The Japanese ideal of lifetime employment in which employees are recruited for and expected to stay at the company for their working lives can be seen as a reflection of the Confucian importance of familial reciprocity and loyalty, even if this ideal is a reality for only a minority of the workforce. In other words, working for the family becomes working for the corporate family.

So in addition to contemporary Western conceptualizations of work that are typically individual-centric—whether serving an individual's and her immediate family's needs for income, psychological fulfillment, social recognition, identity, and caring—work can also serve God, humanity, or one's country, community, or family. In these ways, work can be thought of as service. This view connects to concerns with the invisibility of work because individual-centric norms on work tend to exclude service-based forms of work from definitions of real work and therefore deny service work the same social legitimacy and economic value as afforded to other forms of work.

THE IMPORTANCE OF CONCEPTUALIZATIONS OF WORK FOR INVISIBLE WORK

This framework of ten conceptualizations of work can deepen our understanding of many aspects of work. Of particular interest here are the implications for invisible labor (see the last column of table 2.1 on p. 31). Taken individually, each conceptualization helps reveal why some forms of work are valued more than others. Taken as a set, the conceptualizations explicitly uncover the limits that have been placed on what counts as work and thereby illuminate the aspects of work that need to be added to our mental models of work in order to reduce the invisibility of specific forms of work. Moreover, the set of conceptualizations provides new insights as to why work in general is often invisible in the public imagination, the political arena, and other domains. The next section first discusses the implications of the conceptualizations for the invisibility of specific forms of work and then concludes with implications for the broader invisibility of work.

The Invisibility of Specific Forms of Work

The earliest conceptualization of work as a curse devalues work by seeing it as a predetermined burden, especially for those who are viewed as naturally suited for certain types of tasks. For example, when caring activities are seen as the natural realm of women because of female biological and personality traits, these activities then become less valued as work because they are regarded as women's natural roles. Similarly, if certain types of individuals are seen as being equipped for performing only mundane or other undesirable tasks and as lacking the aptitude or drive for mastering more complex jobs, it then becomes easier for elites who hold these prejudicial views to dismiss concerns about the conditions endured by these workers because they are viewed as these workers' natural burden. In these ways, women and ethnic minorities have been discriminated against for centuries, and their work has been rendered less valuable and therefore invisible by elite segments of society.

When work is conceptualized as a commodity, then what counts as work is that which is perceived as creating economic value by being exchanged in labor markets. Unpaid household work, indigenous activities like hunting, and other nonmarket forms of work are therefore dismissed—as illustrated by the long-standing and prejudicial labeling of indigenous activities as "primitive." Moreover, when markets are seen as the arbiters of value, as in mainstream neoclassical economic thought and in neoliberal market ideology, not only is market exchange required to indicate value creation, but the level of compensation is also taken as an indicator of the value and importance of the work. Lowly paid work is therefore devalued and rendered less visible than highly paid work. The conceptualization of work as disutility reinforces this last implication because from this perspective, the raison d'être of work is supporting consumption, so unpaid or lowly paid work that fails to support high levels of consumption is less likely to be valued and visible.

Those who embrace the commodity and disutility conceptualizations of work generally see markets as natural (witness the rhetorical support for "free markets" and markets' lack of regulation) while also assuming that work is not pleasurable. These views are similar to those associated with seeing work as a curse—just replace the determination of natural forces with the determination of the market. In contrast, a social relations perspective on work sees markets as socially determined via laws pertaining to property rights, contracts, fraud, coercion, and other key elements that ultimately reflect and reinforce power relations between competing groups. A social relations conceptualization of work also emphasizes the importance of social norms. As such, a social relations perspective on work importantly implies that whether specific forms of work are visible or invisible is the result of socially created institutions, power structures, and norms. The invisibility of labor is therefore within our control as a society.

Other conceptualizations highlight different aspects of these norms and thereby illustrate why different forms of work may or may not be invisible. When work is viewed as freedom, then forms of work that fail to achieve economic independence—such as unpaid household caring activities—or that lack creativity, such as low-skilled, repetitive jobs, are less likely to be valued and visible. Similarly, if work is embraced as personal fulfillment, then work that does not provide intrinsic rewards is less likely to be valued and visible, though this viewpoint can be a double-edged sword because if real work is supposed to be hard (recall curse and disutility), then work that is overly pleasurable might be dismissed as not being true work. Work done solely for an individual's pleasure is not recognized by the U.S. legal system as real work and therefore is not covered by employment and labor law (see chapter 13). The conceptualizations of work as caring and service also reveal that when these forms of work fall outside the norms of what is deemed to be work, these forms of work are then rendered invisible. Caring activities, for example, might be seen as acts of love rather than work. Similarly, volunteering might be regarded as a duty, an altruistic activity, or other things, but not as real work. As such, it is invisible.

Individual conceptualizations of work are also important for revealing why invisible labor is a problem. Seeing work as personal fulfillment and identity brings the importance of physical safety, psychological well-being, and the ability to craft a healthy identity to the fore. These standards are harder to achieve when work is invisible because invisible work can have fewer legal protections and less social recognition.

Consequently, all forms of work, including caring and service work, should be valued as real work rather than left as invisible. The occupational citizenship and freedom ways of thinking about work also highlight the connections between work and democracy. Invisible labor can be detrimental to democratic participation by denying workers the resources, the agency, and the skills to be fully deliberative citizens whose voices will be heard. Feminist scholarship that critically explores the conceptualization of work as caring also shows how norms that render household work invisible have negative ramifications in the sphere of paid employment. Specifically, beliefs about the gendered body in the workplace and the caregiving responsibilities of women lead to employment-related discrimination as men and women are segregated into different occupations, given different roles and levels of responsibility, expected to sell or tolerate differing levels of sexuality, and paid differently for performing comparable work.

The General Invisibility of Work

Turning to the invisibility of work generally, the broad set of conceptualizations of work helps us understand why this invisibility is the case. Specifically, the conceptualizations as a set reveal the narrowness with which work is viewed, especially in the dominant neoliberal market paradigm. The combination of seeing work as simultaneously a curse, a commodity, and a disutility reduces work to an unpleasant activity beyond our control—that is, we must take what God, nature, or the market determines. And this activity largely has instrumental benefits, especially productivity for society and income for individuals and their families. From such a narrow perspective, it naturally follows that individuals should be seeking pleasure and deep meaning from other life spheres. Moreover, if work is largely about economic productivity and value, then public policies and organizational strategies will prioritize conditions that are seen as fostering value creation—such as labor market deregulation and unfettered corporate decision-making—rather than prioritize labor standards and worker well-being for all workers.

Note carefully that it takes a broad conceptual foundation to reveal not only how work is conceptualized but also how it is not. The extrinsic emphasis of the neoliberal market ideology overlooks other critical aspects of work that are highlighted by other conceptualizations, especially freedom (and thus democracy), psychological health, identity, caring, and serving others. With a truncated recognition of the deep benefits of work along with a perceived lack of control over work and its conditions, other elements of life are regarded as more important and within our control. So work becomes invisible relative to other spheres.

Lastly, the conceptualizations of work also point to strategies to reduce the invisibility of labor. While seeing work as a curse or a commodity largely puts work beyond our control, the occupational citizenship conceptualization of work advocates institutional intervention to improve market-based outcomes. Even more robustly, a social relations perspective highlights the need to change deeply held social norms, an action that could then bring greater recognition to work generally and also to undervalued and overlooked forms of work. Other conceptualizations point toward the needed changes in norms—we need to reduce the degree to which work is seen as a curse, a commodity, and a disutility while seeing work more inclusively as being a necessary source of psychological health and personal identity as well as a way to care for and serve others.

. . .

The fact that specific forms of work can be invisible underscores the importance of thinking carefully about definitions and conceptualizations of work. Indeed, the argument of this chapter is that our mental models of what work is critically shape our beliefs about who is valued as a worker and what is valued as work. Just as importantly, our intellectual visions of what work is determine what work is not and therefore deny recognition and the corresponding economic, psychological, social, and legal resources to those whose activities are not deemed to be work. Crain (chapter 13), for example, reveals important problems that result from the narrow definition of work used by the U.S. legal system. Moreover, considerations of invisible labor should not overlook the fact that work in general is often rendered invisible because it is overshadowed by other human activities and other sociopolitical/socioeconomic interests. Again, the argument here is that these dynamics reflect, at least partly, the embrace of limited mental models of work that have the unfortunate effect of blinding us to the true depth and breadth of the importance of work.

On multiple levels, then, the extent to which work is visible and valued, or is not, rests in important ways on how we think about work. It is therefore essential that we explicitly identify alternative ways to think about work and understand their implications for invisible labor. To really understand invisible labor, we need to recognize not only what is valued but also what is not. So a broad conceptual framework is needed. In practice, we also need to broaden the dominant conceptualizations of work in order to give all forms of work the recognition that they deserve. Work should not be narrowly seen solely as a commodified economic transaction that provides income but instead should be robustly visible as a fully human activity necessary for reproductive as well as productive activities that have deep importance for our individual and collective material and psychological health as well as for the quality of democracy and other social relations (Boyte and Kari 1996; Budd 2011; Crain 2010).

REFERENCES

Boyte, Harry C., and Nancy N. Kari. 1996. *Building America: The Democratic Promise of Public Work*. Philadelphia: Temple University Press.

Budd, John W. 2004. *Employment with a Human Face: Balancing Efficiency, Equity, and Voice*. Ithaca, NY: Cornell University Press.

———. 2011. *The Thought of Work*. Ithaca, NY: Cornell University Press.

Crain, Marion. 2010. "Work Matters." *Kansas Journal of Law and Public Policy* 19 (Spring): 365–82.

Cropanzano, Russell, and Marie S. Mitchell. 2005. "Social Exchange Theory: An Interdisciplinary Review." *Journal of Management* 31 (December): 874–900.

Deakin, Simon, and Frank Wilkinson. 2005. *The Law of the Labour Market: Industrialization, Employment, and Legal Evolution*. Oxford: Oxford University Press.

Florida, Richard. 2002. *The Rise of the Creative Class: And How It's Transforming Work, Leisure, Community, and Everyday Life*. New York: Basic Books.

Glucksmann, Miriam A. 1995. "Why 'Work'? Gender and the 'Total Social Organization of Labour.'" *Gender, Work, and Organization* 2 (April): 63–75.

Gottfried, Heidi. 2006. "Feminist Theories of Work." Pp. 121–54 in *Social Theory at Work*, edited by M. Korczynski et al. Oxford: Oxford University Press.

Herrnstein, Richard J., and Charles Murray. 1994. *The Bell Curve: Intelligence and Class Structure in American Life*. New York: Free Press.

Hicks, John R. 1963. *The Theory of Wages*. 2nd ed. London: Macmillan.

Jackson, Stevi. 1998. "Feminist Social Theory." Pp. 12–33 in *Contemporary Feminist Theories*, edited by Stevi Jackson and Jackie Jones. New York: New York University Press.

John Paul II. 1981. *Laborem exercens* (On human work). Encyclical letter. Retrieved December 21, 2014 (www.vatican.va/holy_father/john_paul_ii /encyclicals/index.htm).

Knights, David, and Hugh Willmott. 1989. "Power and Subjectivity at Work: From Degradation to Subjugation in Social Relations." *Sociology* 23 (November): 535–58.

Lazear, Edward P. 1995. *Personnel Economics*. Cambridge, MA: MIT Press.

Leidner, Robin. 2006. "Identity and Work." Pp. 424–63 in *Social Theory at Work*, edited by M. Korczynski et al. Oxford: Oxford University Press.

Macpherson, C. B. 1962. *The Political Theory of Possessive Individualism: Hobbes to Locke*. London: Oxford University Press.

Marx, Karl. [1844] 1988. *Economic and Philosophic Manuscripts of 1844*. Translated by Martin Milligan. Reprint, Amherst, NY: Prometheus Books.

Mokyr, Joel. 1990. *The Lever of Riches: Technological Creativity and Economic Progress*. New York: Oxford University Press.

Placher, William C. 2005. "Introduction." Pp. 1–11 in *Callings: Twenty Centuries of Christian Wisdom on Vocation*, edited by William C. Placher. Grand Rapids, MI: Eerdmans.

Portes, Alejandro. 1998. "Social Capital: Its Origins and Applications in Modern Sociology." *Annual Review of Sociology* 24: 1–24.

Spencer, David A. 2009. *The Political Economy of Work*. London: Routledge.

Standing, Guy. 2009. *Work after Globalization: Building Occupational Citizenship*. Cheltenham: Edward Elgar.

Steinfeld, Robert J. 1991. *The Invention of Free Labor: The Employment Relation in English and American Law and Culture, 1350–1870*. Chapel Hill: University of North Carolina Press.

Taylor, Rebecca F. 2005. "Rethinking Voluntary Work." Pp. 119–35 in *A New Sociology of Work?* edited by Lynne Pettinger et al. Malden, MA: Blackwell.

Thompson, Paul, and Kirsty Newsome. 2004. "Labor Process Theory, Work, and the Employment Relation." Pp. 133–62 in *Theoretical Perspectives on Work and the Employment Relationship*, edited by B. E. Kaufman. Champaign, IL: Industrial Relations Research Association.

Turner, Nick, Julian Barling, and Anthea Zacharatos. 2002. "Positive Psychology at Work." Pp. 715–30 in *Handbook of Positive Psychology*, edited by C. R. Snyder and S. J. Lopez. New York: Oxford University Press.

Wallman, Sandra. 1979. "Introduction." Pp. 1–24 in *Social Anthropology of Work*, edited by Sandra Wallman. London: Academic Press.

CHAPTER 3

Maintaining Hierarchies in Predominantly White Organizations

A Theory of Racial Tasks as Invisible Labor

ADIA HARVEY WINGFIELD AND RENÉE SKEETE

Sociological research has been adept at highlighting ways that labor markets and workplaces, far from being neutral, objective structures, can actually serve to perpetuate various forms of inequality. In particular, one of the key ways that markets and work settings accomplish this action is through differential treatment of whites and people of color. Factors like employer preferences, structural discrimination, job queues, differential access to social networks, and other issues collectively work to create stark racial disparities (Kirschenman and Neckerman 1991; Reskin and Roos 1990; Roscigno 2007; Royster 2003). As a consequence, racial minorities are often concentrated into lower-wage, lower-paying jobs and are sparsely represented among the higher-status, more influential positions within organizations and in professions more broadly (Acker 2006; Tomaskovic-Devey 1993; Wilson 1997). Thus, structural and organizational patterns become one way that racial hierarchies are perpetuated in work settings.

While we have many examples of racial incidents at work, there are few theoretical arguments offered that make sense of why such instances occur. Sociologists who study work and race generally lack a theoretical apparatus designed to connect the organizational structure of the workplace to the cultural and social practices within that serve to reproduce racial inequality. We attempt to address this deficiency here by emphasizing the ways that the job requirements and implicit responsibilities associated with work at different levels of the organizational hierarchy are imbued with racialized meanings that impact the practices, behaviors, and actions that occur within the organization. We describe the work that is done in this context as *racial tasks* that ultimately operate to preserve and uphold whites' advantage in work settings. As such, we explore the ways that organizational hierarchies extend to unspoken, often invisible racialized practices that inform and are embedded within racial minorities' work in predominantly white settings.

In this chapter we also explore the ways that racial tasks constitute additional, invisible labor that workers of color are charged with performing. When minority workers do the routine, everyday acts associated with their jobs, we argue that a hidden component of this work involves various tasks and expectations that maintain normative whiteness in organizations. This labor is inconspicuous and easily obscured, and it constitutes an invisible form of racial identity work.

THEORETICAL UNDERPINNINGS OF RACIAL TASKS

Researchers have long noted that organizational structures produce hierarchies and reinforce status inequalities. Within organizations, particularly workplaces, the routine patterns, practices, and expectations that are present can often serve to perpetuate certain groups' advantages over others. Joan Acker (1990) provides a particularly important case of the way this action occurs within organizations wherein assumptions, beliefs, and ideologies are wedded to organizational practices that reproduce gendered patterns. Specifically, Acker's theory asserts that organizations are gendered structures that implicitly hold expectations about which workers are best suited for certain jobs, thus establishing men as natural, ideal workers. Other research has further developed this theoretical argument to find that as organizations "gender" certain occupations, men are often slotted into the jobs that tend to be better paying and hold higher status (Britton 2000; Pierce 1995). Women face difficulties attempting to access and perform in these jobs and are often channeled into "female" positions that are considered more suitable and acceptable for them. Consequently, a great deal of research on gender and work has shown that organizations tacitly establish hierarchies wherein men are rewarded with access to better jobs.

In this chapter we consider the ways in which organizational practices, expectations, and assumptions also serve to reproduce racial hierarchies. Within predominantly white organizations (e.g., many law firms, universities, and financial institutions) there are many employees, often of different races. However, whites tend to be concentrated at the top levels of these organizations (in CEO, director, president, and other senior administrative positions). In 2013, for instance, white males held 73 percent of the board seats at Fortune 500 companies (Alliance for Board Diversity 2013). Some minorities can and do reach these levels, but those who do may find that the rewards associated with this ascent may be negligible as these employees are likely to have less responsibility than whites, supervise primarily other racial minorities, and/or find themselves tracked into submarkets that mostly address racialized concerns (Collins 1997; Durr and Logan 1997; Tomaskovic-Devey 1993). People of color are more likely to be scattered throughout the middle levels (as faculty, associates, and middle managers) and overrepresented at the bottom tiers (in custodial services, administrative support staff, or security work). We seek here to provide a theoretical argument that helps to explain the sorts of racial challenges many workers of color document when employed in these predominantly white workplaces (see, for instance, Feagin and Sikes 1995; Jackson, Thoits, and Taylor 1995; Roscigno 2007). We emphasize the ways in which organizational structures reproduce racialized hierarchies through everyday practices.

PERFORMING RACIAL TASKS

We have defined *racial tasks* broadly as the work minorities do that is associated with their positions in the organizational hierarchy and that reinforces whites' position of power within the workplace. Here, we develop this idea more fully. We argue that racial tasks are present at three levels—ideological, interactional, and physical—and occur in a myriad of ways at each level (see table 3.1). At the *ideological* level, racial tasks involve establishing and/or maintaining an organizational culture that is normatively white and middle class. This labor is mostly done by those at the top level of the organizational hierarchy—CEOs, COOs, and upper-level administrators. As such, racial tasks at this level actively serve to build and/or establish a culture wherein whiteness is normalized and treated as standard. In *interactions,* racial tasks are the routine self-presentation and emotion work done to uphold whites' dominant position in the workplace. Workers at the middle level of organizations—mid-level managers, lower level administrators—are likely to do much of this labor. At the interactional level, the process of completing racial tasks means that through everyday practices and basic interactions, workers are conforming to norms that have already been

TABLE 3.1.   A MODEL OF RACIAL TASKS

Organizational Level of Worker	Type of Work	Racial Tasks
Elites (COOs, upper-level administrators, law firm partners)	Mostly ideological Some interactional	Creating organizational norms, culture
Middle-level workers (middle management, low-level administrators, nurses, professors)	Mostly interactional Some ideological	Upholding/conforming to organizational norms, culture Diversity management Buffering Self-presentation, emotional labor
Low-level workers (janitorial and custodial staff, maintenance)	Mostly physical Some interactional	Building, maintaining, and securing the physical space that houses the institutional and ideological racial tasks of upper-level workers Physical distancing from upper-level workers and clients/customers

NOTE: Table by Adia Harvey Wingfield and Renée Skeete.

set. They also fulfill ideological racial tasks, though in a different capacity than do those at the uppermost levels of the institution. These employees are likely to do the ideological racial tasks of upholding, conforming to, and enforcing the organizational culture and norms established by those at the top. Finally, racial tasks also occur in a *physical* form when workers are responsible for constructing and/or maintaining the infrastructure within which the ideological and institutional forms of racial tasks ensue. This type of labor also includes physical tasks, nonverbal communication, decoration, and spatial organization. Most employees responsible for the physical form of racial tasks will work at the lowest tiers of the organization as maintenance or service workers.

Racial tasks are largely invisible forms of labor. We theorize that they are a type of work that is frequently hidden from white colleagues but that remains essential for minority workers within an organization. In this way, these tasks are similar to the emotional labor Arlie Hochschild (1983) identified long ago as a key part of the way modern organizations commodify service workers' feelings. Racial tasks, however, are structured by organizational hierarchies and subtly serve to reinforce normative whiteness in these spaces by pushing workers of color to gloss over and obscure real or imagined differences.

Racial Tasks at the Ideological Level

Racial tasks include the work that is done to perpetuate the ideological and cultural norms that uphold racial hierarchies in the work environment. Elijah Anderson (1999) describes most professional work environments as normatively white middle-class cultures. We would venture that this description extends beyond professional settings to shape many work cultures more generally, wherein "professionalism" becomes tacitly understood as synonymous with whiteness (see Wingfield 2010 for discussion of how black professionals are expected to conform to emotional norms that deny or minimize racial inequities they face at work and in the broader society). Furthermore, building on Acker's (2006) contention that "decisions about goals, locations, technologies, and investments are made at the top" (p. 112), we argue that those at the top levels of organizations are directly able to set or change the organizational culture and are permitted to do so more directly than employees at the middle or lower tiers are. These employees at the very top levels of an organization are likely to be predominantly white (Acker 2006). As Richard Zweigenhaft and G. William Domhoff (2003) have established, very few workers of color make it to the top ranks of organizational structures due to a variety of systemic and institutional factors. Those who do reach this stratum are likely to be the only minority workers at that level. Thus, minority workers who establish the organizational culture of a work environment (the upper-level administrators, CEOs, and top-tier management) are completing an ideological form of racial task that upholds cultural norms that value and idealize whiteness.

We argue that these low numbers put these minority workers in a position in which they must still do the ideological racial tasks of working to construct and maintain an organizational culture that privileges whiteness. Workers in this situation may be given the responsibility of managing diversity programs, special training and internship programs for workers of color, and other requirements that are seen as the appropriate domain for racial minorities. Although they may have the ability to influence organizational culture as it relates to diversity, top-level workers of color often remain faced with the pressure of maintaining an organizational culture that privileges whiteness. For instance, despite the presence of a few high-ranking individuals of color in various Wall Street firms, Karen Ho's (2009) ethnography of financial organizations reveals that both recruiting and hiring practices are steeped in cultural and racialized premises that result in a disproportionately white upper-class workforce. We expect that while a few racial minority workers may break through to these top levels, their individual presence is not enough to result in broad institutional change to the organizational culture. Hence, we theorize that even those at the top levels of an organization would still find themselves engaged in the invisible work of maintaining racial ideologies that run counter to the inclusion and advancement of workers of color across the board.

However, we do expect that the power that accompanies their high-ranking positions means that workers at this level are freed from doing some, but not all, of the interactional racial tasks expected of workers lower down the ladder. This is not to say that workers at these top levels are completely exempt from this interactional labor but rather that their positions at the top of the organizational hierarchy offer them the ability to do less of this labor than workers of color at the middle levels do.

Sharon Collins (1997) describes this sort of work in her study of black executives in the corporate world. She identifies black managers in diversity-related positions as peacekeepers, crisis managers, and conciliators who often have the responsibility of serving as a buffer between mostly white organizations and minority constituencies. Collins identifies this as "racialized labor," highlighting the ways that black executives are called upon—and often exclusively hired—in order to address concerns related to minority constituents. Collins notes that the prevalence and availability of these jobs are largely linked to the political economy and broader societal support for these sorts of jobs; as such, these positions may be diminishing in a present-day era in which color blindness is the preferred ideological outlook. However, workers who still hold these jobs may find themselves doing ideological racial tasks of upholding the organization's image as a fair and equitable environment despite any racialized practices that may occur to undermine this perception. In addition to the racialized labor that Collins describes of having to address minority group concerns, we argue that at this level workers are also required to help set a racialized ideological culture. Thus, these employees may be responsible for the ideological task of maintaining an organizational culture that obscures or minimizes the challenges facing minority workers.

Research suggests that this situation has become particularly true for present-day diversity officers as well as for those in management positions. As broader societal support for race-related initiatives has waned, workers in this field are likely to find themselves advocating for programs that push diversity as very broadly defined rather than promoting initiatives designed to address institutionalized racial disadvantage. A quotation from a black female manager in David Embrick's (2011) study of executives' perceptions of diversity exemplifies this phenomenon:

> I think about . . . just accepting individuality[,] and that's my definition of [diversity] whether it's race, sex, sexual orientation, . . . or national origin or whether it's . . . [that] one person is from the country, one person's from the city, one person's from a different region, or whether it's age, generational differences[;] it, to me, it's just accepting individuals' different work styles. . . . I have people who are more introverted, I have people who are extroverted, and . . . to me it's just respecting those differences and understanding that they all have some value and not looking negatively on one just because that's not something that you yourself may exhibit and subscribe to. (p. 11)

By constructing diversity as something that includes "individuals' different work styles" as very generally defined, this manager is doing the racial task of helping to construct an ideological culture in which race has little social or cultural significance despite the widespread underrepresentation of people of color in upper-level management and executive roles.

A similar example could be constructed in other organizational settings. Within law firms, partners tend to be those responsible for establishing the culture. In most firms the majority of partners are also white men, though some racial minority men and women of any race can also be counted among these ranks (Pierce 2012). If, in a large firm, partners make it a point to find or retain attorneys who will strengthen their corporate law division (which would service mostly large white-owned companies) over their civil rights/antidiscrimination division (which would presumably provide services mostly to communities of color), such actions help to reinforce what sort of ideological production is valued by the firm. These decisions are market driven in that returns for corporate work are much greater than for civil rights and antidiscrimination law, so to some degree partners are likely driven by financial considerations. However, even to the extent that these are choices shaped by market determinants, these forces still shape organizations in ways that leave workers of color—even partners who are racial minorities—in the position of doing routine acts that reproduce dominant racial paradigms and inequalities. These hiring choices become imbued with racialized significance: in addition to being the basic responsibility of workers in the firm, they are a form of racial task wherein partners reinforce the ideological dynamics that retain racial hierarchies and values within the firm. Hiring decisions thus become an example of an organizational practice that preserves an ideology that maintains racial hierarchies.

In a recent study, Jennifer Pierce (2012) gives some additional examples of how organizational culture is implicitly racialized in law firms. She analyzes the present-day reactions to affirmative action within a large firm and finds that many white male attorneys embrace a narrative of the existence of unqualified, undeserving minorities who have secured jobs within the legal field that they did not truly earn or deserve. Notably, Pierce (2012) contends that white women have actually been the greatest beneficiaries of affirmative action but that the issue has been raced and gendered in such a way that racial minority men and women, particularly black Americans, are seen as unduly "taking jobs" from more deserving white males.

Pierce's (2012) work reveals that white male attorneys are able to establish a culture within the organization in which whites—white men in particular—are tacitly cast as the most suited for the high-status legal work performed in private firms.[1] Additionally, this culture presents black Americans as people who, even when employed by the firm, do not truly deserve to be there. As Pierce (2012) notes, white male elites use institutional memory, gossip about black workers, and reliance on broader cultural narratives as tools to institute an organizational culture that preserves white males' advantages in the firm. Yet, even when they attain partnership status, workers of color in the organization must still do the racial tasks of perpetuating this organizational culture and, even more, presenting the firm as an equitable workplace.

Devon Carbado and Mitu Gulati (2000, 2013) offer a similar analysis, contending that within law firms, racial minorities perform "identity work" in order to assimilate into the organizational norms present in the institution. Citing the concept of *color blindness* and its ubiquitousness in many work cultures, particularly law firms, they contend that "to the extent that an institution expects its workplace culture to be colorblind, people of color bear the brunt of the burden of maintaining this color blindness" (Carbado and Gulati 2000: 1279). We further this argument to suggest that even law partners of color who hold high-ranking positions in firms are likely to find themselves upholding and supporting this color-blind ideal by enforcing sanctions against those who do not do the "identity work" of making themselves palatable to their white peers. We suggest that they take on the racial task of maintaining this ideological culture but that their tasks are shaped by their relationship to the organization and may appear to be different from the expectations assigned to their counterparts who are differently positioned.

When those at the top levels of organizations carry out racial tasks at the ideological level through their efforts to establish an organizational culture, this endeavor has an impact on workers at other levels of the organization as well. Although workers at the middle levels do not have the same agency and ability to determine organizational norms, they are expected to follow the norms that have been set. Thus, these employees do the labor of conforming to the ideological norms that have been established. As such, Asian American workers who take pains not to speak with any trace of an accent are engaging in racial tasks at the ideological level (Chou and Feagin 2006). Black women employees who straighten their hair to fit into professional work environments also are engaging in an especially common ideological type of racial task (Bell and Nkomo 2001; St. Jean and Feagin 1998). In these examples, both Asian American and black women employees are doing the work that maintains the organizational culture and ideological norms that privilege whiteness. These actions do not necessarily involve direct interaction with others in the workplace (hence they are not classified at the interactional level), but they are additional forms of labor that establish the organizational culture of the workplace as a space where whiteness is normal, mainstream, and centralized.

It is critical to note that many of the ideological racial tasks here are largely invisible, additional types of labor that are disproportionately the burden of minority workers. Equally important is the argument that this labor is present among individuals who have ascended to the uppermost levels of an organization. While jobs at the top rungs of an institution can offer greater autonomy, control, pay, and status, we theorize that for racial minorities, they also come with the hidden burden of supporting and perpetuating institutional norms that operate to minority workers' disadvantage.

Racial Tasks at the Interactional Level

Social interactions at work are always key, but for minority workers they can take on outsize importance. Like Collins (1997), George

Wilson and Debra Branch McBrier (2005) have noted that racial dynamics function to black employees' disadvantage in a variety of ways. Studying various aspects of work, including layoffs and promotions, Wilson and McBrier found that black workers are typically given less authority and responsibility than their white peers, a condition that limits them when it comes to promotions and makes them more vulnerable when layoffs occur. Because black employees are more likely to supervise other racial minorities and to have less authority and more narrowly described tasks, they must demonstrate their suitability for leadership positions more overtly and in ways other than those their white colleagues employ. Though he does not use Collins's (1997) specific term of *racialized labor*, Wilson (1997; Wilson and McBrier 2005) nonetheless identifies another aspect of the additional work ascribed to black employees in that their accomplishments are not given the same weight or credence or considered as much indicators of future performance as the accomplishments of their white colleagues are.

We argue here that our concept of *racial tasks* explains another dimension of the occupational responsibilities expected of minority workers through basic, everyday interactions. Researchers have noted that black workers in predominantly white settings must do particular work to prove their capabilities for promotion (Wilson 1997), avoid layoffs (Wilson and McBrier 2005), and otherwise avoid processes of status closure (Tomaskovic-Devey 1993) and discrimination (Roscigno 2007) that would marginalize them and preclude them from accessing high-status positions. Social interactions thus take on critical importance as a site where black workers—and presumably, minority employees more generally—must demonstrate "soft skills" like personableness, geniality, and positivity that can be interpreted as evidence of their capabilities and suitability for promotion to higher-status jobs (Moss and Tilly 1996). Most of the research on minority professionals, in fact, deals with workers at this level and the ways in which social interactions are often fraught with racialized undertones that have implications for their advancement and upward mobility (Cheng 1996; Feagin and Sikes 1995; Kaplan 2006; Pierce 2012). Our theoretical contribution offers a departure from existing studies in that we seek not only to emphasize the unspoken racialized dynamics that are embedded in these everyday interactions but also to connect them to organizational structures and the hierarchies that are implicit within them.

In minorities' interactions with others, racial tasks involve the self-presentation, emotion work, and/or behaviors that are necessary for upholding the racialized power dynamics in predominantly white organizations. When black police officers laugh at racist jokes to ingratiate themselves with white colleagues (Bolton and Feagin 2004) or when black office workers restrain themselves from showing anger because it makes white supervisors uncomfortable, these are examples of racial tasks occurring through interactions (Wingfield 2010). Racial tasks in interactions also involve demonstrating capabilities and competence, as Gladys García-López (2008) indicates in her study of Chicana lawyers: "You do get a lot more questions regarding your ability—they [white men and women] are constantly testing you" (p. 600). When these trained lawyers must answer extensive questions to prove their knowledge and capability in their field, they too are engaging in racial tasks. Through their social interactions in the workplace, they are doing labor that underscores racial hierarchies present within the organization. Doing the work of proving one's capabilities and feigning or hiding emotions about race-related situations is a part of everyday social interaction for minority workers and one that contributes to whites' advantage within the organization.

Racial tasks done at this level are similarly invisible. When workers of color interact with white colleagues in these organizational settings, the types of racial tasks frequently documented by the literature—emotion management regarding racial situations, displaying soft skills that counterbalance assumptions of incompetence—constitute labor that is unseen and easily overlooked. Importantly, these types of racial tasks put minority workers in the position of doing racial identity work even in routinized, informal interactions to compensate for unfavorable stereotypes, assumptions, and biases.

At the middle level of the organization, there are likely to be more employees of color than at the top, though they generally will remain in the minority. Here, we refer to the managers, associates, and professional and semiprofessional workers who constitute the middle tier of an organization's structure. For instance, in the university, these would be the professors, senior staff, and low-level administrators. In a banking center, these employees would include the tellers, managers, and loan officers in a particular branch. These are the workers who are not in positions of power that enable them to set the organizational culture or make major institutional changes, but who may still retain occupational positions with varying degrees of influence, status, and prestige within and outside of the work setting.

Due to their relatively small numbers and their positions in the organization, midlevel workers of color will have to interact primarily with white colleagues, but they will not have the agency and ability to establish organizational culture. Consequently, employees at this level are likely to engage in racial tasks during their everyday interactions—in meetings, when conferring with colleagues, and so forth. In the case of these employees, we theorize that their racial tasks will mostly consist of the work done during daily, routine interactions that maintains whites' privilege and advantage within these spaces—ensuring that whites feel comfortable with them, keeping silent when confronted with expressions of racial bias (Feagin and Sikes 1995; Wingfield 2010). As such, midlevel workers will be more likely to do the emotional labor and self-presentation that comprise racial tasks at the interactional level than they are to carry out racial tasks at the ideological or physical level.

Midlevel workers, especially managers, are those most likely to make routine human resources decisions such as employee hiring, promotion, termination, and training. This responsibility is delegated from organizational elites who establish organizational culture. Midlevel workers interact with potential and current employees to select, promote, and modify behavior appropriate within the organization. As with workers of color at the top levels, diversity work is an important part of the way midlevel workers uphold organizational norms and culture. Following the lead of those at the upper levels of the organization, midlevel workers of color may take on the tasks of easing racial tensions and interpreting and repackaging directives from the top that maintain racial hierarchies in place in the organization.

These midlevel workers may also perform some racial tasks that uphold the ideological norms of the organization, but it is critical to point out that they will do so in a different fashion than would their supervisors, who are higher up the occupational ladder. Following from the previous example of racial labor in a law firm, this means that the attorney hired to do corporate law will produce ideological work that upholds the firm's broader commitment to white corporate interests over those of disadvantaged people of color. However, this attorney is ultimately following more powerful leads—employers' wishes and market-based determinants—in constructing the ideological direction of the firm. More precisely, Carbado and Gulati (2000, 2013) offer additional examples of how midlevel attorneys may engage in everyday practices that uphold color-blind ideologies, even as these practices occur as a consequence of cultural norms established by higher-ranking partners in a firm. When Latino or Latina attorneys avoid each other or carefully monitor their interactions in order to keep white associates from perceiving them as "sticking together," they are doing the racial tasks of supporting a color-blind ideology that they did not create but that permeates the firm nonetheless. As do the other examples cited previously, this one illustrates how racial tasks operate in an invisible, hidden fashion.

Midlevel workers' ideological racial tasks may also take other forms, such as the maintenance of a "professional atmosphere." This activity would include selecting television and radio stations for broadcast in reception areas (e.g., CNN *Headline News* instead of *FOX News* or a top-forty radio station instead of a classical one) and monitoring employees for "inappropriate" conversations and dress. Midlevel workers are given the authority to make these decisions, but their decisions must reflect the wishes of elite workers.

Racial Tasks at the Physical Level

Finally, racial tasks also include the work done that constructs physical space in a way that privileges whiteness. Men of color who work construction may perform racial tasks on multiple fronts: their work may include trying to conform to the white cultural norms of the construction business as well as performing the physical labor of erecting sites that may themselves become spaces where racial labor is performed (Paap 2006). As James Loewen (1999) notes, the existence of buildings or statues named for and dedicated to segregationists, Civil War generals, or military officials involved in massacres of Native Americans sends clear, racialized messages about which groups are valued and prioritized in certain spaces and institutions. The literal physical structure of an organization in which buildings or rooms are named for individuals who openly touted segregationist platforms and advocated for racial inequality serves to privilege whiteness in an unspoken way. Thus, racial tasks can take a physical form when they include efforts to build, shape, and maintain the organizational structure.

Workers at the bottom rungs of the organizational ladder will be those charged with doing racial tasks in their physical form. Very rarely, if ever, will middle- and upper-level employees be responsible for actually constructing or preserving the organization's physical infrastructure. These tasks will fall to workers at the lowest levels of the organizational hierarchy—the janitorial staff, maintenance workers, and so forth. Not coincidentally, this is the level of the organization where people of color are most likely to be overrepresented. Thus, most of these employees will carry out racial tasks that involve protecting, servicing, and caring for the tangible physical structure in which other, higher-status workers do the interactional and ideological forms of racial labor.

Tasks related to decorating and maintaining the physical workspace are often the domain of workers at the bottom of the organizational structure. Decisions about decor, including the types of art and company advertisements displayed, are part of the ideological racial tasks of the elite workers. However, low-level workers are responsible for carrying out the decisions made about the physical environment. In a real estate office, for example, the person responsible for hanging photography featuring smiling white nuclear families in front of large suburban homes is not able to comment as to whether the art reflects the business's clientele. This worker is simply responsible for carrying out the directive to hang the photographs. In keeping with their position in the organizational hierarchy, low-level workers are implicitly charged with performing the physical work necessary for creating and maintaining the organizations that then demand racial tasks from employees.

Another aspect of protecting, servicing, and caring for the physical structure of the organization is the provision of security. Security personnel are more likely to be people of color. They literally are required to use their bodies as a physical barrier between those for whom the space was created and those who do not belong there. Essentially, security and reception personnel are the gatekeepers of these organizational structures. This gatekeeping function inevitably has a raced component. Potential entrants to the space are screened so that people who do not fit the profile of the organization are excluded. Those who tend to be excluded from the space often share racial and socioeconomic characteristics with the security and reception staff. Despite this fact, security and reception staff must blend physical and interactional racial tasks to perform the gatekeeping function.

Racial tasks at the physical level also include maintaining the physical distinction between lower-level workers and mid- and upper-level workers in the organizational structure. Workers at this level, then, are expected to remain minimally engaged with other employees as well as with clients and customers, limiting their interactions with others in the organization to what is required to perform the gatekeeping function or tasks related to physical maintenance of the building. Whereas workers performing the gatekeeping function use the visibility of their bodies to restrict access to the physical space, workers performing other physical kinds of labor must do so while being largely invisible to clients and even to other workers. This type of physical racial task entails workers at the lower end of the hierarchy performing their work in spaces and at hours designed to restrict these workers' visibility. When the preferred invisibility is impossible to maintain, workers performing physical racial tasks must move their bodies in such a way that makes the work they do appear inconspicuous. For instance, janitorial work is usually done outside of work hours, but when janitorial responsibilities need to be performed during work hours, workers are expected to do them quickly and with minimal interruption to higher-level workers. Thus, a cleaning crew charged with janitorial work for a mostly white architectural firm, for instance, could be doing physical racial tasks that reinforce both their invisibility and cultural ideas about people of color as service workers.

Physical distinction between low-level workers and higher-level workers is achieved through both physical and interactional racial tasks on the part of low-level workers as well as through the physical design of the workspace. Low-level workers usually occupy break rooms and workspaces that are separate from those of workers who perform more prestigious tasks within the firm. These spaces are often hidden in basements and other low-visibility locations in the workspace. The confinement of low-level workers, who are more likely to be people of color, to designated spaces with limited visibility serves to reinforce the organization as a white space. Once again, workers at low levels of the institutional hierarchy may find that the racial tasks expected of them perpetuate their invisibility in the organizational structure. Racial tasks, then, require employees of color to become invisible in various ways, depending on their positions in the organizations in which they work.

THE IMPACT OF RACIAL TASKS

In introducing and defining the concept of *racial tasks*, we have attempted to show the ways in which these tasks are connected to organizational practices such as establishing organizational culture hiring, demonstrating skills and qualifications, and even participating in the basic physical construction of the workspace. We have also argued that racial tasks vary, depending on employees' positions within the organizational structure. Basic organizational practices and norms, then, are guided by racialized assumptions that create certain expectations for workers of color and maintain racial hierarchies. Though workers of all races in an organizational structure may engage in this type of labor, it takes its most pronounced toll on minority employees since they must work harder to conform to ideological, institutional, and physical norms that privilege whiteness.

By drawing attention to the concept of racial tasks, it is possible to highlight ways that workplaces create additional stratification and racial inequality between white workers and those of color. When employees of color at the uppermost, middle, and lower levels of an organization undertake the additional work of racial labor, they are engaging in efforts that uphold the institutional norms and practices that keep these spaces relatively unwelcoming for minority workers and more hospitable for whites. Workers of color who engage in racial tasks are doing work that creates a certain organizational climate but that also serves to maintain a racially unequal power structure. Given that racial tasks are linked to the expectations associated with workers at different places within the organizational hierarchy, even workers at the top levels of the institution will still encounter racialized expectations and assumptions that can be detrimental to their work experience.

Related to this occurrence, the theory of racial tasks can also help explain some of the social and structural impediments to occupational ascension that exist for minority workers. Inasmuch as black employees' paths to promotion not only rest on objective criteria like work performance; they—more so than their white peers—must also demonstrate soft skills like personableness and professionalism in order to offset discriminatory practices and be seriously considered for promotion (Moss and Tilly 1996; Roscigno 2007; Wilson and McBrier 2005). We argue here not only that the presentation of these soft skills constitutes just one example of racial tasks at the interactional level but also that such presentation constitutes a bias against workers of color that is inherent within organizations. In other words, within the organizational hierarchy, midlevel workers of color may be judged and evaluated on criteria based on more than their performance; they must also engage in emotion work, show their soft skills, and do impression management. We contend that these interactional processes are expected of minority workers at this level of the organization and constitute institutional barriers to promotion and upward mobility.

For workers at the bottom tier of the organizational ladder, the racial tasks they are expected to do render them even less likely to be promoted to the highest-status, most influential positions. As we have noted, jobs at this level include security, janitorial, and maintenance work and are more likely to be filled by people of color than are jobs at the middle or upper level of the organization. Implicit in these jobs are racial tasks in the physical form, which can involve gatekeeping, establishing a racialized decor, and generally creating infrastructures and spaces that normalize and privilege whiteness. Thus, organizational hierarchies help maintain racial stratification at work inasmuch as workers of color are disproportionately likely to be found in jobs that require the more physical forms of racial tasks.

The theory of racial tasks also sheds light on the tacit, covert processes by which white workers may unwittingly persist in making the workplace an uncomfortable or even hostile space for employees of color. After all, white workers' expectations of racial tasks in the form of self-presentation, behavioral adjustments, and emotion work from their minority colleagues ultimately create additional demands for workers of color. Theoretically, racial tasks can also facilitate the sense of isolation and marginalization many minority workers describe experiencing in predominantly white settings (Feagin and Sikes 1995).

The theory of racial tasks thus also serves to further our understanding of how race operates in the workplace in ways that differ from the mechanisms that maintain gender inequality. As Acker (1990, 2006) notes, the gendered nature of organizations (and jobs) often serves to highlight and in some cases artificially inflate the supposed differences between men and women. Jobs like construction worker, truck driver, and correctional officer are conceptualized as "men's" jobs while jobs like nursing and teaching are gendered female (Britton 2000; Paap 2006; Williams 1995). This process helps to maintain inequality by emphasizing the perceived gender differences in who is best suited for various types of work. When it comes to racial tasks, however, many employees of color must do invisible work that serves to smooth over and conceal perceptions of racial differences. Embedded in the everyday interactions, development of organizational culture, and physical construction and maintenance of worksites is the labor that minority workers do to maintain the normalization of whiteness and to obscure or hide the ways in which they are assumed to be different from the white mainstream. We argue here that while gendered organizations entrench (assumed) divisions between men and women vis-à-vis constructions of work, racial tasks push workers of color to display cultural practices, behaviors, and attitudes in response to race-related situations in an effort to prove their commonality with whites in the organization. In contrast with the way gender inequality is perpetuated, racial inequality is maintained when minority workers do racial tasks that construct whiteness as normative and standard.

Following this dynamic, we suggest that the tacit expectation of racial tasks requires workers of color to engage in labor that is embedded into organizational hierarchies but is largely invisible, uncompensated, and unacknowledged. This theory of racial tasks not only helps illuminate the ways that organizational structures can unwittingly reproduce structural inequalities but also shows how they can push minorities to do identity work in ways that are often hidden from others. Whether maintaining an organizational culture, engaging in emotion management, or cleaning buildings after hours, workers of color routinely perform racial tasks that require them to obscure their racial identity in order to fit into the dominant white racial space of the institution. Yet while these tasks call on workers of color to do invisible forms of work to compensate for a disadvantaged racial identity, the tasks themselves take different forms, depending on the worker's position within the organizational setting.

Empirically, this theory of racial tasks has yet to be explicitly explored. However, there are ways to envision methodological approaches that could be compatible with this theoretical perspective. Given that the theory of racial tasks makes claims about the ways that organizational practices maintain racial hierarchies, an institutional ethnography would be a particularly useful methodological tactic for examining the ways racial tasks occur at various levels of predominantly white work settings. This methodological approach would generate detailed knowledge of an organization's objectives, goals, and mandates as well as its institutional culture and norms. More importantly, it would yield data about the ways that workers at various levels of the organization actually carry out racial tasks, the impact these actions have on their jobs, and the consequences for workers themselves. Another approach might be to use a mixed methods approach that assesses survey data that documents the racial composition of workers in different strata of the organization along with interviews to identify how various workers at different levels perform racial tasks. This strategy would allow for quantitative data that could empirically document the demographic breakdowns within an organization along with the ways that racial minority workers at different levels engage in racial labor.

Ultimately, the theory of racial tasks illuminates the ways that organizational hierarchies are often racially segregated and the fact that the work expected of employees at different levels of the hierarchy includes labor that is invisible and subtly racialized and that continues to perpetuate inequality. Each individual in the workplace contributes to the racialized nature of the organization through her position in the workplace hierarchy and the ways in which she performs the tasks associated with her position. Donald Tomaskovic-Devey (1993) has argued that in the workplace, employees' job descriptions are imbued with racialized concepts that determine who is hired to perform particular tasks. Our theoretical premise extends this claim to explore how in addition to job descriptions, cultural and organizational practices at various levels of the organizational structure push workers to engage in labor that upholds racial hierarchies. Workers of color have a myriad of expectations associated with their positions that white workers do not, particularly the expectation that they will perform certain duties in order to become more palatable to the white majority. Racial tasks are a key mechanism by which this phenomenon happens.

NOTES

Revised version of Adia Harvey Wingfield and Renée Skeete Alston, "Maintaining Hierarchies in Predominantly White Organizations: A Theory of Racial Tasks," *American Behavioral Scientist* 58 (2) (February 2014): 274–87. Used with permission of Sage Publications.

1. An additional example of this phenomenon can be found in the court case of Lawrence Mungin described in Paul M. Barrett, *The Good Black: A True Story of Race in America*. New York: E. P. Dutton, 2000.

REFERENCES

Acker, Joan. 1990. "Hierarchies, Jobs, Bodies: A Theory of Gendered Organizations." *Gender & Society* 4 (2): 139–58.

———. 2006. *Class Questions, Feminist Answers*. Lanham, MD: Rowman and Littlefield.

Alliance for Board Diversity. 2013. "Missing Pieces: Women and Minorities on Fortune 500 Boards." Retrieved June 15, 2015 (http://theabd.org/Reports .html).

Anderson, Elijah. 1999. "The Social Situation of the Black Executive: Black and White Identities in the Corporate World." Pp. 3–29 in *Cultural Territories of Race*, edited by Michèle Lamont. Chicago: University of Chicago Press.

Bell, Ella, and Stella Nkomo. 2001. *Our Separate Ways*. Boston: Harvard Business School Press.

Bolton, Ken, and Joe Feagin. 2004. *Black in Blue: African American Police Officers and Racism*. New York: Routledge.

Britton, Dana. 2000. *At Work in the Iron Cage*. New York: New York University Press.

Carbado, Devon, and Mitu Gulati. 2000. "Working Identity." *Cornell Law Review* 85: 1259–1308.

———. 2013. *Acting White: Rethinking Race in Post-Racial America*. New York: Oxford Press.

Cheng, Cliff. 1996. "We Choose Not to Compete: The 'Merit' Discourse in the Selection Process, and Asian and Asian American Men and Their Masculinity." Pp. 177–200 in *Masculinities in Organizations*, edited by Cliff Cheng. Thousand Oaks, CA: Sage Press.

Chou, Rosalind, and Joe Feagin. 2006. *The Myth of the Model Minority*. Boulder, CO: Paradigm Press.

Collins, Sharon. 1997. *Black Corporate Executives: The Making and Breaking of a Black Middle Class*. Philadelphia: Temple University Press.

Durr, Marlese, and John R. Logan. 1997. "Racial Submarkets in Government Employment: African American Managers in New York State." *Sociological Forum* 12: 353–70.

Embrick, David G. 2011. "The Diversity Ideology in the Business World: A New Oppression for a New Age." *Critical Sociology* 37 (5): 541–56.

Feagin, Joe, and Melvin Sikes. 1995. *Living with Racism*. Boston: Beacon Press.

García-López, Gladys. 2008. "'*Nunca Te Toman en Cuenta* [They Never Take You into Account]': The Challenges of Inclusion and Strategies for Success of Chicana Attorneys." *Gender & Society* 22 (5): 590–612.

Ho, Karen. 2009. *Liquidated: An Ethnography of Wall Street*. Durham, NC: Duke University Press.

Hochschild, Arlie Russell. 1983. *The Managed Heart*. Berkeley: University of California Press.

Jackson, Pamela Braboy, Peggy A. Thoits, and Howard F. Taylor. 1995. "Composition of the Workplace and Psychological Well-Being: The Effects of Tokenism on America's Black Elite." *Social Forces* 74 (2): 543–57.

Kaplan, Victoria. 2006. *Structural Inequality*. Lanham, MD: Rowman and Littlefield.

Kirschenman, Joleen, and Kathryn M. Neckerman. 1991. "'We'd Love to Hire Them, but . . .': The Meaning of Race for Employers." Pp. 203–32 in *The Urban Underclass*, edited by C. Jencks and P. E. Peterson. Washington, DC: Brookings Institution.

Loewen, James. 1999. *Lies across America*. New York: Touchstone Press.

Moss, Phillip, and Charles Tilly. 1996. "'Soft' Skills and Race: An Investigation of Black Men's Employment Problems." *Work and Occupations* 23 (3): 252–76.

Paap, Kris. 2006. *Working Construction: Why White Working-Class Men Put Themselves and the Labor Movement in Harm's Way*. Ithaca, NY: Cornell University Press / Industrial and Labor Relations (ILR) Press.

Pierce, Jennifer 1995. *Gender Trials*. Berkeley: University of California Press.

———. 2012. *Racing for Innocence*. Palo Alto, CA: Stanford University Press.

Reskin, Barbara F., and Patricia A. Roos. 1990. *Job Queues, Gender Queues: Explaining Women's Inroads into Male Occupations*. Philadelphia: Temple University Press.

Roscigno, Vincent. 2007. *The Face of Discrimination: How Race and Gender Impact Work and Home Lives.* Lanham, MD: Rowman and Littlefield.

Royster, Deirdre. 2003. *Race and the Invisible Hand: How White Networks Exclude Black Men from Blue-Collar Jobs.* Berkeley: University of California Press.

St. Jean, Yanick, and Joe Feagin. 1998. *Double Burden.* New York: Armonk Press.

Tomaskovic-Devey, Donald. 1993. *Gender and Racial Inequality at Work: The Sources and Consequences of Job Segregation.* Ithaca, NY: Cornell University Press / Industrial and Labor Relations (ILR) Press.

Williams, Christine L. 1995. *Still a Man's World: Men Who Do Women's Work.* Berkeley: University of California Press.

Wilson, George. 1997. "Pathways to Power: Racial Differences in the Determinants of Job Authority." *Social Problems* 44: 38–54.

Wilson, George, and Debra Branch McBrier. 2005. "Race and Loss of Privilege: African American/White Differences in the Determinants of Job Layoffs from Upper-Tier Occupations." *Sociological Forum* 20 (2): 301–21.

Wingfield, Adia Harvey. 2010. "Are Some Emotions Marked 'Whites Only'? Racialized Feeling Rules in Predominantly White Workplaces." *Social Problems* 57 (2): 251–68.

Zweigenhaft, Richard, and G. William Domhoff. 2003. *Blacks in the White Elite.* Lanham, MD: Rowman and Littlefield.

PART TWO

Virtually Invisible

Disembodied Labor via Technology and Globalization

CHAPTER 4

Virtual Work and Invisible Labor

MIRIAM A. CHERRY

As users post updates on Facebook, pictures on Instagram, and videos on YouTube, an army of content editors works alongside them, unseen. These "digital janitors" winnow out child pornography, beheading videos, and illustrations of torture. Thanks to the editors' behind-the-scenes work, computer users, including teens and the elderly, view social media free from these disturbing images. Most users believe that computer algorithms are responsible for sorting spam, pornography, and other objectionable content from their social media feeds. Currently, however, the algorithms are not sophisticated enough to be able to separate objectionable content properly on their own. Content editors are located mostly offshore, with a large number in the Philippines, where the cost of living is low (Chen 2014). The work the content editors do is hidden from social media users by both technology and distance. These hidden workers are, unfortunately, paid extremely low wages to stare at sick and disturbing images all day. These workers are in the business of making humanity's darkest images invisible—and in so doing, render themselves invisible as well.

Although invisible labor has long existed, the Internet and communications technology have recently added new categories of work that is unseen, with the workers and the work hidden from view. In previous writing I have described how technology has influenced labor market trends as well as new ways of working, which I have termed *virtual work* but which have also been alternately described as labor as a service, digital labor, peer production, microlabor, or "playbor" (Cherry 2011: 962–63; Schott 2010). Technology has allowed not only new ways to buy and sell objects but also new ways to sell one's effort, output, and time, sometimes in small increments. Technology may serve to disembody workers, in some instances separating workers from their work and rendering both the work and workers invisible to consumers. Therefore, this chapter presents a legal and policy analysis at the intersection of virtual work and the theme of invisible labor. In doing so, this chapter ultimately questions how "work" itself is defined.

From telecommuting to meetings in virtual worlds with avatars to workers answering calls directed to them on their cell phones as part of a crowdsourcing effort, virtual work is an increasing trend. Today millions of people worldwide entertain themselves or supplement their incomes—or do both—by working within virtual worlds or casually clicking to make a few dollars by performing simple tasks on crowdsourcing sites like Amazon.com's Mechanical Turk. Because the money in virtual worlds is convertible to real-world money, virtual work is having an impact on real-world economies. Employment agencies such as Manpower and Randstad recruit, collect résumés, and perform interviews with candidates on *Second Life*. In the wake of the economic downturn, Web sites such as Elance, which serves to connect companies seeking short-term help with workers willing to take on short-term assignments, have been doing brisk business (Carew 2009). Throughout cyberspace, workers hold various jobs that, in the words of leading commentators, make it possible to "work in a fantasy world to pay rent in reality" (Lastowka and Hunter 2004: 11).

Technology that enables enhanced communication across distances can also provide remarkable opportunities for those engaged in knowledge work. For example, employers can use virtual spaces to make contacts and recruit talent remotely. Certainly, the possibility of matching workers and jobs in cyberspace creates more opportunities and more efficient labor markets, in many instances crossing national boundaries and legal jurisdictions. These changes can benefit workers, in part by allowing them to find work that may otherwise have been unavailable and by increasing flexibility and allowing workers more control over when and how they are able to perform work. As I have noted in earlier writing, however, virtual work presents many of the same enduring problems that workers' rights advocates have struggled with over the years (Cherry 2009). Some commentators have criticized virtual work as creating virtual sweatshops (Barboza 2005). For years corporations have forum shopped, not only to select the jurisdiction of incorporation that will govern their internal corporate affairs or their tax rate but also to find the jurisdictions with the cheapest labor and the least regulation of employment relationships. In addition to work in virtual worlds, in recent years we have also seen the rise of crowdsourcing, in which complicated tasks are broken down and distributed to thousands of workers throughout the cyberspace, then later consolidated into a finished product (Halbert 2009: 929; Howe 2006). The concern about some types of virtual work—especially crowdsourcing—is that they may be a form of extreme outsourcing that could lead to further acceleration of the race to the bottom and ultimately to the further erosion of workers' rights and benefits.

With that background, the focus of this chapter is on how virtual work renders some types of work and workers invisible. I explore this intersection in several dimensions. Technology may hide workers from a Web site's ultimate users or consumers, who—just as in the example of the content editors—may not even know that a human is working at all. In some instances, this consequence is the result of the technological platform employed; in others, it is the result of the commodification or monetization of small or inconsequential services that would not typically be considered "work" or even be possible without technology. Further, workers who spend their time in virtual worlds use an avatar to represent themselves, an arrangement that may have implications for concepts of identity. Finally, technology may blur the lines between leisure and work through a concept known as *gamification*. Work may be hidden as leisure, experiment, or volunteerism; therefore, this development could obscure what might in other, more traditional circumstances constitute an employer–employee relationship. The last section ends by suggesting how we might analyze the intersection between technology and invisible work through a legal and policy lens, and it provides thoughts about the normative implications of these accelerating trends.

TECHNOLOGY HIDING WORKERS

In some instances, technological platforms divide a person performing work from the consumers who ultimately use the Web site. Web site users might not even know that real people—rather than computer programs, algorithms, robots, or other automatons—are actually working. That misconception may result because—as illustrated by the content editors—some of the work that goes on "behind the Web site" is work that is occurring in another geographic location, sometimes in a remote part of the country or even across the globe. The eventual result is that the Web site users or managers may not think about what type of employment practices are being utilized because they may not realize that there is even a worker there at all. The next section provides concrete examples of this phenomenon. Although the issues arise in two different contexts (work performed behind the Web site and crowdsourcing), they are both illustrated within the same company—Amazon.com.

Hidden Embodied Work in the Warehouse

Most online users are familiar with Amazon.com, which began as an online bookseller much in the style of an old-fashioned mail-order sales catalog. The company achieved success because of Amazon's search function, aggregation of hard-to-find titles, ability to help users find similar products they might like, and willingness to let users instantly see excerpts of many publications. All of these factors, along with the advantage of no sales tax in some jurisdictions, led to Amazon's presenting serious competition for traditional brick-and-mortar retailers, with the large Borders bookstore chain eventually filing for bankruptcy. At the same time, Amazon branched out from its core business of selling and shipping new and used books to begin selling e-readers and the e-books read on them. Recently, Amazon has become a Web site of choice for those shopping for other consumer products, including electronics, clothes, beauty supplies, household goods, and even packaged foods, all of which are ordered online and shipped to customers' homes or businesses.

Subscribers to the Amazon Prime service pay a flat fee for the year and in return receive free shipping on many items. Once the fee has been paid, consumers often decide to use Amazon more frequently for many of their everyday needs since shipping is already a sunk cost. Some users enjoy the convenience, delivery, and ability to compare prices so much that instead of visiting a brick-and-mortar store like Wal-Mart or Target, they will keep a "basket" open at Amazon and order common household items like paper towels as needed, thus avoiding trips to a physical store. Customers enjoy the ease with which the items appear at their homes or offices, seemingly effortlessly, with a few clicks and a credit-card payment. Essentially, due to this ease of use, most customers who use the Amazon.com Web site never think about how their orders are being filled—or who exactly is filling them.

In recent years, however, several press accounts have surfaced recounting various issues with Amazon's workforce in logistics and backroom operations. These stories reveal a disturbing picture of how the various goods that Amazon ships eventually end up at the customer's doorstep (Bernton and Kelleher 2012). A first-person account by a reporter who worked in Amazon's warehouses describes a grueling, almost brutal pace of work filling the orders and running from one part of the warehouse to another in order to ensure that the right items are collected (Soper 2011). One news report describes the heat in the warehouses during the summer, which would sometimes reach more than 105 degrees and resulted in health issues for some workers: "Work in the warehouse is physical, with many employees walking more than 10 miles per shift plucking items from shelves. Workers said those who didn't move at a sufficient pace faced termination. They said quotas were not reduced when temperatures soared. . . . The company installed temporary air conditioning units last year after federal workplace safety regulators began inspecting the facility. But workers said parts of the warehouse, particularly its upper levels, remained unbearably hot even after the temporary air conditioning [had been] installed" (Soper 2012). Other accounts note that in the summer of 2012, ambulances and emergency medical personnel were stationed outside the Amazon warehouses to deal with the workers who would inevitably succumb to the heat. In response to this adverse publicity and subsequent customer and shareholder complaints about working conditions, Amazon announced efforts to improve working conditions and install better climate systems in its warehouses.

Apart from this issue, press accounts have described Amazon's reliance on a contingent and temporary workforce. Specifically, Amazon employs seasonal workers in its warehouses, presumably to deal with high demand during winter holiday shopping and simultaneously to avoid paying benefits for permanent employees. High school or college students available to work during school breaks are one source of labor while the retired are another. Some retirees or others who have chosen a nomadic lifestyle have taken to living in recreational vehicles (RVs), essentially campers or motor homes. These "workampers" will perform day jobs or other work to help pay their bills while traveling the country or seeing family and friends (Soard 2012). What these populations have in common is that they are invisible populations, both temporary and transient. As such, their organizing or otherwise pressing for better conditions is correspondingly more difficult.

Crowdsourcing as Invisible Labor

Another instance in which labor becomes invisible is crowdsourcing. In crowdsourcing, algorithms break large-scale tasks down into their smallest constituent components for which human eyes are needed. Computers connect those who need work done with potentially thousands of computer users who perform small tasks. Usually workers are paid per task, with the aggregate hourly amount often falling below the minimum wage. Upon completion, the individual microtasks are then reaggregated to create the larger project. For example, imagine the intense amount of work it would take to create an online shoe store containing a selection of thousands of shoes, with photographs, materials, and product descriptions for each shoe. While putting the content online for a shoe store would take one person a very long time, crowdsourcing could get the task finished rapidly. In crowdsourcing, hundreds of workers could perform a small task like tagging photographs of individual shoes or writing one or two product descriptions. Each of those tasks might pay twenty-five cents. If hundreds of people participate in these types of microlabor, their descriptions and tagging can then be reaggregated by computers into the one overarching Web site. Thus, a seemingly large task can be accomplished quickly and cost-effectively by harnessing the power of the crowd.

Probably the best-known crowdsourcing service at present is Amazon.com's Mechanical Turk. Named after an eighteenth-century mechanical device that allegedly could beat humans at the game of chess (by using a human chess player hidden inside it), the Mechanical Turk (2013) Web site describes itself as a "market for work" and claims that its services can provide an "on-demand scalable workforce." Individuals or companies formulate and post tasks for the vast crowd of Turkers on the Mechanical Turk Web site. These tasks may include tagging photos, comparing two products, or determining if a Web site is suitable for a general audience. The Turkers are able to browse among the listed tasks and complete them, then receive payment in the form of credits from the Amazon.com Web site.

Requesters have many rights on the Mechanical Turk Web site; Turkers, on the other hand, have far fewer. Requesters may set hiring criteria; they may accept or reject the work product, an action that affects a Turker's online reputation and ability to compete for work in the future. Although Requesters must have a United States address, Turkers can be located anywhere in the world (*Economist* 2006). Amazon.com makes money by charging a service fee for requests, typically 10 percent of the value of the paid labor. Typically, the tasks that Turkers perform are simple and repetitive. According to online accounts, Requesters "do not file tax forms . . . [and] avoid minimum wage, overtime, and workers['] compensation laws" (Mechanical Turk 2013). U.S. Turkers, on the other hand, are still responsible for reporting their income to the Internal Revenue Service (IRS). How many Turkers—especially those who only use the Web site occasionally—actually *do* report these earnings, however, is another question. The ultimate result is a fuzzy gray-market for casual clickwork services, for which there is practically no regulation (Epstein 1994). A recent case, *Otey v. Crowdflower,* challenged the piecework pay system for crowdwork under the minimum wage law, the Fair Labor Standards Act. In July 2015, the case was settled, with Crowdflower compensating the workers to bring their pay up to minimum wage.

Crowdsourcing and other types of distributed work or microlabor are likely to increase in frequency in the years to come. While once Amazon's Mechanical Turk was almost synonymous with crowdsourcing, there are now many more Web sites that promise to help users harness the power of the crowd. In a popular press article, Professor Jonathan Zittrain (2009) sets out a useful typology of crowdsourcing based on the level of knowledge required to complete a given work task. In the level requiring the most skill, companies post a difficult scientific problem and promise a reward for the answer. For example, on the Innocentive Web site, highly skilled scientists try to solve complicated problems in order to reap financial prizes. In the middle skill level, some Web sites rate and grade workers on various tasks to ensure quality control for routine backroom operations such as those performed by customer service representatives. For example, on LiveOps, telephone calls are routed to individual customer-service workers on their cell phones. Finally, at the lowest end, there is work that encompasses tasks that require only minimal awareness, such as the entry of a few characters or the clicking of a mouse in a second or two.

This last type of crowdsourcing, which involves low-skilled workers sometimes located in countries with developing economies, is the type that warrants the greatest amount of thought and attention from a policy and legal perspective. These crowdsourced workers are paid low wages and could be working in a variety of conditions that have low visibility and thus are difficult to assess. Computer workers are largely anonymous, so children or even prisoners could potentially be part of a crowdsourced workforce. The ultimate customer—who may actually care about fair labor—has no way of telling whether a Web site was constructed in a way that would exploit workers. As such, the invisible nature of the work again makes it difficult for anyone to advocate to change or improve working conditions, making this problem akin to others within global labor supply chains.

Avatars That Hide Workers

New kinds of work are also being created in virtual worlds. *Virtual worlds* are defined as "persistent, computer-mediated environments in which a plurality of players can interact with the world and each other" (Bartle 2004–5: 19). Each person who enters these worlds assumes a character—an avatar—that can be tailored to reflect her personality and that will be used as the point of interaction to navigate through the virtual world.

In an earlier article, I examined and classified the types of work available on the virtual world *Second Life* (Cherry 2011). For example, many participants in *Second Life* work as travel agents who advise newcomers about what to see in the virtual world; other players work as greeters who represent a company (or store) and explain its services to visitors. Other work opportunities include "custom avatar designers, party and wedding planners, casino operators, nightclub owner[s], car manufacturers, fashion designers, freelance scripters, [and] game developers" (Ondrejka 2004–5:94). In addition, more "traditional" forms of work can also be conducted in a virtual setting. The work that seems familiar is traditional service or counseling work, essentially tasks similar to those performed in the real world. For example, during tax season, one can receive tax advice in the virtual world in the same way that one would if using a traditional medium such as visiting an accountant's or tax preparer's office or talking to a tax professional on the telephone. The only difference is that the consultation and "meeting" occur in the virtual environment. Thus, virtual work may not change some existing occupations but instead may make them more efficient, obviating the need for in-person consultations or conferences and providing an additional way to stay connected across distance.

What is different is that each person who enters a virtual world adopts a character—an alternate identity—that is of necessity different from his identity in real life. The worker creating an avatar might highlight or even subvert some aspect of her actual identity, such as gender or race. Therefore, some commentators had hoped that technologically enabled forms of work might result in the reduction of recurrent forms of unconscious bias. Why would the "real world" identity of the workers employers hired matter if those workers were only working in a virtual setting? One human resources professional explained: "I interviewed three people on *Second Life,* but I found [doing so] harder than in real life because sometimes you don't know if it's a man or a woman, if they're young or old, and you have to ask more questions to find out what's behind the avatar. . . . [This kind of interviewing] is challenging, but I'm not ready to let go of it yet" (Monaghan 2008: 19). This comment is telling. Although on the one hand, it is perfectly understandable and acceptable for the interviewer to want to know more about the person he is interviewing so as to establish a rapport, on the other hand, some of these characteristics should not be entering into the interview. Why should it matter if the applicant is young or old, male or female? These are protected categories under the employment discrimination laws and factors that should be removed from hiring decisions.

That said, even in a virtual world, there is a very real danger that some forms of existing discrimination could be replicated. For example, a blog article on work in virtual worlds took screenshots of avatars with the caption "All avatars are not created equal. Who would you rather work with?" The first screenshot showed an avatar of a middle-aged white male wearing a crisp white shirt, tie, and pair of dress slacks in what looked like a typical real-world office environment complete with a virtual ficus tree. The second screenshot was of two avatars, one with pink hair who appeared to be androgynous and was wearing a pair of skin-tight leather chaps and a second who was a duck-like character with horns who appeared to be waving a magic wand (Internet Time 2013). The implication was clear: the first avatar was supposed to represent someone trustworthy with whom a person could do business whereas the other two avatars seemed odd and potentially unsettled and did not appear to be avatars one would want to consult for tax advice or entrust with a credit-card number. Given the presence of social biases, it is rather unsurprising that the "trustworthy" avatar in this screenshot was a middle-aged white male. There are implications of hiding one's identity online that will be discussed in the policy section at the end of this chapter.

Hiding Workers through Gamification

Another recent trend that involves hidden labor is the gamification of work. Some Web sites now use fun games to entice users to spend more time on their Internet pages, an activity that in turn increases advertising revenue that these pages derive. For example, Facebook games such as *Farmville* and *Angry Birds* keep users returning and spending more time on the Facebook platform. Other Web sites have set up games that are actually work—and what is done with the user's efforts is sometimes not identified or explained to those users. As such, work is rendered invisible, classified either as volunteerism or as leisure (Anderson 2012).

Gamification includes some forms of work that do not feel like work to the Internet users performing the tasks. Some of these Web sites are up-front about their mission and inform users about how their efforts are being channeled. For example, Foldit.com presents players with puzzles, the answers to which help scientists determine how proteins fold. However, other Web sites, like the now-defunct Games With A Purpose (GWAP), are more oblique. GWAP urged its users to play games and do good at the same time. GWAP, however, had ties to Google, and its games were being harnessed to help Google improve its search engine.

Another example appears in a recently filed court complaint involving hidden work and access to Web sites. In order to prevent their pages from being swamped with spam from automated comment generators or other bots, many sites and blogs require users to type in (recopy) a word or series of letters. This Google software, known as reCAPTCHA, uses the first series of retyped letters to prevent bots (automated programs used by spammers). The second set of letters that the user types, however, actually helps Google digitize books and newspapers by transcribing them one word at a time. The system also allows Google to enlist the help of the crowd in identifying address numbers for Google's mapping system, Google Earth. Although many people use the reCAPTCHA program and are familiar with being asked to enter a word to verify that they are human, far fewer know that this input is also being used to do work for Google. Recently, a group of users filed a complaint in federal district court alleging damages based on a theory of unjust enrichment. The users alleged that Google was essentially running a transcription service through unpaid and hidden labor. As noted in the next section, transparency to users is of great importance in this area.

IMPLICATIONS

The issues this chapter has described thus far provide an update to the existing concerns surrounding invisible labor. Up to this point, this analysis has been fairly descriptive, cataloging ways in which invisible labor intersects with virtual work. The next section of this chapter, however, is normative. Should there be additional regulation, disclosure, or more attention to technology and how it may hide labor? The answer is nuanced and dependent on the particular trend and the ways in which technologies are being used to hide the work or the worker.

The most obvious invisible labor question is perhaps most squarely presented with those workers who engage in labor behind the Web sites in the warehouses of online retailers like Amazon.com. For these embodied laborers, the invisibility of their work is most closely linked to other "backstage" workers, offshore or outsourced workers for whom being hidden may translate into poor working conditions and low pay. These low-skilled warehouse jobs are still very much "old economy," and these workers are at risk of being left behind by technology and knowledge work. Marginalization and poor working conditions are the risks for this group of hidden workers.

However, the invisible labor question becomes more complicated when we turn to crowdsourcing and gamification. Some may argue that, given the low time investments and small amounts of money involved, these forms of work are inconsequential. After all, at least some participants arrive on these Web sites not out of economic need but because they find something about the new technology interesting or enjoyable— or perhaps because they seek a small amount of supplemental income. Since most people do not work—at least not long-term—for free, maybe this employment is just a transitional phase and not of great concern. Some may enjoy volunteering at first but then quit as they find more productive or remunerative pursuits. Others may initially volunteer to work on a Web site, but if it becomes overly commodified or for-profit, these contributors may end up feeling taken advantage of and may even end up withdrawing their support for the project. This was the case with the Huffington Post bloggers. They had originally contributed their writing to a volunteer, unpaid forum that they considered a type of liberal online community. When Arianna Huffington and her financial backers stood to make hundreds of millions of dollars by selling the Web site to AOL Time Warner for $315 million, however, the bloggers brought a lawsuit asking for remuneration. Although the suit was ultimately unsuccessful, the fact that the bloggers felt strongly enough to file a case in court and contest the action is certainly significant. Users will potentially balk if they are continuously asked to contribute free content or if they feel that companies are taking advantage of them.

As such, Web sites that want to keep attracting "workers" or "players" over the long run will need either to make the time an individual spends on the site entertaining or to have a mission that appeals to those who wish to volunteer. If gamified Web sites are fun, then perhaps they are no different from other forms of either passive or active entertainment, and spending time on them should just be considered a hobby. Similarly, volunteerism is alive and well, and the Internet and crowdwork can facilitate those altruistic impulses. For example, thousands of people volunteered to help the online crowdwork in the search for the missing Malaysian airplane in the winter of 2014. Each volunteer could scan a small sector for patterns, and because there were so many volunteers, the analysis could cover a mass area. However, if such Web sites are not particularly entertaining and have not been established for useful, appealing, or noble volunteer causes, they likely will not last long. The issue of hidden or unpaid labor on the Internet might sort itself out, but the hiding of labor via technology may be a trend that is here to stay, at least in some formats. If hidden labor on the Internet is a more permanent feature, ignoring it or failing to consider its ramifications will certainly not lead to the formulation of sound policy options.

As for gamification, there are some highly effective uses of it that can increase worker engagement and happiness, especially if the job involved is tedious or repetitive. Since work is central to one's sense of self as well as one's economic well-being (Schultz 2000: 1890–92), a way to make work more fun would provide widespread hedonic benefits. Workers might find the "play" that a game provides a welcome break from work that could otherwise turn into drudgery. For example, identifying and adding descriptions to pictures is a boring task. However, if one turns the task into a game with a monetary prize for quick completion, it lightens the work and helps to pass the time (von Ahn 2008). We all inherently understand this outcome. Time spent on even the most boring jobs can fly by if we are with friends or have a light-hearted attitude toward the tasks we have been assigned. However, if used in a careless or negligent way, gamification could potentially cause psychological damage—for example, a structure in which the "losers" in a game suffered adverse employment action could be detrimental. If not handled appropriately, this result could trivialize true harm.

Hidden crowdsourced labor presents its own set of policy issues. One major legal issue, as I have noted in my previous writing about virtual work, is the intersection of crowdsourcing and the Fair Labor Standards Act (FLSA), the minimum wage and hour law (Cherry 2009).

While the FLSA provides rather circular definitions of *employer* and *employee*, it does contain certain limitations on volunteer work (§ 203[d], [e][1], [g]; see also Navarro 2008). But these points fail to capture what happens in a game, which is an activity that some people choose to engage in for fun, sometimes helping a for-profit company and sometimes not. The FLSA—which was written during the Great Depression and long before the invention of modern communications technology—does not squarely address whether crowdsourced workers are covered by it. Unresolved by the pending *Otey v. Crowdflower* settlement is whether crowdsourced workers are considered to be independent contractors or employees for the purposes of the FLSA and other labor and employment laws.

When should we become concerned about crowdsourcing as invisible labor from a policy perspective? The issue requires attention when vulnerable or marginalized populations are involved. As many computer workers are obscured or anonymous because of the platforms or third-party vendors involved, the risk is that the work will be exploitative. However, the issues are complicated. Some gamification draws in clickwork from many different countries, all of which have their own sources for rules and standards of minimum wages. The issues of fair labor, global supply chains, and ensuring noncoerced or non-child sources of labor are just as salient here as they are in other forms of labor, such as a situation in which a multinational company uses offshore labor to manufacture goods. But just as there has not been any kind of easily implemented solution in the context of manufactured goods, no answer is easy in the clickwork context, either. These are complicated problems not readily solved, and in the employment area especially, an area that tends to follow demographic shifts and trends, it is difficult to stop a trend—for example, outsourcing—once it has taken hold.

Legal and policy considerations that are important in both the areas of crowdsourcing and gamification are transparency and disclosure. At a minimum, users/workers should be informed about the identity of those whom they are working for, volunteering for, or otherwise assisting—either intentionally or inadvertently. This knowledge is important since many users might not even realize that they are working; therefore, it is vital that this information be transparent. Arguably, some people might want to play a game that helps computers process information faster, but they might be strongly against gaming that has the ultimate result of reinforcing gender stereotypes. In summary, all users should have information about how their time and efforts are being used in order to make fair and full choices about whether they want to participate in an online activity.

In the case of avatars that disguise workers, invisibility may not necessarily be a problem or lead to the same consequence of marginalization that we see with other forms of invisible labor. In fact, if what we are hiding are the traits and cues that trigger forms of racism, sexism, or identity discrimination, then perhaps we need not worry about the issue of invisibility, although we might discuss it, identify it, and be aware of its implications. Obscuring the true identity of a worker might not be of concern at all since it might possibly enable interviewers to "interview blind" and thus perhaps focus on merit rather than on unconscious biases. We might worry that if workers are remote and their identities obscured, these situations might make it more difficult for these workers to be in touch with each other and to organize and protest. However, those issues did not seem to be a problem in September 2007, when more than two thousand employees protested IBM Italy's pay package by having their avatars appear on IBM's headquarters in *Second Life*. This type of protest allowed workers from around the world to join together, an action that would not have been possible without technology (*Economist* 2008). Further, even though the workers were camouflaged by their avatars, the disguises may have benefited those workers—they would not suffer retaliation for their union activity.

. . .

This chapter has described the ways in which technology and the trends inherent in virtual work have rendered certain groups of workers invisible. This situation is present in the separation of the embodied warehouse worker from the Web site user, in the use of crowdsourcing technology to break tasks down into small and menial tasks, and in the disguising of work as a game. We should continue to study and be concerned about some of the forms of virtual work, crowdsourcing, and gamification that create invisible work and invisible workers.

As gamification, crowdsourcing, and virtual worlds continue to increase in popularity, it is important to recognize opportunities and challenges as well as to consider the legal implications—minimum wage and disclosure-related issues—from multiple perspectives, including the worker's experience. The nature of invisibility may in some instances exacerbate existing trends that undermine or erode labor standards. Greater disclosure and transparency are recommended.

REFERENCES

Anderson, Sam. 2012. "Just One More Game . . . : How Time-Wasting Video Games Escaped the Arcade, Jumped into Our Pockets and Took Over Our Lives." *New York Times Magazine,* April 4. Retrieved February 15, 2015 (www.nytimes.com/2012/04/08/magazine/angry-birds-farmville-and-other -hyperaddictive-stupid-games.html?pagewanted=all).

Barboza, David. 2005. "Ogre to Slay? Outsource It to Chinese." *New York Times,* December 9. Retrieved February 15, 2015 (www.nytimes.com/2005/12/09 /technology/09gaming.html?_r=1).

Bartle, Richard A. 2004–5. "Virtual Worldliness: What the Imaginary Asks of the Real." *New York Law School Review* 49: 19–44.

Bernton, Hal, and Susan Kelleher. 2012. "Amazon Warehouse Jobs Push Workers to Physical Limit." *Seattle Times,* April 3. Retrieved February 15, 2015 (http://seattletimes.com/html/businesstechnology/2017901782 _amazonwarehouse04.htm).

Carew, Emma L. 2009. "Tough Times Lead Many into Virtual Work World." *Star-Ledger* (Newark, NJ), July 12, p. 6.

Chen, Adrian. 2014. "The Laborers Who Keep Dick Pics and Beheadings out of Your Facebook Feed." *Wired* 22 (11). Retrieved June 15, 2015 (www.wired .com/2014/10/content-moderation/).

Cherry, Miriam A. 2009. "Working for Virtually Minimum Wage." *Alabama Law Review* 60: 1095–1102.

———. 2011. "A Taxonomy of Virtual Work." *Georgia Law Review* 45: 951–1013.

Economist. 2006. "Technology Quarterly: Artificial Intelligence." June 10. Retrieved February 15, 2015 (www.economist.com/node/7001738).

———. 2008. "On Strike, Virtually." March 15. Retrieved February 15, 2015 (www.economist.com/node/10853751).

Epstein, Richard A. 1994. "The Informal Economy: The Moral and Practical Dilemmas of an Underground Economy." *Yale Law Journal* 103: 2157–78.

Fair Labor Standards Act of 1938, 29 U.S.C. §§ 201–219 (2006) and Supp. (2011).

Games With A Purpose (GWAP). 2013. ESP Game. Retrieved August 12, 2013 (www.gwap.com/gwap/gamesPreview/espgame/).

Halbert, Deborah. 2009. "Mass Culture and the Culture of the Masses: A Manifesto for User-Generated Rights." *Vanderbilt Journal of Entertainment & Technology Law* 11: 921–61.

Howe, Jeff. 2006. "The Rise of Crowdsourcing." *Wired* 14 (6). Retrieved February 15, 2015 (www.wired.com/wired/archive/14.06/crowds_pr.html).

Internet Time. 2013. "Immersive Environments." Wiki. Retrieved August 12, 2013 (http://internettime.pbwiki.com/Immersive+Environments).

Lastowka, F. Gregory, and Dan Hunter. 2004. "The Laws of the Virtual Worlds." *California Law Review* 52: 1–74.

Mechanical Turk. 2013. "How It Works." Retrieved August 12, 2013 (https:// requester.mturk.com/tour/how_it_works).

Monaghan, Gabrielle. 2008. "A Virtual Way to Find Real Talent." *Sunday Times* (London), March 16, p. 19.

Navarro, Monty. 2008. Letter from Monty Navarro, U.S. Department of Labor, Office of Enforcement Policy, Wage and Hour Division, Fair Labor Standards Team, February 29. Retrieved February 15, 2015 (www.dol.gov/whd /opinion/FLSANA/2008/2008_02_29_03NA_FLSA.pdf).

Ondrejka, Cory. 2004–5. "Escaping the Gilded Cage: User-Created Content and Building the Metaverse." *New York Law School Review* 49: 81–101.

Schott, Ben. 2010. "Playbor: The Increasingly Blurred Distinction between Online Play and Labor." Blog. *New York Times,* March 12. Retrieved February 15, 2015 (http://schott.blogs.nytimes.com/2010/03/12/playbor/).

Schultz, Vicki. 2000. "Life's Work." *Columbia Law Review* 100: 1881–1964.

Soard, Lori. 2012. "Amazon CamperForce: Bring Your RV to Work." *ConsumerSearch.* Blog. Retrieved November 1, 2012 (www.consumersearch.com /blog/amazon-camperforce-bring-your-rv-to-work).

Soper, Spencer. 2011. "Inside Amazon's Warehouse." *Morning Call,* September 18. Retrieved February 15, 2015 (www.mcall.com/news/local/amazon /mc-allentown-amazon-complaints-20110917,0,6503103.story).

———. 2012. "Amazon Workers Cool after Company Took Heat for Hot Warehouse." *Morning Call,* June 1. Retrieved February 15, 2015 (http://articles.mcall.com/2012-06-03/business/mc-amazon-warehouse-air -conditioning-20120602_1_warehouse-workers-air-conditioning-breinigsville -warehouse).

von Ahn, Luis. 2008. "Hello World." *GWAP.* Blog. Retrieved May 13, 2008 (www.gwap.com/2008/05/hellow-world.html).

Zittrain, Jonathan. 2009. "The Internet Creates a New Kind of Sweatshop." *Newsweek,* December 8. Retrieved June 15, 2015 (www.newsweek.com /internet-creates-new-kind-sweatshop-75751#.VX9Jqgp-Umg.email).

CHAPTER 5

The Virtual Receptionist with a Human Touch

Opposing Pressures of Digital Automation and Outsourcing in Interactive Services

WINIFRED R. POSTER

The position of a receptionist may seem like a fairly insignificant job. It is generally low skilled, low waged, and monotonous, and it provides mundane services not often regarded as critical to society. However, receptionists are at the juncture of an important struggle for labor in the twenty-first century. It involves a tension among employers over how much humanness and how much physical proximity they want from their workers and what role technology will play in that dynamic. As this chapter will explore, these issues have significant bearing on the visibility of these workers in the future.

Receptionists fall in the category of the service industry, which is generating most new jobs within the formal job sector around the world. From the early 1960s to the late 1990s, the world average of service occupations rose approximately 20 to 50 percent while those in manufacturing fell precipitously. Service jobs, by definition, involve doing something for people rather than making things. A service can also be identified by its nonmaterial outcomes since it does not directly assemble, grow, or extract a product (International Labour Office 2001) or by its relational characteristics since it may provide assistance to customers (MacDonald and Sirianni 1996). *Interactive* services, in particular, are noted for their personal contact with the public.

The receptionist—who greets customers at the front office of a company—epitomizes this personal contact. A major job requirement for a receptionist is literally being the human face of the company. The receptionist position, as such, may seem a highly unlikely job for employers to eliminate, replace, or contract out. Indeed, although service jobs have largely been protected from economic cycles that have eliminated other kinds of jobs in the last few decades, they are now subject to two forms of pressure—from outsourcing, which sends the work outside the firm, and from automation, which replaces the worker and aspects of the work with technological systems.

The automation of services emerged from the fields of artificial intelligence (AI) and human–computer interaction (HCI). Bridging the gap between academic science and the high-tech industry, designers have aimed to create electronic systems that perform the practical tasks of service workers while seeming to appear human as they do so. Firms started replacing some service workers with these systems in the 1980s (e.g., replacing telephone operators with touch-tone phone menus and bank tellers with ATMs). However, something else also happened in the mid-1990s. Advances in science enabled firms to use AI to make those systems seem humanlike, endowing them with voices, appearances, capacity for chattiness and informal talk, and even emotions (Gustavsson 2005; Kerr 2004). The computer programs were then able to interact with customers.

Scholar Lucy Suchman (2007) notes that it is not coincidental for such humanlike, conversational artifacts to be developed within the contemporary context. In fact, this stream of AI emerged closely in connection with the service economy: "As the robot was to industrial imagery, so the software agent is to the desires and fantasies of the service economy. But rather than machines that can do our heavy lifting for us, the dream now is that every one of us can be . . . commanding a staff of servants that gets to know us intimately, watches out for us, keeps us informed in just the ways that we need . . . and represents us faithfully in our everyday affairs (p. 219)." Accordingly, many of the "social agents" or "chatterbots"[1] developed through HCI have reflected a narrative of algorithmic service, assistance, and deference, especially for intimate and domestic labor (such as robotic nurses, maids, and personal assistants). As I will show, this paradigm has crossed over into office services as well.

Yet attention to the automation of receptionists alone ignores the other crucial trend that has reshaped service labor in the last decade or so: outsourcing. The contracting out, and especially the offshoring, of services began to proliferate around 2000 when information and communications systems took a leap forward. Internet connections, fiber optic cables, and satellite communications systems all enabled data and voice to be transferred easily and cheaply among firms. Organizations began to send work processes to outside locations, both local and international. South Asia, with its large educated, middle-class, English-speaking population, became a particularly popular destination of service outsourcing for U.S. firms. Eighty percent of Fortune 500 companies now send work abroad, 50 percent to India alone.[2]

This chapter examines how these two dynamics represent forces that are decomposing the job of the receptionist as well as the live, human, on-site worker who performs it. They pull the tasks of the receptionist outward in two directions, with automation on one side (encouraging employers to move away from the humanness of the worker) and with outsourcing on the other side (encouraging employers to move away from the worker's physical proximity to the firm). In turn, a whole new set of actors—technology vendors, third-party agencies, and international subcontractors—are fighting a vigorous battle to capture the market for these jobs. This is the story of these various actors and their strategies to reshape interactive service occupations.

The visibility of the worker is a primary motivating factor for the utilization of these strategies. Selectively making the worker visible—or else completely invisible—is at the heart of reconfiguring the labor process of these services. Employers are making conscious decisions about what part of their employees' humanness they want customers to interact with: corporeal features like the face and voice; spiritual or mental features like the intellect, emotions, and relational capacities; both kinds—or neither. Sometimes these features are selected independently; at other times, they appear in combination. Sometimes they are recorded from live humans; at other times, they are manufactured digitally through algorithmic code.

Documenting the range of forms among virtual receptionists is the task of this study. The analysis is based on sociological research of the customer service industry in South Asia and the United States that I have been conducting for the past decade. What follows is material from virtual receptionist companies and academic organizations (such as their "webinars" or online videos about their products, promotional fliers, and testimonials from customers) as well as material from my case studies of customer-service call centers in India and Pakistan. Themes of gender, sexuality, domesticity, race, and nationhood will be integral elements of this analysis.

FIGURE 5.1. Spectrum of virtual receptionist business strategies.

LIVE, ROBOTIC, REMOTE: THE AUTOMATION–OUTSOURCING SPECTRUM

As I began to research this phenomenon, I discovered a range of different types of workers—all called *virtual receptionists, secretaries,* or *assistants.* They all do things like greet guests and transfer them to employee offices. However, their duties lie on a spectrum of business strategies that extend outward in two directions (see figure 5.1).

In the center is the classic receptionist. There are more than 1 million of these employees in the United States (U.S. Bureau of Labor Statistics, quoted in National Receptionists Association 2013). The National Receptionists Association includes a range of job titles in its community: "Front Desk Clerk, Operator, Host/Hostess, Information Desk personnel, Maître [d'], and many more." It describes the job in the following way: "Receptionists are the 'front line' personnel in the business setting. They are the first person[s] a client has contact with and the interaction very often sets the tone of the business transaction to follow. Their interpersonal skills, telephone etiquette and communication skills are a very important element in greeting clients, responding to inquiries and representing the company."

In her duties as "frontline personnel," a receptionist has a more important role than a secretary, who sits in the "back" office, does: "A receptionist fields initial company contact and takes [control] of the communication channels with each call during the day. A secretary's role is different because [he] report[s] to someone else in the company and [is] not the initial contact. In fact, most times the receptionist takes the secretary's calls first." This job description represents the traditional mid-twentieth-century model of labor—live and on-site. The job is full-time (with employee benefits such as health care) and relatively stable, with predictable hours, schedules, locations, provisions of living wage, and long-term security. The new virtual receptionist jobs will typically not have these features.

The old-fashioned receptionist job is being pulled in two directions. On one side is automation. It involves strategies designed by technology vendors, and then purchased by firms, to replace human receptionists completely with automated workers. As one moves outward to the left on the continuum, these virtual workers (or software programs) are increasingly more technological and sophisticated. On the other side of the classic human receptionist is outsourcing. It involves strategies to move the job outside the firm to third-party firms and other locations. Therefore, as one moves outward on the right side of the spectrum, the jobs are further distanced from the original employer—geographically but also economically and socially. As we move through examples of virtual receptionists on each side of this spectrum, we will see how their visibility varies to employers, consumers, other workers, and the public.

THE AUTOMATED RECEPTIONISTS

We begin by meeting the *automated* virtual receptionists who are replacing the traditional human ones. With Alice, Ava, and Marve, we see how firms are trying to capture human qualities and insert them into computerized systems. Basic models incorporate some "real" human elements such as a picture, voice recording, or video of an actual person, whereas more advanced models create humanlike features entirely with code.

Partial Automation

Alice. One of the simpler technological models is Alice. Alice is a flat-screen receptionist designed by WinTech corporation (see figure 5.2). She appears as a face on a computer monitor. She uses motion detection to determine when a customer approaches, plays a prerecorded video welcome message, and notifies a staff member when a client has arrived.

She can be found in many places in an office. She may be sitting on the front desk (literally "on" it, not behind it). She may be hung on the wall. She may be lodged in a kiosk. What's curious about these images created by vendor WinTech is that they repeatedly feature a chair next to Alice—one that is always empty. This image reminds us that the human worker is absent, invisible. It is also curious that within the kiosks Alice's "body" may be branded with consumer advertising like Coca-Cola displays. This use follows a trend of employees consuming the identities of the firms for which they work as well as those of other corporations (see chapter 13).

FIGURE 5.2. Alice, the flatscreen receptionist. Reproduced by permission from Wintech LLC. © 2015 by Wintech LLC.

Indeed, even though she is entirely electronic and just a box, Alice is anthropomorphized and gendered.[3] Her *name,* for instance, is feminine. It stands for "A Live Interactive Customer Experience."

Ava. A more sophisticated version of the automated receptionist is Ava, a hologram from Airus Media (see figure 5.3). Through this technology the company gives Ava additional human features to present to the public. She talks to customers as a standing, life-size image. She detects customers with the use of electronic motion systems and, like Alice, plays a greeting, but Ava presents herself in *full-body* form.

Ava is a projection of a live human onto a two-dimensional screen cut to the shape of her body. With three-dimensional digital enhancements, we see the speaking and moving Ava in front of us. She wears professional-looking attire (i.e., black pants, buttoned-down blue shirt). However, her dialogue and intonation in the promotional video from Airus Media (2011) are sexually suggestive. Here's what Ava tells potential "employers" on the Web site:

> My name is Ava, the new virtual assistant that everyone is talking about. You're right: I'm really not here. But I do look pretty good, don't I? I am the latest and greatest in public guidance and advertising. I never take a break, don't charge overtime, hardly ever take sick leave, and I don't need a back-

FIGURE 5.3. Ava, the hologram receptionist. Reproduced by permission from Scott Beale / Laughing Squid. © 2012 by Scott Beale / Laughing Squid.

ground check. I'm so versatile I can be used for just about anything. I can say what you want, dress the way you want, and be just about anything you want me to be. I can advertise your products, promote your facility, and guide your customers. I am so helpful I can even provide instructions and give directions. Even better, it won't be long 'til I can answer questions. How cool is that? I am very cost-effective. I will save you time and money.

Ava saves employers from all the hassles of dealing with live employees—wages, absences, laziness, crime—and gives them new control over her other attributes: her body (dress) and talk (conversation). At the moment, her conversations are one-way. However, Airus Media promises that voice-recognition software will soon enable two-way conversations with the public. Then Ava will be able to serve as a classic front-desk receptionist.

Full Automation

Marve. Marve is the next stage of automation in human–computer interaction—an entirely computerized avatar. He is an experimental virtual receptionist at the University of North Carolina–Charlotte (Babu et al. 2006). Scientists there are equipping Marve with *emotions.* Through this technology virtual secretaries will be able to appear even more life-like to the customer by communicating interactively and with feeling.

Marve can perform the routine receptionist tasks: he takes messages, delivers information, and more for the computer science laboratory. In addition, though, he "interact[s with visitors] using a combination of spoken natural language [and] non-verbal cues . . . that include maintaining appropriate eye contact, facial expressions, and gestures" (Babu et al. 2006: 170). He is programmed to engage in conversation and be social. He makes small talk, chats about the weather and movies, and tells 150 "knock-knock" jokes. In the process, he smiles, laughs, and waves his hands.

Curiously, in the picture provided by the researchers, Marve has the appropriate secretarial props in the background. Even though he is not real, he has a desk, a computer, and pictures of his family. In this way, he has the persona and inhabits the physical environment of a real receptionist. Marve is also marked with specific bodily features as a proxy human: he is male and appears to be white. One wonders, incidentally, if this gender selection was intentional by the designers in order to separate and highlight Marve's emotional qualities. If Marve were female, she would likely be sexualized like Alice and Ava (either by the designers or by the customers), a feature that would in turn overpower or subsume her emotionality.

Marve is a prime example of how software designers are thinking very deliberately about ways to automate not only the *technical functions* of the receptionist (i.e., performing a job's practical tasks) but also the *feeling work* (Hochschild 2003) that receptionists do in their interactions with the public (i.e., making people feel comfortable, discussing friendly topics that have nothing to do with their job, and conveying through subtle visual and corporeal cues that they care about customers).

With Alice, Ava, and Marve, we see the corporate and engineering strategy of replacing live workers with computerized models. Sometimes these models incorporate attributes of the human worker, but underneath, the core platform is algorithmic and digital. The design of this new generation of automated virtual receptionists is being done largely by computer scientists in universities and technical researchers in private firms. What they are moving toward is the digital manufacture of sociability, emotions, and humanlike interactional behaviors.

THE REMOTE RECEPTIONISTS

The other trend in virtual receptionists is outsourcing. Unlike the automated personas discussed above, these are live humans. However, they are not on-site like the traditional receptionists. Instead, they are *remote* virtual receptionists sent outside the firm. This movement happens in two ways: through nearby (local) outsourcing and through offshore (international) outsourcing. As the jobs lie further toward the right on the diagram (see figure 5.1), the workers move geographically and structurally further away from the firm that employs them. Ruby and the At-Home Moms represent local outsourcing options. Margaret and GetFriday Teams represent global outsourcing options. As we will see, these strategies use technology, but in a different way than the cases above. Rather than relying on artificial intelligence, they use communication networks to facilitate interpersonal connection within the context of dispersion.

Local Outsourcing

Ruby. One example of a locally outsourced employee is Ruby, from Ruby Receptionists. She works in an office near, or at least in the same country (the United States) as, that of her client (or boss). Rather than sitting in the front office, she works in a separate location off-site. There, she sits with other virtual receptionists, each working for a distinct boss someplace else.

They represent a pool of workers who are readily available and on call but not physically present in the client's building. For employers, local outsourcing saves money. Centralizing the receptionists in one place makes it more efficient for the outsourcing firm to manage the labor process.

Employers get a variety of "human" qualities with Ruby. First, even though Ruby is off-site, she brings the human back to the office through her *voice*. Office staff and customers can hear her as a live worker communicating over the phone. This may sound like an obvious or trivial thing for a receptionist to do, but Ruby Receptionists knows that clients are considering the alternative of using an automated receptionist, so they amp up this human feature in their advertising and promotions. The company Web site boasts how Ruby will do things like *live* phone answering, *live* call transferring, and *customized* call handling (Ruby Receptionists 2013). These are activities that a human can perform better than a machine can.

A main selling point for the company is how Ruby can do what the automated receptionists cannot. The company's founder says that "in a desert of impersonal customer service and robotic answering machines . . . business owners and callers alike [are] longing for a personal connection. . . . An impersonal answering service or recorded menu won't do. With Ruby, you don't just get a receptionist. You get an exceptional one" (Ruby Receptionists 2013).

Second, they get emotion and enthusiasm: "Ruby is the **smart** and **cheerful** team of virtual receptionists trained to make a difference in your day. From our studio . . . , we handle your calls **with care**. We deliver the perfect mix of friendliness, charm, can-do attitude, and professionalism" (Ruby Receptionists 2013). Ruby sells human spirit. The Web site personalizes the workers on almost every page—for example, by posting individual biographies and photos of the employees. These workers not only look animated; they are downright effervescent (see figure 5.4). In the banner on the site's home page, workers are practically dancing out of their seats. The firm overadvertises the humanness of its workers to contrast them with the robotic offerings of its competitors.

Third, with Ruby, employers receive mental creativity and responsiveness from their receptionists. The Web site lists human "intelligence"—literally—as a quality of their employees: "Intelligent receptionists can distinguish between different types of calls (new clients, current clients, urgent calls, etc.) and handle them according to your instructions" (Ruby Receptionists 2013).

Perhaps most important is the fourth aspect of humanness that Ruby provides. With her voice, Ruby performs crucial relational services for firms: "A phone call is often the first interaction people have with your company. . . . Ruby's cheerful live virtual receptionists *create meaningful connections* with your callers and add sparkle to your image. . . . We

FIGURE 5.4. Ruby, the locally outsourced receptionist. Reproduced by permission from Ruby Receptionists. © 2015 by Ruby Receptionists.

designed Ruby to be tailored to your company and make the most out of interactions. *Ruby does more than answer your phone; we cultivate relationships*" (Ruby Receptionists 2013; italics added). Ruby appeals to customers through the social and interactive elements of their conversations. In fact, the virtual receptionist's voice can raise the status of the firm. It enables an organization to "*sound like* a Fortune 500 company" (Davinci Virtual Office Space and Solutions 2013; italics added).

Thus, local outsourcing firms remove the worker from the workplace but still recapture a range of human capacities through the employee's voice—intelligence, spirit, professionalism, and the capacity to create relationships with customers, clients, and staff.

Work-at-Home Moms. There are other options for the local outsourcing of receptionists. One strategy is to bypass the business office altogether and send the work to the employee *at her own house.* Structurally, this action moves the receptionist further from the employer and out of the market sphere altogether. This outsourcing dynamic crosses the boundary from the public to the private.

The advancement and proliferation of information technology have been crucial for this dynamic. With the spread of communications and computer equipment to the mass consumer market, people now have access to the tools for setting up commerce in their homes: a telephone, computer, and Internet connection. These employees do the same tasks as the local-outsourcing employees (like Ruby) and provide the same voice-based receptionist work—only from their houses.

Many firms have emerged in this market as intermediaries to coordinate and take advantage of the at-home receptionists. Among the larger ones, LiveOps claims to have twenty thousand employees; Convergys has employees in forty-eight states. Also known as a form of *crowdsourcing*, this employment trend incorporates the public into the labor economy through networked technology (see chapter 4). By contracting with Web sites like LiveOps and Convergys, employers recruit a "crowd" of employees whom they will likely never see—in this case because those workers are in their own homes. Crowdsourced labor is known to pay less than on-site labor as whole or full-time jobs are broken down into tiny parts (e.g., single phone calls from customers).

LiveOps states on its Web site that it is "revolutionizing the world of work" by "creating a world without boundaries": "With no constraints on where or when to work, independent agents can work out of their homes or offices and provide call center services to hundreds of well-known clients. . . . LiveOps opens the door to a meaningful work opportunity by providing *the chance to work on your own terms*" (LiveOps 2013; italics added). Benefits for the employee notwithstanding, what these companies are also doing is transferring the infrastructure of work—including the cost—to the employee's home.

This form of local outsourcing is very much predicated on gender, like those previously discussed, but in a different way. At-home receptionist agencies market this employment opportunity to potential workers by utilizing images of motherhood and domesticity. A popular Web site promoting these jobs features a woman wearing a call-center headset—and holding a baby (Kwika.org 2013). Although these outsourcing firms may not specifically mention gender in their ads, they are heavily targeting women for recruitment.

These Web sites highlight not only motherhood but also women's broader roles as care workers for a variety of family members. On the testimonials page of LiveOps (2013), employees say: "First and foremost, I love working from home so I can be with my little guy. I take care of my elderly father. LiveOps gives me the ability to care for him and also help with our family finances. If I were to work for a brick and mortar company, I would have to look for a nursing facility for him. Being an independent contractor means more to me [than] I can express. This has been a lifesaver for me." This form of work is significant as it represents a merging of paid labor as a receptionist with women's other unpaid job as home care worker. In this way, such firms are facilitating the integration of two forms of invisible labor. They are coattailing crowdsourced labor onto domestic labor, taking advantage of women's roles in one to facilitate the other.

By doing work at home, this locally outsourced receptionist becomes physically invisible—out of sight to the employer and the public. Firms selectively retain the detectable humanness of the worker, however, through the sound of her voice.

Significantly, the Work-at-Home companies make a deliberate point of distinguishing themselves from the next case of outsourcing—the offshore receptionists. These firms are very clear to emphasize their localness and their geographical grounding. Some, like LiveOps, are explicitly nationalistic. On the first page of its Web site, LiveOps (2013) describes the basics of its service: "LiveOps was founded on the idea that we wanted people to be able to work out of their homes in the U.S. and that we could provide not only a great work opportunity . . . but also a great customer experience for our clients. Years ago, many companies saw the quality of their customers' experience worsen when they offshored their call center jobs overseas. A lot of those companies have decided to bring those services back to workers in the U.S. and have partnered with LiveOps to handle their calls." LiveOps's narrative suggests a double meaning of the term *home* as a location for virtual assistant work. Along with the literal sense of the house, it provides a figurative reference to the nation as home. By promoting this antiforeignness rhetoric, LiveOps places itself in opposition to the global outsourcing industry discussed next.

Global Outsourcing

A second kind of outsourcing is international. Firms in the United States and other parts of the Global North employ remote receptionists overseas. This practice sends the receptionist job further from the original employer, sometimes halfway around the world. The services that these receptionists provide can be more elaborate than those discussed above, however. Let us start with Margaret.

Margaret (Mussarat). Margaret,[4] like the Work-at-Home Moms, is a live human. But she is distinct in outsourcing in that she recaptures the *body* of the receptionist for employers. Moreover, she does so while sitting at a firm called The Resource Group—in Pakistan. She sits at a desk

FIGURE 5.5. The globally outsourced receptionist. Reproduced by permission from Jessica Tefft. Reproduced by Ann Manwill. Original photo, *Virtual Secretary*, © 2005 by Jessica Tefft.

in Karachi with a video camera pointed at her. Her image is projected to an office in Washington, DC, where a flat screen monitor hangs on the wall of the lobby and a speaker plays her voice (see figure 5.5). There, her bosses, coworkers, and customers in the United States can both see and hear her, treating her as a participant in the firm's daily routines.

Margaret brings personal attention back to the job. First, she does the interactional work with customers and clients. She answers incoming phone calls that are transferred from Washington, DC, via satellite to her desk. She greets people as they enter the office. She directs customers to the coffee room to wait for their meetings. She buzzes in the delivery person through the front door. She can order a cab for a customer or client.

Second, she does personal work for her boss and the staff, attending to their daily routine needs in the office. She orders lunch for meetings from local restaurants. She sits in on meetings to record the minutes. She makes travel arrangements for executives and manages their schedules. She meets with individuals, special interest groups, and others on behalf of executives, committees, and boards of directors.

Margaret is on call for her bosses in the United States. They can interact with her at any time. In these ways, she provides the "office wife" services for the firm that Rosabeth Kanter (1993) discusses in her classic book on corporations—but now from eight thousand miles away. Being able to see Margaret is a big part of what employers are paying for in this day and age.

Let us talk about her name, though—which is in fact not Margaret. It is Mussarat. Even though customers can "see" her, she is told to convey subtly that she is actually in the United States. She does this by changing her name but also by altering her accent (toward American English) and by sitting in front of a theatrical set designed and propped with objects to signify American culture. Behind her, the scene looks like it is in the United States.

Clients pay for Margaret's visibility (often a more high-end service for executives). This case involves not just a gendering of the body, as with the automated receptionists. It also involves a nationalizing of identity, physique, and space.

The GetFriday Team. A more widespread trend of international outsourcing involves another type of virtual receptionist: the virtual assistant "team." In this case, the employees are again live and located overseas, but now they are minimally visible, and at times completely invisible, to the "boss."

This model has arisen in conjunction with the "business process outsourcing" industry in India. This group of more than 2 million employees performs a large range of back-office tasks for Global North firms. Outsourcing firms divide the work processes into voice and nonvoice functions—or, in other words, call centers and data centers. One provides the phone labor of customer service; the other provides clerical and organizational labor.

An example of the latter is GetFriday. It is a company based in Bangalore, India, that provides firms or individuals with virtual assistants. GetFriday has a very different structure for its workforce than does Margaret's company. Instead of employing a single receptionist, customers hire a whole team, most of whom they never see.

The employer is assigned a "primary assistant" with whom he communicates. However, the actual work is then handed off to a "leader," who then parcels out individual tasks to members of a wider "team." When the team has finished, they send the work back up the chain to the primary assistant for transmission to the U.S. employer. Thus, twenty different people may be working behind that one personal assistant. All of this labor is therefore literally invisible to the employer.

Indeed, in the visual image of this scenario on the GetFriday Web site, the employer is represented as a figure sitting at a desk. Her hand is outstretched, and like a puppeteer, she controls strings to a number of tiny workers. They are all in front of computer terminals and located underneath the desk. Supporting them from below is the team leader, who holds them up with a hand over his head.

With this structure, employers can "buy" much more from a single virtual assistant. The list of tasks from which to choose is long (GetFriday 2011). Some tasks are traditional for the receptionist or front-office staff, like customer relations, appointments and follow-up, secretarial work, and travel arrangements. Others are more back-office, like purchasing, organizing, and accounting. Still others are typical for the office wife, such as home assistance and personal chores. These are all the stuff of a classic receptionist, but now that single job is broken down into a multitude of parts that are purchasable individually from a menu. There is less personal contact but far more productivity.

In addition, employers get something else from international outsourcing—*temporal arbitrage* (Nadeem 2011). Shehzad Nadeem defines this term as "the exploitation of time discrepancies between geographical labor markets to make a profit" (p. 60). It happens in two ways at firms like GetFriday.

First, international outsourcing extends the workday. Because the Indian time zone is more or less twelve hours offset from that of the United States—with directly opposite daylight hours—employees can work during their employer's nighttime, producing results overnight. Written work requested at the end of one business day will be completed by the start of business the next morning.

Second, international outsourcing offers continuous live service. With the proliferation of the workforce into rotating shifts, the labor process can operate nonstop. Thus, unlike the labor of the on-site receptionist—or even that of the employees at local outsourcing firms in the United States, who work an eight-hour day and a five-days-a-week shift—the team's labor is continuous. Employers are literally getting more productivity out of the "worker(s)" or the wages they are paying.

The sacrifice, of course, is contact with a live person. This not the video receptionist like Margaret. In fact, communication—even with the primary assistant—is much more limited. A client will contact the receptionist through *written* forms of electronic communication: text, chat, e-mail, and fax (and on occasion, by phone). Therefore, this receptionist, lacking a voice or body, displays the least visible human qualities of all the cases discussed.

Never fear, though. These outsourcing firms ensure that they will provide a "human touch"—even if they are not even talking to you, much less showing their faces. The GetFriday (2011) slogan is "Access to EVERYONE'S SKILLS ... and the PERSONAL TOUCH of one assistant." Moreover, the company can provide this personal touch globally: "Think of us as a regular assistant who is sitting in the next room. Anything that you would ask that assistant to do, we could probably handle. Except that the next room is in another country, so we can't handle anything physical. We can't get you your daily cup of coffee, but we might be able to get someone else to deliver it to you" (GetFriday 2011). The image of the assistant (and his country) "in the next room" is meant to conjure the feeling of proximity and mask the reality of distance. To create a likeness of the traditional receptionist who is sitting in the front office, GetFriday aims to collapse geography through personal attention and individualized service.

DISCUSSION

There are benefits of adaptability and flexibility in these new forms of labor. With the virtual receptionist, employers and employees can overcome space and distance. These groups can coordinate work across geography and public/private spheres. In the process, as Convergys (2013) points out, this industry opens up employment opportunities for workers who may otherwise have difficulty with mobility and joining the labor market—like female, disabled, and rural workers. For consumers, too, there are advantages to automating services: the convenience of banking through automated teller machines at all hours and in many locations.

Hidden and Not-So-Hidden Costs

Still, there are many costs of virtualization and globalization in receptionist work. Some are overt. On the automation side of the spectrum (see figure 5.1), there is the loss of jobs. Digitizing work may replace employees and eliminate some occupations altogether. We see this trend with cases like Alice, Ava, and Marve. They are especially associated with simple service tasks and interactions: greeting customers, directing them to spaces in the building, providing information, and so on.

Ironically though, while Barbara Garson (1988) lamented the dismissal of whole legions of secretarial staff due to computerization of information tasks in the 1980s (and, moreover, predicted its continuation and expansion), we see a different and perhaps reverse pattern in the 2010s. These legions of workers are reappearing and/or being reconstituted through outsourcing locally and globally. We see this development through the cases of Ruby, Margaret, and the GetFriday Team. It suggests that there is a limit to what employers are willing to automate within interactive services. At least for now, they are retaining those workers through strategies of globalization and communication technologies.

The cost of outsourcing, on the other side of the spectrum (see figure 5.1), is a degradation of wages. Outsourcing may be favorable for retaining and even preserving the humanness of the worker but not necessarily for the quality of the work that is retained. Indeed, wages decrease as the distance widens between the receptionist and the firm for which she works. According to one estimate by VPI VirtualSource (2013), the live on-site receptionist earns on average $27 an hour, whereas the work-at-home employee earns $23 an hour, and the off-shore employee earns $13 an hour. Although these figures for live workers may be overinflated (to make VPI's digital worker sound cheaper at $9 an hour), the comparison is warranted in its basic point: all the other options cost the employer less than the live on-site worker does. Whatever the reasons for this disparity, one implication is apparent: when employers do not see the worker or have him nearby, they are likely to pay less for that labor.

Of course, wages for virtual receptionists vary, depending on the particular firm and the context. Some companies, like Convergys, offer full-time, well-paying, at-home jobs and a variety of benefits (including health, retirement, and college tuition). Likewise, jobs sent to India may pay more than other comparable jobs in that labor market. However, these wages are still a mere fraction of those in the United States—sometimes as little as one-tenth. Thus, going overseas further drives down wages in the outsourcing process.

Other costs of virtualization and globalization are more hidden. For instance, there is a consistent gendering of this labor, in which women workers and femininity are devalued and taken advantage of. In the automation cases, the human features inserted within the digital systems and avatars are highly sexualized more often than not (Gustavsson 2005; Weber 2008). Even when the receptionist is just a computer screen, the figure typically displays gendered tendencies to please and serve: feminine names and symbols, eroticized bodies and voices, and deferential language and speech.

Gender is also very integral to the other process in this analysis: outsourcing. Interestingly, relative to the automation narratives, there is *less* sexualization in the corporate rhetoric of outsourcing. The gendering comes in other ways, however. In cases like Ruby's, the worker is not necessarily deferential but rather full of cheerfulness and energy. She offers female-endowed emotional and relational services. And in the case of the At-Home-Moms, the gendering is in imageries and legacies of domesticity. Women's historical responsibilities of caring for family members, old and young, become convenient justifications for transferring the receptionist's work to the home—where these workers already are and where they can double up on paid and unpaid labor.

These features are racialized and nationalized as well. They are "whitened" and "Americanized" in many capacities. Automated receptionists are often designed and presented with white skin and Anglo/Euro facial features. Similarly, the outsourced receptionists undergo aspects of *national identity management* (Poster 2007), altering their accents, their names, and the visual settings of their workspaces to reflect "American" markers. As I have argued elsewhere (Poster 2007), employers institute this process of national identity management (to varying degrees and with varying success) in order to reduce communication troubles across borders, to mask the location of the work, and to hide the process of outsourcing itself. Many insightful books have since reflected on the role of nation in mediating the labor process of Indian call centers (Aneesh 2015; Mirchandani 2012; Nadeem 2011). (For reviews, see Poster 2012; Poster and Yolmo 2016.)

Levels of Invisibility

There are many levels of invisibility embedded in this process. First is the *worker himself*. Sometimes the employee is completely hidden or displaced. At other times, employers are breaking down the live, on-site, whole-person receptionist into parts and taking her out of the workplace. Then, in a seemingly reverse activity, they are recreating these parts digitally or else recapturing them from other locations and reinserting them back into the office. Through technology and outsourcing, the worker as a human is being employed—and presented to the consumer—*selectively:* for the voice and relational capacity, for the body on display, and for the words delivered electronically.

Second, the *labor process* of the virtual receptionist is becoming invisible or at least fragmented. Whether the job involves talking on the phone or doing organizational tasks, the work is reduced to its tiniest elements. We see this process in particular with the cases of GetFriday and the virtual assistant teams. Employers are not hiring the labor of a whole person or whole job anymore. They are hiring a set of "to-dos," picking and choosing particular tasks from a list.

Fragmentation is also evident in wages. Phone work is increasingly paid not by the call, by the day, or even by the hour—but by the *minute*. It is advertised and billed to potential employers in a plan comprised of "minute" levels. Davinci Virtual Office Space and Solutions (2013) announces on its Web site that "live answering minutes will be calculated in *one second increments,* helping you to make the most of your 100 minute plan" (italics added). Industry experts and scholars are referring to this process as "micro labor" (Irani 2012). This term describes how, with networked technology platforms, work is fractionalized and labor is hired on a single-task basis. Along those lines, here we see how the wage is miniaturized as well.

The consequence is an obscuring and masking of the extent of human labor behind the wage. GetFriday (2011) says: "If the task takes 8 man-hours, you will be billed for 8 man-hours, regardless of how many assistants have worked on your task." In classical labor terms, the *man-hour* has referred to the amount of work that an average worker could perform in an hour. Yet in the case of outsourcing, it has little to do with the actual "men" or women who are performing the labor. The multitudes of workers who physically undertake and complete the task are not represented in the billing. They become invisible within the accounting process that tabulates the profits of their labor.

Third, the *workplace* of the virtual receptionist is becoming invisible. In the age of the virtual office, the space of employment is dematerializing and dispersing. This phenomenon is happening in both practical and symbolic ways.

Materially, the physical office space—the infrastructure—is being transferred to new locations. We have examined multiple destinations for the new virtual office. One is the offshore site. Outsource2India (2012) says on its Web site: "Outsourcing to a live virtual receptionist will save you not only the cost of having to hire a full time receptionist but will also save you the space of allotting an extra desk for an actual employee." Firms are motivated to move operations overseas for cost savings not only on wages but also on chairs, tables, walls, and office space. Escaping the financial burden and accountability for the physical upkeep of the building is part of the incentive for creating the virtual office and virtual jobs.

The office is moving to a second place as well—workers' homes—as in the case of the At-Home receptionists. It may seem like an easy thing for an employee to do, at least in the rhetoric of the outsourcing firms: all an employee needs is a cell phone. But that statement is not necessarily true. Being a home-based virtual receptionist requires a large and expensive technological investment, the burden of which is on the worker. He needs a computer, a headset, an Internet connection, specialized software to log in the results of the call, and much more. Dematerializing the workspace for the employer (both the outsourcing company and the company that purchases its services) means rematerializing it for the worker.

The workplace is being reconstituted symbolically as a result. With virtualization, the corporation itself is under threat of becoming invisible. The tasks of the receptionist in maintaining the integrity of the virtual office are crucial here. Given that there may be no actual firm, the receptionist must take on and uphold the identity of the entire organization. Ruby Receptionists' (2013) Web site proclaims: "Ruby's team of professionals can act as the 'glue' that holds your virtual operation together. Callers think we work in your office—even if you don't have one!" As the only point of contact with the public, Ruby's voice represents the firm and rematerializes it as a tangible entity.

In turn, new tasks are being generated for the virtual receptionist—tasks involving deception. We see this with Ruby, who disguises her own location in several ways. She hides from customers the fact that she is physically outside the firm. She also uses specialized technology to keep up the façade that she knows where her bosses are and how clients can reach them, even though they may never be on the premises. Thus, along with displaying pleasing emotions and managing the firm's relations with the public, virtual receptionists perform "corporate" identity management. As an added dimension, offshore receptionists like Margaret perform similar tasks transnationally, combining this corporate identity management with national identity management.

. . .

Employers are increasingly choosing between two alternatives to the live on-site worker: automation and outsourcing. The receptionist job in particular reveals how employers are searching for ways to remove workers, even those who are supposed to be the "face" of the firm.

Aside from the employers, other groups have important roles in this process. Third-party outsourcers and technology vendors are setting the parameters of the platforms, sites, and locations where work can be performed. Striking is the similarity across these virtual receptionist firms—regardless of their position on the spectrum—in the rhetoric they use to vilify the nonvirtual (i.e., human) workers. Sometimes it is about their laziness (taking breaks), sometimes their bodies are weak (getting sick), sometimes it is because they ask for money (raises, overtime, benefits), and sometimes they are just plain irritating: they spend too much time gathering in the parking lot, says Wintech (2012), creator of Alice. Regardless of the alternative labor they are providing, these firms have similar reasons for why humans are basically distasteful.

Negotiating visibility is integral to the process of constructing the virtual receptionist. A spectrum of automation–outsourcing strategies that employers are using illustrates this dynamic (see figure 5.1). At the outer ends of the spectrum, employers are making workers completely invisible. In the automation case, they are getting rid of workers entirely (e.g., the empty chair in the Alice advertisements). In the global outsourcing case, they are shielding workers from view (e.g., the hidden workforce underneath the GetFriday team desk). In the middle range of the spectrum, employers are selecting aspects of the worker to be visible to the customer (and the public). Depending on their business needs, employers use different strategies to determine how much humanness a job needs and which kinds of humanness should be on display. Sometimes it is the employee's voice, sometimes just the face, sometimes the full figure.

Thus, invisibility of labor serves the outsourcing and automation processes well. Through this strategy, a range of actors in the labor process—firms, technology vendors, and outsourcing middlemen—reduce the size of the workforce, the scope of the tasks for a single job, and the infrastructural supports and wages.

The question for future research is whether, by looking at these alternatives to the traditional receptionist job, we are getting a glimpse of a wider trend. These same forces may well be spreading across other service jobs at all occupational levels. There is evidence of automation creeping into lower-skilled jobs like hospital orderlies and hotel bellhops (Miller 2014), midlevel jobs like police officers (McDuffee 2014), and high-skilled professional jobs like doctors, architects, and lawyers (Meltzer 2014).

Yet critics argue that this same alarm has been sounded with every stage of newly introduced technology and that at each point in time, professionals have adapted (Pasquale 2014). Many jobs involve certain kinds of "social intelligence" that cannot be extracted from the human employee. Recently, there are even trends of employers returning to humans after they have tried out various kinds of automated workers. This has happened in industries of travel, home services, and shopping, where consumers have responded with information overload (Manjoo 2015). These consumers are resisting the "work transfer" (Glazer 1993) of tasks once done by employees, especially those of sifting through massive amounts of data, and instead urging firms to rehire skilled employees.

Furthermore, the stability of human labor may be embedded in the peculiar dynamics of the service economy and its "needs." Suchman (2007) astutely notes that the development of the middle class (in many countries) has been predicated on expansions in both service classes of live workers and service classes of digital workers. They do not appear to be mutually exclusive. Thus, as I have argued in this chapter, the future will undoubtedly involve an interplay—and tension—among employer strategies with live on-site workers, remote workers, and digitized workers.

NOTES

Earlier versions of this analysis were presented at the Eastern Sociological Society, the Canadian Industrial Relations Association, and the Intel Science and Technology Center for Social Computing, University of California–Irvine. Danielle Van Jaarsveld and Dan Zuberi organized a wonderful conference on Global Service Work at the University of British Columbia, where the seeds of this project were planted. Much appreciation goes to the participants of my ongoing research in Indian outsourcing zones for their time and stories. I am also grateful for constructive comments by Dorothy Smith, Christopher Andrews, and Melissa Gregg. The Labor Tech reading group, which I co-organize with Kavita Philip, has provided more theoretical and conceptual inspiration than can be described in a small note. Responsibility for all content herein is my own.

1. *Bot* is short for *robot*, referring to software programs that perform automated tasks. A subset of these bots is "embodied agents," which have visual bodies within their digital platforms in order to serve as a graphical front end for the computer systems behind them. They are often represented as cartoons or avatars for customer service Web sites, and as "chatterbots" they are equipped with conversational skills to appear more natural to customers.

2. See Poster and Yolmo (2016) for a lengthier discussion of globalization and outsourcing.

3. *Alice* is a popular name for automated assistants. Lucy Suchman (2007) describes how the winner of the Loebner prize for "most human computer" in 2004 was also an "Alice" (Artificial Linguistic Internet Computer Entity). Her

"body" was a vacuum cleaner, keeping constant with the theme of feminine domesticity that we will see throughout this chapter.

4. Margaret is a composite of several accounts of the video receptionist from my research, including those whom I interviewed and those described in the scholarly literature and news (Kalita 2005; Weightman 2011).

REFERENCES

Airus Media. 2011. Retrieved January 6, 2013 (http://airportone.com /virtualassistancesystem.htm).

Aneesh, Aneesh. 2015. *Neutral Accent: How Language, Labor, and Life Become Global.* Durham, NC: Duke University Press.

Babu, Sabarish, Stephen Schmugge, Tiffany Barnes, and Larry F. Hodges. 2006. "What Would You Like to Talk About? An Evaluation of Social Conversations with a Virtual Receptionist." *Intelligent Virtual Agents* 4133: 169–80.

Convergys. 2013. Retrieved February 3, 2013 (http://careers.convergysworkathome .com/).

Davinci Virtual Office Space and Solutions. 2013. Retrieved February 3, 2013 (www.davincivirtual.com/receptionists/features/virtual-assistant).

Garson, Barbara. 1988. *The Electronic Sweatshop.* New York: Simon & Schuster.

GetFriday. 2011. Retrieved July 28, 2012 (www.getfriday.com).

Glazer, Nona Yetta. 1993. *Women's Paid and Unpaid Labor: The Work Transfer in Health Care and Retailing.* Philadelphia: Temple University Press.

Gustavsson, Eva. 2005. "Virtual Servants." *Gender, Work and Organization* 12 (5): 400–19.

Hochschild, Arlie Russell. 2003. *The Managed Heart.* Berkeley: University of California Press.

International Labour Office. 2001. *World Employment Report 2001: Life at Work in the Information Economy.* Geneva: International Labour Office.

Irani, Lilly. 2012. "Microworking the Crowd." Pp. 1–7 in *Limn: Clouds and Crowds,* edited by Christopher Kelty, Lilly Irani, and Nick Seaver. Seattle: Createspace.

Kalita, S. Mitra. 2005. "Virtual Secretary Puts New Face on Pakistan." *Washington Post,* May 10, p. A1.

Kanter, Rosabeth Moss. 1993. *Men and Women of the Corporation.* New York: Basic Books.

Kerr, Ian R. 2004. "Bots, Babes and the Californication of Commerce." *University of Ottawa Law & Technology Journal* 1: 285–324.

Kwika.org. 2013. Retrieved January 6, 2013 (www.kwika.org/careers/what -are-virtual-assistants.html).

LiveOps. 2013. Retrieved January 27, 2013 (http://join.liveops.com).

MacDonald, Cameron Lynne, and Carmen Sirianni, eds. 1996. *Working in the Service Society.* Philadelphia: Temple University Press.

Manjoo, Farhad. 2015. "The Machines Rose, but Now Start-Ups Add Human Touch." *New York Times,* December 1, pp. B1, 10.

McDuffee, Allen. 2014. "The New Security Robot Watching Over Silicon Valley Is Less RoboCop and More R2-D2." *The Atlantic,* November 2, www.theatlantic.com.

Meltzer, Tom. 2014. "Robot Doctors, Online Lawyers and Automated Architects: The Future of the Professions?" *Guardian,* June 5, pp. 1–8.

Miller, Claire C. 2014. "As Robots Grow Smarter, American Workers Struggle to Keep Up." *New York Times,* December 1, p. A1.

Mirchandani, Kiran. 2012. *Phone Clones.* Ithaca, NY: Cornell University Press.

Nadeem, Shehzad. 2011. *Dead Ringers.* Princeton, NJ: Princeton University Press.

National Receptionists Association. 2013. Retrieved February 6, 2013 (http://nationalreceptionists.com/pressreleases.html).

Outsource2India. 2012. Retrieved July 28, 2013 (www.outsource2india.com /callcenter/virtual-receptionist).

Pasquale, F. 2014. "A More Nuanced View of Legal Automation." *Balkinization.* Retrieved August 22, 2014 (http://balkin.blogspot.com/2014/06/).

Poster, Winifred R. 2007. "Who's on the Line? Indian Call Center Agents Pose as Americans for U.S.-Outsourced Firms." *Industrial Relations* 46 (2): 271–304.

———. 2012. "Review of 'Phone Clones.'" *Industrial and Labor Relations Review* 64 (5): 1005–7.

Poster, Winifred R., and Nima L. Yolmo. 2016. "Globalization and Outsourcing." In *The Sage Handbook of the Sociology of Work and Employment,* edited by Stephen Edgell, Heidi Gottfried, and Edward Granter. London: Sage.

Ruby Receptionists. 2013. Retrieved January 3, 2013 (http://www.callruby .com).

Suchman, Lucy A. 2007. *Human–Machine Reconfigurations.* New York: Cambridge University Press.

The Resource Group. 2009. Retrieved May 22, 2009 (www.resgrp.com).

VPI Virtual Source. 2013. Retrieved January 27, 2013 (www.vpi-corp.com /VirtualSource/).

Weber, Jutta. 2008. "Human–Robot Interaction." Pp. 855–67 in *Handbook of Research on Computer-Mediated Communication,* edited by Sigrid Kelsey and Kirk St. Amant. Hershey, PA: IGI Global.

Weightman, Barbara A. 2011. *Dragons and Tigers.* 3rd ed. Hoboken, NJ: Wiley.

WinTech. 2012. Retrieved January 27, 2013 (www.alicereceptionist.com/).

PART THREE

Pushed Out of Sight

Shielded Forms of Embodied Labor

CHAPTER 6

Hidden from View

Disability, Segregation, and Work

ELIZABETH PENDO

A central goal of the disability rights movement is to enable people with disabilities to fully participate in society and to live complete, independent, and engaged lives. Employment is considered central to this vision and has long been intertwined with ideas of equality and citizenship in the disability rights movement. However, too often people with disabilities are unseen, unwelcome, or simply not present in the traditional workplace.

The employment provisions of the Americans with Disabilities Act of 1990 (42 U.S.C. § 12101) (ADA) were intended to bring working-age people with disabilities into the workplace by providing options for them to seek and gain meaningful, integrated employment. Although the ADA has made significant gains, the rate of progress in employment has been disappointing. For example, in 2012, only 32.7 percent of working-age adults with disabilities were employed, as compared with 73.6 percent of working-age adults without disabilities who were (Institute on Disability 2013). While the lack of progress of people with disabilities in the traditional workplace has received attention, the work done by many, especially those with severe disabilities in segregated workplaces, remains hidden in sheltered workshops.

Sheltered workshops are commonly defined as supervised, segregated workplaces for disabled adults and primarily for adults with intellectual and developmental disabilities. According to a 2001 report by the U.S. General Accounting Office, more than 400,000 people with disabilities are working in sheltered workshops across the country (GAO 2001). The work activities in sheltered workshops typically consist of simple assembly processes performed by hand. Examples include assembling small parts, hand-packaging items, packing or unpacking items, folding, sorting, and collating (pp. 10–12). Sheltered workshops are relatively small settings, each employing an average of eighty-six workers with disabilities, and primarily populated by people with disabilities (p. 10). Sheltered workshops may also include support services such as close supervision, job coaching, and life skills training (p. 13). Sheltered workshops are often characterized as job training programs, but many of them function as long-term and isolating alternatives to competitive employment. Although the invisibility of people with disabilities because of these sheltered workshops may appear to be a dramatic example, it shares similarities with other ways in which such individuals are unseen or simply not present in the traditional workplace. Indeed, there are several gaps or areas of conflict in ADA implementation that operate to obscure, exclude, or divert workers with disabilities from the traditional workplace.

This chapter explores the intersection of the concepts of *disability, invisibility,* and *work* and identifies the ways in which different and conflicting social and legal constructions of disability perpetuate the segregation and invisibility of people with disabilities in the workplace.

HIDDEN FROM VIEW: SHELTERED WORKSHOPS

Sheltered workshops have been present in the United States since at least 1840.[1] The earliest workshops provided job training to people who were blind, with the goal of preparing them for competitive employment. Today, sheltered workshops primarily serve people with intellectual and developmental disabilities (Stefan 2010).

The National Industrial Recovery Act, part of the New Deal policies in 1934, and an executive order signed by President Franklin D. Roosevelt permitting Americans with disabilities to be paid less than the minimum wage set the stage for the growth of sheltered workshops. The Section 14(c) program, as we know it today, was established a few years later in 1938 as part of the Fair Labor Standards Act (FLSA). The program grew in the 1950s and 1960s, when sheltered employment, workshops, or both were seen as a way of providing support and training for those individuals with disabilities who needed the guidance and structure of such an environment.

The Section 14(c) program allows employers to pay employees much less than the minimum wage if they have a physical or cognitive disability that hinders their earning capacity or level of production (Fair Labor Standards Act of 1938, 29 U.S.C. § 201). When Congress passed the 1966 amendment to the Developmental Disabilities Assistance and Bill of Rights Act of 1963, it provided a much broader definition of *disability* that could be used by recipients of Section 14(c) certificates, allowing a larger group of people to be subject to subminimum wages (Public Law 89–601, 42 U.S.C. §§ 15041–15045 [1963]). The 1986 amendment and reauthorization of the FLSA removed any minimum wage floor for those employers that hold Section 14(c) certificates, creating the current sheltered workshop environment (U.S. Department of Labor, Wage and Hour Division 2008). The General Accounting Office's 2001 report found about 424,000 people with disabilities employed under Section 14(c) of the FLSA (GAO 2001).[2]

Sheltered workshops have been seen as job training programs for some or as an alternative to competitive employment for others. Some sheltered workshop programs have been criticized for their lack of meaningful opportunities for the education and training of, lack of meaningful "work" experience for, unnecessary segregation of, and financial exploitation of the disabled. As explained by the Center for Public Representation (2012), a Massachusetts-based nonprofit public interest law firm dedicated to promoting the rights of and improving services for people with mental illness and other disabilities, on its Web site, "For decades, persons with disabilities have been segregated into sheltered workshops . . . and paid far below minimum wage to do rote tasks like stuffing envelopes, sorting [hangers], and sealing bags. Begun seventy years ago as a program of benign paternalism, sheltered workshops exploit employees with disabilities, deny them access to non-disabled peers, and fail to train them for competitive employment. Although persons with disabilities are capable of working in competitive employment, often through supported employment services, many remain segregated in the workshops." Sheltered workshops have also been criticized as being out of line with national policy goals. In its 2011 report *Segregated and Exploited: The Failure of the Disability Service System to Provide Quality Work,* the National Disability Rights Network states that neglect, segregated settings, and a subminimum pay wage all work against the national policy goal of integrating people with disabilities into the community. Instead, unnecessarily segregated workplaces keep people with disabilities marginalized and hidden and create opportunities for abuse, neglect, and exploitation. The report also argues that a subminimum wage reinforces a life of poverty for people with disabilities. This criticism is supported by statistics that show that sheltered employment intended as a vehicle to regular, full-time employment is not working: according to a 2001 investigation by the General Accounting Office, only approximately 5 percent of sheltered workshop participants moved on to a job in the community (GAO 2001: 4).

In light of these and other criticisms, some states are taking steps to eliminate or reduce the number of sheltered workshops. For example, in 2012, a class-action lawsuit was filed in the U.S. District Court for Oregon alleging that the State of Oregon was in violation of the ADA and the Rehabilitation Act for not providing adequate employment opportunities for those with disabilities (*Lane v. Kitzhaber*, 283 F.R.D. 587 [D. Or. 2012]). The plaintiffs alleged that they were entitled to an integrated employment setting as part of their benefits from the Oregon Department of Health Services, and the U.S. Department of Justice intervened on their behalf. Prior to resolution of the case, Oregon governor John Kitzhaber in April 2013 signed Executive Order No. 13–04, which significantly decreased state funding for sheltered workshops and increased employment services for individuals with intellectual and developmental disabilities by July 2015.

However, other states are continuing to support sheltered workshops, at least for some people with disabilities. For example, in New Jersey, after months of petitioning the state legislature and other state officials, families of individuals with disabilities and operators of sheltered workshops succeeded in stopping a process of defunding sheltered employment in the state (Camilli 2013).

The ADA does not strictly prohibit segregated services such as sheltered workshops. Rather, it requires that "people with disabilities must be given a choice of the most integrated service appropriate to their needs and an opportunity to reject segregated services ostensibly provided for their benefit" (Stefan 2010: 878–79). The divergence between approaches of different states appears to be about whether and to what extent sheltered workshops remain an appropriate option for delivering services to people with disabilities. If reliance on sheltered workshops is to be reduced, what might take its place? One possibility is *supported employment*, commonly understood to be "competitive work performed in an integrated work setting where individuals are matched to jobs consistent with their strengths, resources, abilities, capabilities, interests, and informed choice . . . and are provided individualized supports to learn and keep the job" (NDRN 2011: 6).

DISAPPEARING IN THE GAPS: THE ADA

The Americans with Disabilities Act of 1990 (ADA) was intended to bring working-age people with disabilities into the workplace by providing options for them to seek and gain meaningful integrated employment. Title I of the ADA is modeled on Title VII of the Civil Rights Act of 1964 (42 U.S.C. §2000e, et. seq. [1964]), which prohibits discrimination on the basis of race, national origin, sex, and religion. Title I of the ADA prohibits discrimination against a qualified individual with a disability in regard to job application procedures, hiring, advancement, termination, compensation, job training, and other terms, conditions, and privileges of employment (ADA, 42 U.S.C. § 12112[a]). In addition to addressing those traditional forms of discrimination, Title I discusses another form of discrimination—"not making reasonable accommodations to the known physical or mental limitations of an otherwise qualified individual with a disability who is an applicant or employee, unless [the employer] can demonstrate that the accommodation would impose an undue hardship on the operation of the business" (ADA, 42 U.S.C. § 12112[b][5][A]).

Notwithstanding the ADA's significant gains, gaps or areas of conflict in ADA implementation continue to operate to reduce the visibility and participation of workers with disabilities. These include questions of membership in the protected class, issues of disclosure in connection with the reasonable accommodation requirement, and diversion of workers into private benefit systems.

Unlike Title VII, which allows anyone to raise a claim for discrimination based on the protected categories of race, national origin, sex, and religion, the ADA grants standing only to members of the protected class as defined in the statute (ADA, 42 U.S.C. § 12111[8]). The ADA defines *disability* to mean a physical or mental impairment that substantially limits one or more major life activities, or a record of such impairment, or being regarded as having such an impairment regardless of whether the individual actually has the impairment (ADA, 42 U.S.C. § 12102[2]).

After the passage of the ADA, the courts grappled with the questions of who should be protected under the ADA. In several significant decisions, the Supreme Court narrowly interpreted the definition of *disability (Albertson's v. Kirkenburg,* 527 U.S. 555 [1999]; *Murphy v. UPS,* 527 U.S. 516 [1999]; *Sutton v. United Air Lines,* 527 U.S. 471 [1999]; *Toyota Motor Manufacturing v. Williams,* 534 U.S. 184 [2002]).[3] For example, in *Sutton v. United Air Lines* (1999), the Court held that mitigating measures, such as medication, corrective lenses, or other devices, should be taken into account in determining whether a person is disabled for the purposes of the ADA. In other words, because the plaintiffs could fully correct their nearsightedness with contact lenses, they were not actually disabled.

Sutton and the cases like it created a "catch-22": a worker with an undisputed impairment who is rejected for employment because of that impairment has no standing to challenge the rejection if the impairment can be mitigated or corrected. Indeed, courts soon found that individuals with conditions such as epilepsy, diabetes, intellectual and developmental disabilities, bipolar disorder, and multiple sclerosis were not "disabled." According to Ruth Colker's influential 1999 analysis, federal courts resolved approximately 93 percent of employment cases in favor of employers, often on summary judgment ruling based on a determination that the plaintiff was not disabled within the meaning of the ADA (Colker 1999).

The Americans with Disabilities Act Amendments Act of 2008 (Public Law 110–35, 122 Stat. 3553 [2008]) (ADAAA) made clear that the definition of *disability* was to be interpreted broadly. In particular, it explicitly rejected the reasoning of earlier Supreme Court decisions that had narrowed the scope of the ADA's definition of *disability*. Early analysis of post-ADAAA cases suggests that courts are less likely to dismiss cases on the basis that the plaintiff fails to meet the ADA's definition of *disability* and more likely to focus on questions of merit, such as whether the plaintiff is "qualified" within the meaning of the ADA (Befort 2013: 2050–57; Stein et al. 2014: 131–34). Post-ADAAA cases may also bring increased attention to and development of the reasonable accommodation requirement, an outcome that would be welcomed by many advocates and scholars (Porter 2009; Weber 2010).

As noted earlier, Title I requires that employers make reasonable accommodations to the known physical or mental limitations of an otherwise qualified applicant or employee with a disability. The process of reasonable accommodation is intended to be a flexible, interactive process, typically initiated by the employee or applicant. Although the ADA does not require that an individual disclose a disability, disclosure of disability-related information may be required to support a request for reasonable accommodation. Therefore, individuals with disabilities may experience the issue of disclosure as a different type of catch-22. As defined by the ADA, *disability* is a diverse category that includes a wide range of impairments and conditions. Some disabilities may affect an individual's ability to do her job, and some may not. *Disability* is also a fluid category since impairments can be acquired at any point in the life span, and the severity and impact of impairments can change or fluctuate over time. In addition, some disabilities are obvious or easily observed, either directly or through cues such as the use of a cane, hearing aid, or service animal. Other disabilities are hidden or less easily observed, such as mental conditions, intellectual impairments, infertility, or chronic pain. There is a robust literature on the pressures felt by people with disabilities to downplay or deny their disabilities in the workplace, often through strategies similar to those employed by members of other marginalized groups. Such strategies include *passing,* in which an individual hides his identity, or *covering,* in which an individual acknowledges her identity but suppresses outward signs or aspects of the identity (Goffman 1963 [definitions of terms], discussed in Yoshino 2006: 18; Gulati and Carbado 2000). Many people with hidden disabilities choose not to disclose their disabilities in the workplace to avoid stereotyping, stigmatizing, and discrimination (Bouton 2013).

Another reason that workers with disabilities are not visible in the workplace is that they may be diverted from the workplace into private benefits systems.[4] The ADA prohibits an employer from discriminating on the basis of disability in regard to, among other things, fringe benefits, including participation in an employer-sponsored disability benefits plan (29 C.F.R. 1630.4[f] [1993]). Disability benefits plans provide income-replacement benefits to employees who are unable to work because of illness or accident. The purpose of such plans is to replace some or all of the income lost when an employee is suffering from a disability as defined by the policy at issue. The definition of *disability* in these plans is frequently keyed to the individual's ability to perform his job.

Most employer-sponsored welfare plans, including disability benefits plans, are governed by the Employee Retirement Income Security Act of 1974 (29 U.S.C. §§ 1001–1461) (ERISA). As explored in my prior work, ERISA–regulated disability benefits and the structure of ERISA's remedial scheme can be used by employers to avoid the duty of reasonable accommodation of employees with disabilities (Pendo 2002: 1186–91). Consider an employee with epilepsy who is treated effectively with regular medication to prevent seizures. She is ready and able to work, and requires regular breaks to take medication, which are reasonable under the circumstances of her employment. She notifies her employer of the disability, and depending on her familiarity with the ADA, she may or may not request breaks as an accommodation of her disability. Imagine that the employer is unaware that the employee needs frequent breaks (or is unwilling to provide them) and instead suggests, encourages, or forces the employee to leave the workplace on temporary or permanent disability leave. Because employer-sponsored disability plans rarely define *disability* with reference to reasonable accommodation, it is entirely possible that the employee may receive disability benefits even though she is able to perform her job with the reasonable accommodation of frequent breaks. As a result, the employee falls into a gap between the definition of *disability* contained in her employer's disability leave policy and the definition of *disability* contained in the ADA. This situation often results in an individual's exclusion from the workplace, isolation, and economic dependence—the very problems that the ADA seeks to remedy (Pendo 2002: 1186–91).

UNDERLYING TENSIONS: DISABILITY AND WORK

The gaps and contradictions within ADA jurisprudence identified above suggest a continuing debate on fundamental questions about the scope and purpose of the ADA. Who should the ADA be protecting? Who should be reasonably accommodated in the workplace—and at what cost? What types of "work" are performed in sheltered workshops, and why? Are sheltered workshops a choice that should be made available or a form of unjustified segregation and possible exploitation? What legal rights or other forms of regulation should adhere?

Both debates point to fundamental and unresolved questions surrounding disability and work, which often appear as dichotomies: disabled or worker, work or therapy, independence or assistance, integration or segregation, protection or exploitation, rights or benefits. The tensions surrounding disability and work are not surprising since *disability* has historically been defined in opposition to *employment* (Crossley 1999). Political scientist Richard Scotch (2000) identified a series of theoretical paradigms to explain how disability has been conceptualized historically in Western society: the moral model, the medical model, the economic model, the social model, and the civil rights model. The interchange and layering of these models are a helpful framework for drawing out some of the tensions and contradictions apparent in these debates.

In modern times *disability* has been defined in predominantly medical terms as a specific trait of an individual that can be traced to a physical or mental impairment (Crossley 1999; Scotch 2000). The disabled individual is viewed as biologically different and inferior. According to this model, the primary problem faced by people with disabilities is their incapacity to work and otherwise participate in society. The incapacity is the natural product of a person's impairments. Consequently, the best way to help the disabled person is to cure or ameliorate the impairment, or to use rehabilitation techniques to enable the person to adjust to or overcome the impairment.

A variant of the medical model, the economic model, which arose after the advent of World War II, views disability as a "phenomenon that lies at the intersection of human impairment and the market for labor" (Berg 1999: 8). Disability is assessed according to how much it restricts people from performing the work, and the goal is to promote their economic self-sufficiency by increasing their participation in the traditional workplace. Because disability is constructed as the inability to work, many people with disabilities are not "seen" working or as workers.

In contrast to the medical model, the social model of disability suggests that disadvantages or "disablement" flows from social systems and structures rather than from impairments (Crossley 1999). A major premise of this model is that disability is a social construct rather than a biological fact. Thus, the disadvantaged status of persons with disabilities is the product of a hostile or inhospitable social environment, not simply the product of physical or mental impairments. In this view, barriers embedded in social structures and attitudes also construct disability. The classic example distinguishing the social model from the medical model is a person who uses a wheelchair who is unable to enter a building because the only means of entry is a staircase. The medical model suggests that the impairment and use of the wheelchair are the problem. The social model suggests that the socially created barriers, such as a building design that involves the use of stairs and fails to include a ramp or lift, are the source of disablement.

An example in the employment context is a continued deference to employer rule-making that permits the "disabling" and exclusion of employees. Consider the facts of a Supreme Court case from 2002, *Toyota v. Williams*.[5] Ms. Williams began working on the engine fabrication assembly line at an automobile manufacturing plant in 1990. When use of the pneumatic tools on the assembly line caused pain in her hands, wrists, and arms—injuries diagnosed as bilateral carpal tunnel syndrome and bilateral tendonitis, she was transferred to modified duty jobs. She worked on modified duty until 1993, when she was transferred to a paint and body inspection line that required visual and manual inspection tasks. In light of her medical restrictions, she performed only the visual inspection for a few years without incident. In 1996, her employer instituted a new requirement that all paint and body inspection line employees perform both visual and manual inspections. When she started doing manual inspections, she once again began to experience pain in her neck and shoulders that interfered with her ability to perform her job. Employers continue to hold the power to define work and normal workplace standards; in this case, Ms. Williams was transformed from an adequate worker to an inadequate one by virtue of her employer's policy change.

In the realm of disability policy, the idea that rules can disable is not new. In fact, the *Oxford English Dictionary* defines the word *disabled* as "incapacity recognized or created by law; legal disqualification." To disable a person is to disqualify legally, to pronounce legally incapable. The "disabling" of employees who could perform the essential function of their jobs with reasonable accommodation is particularly disturbing because people with disabilities want to work. According to a recent analysis of the 2006 General Social Survey, 80 percent of unemployed working-age people with disabilities reported that they would like to be working now or in the future (Ali, Schur, and Blank 2011: 202).

From the social model grew the civil rights model, which is based on the civil rights movement of the 1950s and 1960s (Drimmer 1993). In this view the legal status and social status of disabled persons reflect underlying social attitudes and assumptions concerning disability. Above all, the civil rights model seeks to "unmask the false objectivity that allows society to label some of its members 'disabled' and treat those citizens as less than equal" (p. 1356). Borrowing from earlier civil rights movements, this model has a first goal of eradicating perceptions of inferiority and all other irrational reactions. The second goal is eliminating discrimination that results from such prejudices. Finally, the model "pursues a 'level playing field,'" or equality of opportunity, by aggressively securing access to, and independence in, all aspects of society" (p. 1358).

These models are overlapping rather than progressive and often implicit and unacknowledged: they form what Professor Mary Crossley (1999) evocatively termed "the disability kaleidoscope." For example, although the ADA can be viewed as ushering in the age of the civil rights model, assumptions about disability linked to the medical and economic models can still be seen in programs that link benefits to an individual's perceived incapacity to work, such as the Social Security Disability Insurance (SSDI) program, which provides a subsistence income to persons with total, long-term disabilities (42 U.S.C. § 423 [1994] [SSDI]; 42 U.S.C. § 1382 [2013]) [SSI]). Similarly, employers' ability to rely on employer-sponsored long-term disability benefits to avoid, consciously or unconsciously, the duty of providing reasonable accommodations for employees with disabilities also reflects medical and economic models of disability.

TOWARD INCLUSION AND INCREASED VISIBILITY

A key insight of disability studies is that the lives and life experiences of people with disabilities are invisible to many in the nondisabled community. As disability studies scholar Lennard Davis (2006) asks: "Why have the disabled been rendered more invisible than other groups? Why are . . . issues about perception, mobility, accessibility, distribution of bio-resources, [and] physical space . . . difference[s] not seen as central to the human condition?" (p. xv). In prior work, I have drawn attention to the considerable evidence that people without disabilities are unable to identify with people with disabilities, including empirical evidence indicating that people without disabilities significantly and unreasonably devalue the lives of people with disabilities (Pendo 2002, 2003). In the workplace, this situation means that too often people with disabilities are unseen, unacknowledged, or simply not present.

Calling attention to how and why people with disabilities are segregated, obscured, or excluded in the workplace is an important first step. Next, promoting greater opportunity and integration through legal and regulatory structures could serve as a way forward from the false dichotomies that contribute to the invisibility of workers with disabilities. Rather than choosing between "disabled" or "worker," the use or reasonable accommodation of supported employment could be increased. Rather than choosing between "independence" or "assistance," services and opportunities can be provided to people with disabilities in a manner that allows them to live as independently as possible.

Recent amendments to the ADA provide a chance to expand opportunities and visibility. However, it remains to be seen whether this situation will result in more positive outcomes for workers with disabilities or whether the courts will interpret qualification, the reasonable accommodation requirement, or both narrowly.

In terms of sheltered workshops, scholars and advocates have argued that the principle of the Supreme Court's 1999 decision in *Olmstead v.*

L. C. ex rel. Zimring, 527 U.S. 581 (1999) that persons with disabilities have a right to spend their lives in the most integrated setting appropriate for them as individuals should be applied to employment (Bagenstos 2011; *Olmstead* 1999; Stefan 2010). In that case, Lois Curtis and Elaine Wilson had mental illness and developmental disabilities and were voluntarily admitted to the psychiatric unit in the state-run Georgia Regional Hospital. After their treatment, their doctors stated that they were ready to move to a community-based program. However, the women remained confined in the institution for several years. They filed suit under the ADA for release from the hospital. The Supreme Court held that unjustified segregation of people with disabilities constitutes discrimination in violation of Title II of the ADA. The Court held that public entities must provide community-based services to persons with disabilities when such services are appropriate and not opposed by the affected person and when community-based services can be reasonably accommodated, taking into account the resources available to the public entity and the needs of others who are receiving disability services. The Court explained that its holding was based on two important principles. First, "institutional placement of persons who can handle and benefit from community settings perpetuates unwarranted assumptions that persons so isolated are incapable of or unworthy of participating in community life" (*Olmstead* 1999: 600). Second, "confinement in an institution severely diminishes the everyday life activities of individuals, including family relations, social contacts, work options, economic independence, educational advancement, and cultural enrichment" (p. 601).

When these principles are applied to employment, it is clear that people with disabilities can and should live and work independently in their communities, as envisioned by the ADA. "The truth is that people with disabilities can—and do—work in all areas of the American workforce. They thrive when they fully participate in their communities, and in turn, the nation thrives" (NDRN 2011: 3; Whittaker 2005). The integration mandate of *Olmstead* supports increased reliance on the supported employment model. In the words of Susan Stefan (2010), "People with disabilities do not need to be sheltered from the world; they need to be welcomed into it" (p. 935).

. . .

Twenty-five years after passage of the ADA, people with disabilities are too often unseen, unacknowledged, or simply not present in the workplace. Although sheltered workshops and traditional employment may seem very different, they both operate in some circumstances to remove willing and capable workers from the workplace. In both cases, contradictions in the construction of disability and tensions within the disability rights movement contribute to the segregation and invisibility of people with disabilities in the workplace. In both cases the practical result—exclusion, isolation, and economic dependence—is the very problem that the ADA seeks to remedy.

The ADA is more than a specific protection from discrimination—it is also a policy commitment to the social inclusion of people with disabilities (Scotch 2000: 216). Promoting greater opportunity and integration through legal and regulatory structures is a way forward from the beliefs and dichotomies that contribute to the invisibility of people with disabilities in the workplace. Greater integration of people with disabilities into every avenue of American life, including the workplace, would also provide an opportunity for the currently nondisabled majority to become educated about the reality of life with a disability and to dispel certain stereotypes based on fear and ignorance (Pendo 2003).

NOTES

1. For a fuller history of sheltered workshops in the United States, see Stefan 2010, pp. 875, 868–902; and NDRN 2011.

2. Of that total, about 95 percent of 14(c) employees who receive subminimum wages are employed by public, nonprofit entities rather than by private, for-profit businesses.

3. All decisions were overturned due to legislative action in Public Law 110–325, January 1, 2009.

4. The following two sections are based on research published in Pendo 2002. Used with permission of the *University of California–Davis Law Review.*

5. This case was overturned due to legislative action in Public Law 110–325, January 1, 2009. The Court in *Toyota Motor Manufacturing v. Williams* (534 U.S. 184 [2002]) had held that the terms *substantially* and *major life activity* in the ADA's definition of disability "need to be interpreted strictly to create a demanding standard for quality as disabled" (*Toyota,* 534 U.S. at 197 [2002]). The ADAAA explicitly overturned the ruling in *Toyota v. Williams* that the terms *substantially* and *major* created a demanding standard and that to be substantially limited in performing a major life activity under the ADA, "an individual must have an impairment that prevents or severely restricts the individual from doing activities that are of central importance to most people's daily lives" (ADAAA, Sec. 2 [b][4]). Although the ADAAA overturned the specific ruling of the case, the facts remain instructive.

REFERENCES

Albertson's v. Kirkenburg, 527 U.S. 555 (1999).

Ali, Muhammed, Lisa Schur, and Peter Blank. 2011. "What Types of Jobs Do People with Disabilities Want?" *Journal of Occupational Rehabilitation* 21: 199–210.

ADA (Americans with Disabilities Act of 1990), 42 U.S.C. §§ 12101–12213.

Americans with Disabilities Act Amendments Act of 2008, Public Law 110–35, 122 U.S. Statutes at Large 3553 (2008).

Bagenstos, Samuel R. 2011. "*Olmstead* Goes to Work." Remarks delivered at Case Western Reserve University School of Law, March 15, Cleveland, OH. Retrieved January 6, 2015 (www.ada.gov/olmstead/documents/bagenstos _speech_cwru.pdf).

Befort, Stephen F. 2013. "An Empirical Analysis of Case Outcomes under the ADA Amendments Act." *Washington & Lee Law Review* 70: 2027–71.

Berg, Paula E. 1999. "Ill/Legal: Interrogating the Meaning and Function of the Category of Disability Anti-Discrimination Law." *Yale Law & Policy Review* 18: 1–51.

Bouton, Katherine. 2013. "Quandary of Hidden Disability: Conceal or Reveal?" *New York Times,* September 22, p. BU8.

Camilli, Danielle. 2013. "State Saves Sheltered Workshops for Adults with Developmental Disabilities." *Burlington (NJ) County Times,* July 29. Retrieved January 6, 2015 (www.burlingtoncountytimes.com/news/local/breaking -news/state-saves-sheltered-workshops-for-adults-with-developmentally -disabilities/article_od59d5c4-d54b-54d7-bfca-516c113fac88.html).

Center for Public Representation. 2012. "Integrated Employment." Retrieved January 6, 2015 (www.centerforpublicrep.org/litigation-and-major-cases /litigation-major-cases).

Civil Rights Act of 1964, 42 U.S.C. §§ 1981–2000 (1964).

Colker, Ruth. 1999. "The Americans with Disabilities Act: A Windfall for Defendants." *Harvard Civil Rights–Civil Liberties Review* 34: 99–162.

Crossley, Mary. 1999. "The Disability Kaleidoscope." *Notre Dame Law Review* 74: 621–716.

Davis, Lennard J., ed. 2006. *The Disability Studies Reader.* New York: Routledge.

Developmental Disabilities Assistance and Bill of Rights Act of 1963, 42 U.S.C. §§ 15041–15045.

Drimmer, Jonathan. 1993. "Cripples, Overcomers, and Civil Rights: Tracing the Evolution of Federal Legislation and Social Policy for People with Disabilities." *UCLA Law Review* 40: 1341–1410.

Employee Retirement Income Security Act of 1974, 29 U.S.C. §§ 1001–1461.

Fair Labor Standards Act of 1938, 29 U.S.C. §§ 201–219 (2006 & Supp. 2011).

GAO (General Accounting Office). 2001. "Centers Offer Employment and Support Services to Workers with Disabilities, but Labor Should Improve Oversight." *Special Minimum Wage Program.* GAO-01–886. Washington, DC: GAO.

Goffman, Irving. 1963. *Stigma: Notes on the Management of Spoiled Identity.* Englewood Cliffs, NJ: Prentice-Hall.

Gulati, Mitu, and Devon W. Carbado. 2000. "Working Identity." *Cornell Law Review* 85: 1259–1308.

H.R. Rep. No. 101–485, 101st Congress, 2nd Session, pt. 2 (1990).

Institute on Disability. 2013. "Statistics." *Disability Compendium.* Retrieved January 6, 2015 (www.disabilitycompendium.org/compendium-statistics /employment).

Kaplan, Deborah. 2000. "The Definition of Disability: Perspective of the Disability Community." *Journal of Health Care Law & Policy* 3: 352–64.

Lane v. Kitzhaber, 283 F.R.D. 587 (D. Or. 2012).

Murphy v. UPS, 527 U.S. 516 (1999).

NDRN (National Disability Rights Network). 2011. *Segregated and Exploited: The Failure of the Disability Service System to Provide Quality Work.* Washington, DC: NDRN.

Olmstead v. L. C. ex rel. by Zimring, 527 U.S. 581 (1999).

Pendo, Elizabeth A. 2002. "Disability, Doctors, and Dollars: Distinguishing the Three Faces of Reasonable Accommodation." *University of California– Davis Law Review* 35: 1175–1227.

———. 2003. "Substantially Limited Justice? The Possibilities and Limits to a New Rawlsian Analysis of Disability-Based Discrimination." *St. John's Law Review* 77: 225–75.

Porter, Nicole B. 2009. "Relieving (Most of) the Tension: A Review Essay of Samuel R. Bagenstos, *Law and the Contradictions of the Disability Rights Movement.*" *Cornell Journal of Law and Public Policy* 20: 761–806.

Scotch, Richard K. 2000. "Models of Disability and the Americans with Disabilities Act." *Berkeley Journal of Employment and Labor Law* 21: 213–22.

Social Security Act of 1935, 42 U.S.C. §§ 301–1937 (1994).

Stefan, Susan. 2010. "Beyond Residential Segregation: The Application of *Olmstead* to Segregated Employment Settings." *Georgia State University Law Review* 26: 875–935.

Stein, Michael Ashley, Anita Silvers, Bradley A. Areheart, and Leslie Pickering Francis. 2014. "Accommodating Every Body." *University of Chicago Law Review* 82: 101–67.

Sutton v. United Air Lines, 527 U.S. 471 (1999).

Toyota Motor Manufacturing v. Williams, 534 U.S. 184 (2002).

US Department of Labor, Wage and Hour Division. 2008. "Fact Sheet No. 39: The Employment of Workers with Disabilities at Special Minimum Wages." Retrieved January 6, 2015 (www.dol.gov/whd/regs/compliance/whdfs39.pdf).

Weber, Mark C. 2010. "Unreasonable Accommodation and Due Hardship." *Florida Law Review* 62: 1119–78.

Whittaker, William G. 2005. "Treatment of Workers with Disabilities under Section 14(c) of the Fair Labor Standards Act." Federal Publications Paper No. 209. Retrieved January 6, 2015 (http://digitalcommons.ilr.cornell.edu /key_workplace/209).

Yoshino, Kenji. 2006. *Covering: The Hidden Assault on Our Civil Rights.* New York: Random House.

Simply White

*Race, Politics, and Invisibility in Advertising
Depictions of Farm Labor*

EVAN STEWART

Troubles with race in the world of contemporary labor are intimately linked to troubles with visibility. This chapter considers one industry in which these connections are especially prevalent: migrant farm labor in the United States. The history of race relations in the United States is fraught with stories of interpersonal violence such as harassment, arson, assassination, and the like. However, when we talk about race, we also must consider structural violence—the way that social institutions such as the law and the workplace perpetuate inequality without the aid of any single individual's bad intent. In farm labor, an occupation in which dangerous and exploitative working conditions fall disproportionately along lines of race and citizenship, invisibility is a key factor in perpetuating this structural violence. Overcoming that invisibility is a key strategy of movements resisting and changing these working conditions. To understand why this endeavor is important, we have to understand a fundamental paradox: how do companies relying on migrant farm labor demonstrate the work and value that went into the cultivation of their products without revealing the underlying racial power structure that keeps their workers in a profitable, but highly precarious, state? The following analysis draws insights from ethnographic literature, studies in race and food production, and visual sociology to demonstrate how racialized structures permeate deeply enough to influence even the visual composition of advertisements in the U.S. agricultural industry. This results in commercials that cast the very act of food

consumption as a whitewashed activity—one in which conversations about labor and production are much less likely to occur.

Migrant farm labor is an exemplary case in which we can understand intersectional struggles over workers' rights and recognition through the metaphor of visibility. According to data from the Census of Agriculture, the National Agricultural Statistics Service, and the U.S. Department of Labor reported by Philip Martin (2012), average annual farm labor employment was 1.2 million workers between 2001 and 2008, but high turnover rates led to doubling estimates to 2.4 million. The data also show that two-thirds of crop farm employees were Mexican born, one-third were U.S. citizens, and about half were unauthorized employees. Scholarship on immigrant labor in a variety of institutional contexts shows that employers do not just desire these conditions but also actively work to create and optimize a sense of flexibility through the recruitment and constant management of migrant workers and their social networks (Miraftab 2012; Wells 1996; Zlolniski 2003).

Within this broader field, citrus farming is a key industry and the focus for this chapter. In the 1980s, Richard Mines and Philip Martin (1984) reported that citrus farms "employ[ed] more alien workers than any other agricultural sector" (p. 139). More recently, according to the Southern Poverty Law Center (2010), there were about twenty thousand undocumented workers picking oranges in Florida in 2010, and their labor composed the main source of U.S. orange juice production. As the products of U.S. growers continue to compete with imported oranges in the marketplace, these workers are increasingly subjected to a "race to the bottom" production process that their undocumented status makes increasingly difficult to challenge.

These trends produce working conditions that are far from ideal. Despite use of mechanization in farm labor, specialty fruit and vegetable industries maintain a high demand for migrant workers' "hand labor" to ensure a more delicate and thorough harvest (Arcury, Quandt, and Russell 2002). Juan Palerm (1992) points to these developments as an explanation for the "Mexicanization" of farm labor after World War II. Citrus farming is a key example of the trend. Mines and Martin (1984) observe: "Harvest workers, wearing heavy gloves, padded sleeves, and helmets to protect themselves from thorns, mount ladders that are 8 to 12 feet tall, clip each fruit with curved clippers, drop it into a packing bag, and dump the full bag into a bin on the ground" (p. 140).

These conditions often directly translate into health disparities across racial, ethnic, and legal boundaries of citizenship. First, migrants are subjected to the occupational hazards of the farms themselves. In one research account a young man harvesting oranges fell from a tree for the "fifth time in three days" (Palerm 1992: 362). Seth Holmes (2007) describes the temporary living conditions on or near the farms, which often amount to "tin-roofed tool sheds" (p. 40). The nature of hand labor also creates a higher risk for pesticide exposure, causing even more extreme long-term effects than the physical labor itself. Second, the social relationships structured around employment and race on these farms compound the work's direct effects on health. In their interviews with 283 Latino farmworkers, Thomas Arcury and his colleagues (2002) demonstrate how a perceived sense of control on the job is just as important as a perceived sense of risk in workers' adoption of safety policies to prevent the negative consequences of pesticide exposure. However, the precarious nature of these workers vis-à-vis race and citizenship means this sense of control is often not present. Holmes's (2007) ethnographic work with berry pickers reports, "Segregation is not conscious or willed on the part of the farm owners or managers. Much the opposite[,] larger structural forces, as well as the anxieties they produce, drive these inequalities" (p. 48).

Holmes's work reminds us that racial inequality is not only caused by individual racism itself but also advanced in the way farm labor is organized as a social system including both work and everyday life. It also argues that more traditional accounts of labor struggles for recognition also require an awareness of race and environmental justice when applied to the case of farm labor (Edwards 2011; Holmes 2006).

A key strategy to resist racial and labor inequality is rooted in visibility. Michelle Edwards's (2011) work on community organizing among farmworkers in Texas speaks to this issue in metaphor by inviting different fields to "see" each other. This analysis emphasizes workers' strategies to "integrate human and environmental issues" and introduces the race-conscious perspective of environmental justice to more classic Marxist and treadmill of production accounts of industrialized farming. Christian Zlolniski's (2003) study of immigrant janitors in Silicon Valley and Faranak Miraftab's (2012) account of immigrant workers in the meatpacking industry address this point more literally. In both of these works, a central aspect of workers' organizing for improved labor conditions is the "persistent creation of a public presence" (Miraftab 2012: 1219) through struggles for recognition and dignity. For the janitors in Zlolniski's study, visibility was a key part of the struggle for racial justice, both because symbolic recognition through "defense of their dignity and respect in the workplace played a key role" in building support for unionization and because public support mobilized by the union ultimately led to success in reform efforts (pp. 43–47). As discussed earlier, this sense of agency and control is also linked to increased safety on the farm.

However, contemporary racial power structures are often predicated on the invisibility of race created by the systematic denial of race's significance to the inner workings of social organizations (Bonilla-Silva 2003). For studies of labor, a white racial consciousness has historically intertwined with working-class identities in the United States (Roediger 1991).

Meredith Reitman (2006) discusses workplaces as "whitewashed" spaces defined by an explicit denial of racial identity in an attempt to remove "undesired racial politics" (pp. 268, 279). In a comparative study of contemporary nonfiction and novels about America's food production, Sarah Wald (2011) illustrates how the realities of immigrant farm labor are often neglected through a process of whitewashing since "major food movement texts privilege consumer citizenship over a politics of production" that serves to maintain the "relationship between land ownership and white citizenship" (pp. 568, 571). The result is a "public gaze . . . trained away from . . . migrant farm workers" (Holmes 2007: 41).

This chapter extends Wald's work with text to visual media through an analysis of how a particular agricultural industry—citrus growers and producers of orange juice—depicts its workforce in television commercials and print advertisements. These commercials contain an inherent tension between the demonstration of the labor that goes into the cultivation of these products, which makes them valuable, and the denial that this labor is in any way contested or controversial. Thus, while each commercial directly references labor in the process of producing orange juice, these commercials share structured practices of whitewashing either by coding that labor as a "white" activity or by obliterating any kind of embodied labor in the presentation of the product. Instead of serving as a neutral platform to promote orange juice, the internal communicative logic of these commercials instead acts as a barrier to public understanding of the contested nature of racial inequality in the industry.

METHODOLOGY AND VISUAL SOCIOLOGY

The misrepresentation of working-class labor in public images is not a new phenomenon. In his classic work *Ways of Seeing,* John Berger

(1972) observes seventeenth-century oil paintings in which artists portray poor laborers with wide smiles to appease upper-class viewers. The artist's choice to represent emotion in this manner serves to legitimize the power relationship exercised between the rich observer and the poor subject because it communicates that "the poor are happy . . . and that the better off are a source of hope for the world" (p. 104). Critical sociological analyses of media—such as Max Horkheimer and Theodor Adorno's (1944) writing on the culture industry—have historically emphasized a similar "unpacking" of cultural artifacts to uncover their ideological assumptions about the social world (Holliday 2000).

Since the 1940s, a prolific field of visual sociology has developed to explicitly address methodological questions that extend beyond a class-based critique of media representation. Bernt Schnettler (2013) outlines three main approaches to the study of visual images in sociology. The first, a documentation approach, emphasizes images as a way to "produce a record" of a given external social reality (p. 50). The second, an analytical approach, has its roots in mid-twentieth-century microsociological and psychological methods. This work emphasized scrutinizing small physical movements as a means to understand and interpret social interactions rather than to merely document them as a companion to analysis. The final approach, situated within later developments of the analytical approach, is an interpretive method. Here, sociologists took up the intellectual tradition of Peter Berger and Thomas Luckmann's *The Social Construction of Reality* (1967), which concerns itself with the sociology of knowledge: how continued relationships between people take subjective beliefs and "crystalize and stabilize" them into an objective reality of shared beliefs (p. 38). This work focuses on how images are part of the "communicative construction of reality," analyzing how images construct and produce, rather than document, a social reality in the course of visual communication (Schnettler 2013: 57).

It is this third approach that presents the most potential for a vigorous union of visual methodology and sociological analysis, as elaborated by Ralf Bohnsack (2008). In Bohnsack's approach, an image illustrates its creator's practice of Karl Mannheim's "tacit knowledge"— actions based on habit and routine that structure how we engage with the social world rather than what we consciously communicate to each other. In this sense, social reality is created through the composition of a picture or video, and what the composer says is less important than how she says it. Scholars often talk about pictures as systems that represent some conscious knowledge (an iconographic approach), but this

approach looks at images as a site where people employ tacit knowledge to produce a way of seeing (an iconological approach). We have to
ask how the composition of a video produces a particular social reality
for the viewer—rather than question deeper symbolic meanings or
authorial intent—in order to use "style as a gateway to the norms and
values . . . of a culture" (Pauwels 2010: 204). We can consider three key
dimensions of an image's composition to understand the underlying cultural assumptions of its authors (Imdahl 1996, paraphrased in Bohnsack 2008: para. 41):

> *Planimetric structure:* Where are individuals located and framed on a plane
> in the photograph? Are they observed on different levels; if so, do they
> look across these levels or remain separated?
>
> *Scenic choreography:* How are the individuals arranged in relation to one
> another, the scenery, and the objects in a photograph?
>
> *Perspectivity:* Where is the vanishing point in the image, and where is the
> camera focused? Where are the individuals in the photograph looking?

These three concepts invite us to look at the way a scene's structure
represents social relationships. If figures all fall on an equal plane across
the image, looking directly across at each other or at a viewer—with
none above, below, in front of, or behind another—the image's composition conveys a sense of equality independent of who or what is pictured. On the other hand, figures sitting on different planes can convey
assumptions about hierarchy: who or what must be "featured" in the
final product.

To maximize our theoretical purchase in the following cases, given
that television combines auditory and visual information, I use an
iconological approach to add a visual dimension to more standard sociological analyses of the text in recent television and YouTube commercials from the orange juice industry. This process aims to draw conclusions about the advertisements' visual structure to illuminate practices
of whitewashing the representation of farm labor. Though these cultural artifacts are television commercials first, they belong to a new
generation of television advertising that straddles the line between
broadcast and online media—each is widely available on YouTube,[1]
and one even went viral in the wake of its debut during the television
broadcast of the 2013 Superbowl. Lisa Nakamura (2002) argues that
advertisements in these digital spaces "remaster race" by simultaneously deconstructing a "corporeal self anchored in familiar categories
of identity" and "discursively fix[ing]" minority groups to preserve a

white, Western space in digital media (pp. 12–13, 20). Whitewashing denies a racial identity in order to create a "natural, biological category of race that creates a particular type of culture" (Reitman 2006: 276) and thus reinforces the racial dimensions of what Wald (2011) identifies as food advertising's key denial of embodied labor: "The pastoral image of the farm girl captured on the Sun Maid raisin box obfuscates the physical difficulty of farm workers' work and the economic insecurity and immobility of their migrant lives. . . . [S]he shares the bounty of nature with the consumer" (p. 574).

FARM LABOR IN ORANGE JUICE ADVERTISING

The first commercial, titled "Simply Orange Plant Tour," begins in a serene orange grove. It opens with a shot of two bottles of orange juice centered on a rustic picnic table and framed by a whole orange, an orange blossom, and two orange segments. The camera zooms in and fades to a wide shot of an orange tree in the center of the frame as the narration begins.

"Welcome to the Simply Orange® Tour. This is our plant, these are our workers," our narrator indicates as the image fades into a close-up of oranges and blossoms on a branch, panning from left to right, "and this . . . is upper management." The shot fades to the sky; a bright sunrise is centered in the frame as the narration continues. We hear, "But what you won't find around here . . . is any freezing, flavoring, or concentrating" while the camera provides a second panning shot of an orange branch from right to left, transitioning to two more close-ups of plump oranges centered in the frame. The narrator concludes, "Which brings us to our end product. Simply Orange. Honestly Simple®." The last orange fades into the label, on a close-up shot of the bottle in center frame, which zooms out to give the viewer a final look at the two bottles and oranges now accompanied by a full glass of juice (Simply Orange Juices 2011).

A commercial for Tropicana Pure Premium Orange Juice takes place in a similar serene grove, but it portrays a series of animated oranges leaping into an empty bottle and ultimately squeezing themselves into a juice: "There are sixteen fresh-picked oranges squeezed into each bottle of Tropicana Pure Premium and absolutely no space for added sugar, water, or preservatives. Tropicana. We put the 'good' in morning" (Tropicana 2011).

These two commercials share a unique iconological approach to their visual communication. Both directly reference the production of orange juice, but neither features human workers in the planimetric composition of its shots. Instead, shots in which work or workers are mentioned in the accompanying narrative feature the oranges themselves, and the oranges dominate the scenic choreography across the visual field. In both of these shots, the oranges have visual priority in the foreground and are staged on an equal horizontal plane across the frame. These visual traits convey two claims about the orange juice. First, the oranges' visual priority shows that they are the most important part of the production process. The Tropicana commercial even attributes an agency to the oranges as they bound toward their newfound container. The oranges are a product, not a producer, yet, as in Wald's (2011) account of popular nonfiction's descriptions of food production, the anthropomorphized oranges serve as a way to merge images of the workers with images of production and thus erase workers' contributions to the process. Instead, the viewer's focus moves toward a product-centered presentation of the manufacturer's juice. Second, by placing the oranges on an equal horizontal plane across the frame, both commercials convey a sense of equality and normality across the materials that go into the juice. The equal presentation implies that each individual orange is of similar (high) quality and status to all others.

The texts of these commercials further supplement an erasure of production. In the Simply Orange commercial, the narrator tells the audience directly that these oranges are the workers, and the narrator's passive voice in the Tropicana commercial emphasizes to the audience that sixteen oranges (already "fresh-picked") "are . . . squeezed" into each bottle. This claim begs the question of who does the squeezing, which in the world of the commercial appears to be the oranges themselves. Both of these advertisements claim their juice production is simpler than that of their competitors, touting their products as uncorrupted by added sugars or complicated production processes. In turn, they portray the labor process as equally pure and uncorrupted. All the productive effort is condensed into the image of an orange blossom, as if it can be assumed that such production will naturally occur like an annual blooming. Simply Orange's portrayal of the tree as a factory and the sun as upper management naturalizes both the production process itself and the relationships between workers and management (represented as the sun), an image that serves to undercut the public presence of workers' concerns about labor practices.

Figure 7.1 shows an example of these stylistic choices in Simply Orange print advertisements. Here, the tagline "Simple juice. Simply

FIGURE 7.1. The "simplified" production process. Print advertisements for Simply Orange employ a visual composition similar to that of corresponding television advertisements. They both employ naturalistic scenes with the fruit foregrounded, but pair them with a discussion of the juice production process. The result is an image that distinctly omits representations of labor, particularly farm labor. Photograph by Rob Nguyen, posted August 19, 2010 (https://www.flickr.com/photos/rob_nguyen/4906552636). Licensed under CC BY 2.0.

made" and descriptions of the production process reference how the juice is manufactured (particularly telling what the production process *never* does in the quest for natural juice), but those descriptions are accompanied by images of natural growth rather than of farm labor.

Lest we take these pieces too literally, the point of presenting the workers' disembodied labor is not that consumers are actually supposed to believe that enchanted jumping oranges are an acceptable substitute for the people who make their juice. We must bracket the question of authorial intent and should not attribute any kind of sinister hidden motives to the production of these commercials. Rather, it is the internal communicative logic of the commercials and print advertisements in which human workers play no role in the production process that is striking on its own terms. This internal logic forms a structure in which discussions of labor are immediately superseded by images of the product produced directly by nature. Lisa Nakamura (2002) argues that such naturalistic visions are a "timeless primitive" and are threatened by the visibility implied by modern media (p. 17), and here we see these commercials directly contributing a structure in which these threats are less likely to occur. Also, this pattern is not limited to these two commercials and may actually be spreading internationally. While both the Tropicana and Simply Orange commercials appeared on YouTube in 2011, commercials touting very similar visual compositions ran on YouTube in 2011 and 2013 for the European firm Innocent Juice and featured a dancing bottle along with the telling line "Nature does the hard work; we just squeeze her best bits" (Innocent Juice 2011, 2012).

Two challenges limit the implications of these commercials for drawing broader conclusions about the racial nature of contemporary representations of farm labor. First, it is a stretch to say that commercials in which no people are present are explicitly racialized. However, because they generate value from a "pure" production process linked to images of natural growth and the denial of labor's embodiment by not depicting people with racial identities, these commercials do contribute to consumer privilege, which other scholars identify as a particularly white consumer culture (Nakamura 2002; Rietman 2006; Wald 2011). Here, whiteness creates an environment of privilege in which consumers can prefer the orange juice untainted by the messy realities of racialized farm labor and production. Second, if these companies source their raw materials from independent orange growers, the internal communicative logic of their commercials may come from the advertising preferences of a firm for which farm labor is simply not important rather than from a denial of the firm's employees and their lived experiences.

To better address this issue, we can also examine how similar commercials from the citrus industry portray actual farmworkers. Florida's Natural advertises its brand of orange juice by presenting farmers front and center. The firm is a growers' co-op organized in 1933 that owns the land, raises and harvests the fruit, and produces and packages the juice. Perhaps its best-known commercial is "Restock," in which a grocery store manager sees a mother approaching the orange juice aisle, where the juice is out of stock, and calls directly to the orange grove for a new carton. As the mother reaches toward the empty shelf in the grocery store, a farmer from the grove heroically sprints in slow motion down the field and ultimately pitches the carton into her grasping hand at the last second (Florida's Natural 2006).

A second commercial for this brand speaks to an average consumer's concerns about what goes into Florida's Natural's product: "Let's raise a glass to raising oranges the natural way. Here's to growing oranges on our own soil. To a co-op of growers working hard and having something to show for it. Here's to a built-in afternoon snack, to an office with a view; here's to orange juice raised right. Florida's Natural" (Florida's Natural 2012). As in the "Restock" commercial, this self-titled advertisement pairs its references to labor with distinct textual and visual elements. The narrator refers to the people pictured as "growers" and members of the co-op, and the workers shown are all light-skinned men. Here, with a horizontal planimetric composition almost identical to that of Tropicana's bouncing sixteen oranges, "Florida's Natural" shows the growers working on the farm in a feature shot stretched across the span of the image. The workers all remain on a level plane with one another, even while climbing ladders in coordinated pairs, but they also maintain a vertical visual relationship to their products. Their gazes always project either horizontally at each other, demonstrating an equal standing, or downward upon the oranges in their hands in a display of power over the product. There is almost no bending, straining, or other extensive physical display of exerted labor other than a man climbing a ladder. In one scene, a grower slices and eats a freshly picked orange, and another enjoys a glass of orange juice at the end of the commercial.

The federated structure of the Florida's Natural co-op actually contains a number of smaller farms owned and operated by these "growers." The internal communicative logic of these commercials portrays growers who are intimately involved in the care and harvest of oranges but who work from a position of power over their products. They gaze down upon the oranges and sample them frequently—actions that convey a degree of ownership. The growers are also visually positioned in a relationship of equality with one another in which no grower takes a managerial position or demonstrates authority over any other. This construction of the "grower" also goes beyond advertising—the co-op also uses it when posting notices at the boundaries of its orange groves to indicate that passersby should allow only growers to pick the fruit (see figure 7.2). This depiction removes both images of migrants and migrant labor relationships from the production process. Not only do these farms often employ migrant workers, but also workers of color do not have the luxury of holding such a position of power over the oranges they pick. Migrant bodies of different races reach, strain, and suffer structural forms

FIGURE 7.2. The orange growers. A sign posted alongside a Florida's Natural orange grove illustrates the co-op's approach to defining labor and employment. Farmworkers are "growers" who cultivate the crops rather than "harvesters" who work to gather them. Photograph by Sam Howzit, February 6, 2010 (https://www.flickr.com/photos /aloha75/4417953913/in/photolist-7JpaQZ-s2vJAF-rHftwgrJZ2Q5-rJZ14u-rK18Uj -8TZ7JR-7JpaMc). Licensed under CC BY 2.0.

of violence in their relationship to their employers on the farms (Holmes 2007). These commercials' images racially code the farmworkers as white and conflate ownership with labor, rendering the contributions of workers of color invisible. The text also directs viewers to Wald's (2011) product-centered, rather than production-centered, perspective—a whitewashed space of attention predicated on the unimportance of race to "natural" juice. Wald (2011) maintains: "Mainstream celebrations of local and organic produce continue to privilege a relationship between land ownership and white citizenship through the romanticizing of the family farm (ignoring the labor needs of such farms)" (p. 572).

BROADER IMPLICATIONS: RACE TO THE VIEWER

Other early work on racialized representations of farm labor identifies similar racial structures across advertisements for various products created by and related to the field (Harsh 2013). The most notable recent example of romanticizing the (usually white) family farmer was a 2013

FIGURE 7.3. *The American Farmer*, a 1943 painting by Benton
Henderson Clark. This was used as an illustration in a 1944
Country Gentleman magazine advertisement for John Deere
tractors. It presents the visual myth of the white yeoman farmer: an
individualistic worker who often owns the land on which he farms.
Photograph by Don O'Brien, taken April 18, 2015 (https://www
.flickr.com/photos/dok1/17004023240/). Licensed under CC BY 2.0.

Superbowl television advertisement for Ram Trucks, a division of the
Chrysler Group. The commercial uses a recording of broadcaster Paul
Harvey's (1978) speech "So God Made a Farmer" juxtaposed with images
of American farmers at work and at home. The text of the commercial
relies on the romantic, racialized notion of the white yeoman farmer, a
self-reliant combination of landowner and entrepreneurial producer that
has distinct cultural significance in the history of American food production (Wald 2011) (see figure 7.3). In one excerpt from Harvey's speech,

> God said, "I need somebody strong enough to clear trees and heave [bales]
> yet gentle enough to tame lambs and wean pigs and tend the pink-combed

pullets, who will stop his mower for an hour to splint the broken leg of a meadow lark." It had to be somebody who'd plow deep and straight and not cut corners. Somebody to seed, weed, feed, breed and rake and disc and plow and plant and tie the fleece and strain the milk and replenish the self-feeder and finish a hard week's work with a five-mile drive to church. (Harvey 1978, quoted in Ram Trucks 2014)

In total, the extended version of the commercial depicts thirty-five farmers of various ages, genders, and racial origins. While the majority are light skinned or Caucasian, it is less useful to count the representations of racial groups in this commercial than to consider a distinct artistic choice in the visual composition: the races of many of these farmers are obscured by the commercial itself. Eight of the farmers are depicted in either black and white or with a sepia color filter on the image, obscuring or in some cases removing physical racial signifiers of skin tone. Five shots depict farmers from behind or wearing protective equipment, and three show only hands, at times obscured by produce or farm animals. In total, nearly half of the images of people in the commercial somehow obscure or conceal their races. These depictions provide an example of how an absence of racial signifiers can code an image as a white space because the underlying cultural mechanisms at work in the image of the white yeoman farmer are not directly contested by the ambiguous bodies portrayed by these portraits. Any farmer in protective equipment could be the white farmer endemic to classic advertisements for agricultural equipment (see figure 7.3) and could be viewed as such by consumers. Given the demographics of contemporary farmworkers, however, the person doing the real work is equally likely to come from a different racial and social standpoint (see figure 7.4).

This Ram Trucks commercial encompasses a number of broader conclusions we can draw from the orange juice industry about the racial nature of depictions of farm labor in the United States. All of these commercials want to convey the value of farm labor—value that directly translates into the quality of the produce. However, if they were to show this labor as it actually happens, viewers would be more likely to balk at the harsh and unsafe conditions of the majority-migrant workforce that actually harvests the products. This image would both trouble the cultural narrative of the farmer in American national identity and undercut consumers' assumptions about the quality of their juice. So instead, the commercials *talk* about the quality of labor in general terms but *illustrate* it with a visual style than can communicate the unspoken assumptions about that labor. This style either explicitly codes the

FIGURE 7.4. Migrant workers harvesting corn. The reality of contemporary farm labor often clashes with the myth of the individualistic, white, yeoman farmer. As shown in this USDA photo, migrant workers (often women of color) work long hours in large groups to gather the harvest under the purview of landowning management. Photograph by Bob Nichols, Uesugi Farms, Gilroy, California, August 28, 2013. U.S. Department of Agriculture (www.flickr.com/photos/usdagov/9622528306/). Licensed under CC BY 2.0.

farmworkers as white, equating them with positions of farm ownership and power over their products, or pushes race to the sidelines by obscuring or eliminating embodied signifiers of racial identities and physical labor. We must remain agnostic as to whether these composition choices were intentional on the part of the commercials' producers and instead see them as examples of a tacit knowledge—a part of racialized structural violence that marginalizes the race of more than two-thirds of farmworkers today.

In this symbolic field, public recognition of the presence of farmworkers of color is less likely to occur. Previous research on organizing practices among migrant workers indicates that such a persistent public presence is not only often a primary goal of workers' movements but also a key factor in securing the public support necessary to affect change and alleviate inequalities in these industries. In her groundbreaking work on the emotional labor of flight attendants and others in the service industry, Arlie Hochschild (1983) writes of a "doctrine of feelings" in which "a person of lower status has a weaker claim to the right to define what is going on" (p. 173). An unintended side effect of these commercials is that they maintain such a doctrine for the feelings of migrant workers. Their racialized visions of working-class identities supplement material inequalities because migrant workers are not just alienated from the production process; they are rendered invisible and denied credit for even participating in the first place. Without this public recognition, the workers' "right to be angry" is undercut, and efforts to reform the industry are less likely to be successful (Hochschild 1983: 112).

Furthermore, these commercials and print advertisements illustrate how advertising is not a neutral process that only conveys the value of a product, even if that is what the advertiser intends. Instead, it relies on particular visual characteristics that whitewash public space and appeal to consumers' notions of racial value to determine labor value. Here, race as a symbol is deeply intertwined with the material value of goods and services in the market. Even though agricultural companies are only consciously trying to sell a product, the logic of race forces their commercials and advertisements to go beyond the simple act of showing labor value; it bends their implicit methods of communication around cultural norms that cannot speak of certain kinds of labor done by certain kinds of people lest the product lose a sense of quality or legitimacy. Therefore, the place of invisible labor in the relationship between producer and consumer is not clear-cut. It may either increase or decrease the value of a product, depending on the way it communicates labor value alongside a whole host of racialized assumptions about the way that an industry operates. By excluding the migrant workforce, which arguably contributes the most valuable labor to agricultural production in the United States today, these orange juice advertisements show how selling a product often requires selling just as many assumptions about *who* made it as about *how* it was produced.

NOTE

1. All commercials were viewed directly on the official YouTube channels of the parent juice companies, with the exception of a Florida's Natural (2012) commercial produced by Trailblazer Studios, from which footage is also viewable on the Florida's Natural Web site.

REFERENCES

Arcury, Thomas A., Sara A. Quandt, and Gregory B. Russell. 2002. "Pesticide Safety among Farmworkers: Perceived Risk and Perceived Control as

Factors Reflecting Environmental Justice." *Environmental Health Perspectives* 110 (2): 233–40.

Berger, John. 1972. *Ways of Seeing.* New York: Penguin.

Berger, Peter L., and Thomas Luckmann. 1967. *The Social Construction of Reality: A Treatise in the Sociology of Knowledge.* Garden City, NY: Doubleday.

Bohnsack, Ralf. 2008. "The Interpretation of Pictures and the Documentary Method." *Forum Qualitative Sozialforschung / Forum: Qualitative Social Research* 9 (3), Art. 26, numbered paragraphs.

Bonilla-Silva, Eduardo. 2003. *Racism without Racists: Color-Blind Racism and the Persistence of Racial Inequality in the United States.* New York: Rowman and Littlefield.

Edwards, Michelle L. 2011. "Our People Are Still Resisting: Farmworker Community Organizing and the Texas Agricultural System." *Organization Environment* 24 (2): 175–91.

Florida's Natural. 2006. "Restock." Video advertisement, 30 sec. YouTube Web site. Posted August 4, 2006. Retrieved September 1, 2014 (www.youtube.com/watch?v=DlA7J4rFNTM).

———. 2012. "Florida's Natural." Video advertisement, 30 sec. YouTube Web site. Posted January 3, 2012. Retrieved September 5, 2014 (www.youtube.com/watch?v=QuqBW7sfKKA).

Harsh, Cameron. 2013. "Farmers' Marketing: White-Washing Our Nation's Farmers." *Farmers, Fairness, & the Farm Bill.* Retrieved September 9, 2014 (www.farmbillfairness.org).

Harvey, Paul. 1978. "So God Made a Farmer." Speech presented at the annual convention of the National Future Farmers of America (FFA), November 1978. Transcribed from audiotape by Michael E. Eidenmuller. Retrieved December 30, 2014 (www.americanrhetoric.com/speeches/paulharvey sogodmadeafarmer.htm).

Hochschild, Arlie Russell. 1983. *The Managed Heart: Commercialization of Human Feeling.* Berkeley: University of California Press.

Holliday, Ruth. 2000. "We've Been Framed: Visualizing Methodology." *Sociological Review* 48 (4): 503–21.

Holmes, Seth M. 2006. "An Ethnographic Study of the Social Context of Migrant Health in the United States." *PLOS Medicine* 3 (10): 1776–93.

———. 2007. "'Oaxacans Like to Work Bent Over': The Naturalization of Social Suffering among Berry Farm Workers." *International Migration* 45 (3): 39–68.

Horkheimer, Max, and Theodor W. Adorno. [1944] 2002. *Dialectic of Enlightenment.* Reprint, Redwood City, CA: Stanford University Press.

Innocent Juice. 2011. "Intro-juicing New Innocent Orange Juice." Video advertisement, 31 sec. YouTube Web site. Posted February 24, 2011. Retrieved September 10, 2014 (www.youtube.com/watch?v=didBPhx25hg).

———. 2012. "Innocent Juice TV-Advert 2013." Video advertisement, 31 sec. YouTube Web site. Posted December 21, 2012. Retrieved September 10, 2014 (www.youtube.com/watch?v=zY_OaZAlaFA).

Martin, Philip. 2012. "Immigration and Farm Labor: Policy Options and Consequences." *American Journal of Agricultural Economics* 95 (2): 470–75.

Mines, Richard, and Philip L. Martin. 1984. "Immigrant Workers and the California Citrus Industry." *Industrial Relations* 23 (1): 139–49.

Miraftab, Faranak. 2012. "Emergent Transnational Spaces: Meat, Sweat and Global (Re)Production in the Heartland." *International Journal of Urban and Regional Research* 36 (6): 1204–22.

Nakamura, Lisa. 2002. *Cybertypes: Race, Ethnicity, and Identity on the Internet.* New York: Routledge.

Palerm, Juan Vicente. 1992. "A Season in the Life of a Migrant Farm Worker in California." *Western Journal of Medicine* 157 (3): 362–66.

Pauwels, Luc. 2010. "Visual Sociology Reframed: An Analytical Synthesis and Discussion of Visual Methods in Social and Cultural Research." Pp. 193–226 in *SAGE Visual Methods,* edited by Jason Hughes. London: Sage.

Ram Trucks. 2014. "'Farmer': Long Version." Video advertisement, 2:42. YouTube Web site. Posted January 28, 2014. Retrieved September 1, 2014 (www.youtube.com/watch?v=H7yZdOl_e_c).

Reitman, Meredith. 2006. "Uncovering the White Place: Whitewashing at Work." *Social and Cultural Geography* 7 (2): 267–82.

Roediger, David. 1991. *The Wages of Whiteness: Race and the Making of the American Working Class.* New York: Verso.

Schnettler, Bernt. 2013. "Notes on the History and Development of Visual Research Methods." *InterDisciplines: Journal of History and Sociology* 4 (1): 41–75.

Simply Orange Juices. 2011. "Simply Orange Plant Tour." Video advertisement, 31 sec. YouTube Web site. Posted January 21, 2011. Retrieved September 3, 2014 (www.youtube.com/watch?v=kSPuqC-a7ZU).

Southern Poverty Law Center. 2010. "Food-Specific Industries." Retrieved September 4, 2014 (www.splcenter.org/get-informed/publications/injustice-on-our-plates/food-industries).

Tropicana. "Tropicana Pure Premium Puts the 'Good' in Morning." Video advertisement, 30 sec. YouTube Web site. Posted February 1, 2011. Retrieved September 1, 2014 (www.youtube.com/watch?v=oxyNNlU4ct8).

Wald, Sarah D. 2011. "Visible Farmers/Invisible Workers." *Food, Culture, and Society* 14 (4): 567–86.

Wells, Miriam. 1996. *Strawberry Fields: Politics, Class, and Work in California Agriculture.* Ithaca, NY: Cornell University Press.

Zlolniski, Christian. 2003. "Labor Control and Resistance of Mexican Immigrant Janitors in Silicon Valley." *Human Organization* 62 (1): 39–49.

CHAPTER 8

Producing Invisibility

Surveillance, Hunger, and Work in the
Produce Aisles of Wal-Mart, China

EILEEN M. OTIS AND ZHENG ZHAO

I entered the capacious Wal-Mart located on a broad, busy street of the arid northeastern Chinese city of Changchun and made my way through aisles of food to the produce section where Zheng was working. When I finally spotted him, the affable, soccer-loving graduate student was barely recognizable. In the month since he had begun working in the produce section of Wal-Mart, he had become gaunt. Misery and despondency registered on his face. His clothes were ragged and dirty. When I wandered by him, he did not even notice me. It was hard to imagine that just a few months earlier he had been guiding me around the aisles of a Wal-Mart in Stony Brook, Long Island, explaining how much money he had saved on various items by shopping there. As a U.S. graduate student living on a low income, he had done most of his shopping at the retailer. In Changchun I watched as Zheng and his fellow workers straightened oranges, mangosteen, lychees, cabbage, and spring onions on the shelves; it looked like tedious and tiring work. Later that week Zheng and I visited another Wal-Mart in the city, where he immediately began criticizing the sloppy state of the produce shelves. He even straightened a few vegetables. He could not help himself.

Zheng toiled for a month in the produce section of this Changchun Wal-Mart. He was paid minimally for his efforts, a condition that, of course, troubled him. These efforts were largely invisible, a situation that pleased him. Why did he prefer this state of invisibility? Feminist scholars contend that many forms of modern labor that are largely performed by women are devalued due to their invisibility. The reference point of this concealment is domestic labor, which is sentimentalized as the love of mothers and wives and executed in the decommodified private sphere. Such efforts are not recognized as "real work"; they are unwaged and offer no formal benefits. Considered an expression of affection, the activity unfolds in a world—and is judged by criteria—largely incommensurable with waged labor. The condition of invisibility follows women into the workplace since labor related to care and affection is devalued. If feminist scholars are right that invisibility is a source of disempowerment for labor, why do workers like Zheng and his colleagues go to great lengths to conceal their labors, as we have found? Why are workers who are paid wages and who work within a commodified space in proximity to those who consume their labor, in effect, invisible?

To answer these questions, this chapter considers relationships between visibility and invisibility in the modern retail workplace, presenting ethnographic data collected from a produce section of a Wal-Mart in China where Zheng Zhao worked for one month.[1] Work in the produce section involves cleaning, ordering, packaging, bundling, and placing fruits and vegetables on shelves for customers to purchase. It also involves interaction with customers as the occasion arises. Most studies of labor in the consumer service sector focus on the "front stage" work of managing interactions with customers. In contrast, produce workers toggle between the "backstage" area of the store (the storage cooler) and the "front stage" (the retail sales floor). As employees in the Changchun Wal-Mart produce section became aware of multiple forms of surveillance, they strategically maneuvered between these spaces to minimize their visibility and thereby elude the physical, social, and cognitive effects of panoptic power.

LABOR INVISIBILITY

The degree of labor's visibility, and visibility's linkage to status and wages, has been an enduring theme in labor studies. Feminists developed a concept of *invisible labor* (Daniels 1987), which refers to value-adding activity that is unrecognized as legitimate work largely because it occurs in the decommodified space of the home. This labor encompasses physical maintenance of the household in the form of housework (like cleaning and provisioning) as well as the coordination of activities of household members (DeVault 1991; Lareau and Weininger 2008).

The origins of such unremunerated, unrecognized labor can be traced to the emergence of two spheres during the English Industrial Revolution. At that time the waged labor of the public sphere was cleaved from the work of the private sphere, which came to be associated with a middle-class sentimentalization of the home (Cott 1997). Deprived of the status of productive labor, work in the domestic realm came to be understood as an expression of affection commensurate with a mother's reproductive role. However, even as domestic labor, along with related forms of caregiving in public settings, has become commodified, it continues to suffer from a devalued, invisible status (Hochschild 1983). For example, in her classic research on paid domestic labor, Judith Rollins (1985) found that employers treat workers as socially invisible despite their physical presence, exhibiting sometimes cruel disregard for domestic employees by discussing inappropriate personal matters in front of them, referring to them in the third person (as if they were not present), and in one case reducing the thermostat to an uncomfortably low temperature, leaving the worker to labor in the frigid cold. To remedy the invisibility problem, feminist scholarship has developed a battery of analytic terms to show that productive activities that are traditionally cast as irrelevant to the economy are, in fact, legitimate forms of labor central to its functioning. Terms such as *reproductive labor, affective labor, emotion work, the second shift,* and *care work* illuminate the effort and skill required to perform relational activities (Boris and Klein 2012; DeVault 1991; England 2005; Glenn 1986; Hochschild and Machung 2012; Stacy 2011).

Retail work—as a type of service labor in which workers are formally defined as *employees*, are paid a wage, and have regular, direct contact with customers—would seem to be irrelevant to a discussion of invisible labor. It turns out that key features of the work are in fact invisible. Arlie Hochschild (1983) unearthed the hidden labor required when workers must regularly arouse a particular sentiment in a customer. Moreover, the aesthetic labor that workers perform on their bodies to appeal to certain classes of markets is often concealed because employers hire workers already socialized in particular class aesthetics or train them to enact the desired aesthetic in the backstages of the workplace (Otis 2011; Warhurst and Nickson 2007; Williams and Connell 2010). Once these features of work are exposed, employees might be recognized for the entire range of their efforts, not just the visible bits.

Puzzlingly, instead of seeking visibility and recognition from customers and managers, Wal-Mart produce workers in Changchun endeavored to conceal themselves—and their labor—as much as possible. If we understand how visibility is adopted as a mode of labor control, we can better grasp the dilemma workers face when navigating between recognition of their work and control of their time and bodies. Michel Foucault (1995) describes the organizational use of panoptic technologies that create individual-level consciousness of surveillance. The panoptic originated in a cylindrical prison designed by Jeremy Bentham in the late eighteenth century. In it, prisoners' cells were arrayed along the circumference of a radial, each cell visible from an internal hub occupied by guards who could invisibly survey many prisoners simultaneously. Regardless of whether they were actually under surveillance at any particular moment, the design instilled a consciousness of constant visibility among prisoners, who would thus behave "as if" they were watched by guards and therefore adhere to prison rules. According to Foucault, Bentham's prison design is an apt metaphor for modern forms of power that exert control by instilling a consciousness of visibility, a sense of being at any time potentially under the surveillance of an authority. Foucault did not specifically examine how such power relations might condition flight into the recesses of invisibility, although he did recognize that power is never total.

Scholars have begun to conceive of panoptic surveillance as a social construction, the effects of which are constituted by all participants, observer and observed alike, although not in equal measure. The approach restores an experience of agency to workers subjected to observation (Anteby and Chung 2014; Monahan, Phillips, and Wood 2010). One corrective the perspective offers is that surveillance is not an airtight system of control and introduces various possibilities for response, if not resistance (Anteby and Chan 2014; Fernandez and Huey 2009). Research on TSA employees laboring under tight video surveillance at airports has found that employees endeavor to become invisible by making themselves as anonymous as possible to travelers, managers, and surveillance technology (Anteby and Chan 2014). On the other hand, Leslie Salzinger (2003) found that women workers in a Mexican maquiladora (foreign-owned factory) basked in the glow of attention afforded by surveillance.

The present research in the perhaps more mundane space of a retail store shows that panoptic techniques condition employees to seek physical invisibility. This invisibility allows them space to achieve limited autonomy of activity and consciousness. They engage in rule-breaking behavior that in effect smuggles activity necessary to their labor (eating) into the invisible corners of the workplace. Even within the semiautonomous space created by invisibility from surveillance, workers' rulebreaking serves the purposes of the firm.

Wal-Mart, China, and Changchun

As China integrated into world markets, global retailers flocked to the country, launching more than four thousand outlets by 2005 (Ernst and Young 2006). Given the rapid development of its economy, unprecedented increase in disposable household income, and new consumer appetites for goods and services, China is one of the most important growth markets for retailers. Wal-Mart is the largest global retailer operating in China, in terms of revenue and employment, while two domestic retailers rank above it. Having established its first China outlet in Shenzhen in 1996, Wal-Mart now owns 400 stores in 160 sites across the country, employing 90,000 workers (Roberts 2013). The retail industry has certainly contributed its share to the massive employment growth in China's service sector. In 2011, service sector jobs represented 35 percent of all employment, outstripping employment in manufacturing by 5 percent (China Statistical Yearbook 2013).

Wal-Mart is of central importance as a model of mass merchandizing success (Lichtenstein 2009). The firm leads the Fortune 500, and it was the first retailer to achieve that position. Its success as a retailer can be traced to its adoption of logistics technology to optimize supply chain efficiency. It harnessed the bar code to coordinate and centralize the distribution and delivery of products, allowing stores to diversify goods and at the same time lowering labor costs associated with price changes, inventory, stocking, and checkout. Pairing bar code and satellite technology, Wal-Mart stores link directly to supplier factories; information about supply generated from the computerized checkout register travels almost instantly to the manufacturer in a tightly choreographed commodity chain (Lichtenstein 2009).

Wal-Mart has opened four outlets in Changchun, the host city of the present research. Located in northeast China, Changchun is the capital of Jilin Province and has a population of 3.4 million. Wal-Mart's entry into Changchun and other Chinese cities is part of a transformation in local consumption practices. Until the 1990s, urbanites were accustomed to purchasing fresh produce directly from farmers at local outdoor markets, where they negotiated the price of each food item. These markets still exist in urban centers, but now they compete with retail supermarkets and modern grocery stores. In 2009, 60 percent of urban dwellers in China purchased food in stores like Wal-Mart. Instead of negotiating with the people who grow their food, today they simply select fresh produce from store shelves, place it in shopping carts, and make their purchases. The farmer is now invisible, and so is the produce worker.

Researching Retail

In the summer of 2007, Zheng Zhao accepted a job as a produce worker at a Wal-Mart in Changchun, where he had attended college some years earlier. Zheng used personal connections to secure a job at one of the outlets. He was assigned to work in the produce section of the store. He spent one month in this job, working six days a week. Zheng compiled detailed field notes from memory after each day of work. He recorded observations relevant to the formal structure of employment, the labor process, and the workers' employment experiences and concerns as well as those documenting his interactions with managers and customers. He used both English and Chinese in these notes. He then passed the notes to Eileen Otis, who coded them for thematic patterns. Otis consulted with Zheng about his notes, discussing interpretive and analytic issues in addition to clarifying details.

Otis visited the store where Zheng worked on one of his last days of employment and spent the subsequent three days at the store conducting observations and interviewing workers informally. Otis has also conducted observations and interviews at Wal-Mart outlets in Beijing, Shanghai, and Kunming. This chapter focuses on Zheng's research in Changchun supplemented with material from Otis. The names of all individuals mentioned have been changed, and the chapter uses English names that reflect the names workers used on their badges at the store. The chapter also excludes information identifying details of the particular outlet employing Zheng. The authors adopt Michael Burawoy's (1998) extended case method and use the data to engage and rebuild existing theories of labor visibility.

WORKING AT WAL-MART, CHANGCHUN

Zheng was hired as a part-time Wal-Mart employee. His first day of work began with a three-hour training session, during which trainees were introduced to the retailer's corporate culture. The training manager discussed Wal-Mart's three basic principles: respect the individual, the customer comes first, and strive for excellence. Expanding on principle 2, he explained that customers are "everyone's boss." He warned that customers could fire anyone at any time. Some of these customers, he revealed, might very well be plainclothes Wal-Mart inspectors dispatched to secretly assess worker performance and attitudes. Therefore, workers could not be sure of the identities of those who watched them on the service floor. This revelation was Zheng's introduction to one type of panoptic surveillance used by the retailer: any customer might be an agent of management; therefore, workers should treat all customers as if they were supervisors.

The manager also warned employees against "stealing time." Employees were expected to be fully engaged in value-adding activities at all times while at work. Failure to keep busy at work constituted theft from the firm, so worker inactivity or a slowing of work pace was cast as criminal. Amid the onslaught of warnings and urgings brought forth by the manager, there was one feature of the workplace that gave workers hope in the fairness of the firm. That was an emphasis on symbolic democracy evident in the badge system: all employees, including managers and supervisors, were to be called by their first names, and the use of titles was completely eschewed. Workers were to select English names for their work badges.

At the end of the training, management dispatched Zheng to the produce section, which occupies substantial space in the store. Aisles were wide, and the produce was arranged in display shelving with signs describing varieties and listing prices hanging overhead. The selection was plentiful: bok choy, long beans, spinach hearts, bitter melons, skinny eggplants, cucumbers, lychees, mangos, apples, bananas, durians, and round pears were all stacked in rows, piles, and pyramids under neon lights.

At that time the produce section employed two supervisors, thirteen full-time workers, and three part-time workers. Most were male, with the exception of three female workers who packaged, weighed, and affixed prices to produce that customers purchased at the centralized checkout stands along with other items. Workers' ages ranged from twenty to forty. One of the full-time workers was a manager-in-training, officially known as a lead employee. A single manager headed the department; he was assisted by a department vice manager. Employee pay met local minimum wage standards, but as in many cities across the country, those standards were not sufficient to afford workers a decent livelihood (Cheung 2012). For part-time work, Zheng earned $13 per week (105 yuan). Full-time workers earned wages at about the same rate. For example, Zheng's coworker Phil earned a monthly salary of $112 (900 yuan). These earnings were supplemented by 600 yuan ($75) in rental income from an apartment he owned, but he still struggled to support his wife and newborn.[2] There were additional hardships. Morning shifts began before bus service was available, so Zheng rode a bike to work, as did his coworkers. Some days the sky opened and poured rain over him, so he arrived at work drenched.

While the retailer was open to customers from 7 A.M. to 10 P.M., the produce employees worked in shifts covering twenty-four hours to take deliveries of fresh vegetables and fruits, many of which arrived after midnight. The produce section had the largest customer volume and most sales transactions in the entire store. Employees in the section performed some of the most grueling labor. Throughout their shifts, produce workers continuously move heavy loads of fruits and vegetables from the warehouse in the back of the store to refill the display shelves on the sales floor. They keep stacks, rows, and pyramids of produce full and tidy. The work is labor-intensive and exhausting. Sometimes workers use a forklift to move boxes of produce to the retail floor, but they mostly roll handcarts from the storage room into the brightly lit aisles of the store. Along with his coworkers, Zheng restocked shelves once or twice per hour, depending on customer volume. Like folding shirts in a busy retail store or working on an assembly line, labor in produce presents an endless cyclical repetition of tasks. For five hours each day, Zheng repeated the same work routine: surveying the fruits and vegetables, noting which shelves required refilling, pulling his handcart about thirty meters to the cooler in the warehouse, loading vegetables onto the cart, pulling it to the vegetable section, unloading the produce, and finally, arranging the items.

As a produce neophyte, Zheng discovered some of the challenges of what might at first glance appear to be simple labor. There were more than fifty kinds of vegetables and fruits sold in the section. Zheng found some of them confusing. For example, he had difficulty distinguishing among the five types of apples sold. Before a restocking trip, he had to commit to memory which items needed to be refilled and estimate the necessary quantity by considering how quickly each tended to sell. As a new worker, Zheng often forgot items on the way and was forced to return to the shelves to recheck supplies. His supervisor, Mike, was not happy about Zheng's short memory; unnecessary trips wasted his labor on the service floor. Mike told Zheng to write down items that needed restocking before he ventured to the storage area—at least until he became more familiar with the various types of produce. This restocking routine became even more complicated when customers filled the produce aisles.

Invisibility and Visibility to Customers on the Retail Floor

Zheng and his coworkers performed most of their labor directly under the noses of customers, yet they were effectively invisible to them. When customers were scarce, workers might expend almost an hour and a half on a round of reloading shelves, but when the volume of customers increased, the pace intensified, and the same work had to be completed in between thirty and forty-five minutes. Workers experienced customers, therefore, as the cause of their increased toil. To make matters worse, Zheng found that customers seemed oblivious to his efforts. His careful placement of vegetables and fruits into pyramids, stacks, and neat rows was almost immediately undone by customers who disrupted the order to find the perfect mango or cucumber. In a typical field-note entry complaining about customers, Zheng writes: "It takes ten minutes to arrange the shelves, but when you come back ten minutes later, it could be all messed up. Some customers drop goods they take from other departments on your shelves, and you have to take [them] out." Again, Zheng vents, "Chinese customers are picky about food, so they always mess up the organized vegetables. So I have to walk around all the time to organize the vegetables."

In Otis's observations of produce sections, she also found that customers spent a considerable amount of time and effort sorting through produce for the perfectly ripened item. Customers looking for the freshest produce frequently dug through the piles and stacks and unwittingly pushed produce into shelves where it did not belong. The perpetual need to clean up after customers pitted workers against them since workers' reorganizing and reshelving labor was not recognized by customers, who seemed unconcerned about who would clean up the mess they had made on the shelves in their quest for the ideal pear, peach, or tomato.

During busy hours, when Zheng dragged his handcart full of produce to the display bins, customers swarmed around picking from the cart at will with complete disregard for him. With the mothers, wives, grandmothers, and occasional father closing in, he was stopped in his tracks, unable to reach the display bins and often pushed by shoppers out of reach of the cart. He could only helplessly watch as customers slowly emptied his cart. In their incessant disruption and emptying of the produce shelves, customers became a nuisance to workers.

Workers used tactics to economize their labor, especially endeavoring to slow sales down in order to find some respite from the constant moving and stacking. Their interests in moderating physical output come into direct conflict with their employer's interest in a high volume of purchases. Zheng discovered one tactic when his colleague Sam offered him a tip: "If you need to refill cucumbers, use the ones in the white box first because cucumbers in that particular box are the ugliest. That will slow down the sales." Zheng learned from fellow workers to place the occasional rotten vegetables or fruits in the display bins to slacken sales, offering workers some reprieve from the endless cycle of refilling shelves. When workers saved labor time, they frequently retreated to the space where their activities were concealed from customers, managers, and surveillance cameras: the cold storage room.

Since customers not only were a cause for the intensification of their labor but also disrupted the flow of their activity, workers avoided interacting with them as much as possible. When Otis visited Zheng at work, he failed to notice her despite the fact that she wandered quite close to him and was the only foreigner present in the section (see page 148). Zheng's tunnel vision resulted from his studied inattention to customers. But he had not always felt this way about them. During Zheng's first days on the job, he had actually enjoyed talking with customers. He comments in his field notes: "Most of the customers are nice and polite, even though they are really picky about their vegetables. They frequently ask me if the vegetables are good [and] fresh and how to cook certain vegetables. Obviously, for most of those questions, I don't know the answers. But I still like to talk with them if I know a little bit about the vegetables in [which] they are interested."

However, Zheng quickly became jaded as he watched customers disrupt his stacking and piling work. Over time, customers who inquired about the quality, flavor, and use of various vegetables came to irritate him. Like his colleagues, he would grumble in a low voice, conveying that he knew little about preparing the produce he managed. Customers simply got in the way of his work and created more labor for him. He grew spiteful of them. This sentiment was shared by his coworkers, who offered customers no interactive amenities. In his field notes, Zheng relates: "For example, . . . a customer asked me if [she] might buy a half of a certain fruit. As I hesitated, John [the lead employee] blurted out . . . in an impatient tone that [customers] can't do that. Then, John dragged me aside, told me that customers are crazy and that I should not behave too nicely." In another incident his coworker Tim caught a customer trying to open a bundle of celery. Tim stopped the customer, scolding, "No, that's not allowed! You can't open those." Reflecting on lessons he had learned while interacting with customers, Zheng writes, "All your words must be formal and sound reasonable[;] however, you have to speak in a tough tone. In this way, your customers can't catch you making a mistake, and at the same time they are intimidated by your tone, which [will] help silence them." In the view of Zheng and his coworkers, customers must be managed firmly in order to moderate demands on employees' labor.

By minimizing interaction, workers tried to limit customers' control over them and, in some cases, exert control over customers. However, by withdrawing from interaction and withholding "care," the workers also limited their own potential to develop and demonstrate expertise in selecting and using the items they sold. Moreover, they may have undermined the potential for customers to feel sympathy for their hard labor. It is surely easier for a customer to disrupt stacks of produce when a worker avoids eye contact and verbal exchanges, even easier if the worker is gruff and uncooperative.

Management and Surveillance

As it was, workers not only avoided the attention of customers; they also did their best to evade the regulatory efforts of management on the retail service floor. Managers control employees' labor efforts both directly and indirectly. They oversee produce delivery, storage, preparation, and stocking. They also schedule worker shifts and monitor employee breaks and shift changes. Managers directly observe workers in real time and indirectly observe them through video surveillance cameras. At the Changchun Wal-Mart, these cameras floated above employees in the produce aisles, warehouses, and cooler, recording their every move. However, employees quickly learned the limits of vision of the mechanical-managerial eye, moving into corners to eat and ducking underneath shelves and bins to make phone calls and text. Of course, cameras did not record speech, so if workers accommodated their physical demeanor to conform with work expectations, they could be fairly well assured that their speech was unmonitored, at least while managers were absent. Whenever possible, workers arranged their tasks so that they might retreat to a section of the storage cooler out of the view of cameras, where they could socialize, share work strategies, rest, and replenish calories expended during work.

During Zheng's tenure as a produce worker, tensions between managers and employees became evident. These tensions revolved around how to manage the produce, which was, in fact, a struggle over the intensity and pace of workers' labor. As discussed earlier, workers developed strategies to slow the pace of their labor, but managers urged workers to carry out tasks at a rapid clip. Zheng learned early on, for example, that overstocking the produce displays was frowned upon by management, who wanted the shelves just full enough so that vegetables did not linger too long out of cold storage in the warm store environment, where the ripening cycle accelerated. As a new worker, Zheng was anxious about his performance and tried to work as fast as possible. But his strength was quickly depleted, and he was exhausted after each five-hour shift. Phil, a coworker, urged him to keep a steady pace through the duration of his shift—"not so slow and not so fast." Phil elaborated, "Supervisors cannot say anything to you as long as you keep working. It's not your own business, and you don't have to hurry unless you really want a promotion." The sentiment that the business was not their own was frequently repeated in fellow employees' comments to Zheng. The mantra, a refusal to identify with the firm, reminded workers that they did not need to adopt management's concerns about customer volume and business profit. Hence, they could enjoy a certain critical distance from their work and regulate its intensity according to their own physiological, psychological, and social needs. Like assembly-line workers who push themselves to complete their tasks in advance in order to squirrel away a few moments for rest and a brief delivery from the dull and incessant pace of the line, the produce workers' strategic deployment of effort provided them a respite from the interminable pace of labor as they asserted control over their time and ultimately also regained a certain autonomy over themselves.

One day as Zheng was carrying out Phil's injunction to moderate his pace, the store vice manager and two supervisors entered his orbit of activity to observe. Zheng placed bean sprouts on a shelf half full of sprouts that had already blackened. The vice manager instructed: "The bean sprouts are full of moisture; you cannot put so much out at the same time; put[ting] a thin layer is enough." He pointed out that the section's net profit suffered because of losses from produce disposal. Zheng listened to the manager, acknowledging his point. However, once the managers departed, he continued to overfill the shelves, as did other workers. Despite being scrutinized by dozens of cameras suspended above them, workers knew that the surveillance cameras were not used to enforce any nuance in shelving practices, so they disregarded managerial directives about them.

On another occasion, as Zheng stacked cucumbers, a man in a casual shirt startled him, appearing, as Zheng describes in his notes, "like a ghost." The man's badge indicated he was also an employee, but since badges do not display rank, Zheng could not discern whether he was a coworker or manager. He began showing Zheng how to organize the cucumbers, instructing him not to put too many in the display baskets: "Instead, just keep refilling it." Later Zheng discovered that he was the vice manager of the fresh food section. Zheng realized that the company's practice of omitting rank indicators from uniform badges, reputed to be an indicator of symbolic equality, in practice meant that any worker with whom one was not already familiar might be a manager or supervisor. Ultimately, this policy had a panoptic effect. In response to the vagaries introduced by the omission of rank information on badges, workers learned to exercise caution and act as if colleagues from other departments might be supervisors. This strategy discouraged any immediate camaraderie workers might have felt for other rank-and-file employees.

Eventually, Zheng, like his colleagues, discerned the timetable of managerial supervision. To contain labor costs, Wal-Mart limits the number of managers it employs (Lichtenstein 2009). With managers scarce, workers were not constantly under direct, personal supervision. Managers visited the produce section to check on the state of displays in the morning, so workers arranged the fruit and vegetables in accordance with store policy at that time. But later in the day, workers piled produce high to avoid running back and forth to the storehouse to replenish shelves.

Another method workers used to limit their expenditure of time and effort was to throw away any otherwise perfectly edible produce that customers unbundled. When customers opened bundled items, store policy required that they be rebundled. Instead, employees discarded the disassembled food because doing so saved them time and effort. This practice also reflected the degree to which they had become indifferent to waste. During a slow evening shift, Zheng's coworker Stan started joking around: He leaned next to Zheng, who was stacking bundles of bok choy, and squeezed a plastic-wrapped pickled egg, enthusing, "See, I can even squeeze the oil out." The egg was destroyed. Reacting to the disapproval registered on Zheng's face, Stan disclaimed,

"Don't worry; the waste of the corporation is huge. Like these vegetables—most of them on the shelf, if not sold today, will all be thrown away." Management requires employees to discard all leafy vegetables each night, no matter what their condition.[3] Thus, the retailer's disposal practices inured workers to waste.

Ironically, in the midst of food abundance, not to mention wasteful disposal practices, many produce workers went hungry. Zheng found that employees' normal eating schedules conflicted with work scheduling, and they became hungry well before break time. When workers retreated to the cooler, therefore, they not only chatted with colleagues and rested a bit but also replenished much-needed calories. In his field notes, Zheng describes his own experience: "Hunger is really a problem. I experienced this today. I worked the 10 [A.M.] to 3 [P.M.] shift today. I ate breakfast at 7:30 in the morning and rode 45 minutes on my bike to work. Around noon I got really hungry and couldn't manage to move any heavy boxes. I had to eat a couple of plums in the corner of the cooler to sustain myself until 3." Before his morning shifts, which started at 6 A.M., Zheng would force down one or two rice buns despite having no appetite at all. This amount was scarcely enough food to sustain five hours of virtually continuous labor. Produce workers were perpetually underfed and hungry as a result of scheduling arrangements that did not take into account time between breakfasts and late lunches. Employees were, in theory, entitled to one free meal in the canteen for each four hours they labored. If a worker's shift started at 10 A.M., he would grow quite hungry by noon; by 2 P.M., when freed for lunch, his hunger would have reached ravenous proportions. This situation was compounded by workers' long-established habit of eating breakfast at 8 A.M. Shifts changed from week to week, so it was challenging for workers to adapt their bodies to new eating schedules with each shift cycle. Eating schedules, to which workers had become habituated over a lifetime, were difficult to adjust. If employees could not manage to force down a substantial meal before their shifts, they would go hungry as they labored. When Zheng complained about his fatigue to Tony, one of the full-time workers, Tony described his own challenges. He faced shifts that began at 4 A.M. with breaks that did not correspond to normal eating times. These morning-shift workers disposed of old produce, cleaned the cooler, and filled the produce shelves before the store opened. Tony rode his bike one hour each way to and from work, rising at 2:30 A.M. for his morning shift. He was not hungry before his shift, but by the time his first break approached, he was famished.

He struggled to eat enough on the job to sustain himself until break time, which was not until 11 A.M., when the canteen opened. After working so many hours continuously, Tony moaned, "we are too hungry to stand." He continued, "You see, we [the produce workers] do not have fat. When I started working here, I was 150 pounds; now I'm only 125 pounds."

At other times workers intentionally delayed their meals so they might be ensured of eating at the beginning of the dining period in the canteen. Doing this would guarantee them a plentiful supply of dishes. Strategizing to obtain optimal work meals meant that workers would starve themselves for hours and labor on very little energy. On unusually busy days when too few workers were scheduled, managers forced workers to labor through their break, so their hunger became especially acute. One employee, Sam, arrived at work at 4 A.M. and waited until 12:30 for the first meal of the day while Tim arrived at 6 A.M. and worked until 2 P.M. Around 1 P.M., Tim told Zheng that he was so energy depleted that he could not move. He groaned, "My chest is sticking to my back" (前胸贴后背). Zheng suggested, "Some fruit may help." Tim ate a handful of grapes, hiding in the corner of the cooler out of the surveillance camera's range while Zheng kept watch for managers.

Management pushed these workers to the limits of their physical energy, draining them of their energy without offering regular and reasonable opportunities for restoration. Not surprisingly, workers dipped into the bounty of fruit surrounding them. Because eating on the job was forbidden, produce workers strategized and cooperated to surreptitiously obtain the calories they needed to continue their physical labor. Defiance of employment rules in this case actually served employer goals. The hidden consumption of necessary calories, as well as the concealed effort to coordinate strategies to access them, is labor that allowed workers to continue expending effort on the service floor and at the same time ostensibly conform to formal work rules.

Once workers were allowed to go on break and made their way to the cafeteria, they often found no meat dishes. Zheng speculated that with the rapid rise of inflation in the city, meat had been taken off the menu. Instead, workers ate tofu, rice, and a variety of vegetables under the watchful electronic eyes of security cameras and amid a sea of wall posters describing penalties for breaking store rules. One sign told of an employee who had been fired for eating candy during work time. Breaking the rule prohibiting eating on the job, stowing away invisibly in the cooler to fill up on fruit, put these workers simultaneously at odds and in concordance with management, a situation that certainly did not encourage identification with the firm and its objectives.

. . .

Zheng was relieved when it was time to leave his job, but he feared that quitting would be almost as difficult as getting his Wal-Mart job had been. Upon informing the Human Resources Department of his intention to resign, an administrator in the department presented him with a form requiring the signatures of managers from eight separate sections of the store. Zheng worried that it would take excessive time and effort to find all of these people, but he was lucky and completed the task in half an hour, his final half hour of invisible labor for the retailer. On days or shifts when managers might not be present, one can imagine the process could move at a snail's pace.

The question of labor's visibility is central to feminist analyses, which maintain that work is devalued by way of its concealment in domestic space. Invisibility, however, is not limited to the private sphere of the home and to workers who perform domestic labor; it is a condition of a multitude of jobs in the waged economy in which the activity invested in executing work tasks goes unrecognized as labor per se. It would seem that retail work places employees front and center, clear as daylight, as they perform labor directly under the gaze of customers, not to mention the view of management and surveillance cameras. However, even though produce work might seem quite visible, it is nonetheless socially invisible, much like the labor of domestic workers studied by Rollins (1985). Employees like Zheng labor next to shoppers, but through a variety of organizational, individual, and social processes, including their own unwillingness to interact with customers, these retail workers are often little more than a shadowy presence on the service floor.

This case study of produce labor has shown how workers strategically maneuver between visible and invisible space. The produce workers fled the surveillance of cameras, customers, and managers in order to resculpt the content of their time and reclaim a modicum of control over their own labor process. Therefore, this chapter argues that workers seek out invisibility because they gain autonomy by evading management and the public, even as they may be sacrificing some possibility for recognition of their efforts. For these workers, invisibility offers a kind of situated empowerment, affording them some ease of movement and discretion over activities away from monitors. Researchers have found additional instances in which visibility is problematic. To take a classic example, the tokens in Rosabeth Kanter's *Men and Women of the Corporation* (1993) who were hypervisible—and taken to represent, act on behalf of, and speak for an entire category of (disadvantaged) people, in this case, women—were burdened and constrained by their "over" visibility. But, unlike the produce workers, some embraced the spotlight and overperformed. A number, however, did retreat into social isolation and invisibility. A question for future research, then, is under what conditions and with what consequences do workers seek cover?

What we do know is that when workers and their labor are invisible, it is impossible for anyone to recognize the value that they add to the economy. Invisibility can only compound wage and status disadvantage. A classic example of activity that adds value to the economy but remains invisible is emotion work. When firms fail to include in formal job evaluations assessment of the emotion work that employees perform, an important part of the workers' job content is overlooked, and workers are therefore not adequately compensated for the spectrum of tasks they have been hired to execute (Otis 2011; Steinberg 1999).

Foucault (1995) examined technologies that use modes of vision as a form of social control to foster adoption (internalization) of rules and norms among those under surveillance, yet few have understood the dynamics of invisibility introduced into the workplace, especially the retail workplace, by these technologies. In seeking concealment from surveillance, Wal-Mart produce employees in this study refused to internalize the objectives and culture of the firm. This response was most clearly expressed when the workers reminded each other that they were not owners of the firm, so they therefore did not need to fret over profits or performance and could moderate their pace of work. But this situation is not a clear-cut case of agency or resistance: employees defied some work rules that required them to engage in continuous labor in order to fulfill their responsibility to their employer; by using the work time gained after taking surreptitious breaks to consume needed calories, they were actually able to perform their assigned tasks. Here feminist notions of "reproductive labor" (Glenn 1986) take on new significance since these workers struggled not only to replenish their energy (eating is perhaps the quintessential reproductive work) but also to expend effort to conceal this activity from management.

One means by which workers might attain greater visibility is through collective worker action. Since 2006, Wal-Mart outlets in China have been unionized by the All-China Federation of Unions, which is operated by the state. Managers usually serve as store-level union chairs, and workers' concerns are rarely addressed by the union. One exception, however, was a movement by workers at a Wal-Mart outlet in Changde, Hunan Province, which closed its doors without providing workers sufficient notice or compensation. These workers used union channels to pressure the firm into meeting its legal obligations to them. This outcome provides some limited hope that the union may under the right circumstances support other worker mobilizations that might illuminate and valorize workers' labor.

NOTES

1. Zheng Zhao collected data in 2007 in an outlet located in the city of Changchun, Jilin Province, China. The data this chapter presents are from Zheng's ethnography. These data are supplemented for general understanding by observations and interviews conducted by Eileen Otis between 2006 and 2013 in various Chinese cities, including Changchun, Kunming, Beijing, and Shanghai.

2. A branch of the All-China Federation of Trade Unions formally represented workers at the outlet. Workers paid one yuan in monthly dues to the union. When Zheng listened to his colleagues complain of their meager wages, he suggested that they approach the union about the issue. The workers responded by laughing in unison at their new colleague's naiveté. They held little hope that the state-run union would represent their interests.

3. One scale operator estimated that daily produce waste amounted to, on average, 3,000 yuan ($375) and that on holidays it might reach 16,000 yuan ($2,000). The losses are partially shouldered by suppliers. A Receiving Department employee told Zheng that the firm paid for only about 80 percent of the weight of produce shipments, assuming the final 20 percent of the weight to be packaging, water, and rotted items. For example, if 1,000 pounds of potatoes are delivered, the supplier is paid for 800 pounds. The Receiving Department employee estimated that in fact only about 5 percent of the weight of produce consisted of packaging, water, and inedible items.

REFERENCES

Anteby, Michel, and Curtis Chan. 2014. "Being Seen and Going Unnoticed: Working under Surveillance." Paper presented at a meeting of the Eastern Sociology Society, February 2014, Baltimore, MD.

Boris, Eileen, and Jennifer Klein. 2012. Caring for America: Home Health Workers in the Shadow of the Welfare State. Oxford: Oxford University Press.

Burawoy, Michael. 1998. "The Extended Case Method." Sociological Theory 16: 1–31.

Cheung, Jennifer. 2012. "Minimum Wage Increases in 2012 Fail to Provide Workers with a Living Wage." *China Labour Bulletin*, December 13. Retrieved November 16, 2013 (www.clb.org.hk/en/content/minimum-wage -increases-2012-fail-provide-workers-living-wage).

China Statistical Yearbook *[Zhongguo tongji jinian]*. 2013. Beijing: China Bureau of Statistics.

Cott, Nancy. 1997. *The Bonds of Womanhood: "Woman's Sphere" in New England, 1780–1835*. New Haven, CT: Yale University Press.

Daniels, Arlene Kaplan. 1987. "Invisible Work." *Social Problems* 34: 403–15.

DeVault, Marjorie. 1991. *Feeding the Family: The Social Organization of Caring as Gendered Work*. Chicago: University of Chicago Press.

England, Paula. 2005. "Emerging Theories of Care Work." *American Sociological Review* 31: 381–99.

Ernst and Young. 2006. "Retail Revolution—A Look at Mergers and Acquisitions in China's Retail Industry." Posted September 2006. Retrieved June 19, 2013 (www.ey.com/Global/assets.nsf/China_E/260906_RCP_Report_Eng /$file/260906%20RCP%20Report_Eng.pdf).

Fernandez, Luis, and Laura Huey. 2009. "Is Resistance Futile? Thoughts on Resisting Surveillance." *Surveillance & Society* 6 (3): 198–202.

Foucault, Michel. 1995. *Discipline and Punish: The Birth of the Modern Prison*. New York: Vintage.

Glenn, Evelyn. 1986. *Issei, Nisei, War Bride: Three Generations of Japanese American Women in Domestic Service*. Philadelphia: Temple University Press.

Hochschild, Arlie Russell. 1983. *The Managed Heart: Commercialization of Human Feeling*. Berkeley: University of California Press.

Hochschild, Arlie Russell, and Anne Machung. 2012. *The Second Shift: Working Families and the Revolution at Home*. New York: Penguin.

Kanter, Rosabeth Moss. 1993. *Men and Women of the Corporation*. New York: Basic Books.

Lareau, Annette, and Elliot Weininger. 2008. "Time, Work, and Family Life: Reconceptualizing Gendered Time Patterns through the Case of Children's Organized Activities." *Sociological Forum* 23: 419–54.

Lichtenstein, Nelson. 2009. *The Retail Revolution: How Wal-Mart Created a Brave New World of Business*. New York: Metropolitan Books.

Monahan, Torin, D.J. Phillips, and D.M. Wood. 2010. "Surveillance and Empowerment." *Surveillance & Society* 8 (2): 106–12.

Otis, Eileen. 2011. *Markets and Bodies: Women, Service Work and the Making of Inequality in China*. Redwood City, CA: Stanford University Press.

Roberts, Dexter. 2013. "Wal-Mart's China Expansion Aims to Tap Urbanization." *Bloomberg Businessweek*, October 24. Retrieved November 11, 2013 (www.businessweek.com/articles/2013-10-24/walmarts-china-expansion -aims-to-tap-urbanization).

Rollins, Judith. 1985. *Between Women: Domestics and Their Employers*. Philadelphia: Temple University Press.

Salzinger, Leslie. 2003. *Genders in Production: Making Workers in Mexico's Global Factories*. Berkeley: University of California Press.

Stacy, Clare. 2011. *The Caring Self: The Work Experiences of Home Care Aides*. Ithaca, NY: Cornell University Press.

Steinberg, Ronnie. 1999. "Emotional Labor in Job Evaluation: Redesigning Compensation Practices." *Annals of the American Academy of Political and Social Science* 561: 143–57.

Warhurst, Chris, and Dennis Nickson. 2007. "A New Labour Aristocracy? Aesthetic Labour and Routine Interactive Service." *Work, Employment and Society* 21: 785–98.

Williams, Christine, and Catherine Connell. 2010. "Looking Good and Sounding Right: Aesthetic Labor and Social Inequality in the Retail Industry." *Work and Occupations* 37: 349–77.

PART FOUR

Looking Good at Work

Invisible Labor in Plain Sight

CHAPTER 9

The Female Breast as Brand

The Aesthetic Labor of Breastaurant Servers

DIANNE AVERY

Breastaurants are casual dining establishments such as Hooters where all the servers are attractive young women who are dressed in revealing, sexually provocative costumes. The breastaurant server's job is to sell food, beverages, and branded merchandise while simultaneously offering customers vicarious sexual entertainment and simulated intimacy. The vulnerabilities of these young women as workers arise in part from the economics of the restaurant industry in general and from the gender and racial inequity of its labor markets. The success of breastaurants in the highly competitive food and beverage industry depends on the consistent and low-cost delivery of the eroticized brand by unskilled, low-wage female servers. This internal branding is accomplished through recruitment practices, work rules, gendered uniform and appearance requirements, and tipping norms that shape and control the emotional and aesthetic labor expected of the breastaurant servers. But federal and state wage and hour laws also play a role, allowing breastaurants to pay their servers a minimum or subminimum wage and to use high customer tips to subsidize the costs of delivering the sexualized brand.

This chapter will explore how the demographics and economics of the restaurant industry, in conjunction with the laws and social norms affecting tipped wages of restaurant servers, enable breastaurants to extract economic rent from their female servers, to appropriate for the employer the value of much of their servers' aesthetic labor and erotic capital, and to keep the servers on brand. The management practices, legal rules, and social norms that are part of the business model of operating a breastaurant in the United States hide from view many costs to the servers—as well as the benefits to the employers—of these jobs. Unlike workers who are located in an offshore call center or a remote warehouse or are otherwise "hidden" from the customer by technology or geography, breastaurant servers are highly visible to customers. The female servers are expected to display their bodies and project their personalities in order to entice and engage their (predominantly male) customers. Their labor is perceived as embodied and personal rather than disembodied and anonymous. What seem to be "hidden" are the gender-based labor dynamics, pay structures, and other business practices that exploit young women but are not always apparent to the workers themselves.

THE ECONOMICS OF THE BREASTAURANT BUSINESS, EROTICIZED SERVICE, AND TIPPED WORK

The first Hooters restaurant was opened in 1983 in Clearwater, Florida, taking its name from a slang term for female breasts (Brizek 2011; Original Hooters 2015). Hooters has been described as "the nation's first 'breastaurant'" (Funding Universe 2005). In addition to its South Florida beach-themed decor, the Hooters brand was built around its all-female servers—young shapely Hooters Girls dressed in tight white tank tops bearing the Hooters trademarked owl logo, orange running shorts, suntan panty hose, white crew socks, and white sneakers (Rowe 2013: 34–35). In 1991, the Equal Employment Opportunity Commission (EEOC) initiated a controversial Title VII sex discrimination complaint against Hooters because of its refusal to hire male servers (Rowe 2013: 34n93; Schneyer 1998: 567–68). Eventually, the government caved in to the company's expertly orchestrated publicity campaign (Rowe 2013: 45–46; Schneyer 1998: 574–92), and Hooters has settled subsequent sex discrimination suits brought by men seeking front-of-the-house server jobs at Hooters restaurants. These settlements have permitted Hooters to continue its practice of hiring only female servers in order to provide its customers with a service that its president, Rick Akam, described as "vicarious sexual entertainment" (quoted in Helyar 2003).

Sociologists Chris Warhurst and Dennis Nickson (2009) note that "any deliberate strategy of sexualization by organizations tends to centre on advertising and marketing rather than labour. In other words, some organizations promote an image of sexualized labour but do not actually intervene and prescribe that labour" (p. 396). In a "significant" departure from the general practice of firms, however, "Hooters is explicit in the sexualized labour that features as part of its product" (p. 396). Breastaurants like Hooters, which have built their brand around the fetishized female breast, provide the front stage and costumes for their female servers to perform emotional labor (Hochschild 1983; Loe 1996: 404–6) and sexualized aesthetic labor (Warhurst and Nickson 2009), allowing customers to monitor and control the delivery of this labor through giving or withholding tips.

By 2012, signage with the "Hooters" trademarked owl graced the premises of 160 restaurants owned by the original Florida-based Hooters, Inc., in addition to more than 430 restaurants—in forty-four states and twenty-eight countries—operated or franchised by Atlanta-based Hooters of America, LLC (Hooters 2012; Original Hooters 2015). But a business model built on the not-so-novel marketing concept that sex sells—and particularly that sexy, skimpily clad female servers can enhance sales in the casual dining sector of the food and beverage industry—was not too difficult to copy. Initially, Hooters attempted, unsuccessfully, to stave off competition through trademark, trade secret, and trade dress lawsuits (Avery and Crain 2007: 29–30; Brizek 2011: 6; Jamieson 2011). Even in recessionary times, when many casual dining restaurants have been going out of business, new breastaurants—either company owned or franchises—reportedly can bring in gross sales of up to $5 million a year at each location (Thompson 2011), so the "breastaurant" business is thriving. Today we have, among others, Tilted Kilt, Twin Peaks, Brick House, Show-Me's, Canz-a-citi, Bone Daddy's, and the Heart Attack Grill, which features "Naughty Nurses" (Agar 2011; Berman 2015; Valverde 2013). Other names adopted by firms that have entered or attempted to enter the breastaurant business also connote the female breast: Bazookas, Grand Tetons, Northern Exposure, Knockers, Melons, and Mugs 'n' Jugs (Kuebelbeck 1993). In 2012—in a telling acknowledgment of the symbolic commodification of the female breast in the restaurant industry—the owner of the Bikini Sports Bar and Grill in Bikinis, Texas, registered the term *Breastaurant* with the U.S. Patent and Trademark Office.

Breastaurants are now the fastest growing sector of the casual dining industry (Berman 2015; Daley 2011; Giang 2011). In 2008, at the beginning of the Great Recession, when many chain restaurants were closing, Hooters reported nearly a billion dollars in sales, a 2 percent increase from the previous year (Owens and Karar 2009). Nevertheless, industry analyst Techonomic reported that between 2008 and 2011 Hooters' U.S. sales declined and some outlets closed, in part because of the recession but also because of the fierce competition from new breastaurants (Techonomic data, cited in Sanburn 2012). By the end of 2014, several breastaurant enterprises—Tilted Kilt, Twin Peaks, and Brick House—had experienced double-digit growth in sales, outpacing the overall 3.5 percent growth in full-service chains and the more modest 3.1 percent growth in Hooters' sales (Techonomic data, cited in Berman 2015). To keep up with the competition from the proliferating breastaurants, Hooters is now updating its menu, logo, and decor, and—in a novel development—even attempting to appeal to female customers (Sanburn 2012), although it intends to keep its sexy Hooters Girls.

Without question, breastaurant servers are hired to engage in a sexualized display and performance, and their jobs should be considered, at least in part, as a form of sex work. Joshua Burstein (1998), for example, described Hooters as "an intermediate step between airline flight attendants and cocktail waitresses at one end, and nude dancers at the other" (pp. 291–92). And Kimberly Yuracko (2004) goes further, arguing that "Hooters' primary product is its sexualized environment, offering a particular soft-core porn sexual fantasy involving the 'All-American Cheerleader/Surfer-Girl-Next-Door.' Cognitively, the choice to be a Hooters Girl looks a lot like the choice to be a stripper" (p. 204). A breastaurant's primary products, however, are its food, beverages, and branded merchandise, and the company uses female servers both to perform the ordinary frontline service work needed to sell and deliver these items to customers and to create the eroticized brand through sexualized bodily display and performance, that is, sexualized aesthetic labor (Warhurst and Nickson 2009). In this sense, breastaurants are what Yuracko (2004) describes as "plus-sex" businesses "in which employers seek to sell sexual arousal, generally through the provision of gaze objects, along with some other nonsexual good or service" (p. 158). She also notes, "Hooters restaurants are perhaps the most obvious current example of a plus-sex business. [And] no court has ruled on Hooters' policy of hiring only women as food servers, or 'Hooters Girls'" (p. 158n28).

The spatial setting of a full-service restaurant and the physical demands imposed on the bodies of its food servers provide the conditions that both create and limit the possibilities of sexualized aesthetic labor. In her ethnographic study of a small neighborhood restaurant, sociologist Karla Erickson (2009) described how the restaurant utilized the embodied labor of its food servers: "The ambience of the restaurant is displayed on their bodies as uniforms and also seeps into their skin as aroma, cuts, burns, and wanted and unwanted touches. Their skin absorbs the smells, the touch, the approving looks, and the insulting glares of their customers and coworkers. In service work, bodies are both a source of skill and a site of vulnerability. Bodies are also resources mined for strength, for agility, for energy when face and feelings grow tired, and for decoration: servers' bodies are part of the scenery" (p. 21). The aesthetic labor of a breastaurant server goes beyond the physical and emotional labor of waiting on tables; it is similar to the body labor described by Miliann Kang (2010) in her study of manicurists: "The term *body labor* designates commercialized exchanges in which service workers attend to the physical comfort and appearance of the customers, through direct contact with the body (such as touching, massaging, and manicuring) and by attending to the feelings involved with these practices" (p. 20). While breastaurant servers are not engaged in "body labor" because—unlike manicurists—they may only casually and incidentally touch the bodies of their customers, they are engaged in a form of bodily display and movement that is intended to be sexually provocative and aesthetically pleasing to the customer—much like that of an exotic dancer. The close proximity of a breastaurant server's body to her customer during the service exchange (and the implicit prohibition against sexual touching) produces in the customer the desired feelings of sexual excitement and intimacy. The server is not just a gaze object or "part of the scenery"; she is the embodied brand of the breastaurant.

Examining the job of breastaurant server inevitably raises questions of agency and invokes the debates among and between feminist and postfeminist scholars over whether sex workers or "plus-sex" workers are subordinated or empowered by their work. Feminist scholars have written extensively about the legal regulation of sex work such as prostitution, the pornography industry, and exotic dancing. For example, Noah Zatz (1997) has analyzed some "competing narratives of prostitution" that draw on "approaches of liberal feminism, Marxist feminism, radical feminism, and sex radicalism" (p. 282). While these ideological debates inform this chapter's analysis of the labor aspects of the breastaurant industry, they are not the chapter's central focus. We cannot begin to address the debate over free choice versus exploitation without a complete understanding of the social, legal, and economic contexts that shape the job of the breastaurant server. Moreover, for many frontline service workers, the boundaries between the worker's free agency and the coercion of the labor market are not always clear. For example, in her study of food servers, Erickson (2009) found that "autonomy and exploitation are not opposites; rather, autonomy blends with structural disadvantage and even exploitation" (p. 39).

FRONTLINE SERVICE WORK IN THE CASUAL DINING INDUSTRY: THE ROLE OF TIPPING

While the restaurant industry as a whole is a major employer of millions of low-wage employees in the United States, it is also a source of billions of dollars per year in tips for low-wage hourly workers. Because of the social norm of tipping in the United States, "people tip billions of dollars per year in restaurants, both those that they frequent and those that they will never visit again" (Conlin, Lynn, and O'Donoghue 2003: 297). Using 2005 U.S. Bureau of the Census data on the sale of "food and alcoholic beverages to consumers in full-service restaurants, snack and nonalcoholic beverage bars, bars and taverns, and lodging places," Ofer H. Azar (2009: 1917) has estimated annual tips in U.S. restaurants at $41.8 billion. Azar (2004) had previously estimated annual restaurant tip income at $27 billion based on 2002 U.S. Bureau of the Census data that excluded "snack and nonalcoholic beverage bars" (p. 170). With customers' tips supplementing their employer-paid cash wages, servers at breastaurants can expect to earn income well in excess of the federal or state minimum hourly wage. In addition, substantial amounts of cash tips are unreported and therefore untaxed as income to the employee (Estreicher and Nash, 2004: 4; Margalioth, 2006: 130–39; Seltzer and Ochs 2010: 1). More importantly, breastaurant owners, franchisees, and managers can use the low- or no-cost tipping system to keep female servers "on brand"—using customers to monitor work performance and using the lure of increased tips as incentives to keep the appearance and behavior of individual servers sexualized appropriately to fit the brand image (Azar 2011; Ogbonna and Harris 2002). Together with the legal regime of at-will employment, which facilitates strict top-down corporate or franchisor control of how breastaurant servers embody and deliver the brand, the system of tipped service work situates breastaurant servers collectively as central and critical to the success of the enterprise while at the same time they are individually—as workers—marginal and fungible.

Although the servers at a breastaurant may earn a premium in tips for their sexualized appearance and services, customers do not pay the enterprise a cover charge, service charge, or additional fee for "entertainment" by female servers. Thus, a breastaurant—unlike a club for exotic dancers—is essentially a full-service restaurant engaged in the business of selling food and beverages. None of the restaurant's revenue stream is derived from the sale of sexual entertainment. For example, Hooters of America reported on its Web site in 2007 that, systemwide, 100 percent of the sales revenue generated by its restaurants was derived from the sale of food items (72 percent), alcoholic beverages (23 percent), and branded merchandise (5 percent) (Brizek 2011: 6). This accounting does not mean that the sexualized service of a Hooters Girl is "free"; it just means that the cost of providing this type of service is shifted to the customer and to the server. This cost shifting can only be accomplished because of the economic structure of the labor market in the food and beverage industry and because of the legal rules and social norms surrounding tipping practices in the United States.

Though many of the jobs available in food services and drinking places are low-wage and part-time, they are not an insignificant part of the overall service economy. Food preparation and serving-related occupations in the United States accounted for the employment of nearly 12 million workers in 2013 (BLS–OES 2013). In May 2013, more than 2.4 million individuals worked in the occupation classified by the U.S. Bureau of Labor Statistics as "waiters and waitresses," with an hourly mean wage (including tips) of $10.04 and annual mean wage of $20,880 (BLS–OES 2013). The median hourly wage for this occupation was $8.94, and the median annual wage was $18,590. Servers in the ninetieth percentile earned a median hourly wage of $14.33 and a median annual wage of $29,810 (BLS–OES 2013). Nearly 2 million of these waiters and waitresses worked in full-service restaurants in 2013, with an hourly mean wage of $9.87 and an annual mean wage of $20,530 (BLS–OES 2013). Restaurants like Hooters, Twin Peaks, and the Tilted Kilt are considered full-service restaurants because the food and beverages are sold and consumed on the premises, the servers wait on patrons at a table or booth, and patrons are presented with a bill for payment after the food and beverages have been consumed (U.S. Bureau of the Census 2012). In 2007, economists at the Center for Economic and Policy Research and at the Center for Social Policy at the University of Massachusetts reported that the occupation of waiter or waitress was number six on the list of "the ten worst jobs in America," which are defined as "bad" jobs because of their low pay and lack of benefits (Mantell 2007).

THE GENDER WAGE GAP

Since the 1970s, labor economists have published data showing a substantial gender-based difference in wages and tips in the food service industry (Segrave 1998: 117–18). These disparities have persisted despite sex discrimination lawsuits brought against upscale restaurants that hired only male servers (OAG–NY 2000). For example, a 2010 study of New York City restaurants reported that "female workers pay a 'gender tax' in the form of 21.8 [percent] lower earnings than [those of] their male counterparts with the same qualifications" (ROC–NY 2010: 2, 9). And relatively few women have had access to the highest-paid serving positions such as the jobs in New York City's "most expensive restaurants," where "some servers can earn total annual compensation of $100,000 or more" (OAG–NY 2000: *in*1). Available wage data for all waiters and waitresses in the U.S. food and beverage industry who worked full-time in 2013—883,000 individuals—reveal a substantial gender disparity in employment numbers as well as a significant gender wage gap: 325,000 men earned a median weekly wage of $449, and 558,000 women earned a median weekly wage of $400 (BLS–CPS 2013). Thus, nearly twice as many women as men worked full-time as servers (a female-to-male ratio of 1.72:1), but female servers' median weekly wages were 89 percent of male servers' median wages. Full-time female servers would have to work longer hours than full-time male servers to achieve the same take-home wages (which would by definition entail overtime work). In 2012, about half of all waiters and waitresses were part-time employees (BLS–OOH 2014b). Consequently, many servers—both male and female—do not have the option of earning premium pay for working overtime.

Instead of working longer hours than their male counterparts, female servers who are young, shapely, attractive, and sexy—and particularly women who are Caucasian (Cook 2011; Cook 2012)—may be able to work the same hours that male servers do and make up the gender-based wage gap by offering male patrons sexualized "entertainment" along with the food and beverage service for higher tips. Breastaurants facilitate this type of exchange. The gendered and racialized aspects of *lookism*—employment discrimination based on appearance—and the wage premium for attractive individuals have been explored by legal scholars (Rhode 2010; Wang 2014), economists (Hamermesh 2011), and sociologists (Warhurst et al. 2012), among others. By hiring only attractive young female servers who embody a certain "branded," sexualized—and predominantly racialized—image, breastaurants enable some young women to turn an occupational gender-based wage penalty into a gender-based wage premium.

Not surprisingly, the U.S. Bureau of Labor Statistics reports, "Waiter and waitress jobs are a major source of part-time employment for high school and college students, multiple job holders, and those seeking supplemental incomes" (BLS–OOH 2014b). Many restaurant server jobs, particularly in the fast-food and casual dining sectors, have minimal requirements for education, training, and experience; and many entry-level waiters and waitresses "are in their late teens or early twenties and have less than a high school education" (BLS–OOH 2014b). In fact, many teenagers obtain their first job—and their "worst-paying job"—in the food-and-beverage service industry, particularly in fast-food outlets (Newman 2006: 335–36n2). "Compared with all other occupations, a much larger proportion of food and beverage serving and related workers were 16 to 19 years old in 2012" (BLS–OOH 2014a). If they serve alcoholic beverages, however, breastaurant servers generally must be at least eighteen to twenty-one years old, depending on the minimum age requirement of the local alcoholic beverage control law (NIH–APIS 2014). Nevertheless, in some states women as young as age seventeen may begin their training at breastaurants in hostess jobs, in which they do not serve alcohol (Mikin 2012). For an attractive, curvaceous, outgoing woman in her late teens or early twenties with only a high school education and limited work experience, someone who needs to work part-time and wants flexible hours to accommodate the demands of postsecondary education or child care, a breastaurant server job appears to be one of the best-paid jobs available in the United States. Why is this so?

The answer lies in the incentives created by the social norms and legal rules of tipped work. Restaurant servers are "nonexempt" employees covered by the federal minimum wage and overtime provisions of the Fair Labor Standards Act of 1938 (FLSA, 29 U.S.C. §§ 203[m][t], 206[a][1]), and if they "customarily and regularly [receive] more than $30 a month in tips," they are defined as "tipped employees" (29 U.S.C. § 203[t]). Under federal wage and hour law, tipped employees may be paid as little as $2.13 an hour in cash wages by their employer as long as they receive tips from customers in an amount that satisfies the federal minimum wage, currently $7.25 an hour (29 U.S.C. § 203[m]). The employer receives a "tip credit" for the $5.12 difference between the employer-paid cash wage and the minimum wage. Thus, a maximum of $5.12 an hour of tip credit, which is paid to the server by the customer (ostensibly as a gratuity), plus $2.13 cash wages, which are paid by the employer, satisfy the current federal minimum wage obligation.

Because the federal minimum wage is a floor, state and local wage and hour laws can provide for a minimum wage that is higher than the federal minimum wage or have more generous rules for tipped employees. Several states require that the state minimum wage be satisfied entirely with cash wages, even for tipped employees, whereas other states have a much higher minimum cash wage for tipped workers. For example, as of December 31, 2014, the New York minimum cash wage for tipped food service employees was $5.00, and a maximum tip credit of $3.75 an hour was allowed to satisfy the state minimum wage of $8.75 an hour. In 2015, Washington established a minimum wage for all employees—including tipped workers—of $9.47 an hour and does not permit a tip credit to satisfy the minimum wage. Indiana tracks the federal law by requiring a minimum cash wage of $2.13 an hour for tipped employees and permitting employers to take a maximum tip credit of $5.12 an hour against the state minimum wage of $7.25 an hour (DOL–WHD 2015).

Although the federal subminimum wage for tipped employees, first enacted in 1966, was originally indexed to the minimum wage, it had risen to 60 percent of the federal minimum wage over the years, but it had never fallen below 50 percent of the federal minimum wage until 1996 (Allegretto and Filion 2011:3). When Congress amended the Fair Labor Standards Act in 1996, the tipped subminimum wage was decoupled from the minimum wage (pp. 1, 3). At the time, the tipped subminimum wage, which had been set in 1991 at $2.13 per hour, was 50 percent of the minimum wage (p. 3). Because Congress subsequently raised the federal minimum wage but allowed the tipped minimum wage to remain frozen at the rate that was set in 1991, the ratio of the federal tipped minimum wage to the federal minimum wage in 2011 had fallen to 29.4 percent (p. 3). In the view of labor economists, "the tip credit is an employer subsidy provided by customers through their tips [that] decreases labor costs" (p. 4). Significantly, under federal law today, "the subsidy afforded employers ($5.12) is now more than twice as much as the base wage given to tipped workers" (p. 3).

At full-service restaurants the tipping rates vary, depending in part on the type and location of the restaurant (Bodvarsson and Gibson 1997: 195–97; BLS–OOH 2014b). For example, "tips appear to be higher on the East Coast and the West Coast. Servers seem to get 18–20% on the coasts and 14–15% in other areas" (Seltzer and Ochs

2010: 254). Yoram Margalioth (2010) reports, "The expected tip in restaurants in the [United States] is currently slightly above nineteen percent[,] and it is fifteen percent in Canada" (p. 563). Moreover, "tips are generally much higher in upscale restaurants in major metropolitan areas and resorts" (BLS–OOH 2014b).

Expensive restaurants tend to employ more men than women in front-of-the-house positions (LaPointe 1992: 380; ROC–United 2012: 19), and male servers generally tend to receive higher tips than female servers (Hall 1993; Wang 2014). Historical gender-based status distinctions and stereotypes are evident in customers' perceptions of waiters and waitresses today, and "stereotypical social preferences" contribute to the overall gender-based wage gap in tipped wages (Wang 2014: 135–39). Eleanor LaPointe (1992) observed: "Waiters are often considered more prestigious and skilled, but waitresses are seen as simply doing a job that comes 'naturally' to them" (p. 387).

In the casual dining segment of full-service restaurants—"defined by moderate menu prices, casual atmosphere, and table service" (Brizek 2011: 3)—tips will depend on the volume of business, whether servers are assigned to high-traffic areas of the restaurant, and whether customers (who by definition have sought out a moderately priced restaurant) choose to tip up to 20 percent or more for the services of the wait staff. In her study of a family-style restaurant in New Jersey, cultural anthropologist Greta Foff Paules (1991) described the various strategies that waitresses used to increase their tips from the customer (pp. 23–47), "who is perceived as material that is to be processed" (p. 34). In a wage and hour lawsuit brought against an Outback Steakhouse in Florida in the late 1990s, the plaintiffs claimed that their tips "frequently fail[ed] to reach the 'standard' 15 percent level" and that "'it was not uncommon for customers to tip less than 10 percent'" (*Kilgore v. Outback Steakhouse*, 160 F.3d 294, 296 [6th Cir. 1998]). As the court noted, "Servers at Outback perform the traditional tasks of waiters and waitresses. They take orders, deliver food and drinks, and take care of other customer demands" (*Kilgore*, 160 F.3d at 296). But the "customer demands" in a generic casual dining restaurant pertain to the speed and quality of the food and beverage service, not to demands for "vicarious sexual entertainment," the hallmark of a breastaurant. One commentator noted, "The amount of service at Hooters is comparable to that of various other chain casual-dining restaurants with one exception. This service is to be administered by the world famous Hooters Girls who fit the profile of attractive females with friendly attitudes and table-waiting skills" (Brizek 2011: 3).

Enabling a female server to trade on her attractive appearance and sexualized behavior while she is serving moderately priced food and beverages to male customers can make all the difference in the amount of the tips she receives (Segrave 1998: 139). A study by Michael Lynn (2009) showed that "waitresses in their 30's and those with large breasts, blond hair, and/or slender bodies received larger average tips than their counterparts without these characteristics" (p. 743). In exploring the relationship between sex and money, intimacy and the market, Viviana Zelizer (2011) observed that "not only the form of payment but also the location, dress, personal style, and practices of the service provider identify the special properties of the relationships between sex workers and their clients" (p. 156). The social meaning of a tip given to a breastaurant server is ambiguous, for both the server and the customer. Is it payment for a form of ("vicarious") sex work? Is it charity for a low-wage worker? A customary gratuity for a satisfying meal well served? Or a bribe for the opportunity to gaze freely (and often) at the breasts and buttocks of scantily clad young women? In the early twentieth century, "a man's tips were suspect as dangerous enticements to prostitution" (Zelizer 1994: 102). Even today, as anthropologist David Sutton (2007) writes, "any time that money changes hands so directly between men and women, we might surmise, there is some hint of a sexual transaction, which is why some restaurant owners and managers, and in some cases servers themselves, may attempt to exaggerate that dimension through the use, for example, of revealing uniforms, with 'Hooters' restaurants representing simply one end of a long continuum" (p. 202).

A server at a breastaurant offers her customers more than "traditional" food and beverage service, and she is, apparently, tipped well for this added value. She is "eye candy," a friendly and desirable table companion, a buxom "girl" who plays children's games with grown men; and the tipping system creates incentives for her—as it does for waitresses generally—to invite the sexual attention of male customers and managers, to tolerate their crudeness and vulgarity, and even to endure their sexual harassment and abuse (Cobble 1991: 44–45; Loe 1996: 412, 416–19; Segrave 1994: 129–34; Tibbals 2007: 740–44). A recent survey concluded that "sexual harassment is endemic across the restaurant industry," but it has "a greater impact on women, and its greatest impact on women in tipped occupations in states that have a sub-minimum wage of $2.13 per hour for tipped workers" (ROC–United 2014:30). Suggestive uniforms for female servers working for tips amplify the risks of sexual harassment (ROC–United 2014: 25).

Nevertheless, sexual harassment lawsuits brought under Title VII by women who chose to work in sexualized environments wearing revealing costumes have proved to be problematic (see, for example, Beiner 2007; Cahill 1995; McGinley 2006; McGinley 2007; Rhee 1997). There is evidence that female restaurant servers "are reluctant to label blatantly offensive behavior as sexual harassment" (Giuffre and Williams 1994: 387) and that, even when waitresses labeled offensive workplace behavior as sexual harassment, "they said it was unacceptable behavior but something they endured to receive tips and maintain employment" (Huebner 2008: 80).

The FLSA mandates that employers must allow a tipped employee to retain "all tips *received by such employee*" unless the tips are pooled "among employees who customarily and regularly receive tips" (29 U.S.C. § 203[m]). Many full-service restaurants mandate tip-pooling or tip-splitting arrangements, which the employer uses to subsidize the cash wages of certain front-of-the-house workers like bussers or hosts. Minimum-wage employees working in back-of-the-house occupations such as cook, dishwasher, or janitor are not "customarily and regularly tipped employees" because they do not receive tips directly from patrons or work in view of patrons, and as a general rule under federal law, an employer cannot require servers to share their tips with them. In upholding the legitimacy of a mandatory tip-splitting arrangement, one court reasoned that

> to permit a waitress to determine what if anything she should share with the busboy based upon what she deems to be the worth of his service can only lead to the surrender of the employer's prerogative to run his own business, dissension among employees, friction and quarreling, loss of good employees who cannot work in such an environment, and a disruption in the kind of service the public has a right to expect. An employer must be able to exercise control over his business to ensure an equitable sharing of gratuities in order to promote peace and harmony among employees and provide good service to the public. (*Leighton v. Old Heidelberg, Ltd.,* 268 Cal. Rptr. 647, 653 [Ct. App. 2d Dist. 1990], as quoted in Estreicher and Nash 2004: 22)

Even with mandatory tip pooling or tip sharing, a tipped restaurant server can be seen either as an entrepreneur who essentially works for herself or as a piece-rate worker "with an immediate interest in the productive goals of the firm" (Alpert 1986: 48). Economists have recognized that "tipping partially separates waiters from restaurants as entities. The waiter is not simply an agent of the restaurateur, but is, to some extent, a separate entrepreneur" (Bodvarsson and Gibson 1997: 189). Moreover, "gratuities resemble piece rates and are a form of remuneration in which performance is monitored by customers" (Pencavel 1977, cited in Bodvarsson and Gibson 1997: 187). One Hooters Girl who was interviewed about her work reported that her managers "would tell us, 'Treat this like it's your business'" (Cook 2011: 82). But, of course, it is not the Hooters Girl's business, and she owns no part of it. In fact, she may have to share her tips with other workers in a valid tip pool. The ubiquitous Hooters Girl is just a nonunion, low-wage hourly employee paid a cash wage, which is likely to be a fraction of the minimum wage. She must engage in a scripted, sexualized performance in a body-revealing uniform (not of her choosing and which she cannot sell) and submit to continual surveillance by managers and coworkers while working constantly under the "male gaze" of her customers. The corporation appropriates her face and body and may even give her a new name (not of her choosing) to use on promotional materials. For all this she may receive a premium in tips on good shifts. But she is still a tipped worker, particularly vulnerable to sexual harassment and subject to all the potential employer violations of the wage and hour laws that are experienced by tipped workers throughout the restaurant industry—such as employers demanding work off the clock, denying mandated meal and rest breaks, denying overtime pay, refusing to pay for required uniforms, charging for breakage and walkouts, and diverting tip-pool funds to managers, owners, or kitchen workers. These illegal management practices create the opportunity for employee resistance, and the fact that Hooters servers in California have brought several class-action lawsuits under state wage and hour laws (Wollan 2010) suggests that other forms of collective action and opposition may not be out of the question.

Nevertheless, even with a hefty tip premium and robust employer compliance with labor and employment laws, breastaurant servers are selling themselves short. Many have invested their own time and money in breast implants, gym memberships, expensive undergarments, makeup, hair extensions, and beauty treatments—and perhaps even succumbed to eating disorders—in order to embody the brand and ensure the flow of high tips. Catherine Hakim's (2011) theory of "erotic capital" would suggest that such expenditures are a good investment on the assumption that "even without physical sex as such, heterosexual men around the world are ready to spend substantial sums of money to enjoy the company of women with high erotic capital" (p. 144). Yet a breastaurant server's short-term return on her investment in erotic capital—measured in tips received—should take into account "the damage caused by the sexualization of social relations," which Hakim fails to consider (Warhurst 2012:

1037). And the notion that breastaurant servers—like other frontline low-wage workers—acquire "skills" in performing emotional labor is open to serious scholarly debate (Payne 2009). Importantly, the employer appropriates all the brand value of the workers' display of their faces and bodies, whether in person to customers at the point of the service exchange or to the public at promotional events like swimsuit pageants and bikini car washes or in photos lining the breastaurant walls, in company merchandise like magazines and calendars, or in online videos and television advertising. Much of this "brand work" may be performed off the clock, and the worker has at most improved her chances for obtaining a modeling job or work as a product demonstrator, jobs that were also included in the 2007 listing of "the ten worst jobs in America" (Mantell 2007). Sociologist Ashley Mears (2011) described these jobs in "the cultural industries" as "sociologically speaking, 'bad jobs' akin to irregular work arrangements in the secondary-employment sector, such as day laborers and contingent workers who piece together a precarious living" (pp. 11–12).

In their study of aesthetic labor, sociologists Ann Witz, Chris Warhurst, and Dennis Nickson (2003) observed: "The concept of aesthetic labour opens up the possibility of seeing how, through the embodied performance of interactive service work, the physical capital of employees is valorized and converted into economic capital by and for organizations" (pp. 40–41). Tipping rules and norms are an important aspect of the work practices that enable breastaurant managers to control their servers' eroticized aesthetic labor in order to sustain the breastaurant brand. Their function may not be as obvious as the social and psychological constraints imposed by sexualized appearance codes and uniform rules, which literally impose the brand on the worker's material body. But high tips are an essential part of the bait that lures young women to a job that promises a sort of lowbrow eroticized glamour and celebrity status. The switch is that they are really just vulnerable low-wage waitresses whose employers pay them in cash wages far less than they are worth to the enterprise.

The commercialization of the female breast is not a new phenomenon in the history of advertising and entertainment (Yalom 1997: 183–202), but it has assumed a new cultural legitimacy for companies marketing goods and services with interactive service workers. If young attractive female workers with large breasts in sexy, revealing outfits can increase sales and enhance the brand for midpriced restaurants, what other goods and services can they sell? We know some of the answers to this question: for coffee shops we have, among others, Bikini Espresso, Cowgirls

Espresso, Java Juggs, Java Divas, Sexpresso, and Bikini Baristas; for hair salons we have Knockouts, Exposed Hair Salon, Barber Babes, the Bikini Barbershop, and A Little Off the Top Salon; for housecleaning services we have Fantasy Maids and Hotties Cleaning Service; for lawn care we have Tiger Time "Bikini" Lawn Care; for car-wash businesses we have Baywash Bikini Car Wash, Barbies Bikini Car Wash, Wet N Wild Bikini Car Wash, and Naughty Butt Nice Car Wash. Are these sex workers using their bodies to earn high tips? Or just young women with low-wage jobs serving coffee, cutting hair, cleaning houses, mowing lawns, and washing cars?

While these jobs foreground the female body—making it visible to the customer—the labor aspects of the job are largely invisible to the worker. Until we fully appreciate how and why the market for low-wage service work intersects with and shapes the market for the display of the female body, particularly the female breast, we will not be able to adequately and fairly address the labor dimensions of these eroticized jobs. This research suggests that banning tips, or abolishing the subminimum wage for tipped employees and raising the minimum wage, might compel employers to pay the true cost of using the sexualized labor of young women to sell products and services—and very likely make the most marginal (and exploitative) enterprises unprofitable. Robust enforcement of sex discrimination laws could prohibit employing only females in server positions at breastaurants under a dubious bona fide occupational qualification rationale and also remedy the underemployment of women at high-end upscale restaurants. Using discrimination laws to address the problem of sexual harassment in the food service industry as a whole could benefit the working conditions of breastaurant servers who, because of their provocative dress and appearance, are prime targets of harassment by customers and managers. In the end, gendered social norms and cultural stereotypes, as well as consumer demand, may trump even the best-intentioned efforts to use the law to mitigate the potential harms to workers of sexualized aesthetic labor. At the very least, we can attempt to make breastaurant servers fully aware of the labor dimensions of selling the female breast as brand.

REFERENCES

Agar, Selim. 2011. "Breast-aurant Battle: LI Upstart Takes on Hooters." *New York Post*, June 13. Retrieved December 10, 2014 (www.nypost.com/p /news/local/breast_aurant_battle).

Allegretto, Sylvia A., and Kai Filion. 2011. "Waiting for Change: The $2.13 Federal Subminimum Wage." Briefing Paper No. 297. Washington, DC: Economic Policy Institute and Center for Wage and Employment Dynamics. February 23, 2011. Retrieved December 10, 2014 (www.epi.org/publication /waiting_for_change_the_213_federal_subminimum_wage/).

Alpert, William T. 1986. *The Minimum Wage in the Restaurant Industry*. New York: Praeger.

Avery, Dianne, and Marion Crain. 2007. "Branded: Corporate Image, Sexual Stereotyping, and the New Face of Capitalism." *Duke Journal of Gender Law and Policy* 14 (1): 13–124.

Azar, Ofer H. 2004. "Optimal Monitoring with External Incentives: The Case of Tipping." *Southern Economic Journal* 71 (1): 170–81.

———. 2009. "Incentives and Service Quality in the Restaurant Industry: The Tipping–Service Puzzle." *Applied Economics* 41 (15): 1917–27.

———. 2011. "Business Strategy and the Social Norm of Tipping." *Journal of Economic Psychology* 32 (3): 515–25.

Beiner, Theresa M. 2007. "Sexy Dressing Revisited: Does Target Dress Play a Part in Sexual Harassment Cases?" *Duke Journal of Gender Law and Policy* 14 (1): 125–52.

Berman, Jillian. 2015. "Breastaurants Booming as the Restaurant Industry Struggles." HuffingtonPost.com, January 13. Last modified January 15, 2015. Retrieved January 17, 2015 (www.huffingtonpost.com/2015/01/13 /breastaurants-growth_n_6443274.html).

BLS–CPS (US Bureau of Labor Statistics—Current Population Survey). 2013. "Labor Force Statistics from the Current Population Survey: Household Data, Annual Averages." Table 39: Median Weekly Earnings of Full-Time Wage and Salary Workers by Detailed Occupation and Sex. Last modified February 26, 2014. Retrieved January 14, 2015 (www.bls.gov/cps/cpsaat39 .htm).

BLS–OES (US Bureau of Labor Statistics—Occupational Employment Statistics). 2013. "Occupational Employment and Wages, Waiters and Waitresses," SOC Code 35-3031. May 2013. Last modified April 1, 2014. Retrieved January 14, 2015 (www.bls.gov/oes/current/oes353031.htm).

BLS–OOH (US Bureau of Labor Statistics—Occupational Outlook Handbook). 2014a. "Food and Beverage Serving and Related Workers: Work Environment." January 8, 2014. Retrieved January 14, 2015 (www.bls.gov /ooh/food-preparation-and-serving/food-and-beverage-serving-and-related -workers.htm).

BLS–OOH (US Bureau of Labor Statistics—Occupational Outlook Handbook). 2014b. "Food Preparation and Serving: Waiters and Waitresses." January 8, 2014. Retrieved January 14, 2015 (www.bls.gov/ooh/food -preparation-and-serving/waiters-and-waitresses.htm).

Bodvarsson, Örn B., and William A. Gibson. 1997. "Economics and Restaurant Gratuities: Determining Tip Rates." *American Journal of Economics and Sociology* 56 (2): 187–203.

Brizek, Michael. 2011. "It's More Than Just the Perceived Exploitation of Women: Contemporary Issues Facing Hooters Restaurants." *Journal of Case*

Research in Business and Economics 3 (August): 1–13. Retrieved December 10, 2014 (www.aabri.com/manuscripts/10431.pdf).

Burstein, Joshua. 1998. "Testing the Strength of Title VII Sexual Harassment Protection: Can It Support a Hostile Work Environment Claim Brought by a Nude Dancer?" *New York University Review of Law and Social Change* 24 (2): 271–314.

Cahill, Kelly Ann. 1995. "Hooters: Should There Be an Assumption of Risk Defense to Some Hostile Work Environment Sexual Harassment Claims?" *Vanderbilt Law Review* 48 (4): 1107–54.

Cobble, Dorothy Sue. 1991. *Dishing It Out: Waitresses and Their Unions in the Twentieth Century*. Urbana-Champaign: University of Illinois Press.

Conlin, Michael, Michael Lynn, and Ted O'Donoghue. 2003. "The Norm of Restaurant Tipping." *Journal of Economic Behavior and Organization* 52 (3): 297–321.

Cook, Rachel E. 2011. "You're Wearing the Orange Shorts? African American Hooters Girls and the All American Girl Next Door." Master's thesis, Georgia State University. Women's Studies Theses, Paper 21. ScholarWorks@ Georgia State University. Posted April 26, 2011. Retrieved December 10, 2014 (http://scholarworks.gsu.edu/wsi_theses/21).

———. 2012. "Black Skin, Orange Shorts: A Hooters Girl Narrative." *Ebony*, August 2. Retrieved December 10, 2014 (www.ebony.com/news-views /black-skin-orange-shorts-a-hooters-girl-narrative#axzz3LWrSLxgd).

Daley, Jason. 2011. "'Breastaurants' Ring Up Big Profits." *Entrepreneur*, May 24. Retrieved December 10, 2014 (www.entrepreneur.com/article /219606).

DOL–WHD (US Department of Labor—Wage and Hour Division). 2015. "Minimum Wages for Tipped Employees." January 1. Retrieved January 12, 2015 (www.dol.gov/whd/state/tipped.htm).

Erickson, Karla A. 2009. *The Hungry Cowboy: Service and Community in a Neighborhood Restaurant*. Jackson: University Press of Mississippi.

Estreicher, Samuel, and Jonathan R. Nash. 2004. "The Law and Economics of Tipping: The Laborer's Perspective." Paper No. 54:1–24. American Law and Economics Association Annual Meetings. Retrieved December 10, 2014 (http://law.bepress.com/cgi/viewcontent.cgi!article=1068&context=alea).

Fair Labor Standards Act of 1938, 29 U.S.C. §§ 203 (m) (t), 206(a)(1).

Funding Universe. 2005. "Hooters of America, Inc. History." Retrieved December 10, 2014 (www.fundinguniverse.com/company-histories/hooters-of -america-inc-history/).

Giang, Vivian. 2011. "How 'Breastaurants' Took Over the Casual Dining Industry." *Business Insider*, June 2. Retrieved December 10, 2014 (www .businessinsider.com/breastaurant-2011-5).

Giuffre, Patti A., and Christine L. Williams. 1994. "Boundary Lines: Labeling Sexual Harassment in Restaurants." *Gender and Society* 8 (3): 378–401.

Hakim, Catherine. 2011. *Erotic Capital: The Power of Attraction in the Boardroom and Bedroom*. New York: Basic Books.

Hall, Elaine J. 1993. "Waitering/Waitressing: Engendering the Work of Table Servers." *Gender and Society* 7 (3): 329–46. doi: 10.1177/089124393007003002.

Hamermesh, Daniel S. 2011. *Beauty Pays: Why Attractive People Are More Successful.* Princeton, NJ: Princeton University Press.

Helyar, John. 2003. "Hooters: A Case Study: 'This Thing Has Incredible Legs,' an Early Investor Said. Twenty Years Later, the Restaurant Chain Has Finally Hit Its Stride." *Fortune,* September 1, pp. 140–46. Retrieved December 10, 2014 (http://archive.fortune.com/magazines/fortune/fortune_archive/2003/09/01/348187/index.htm).

Hochschild, Arlie R. 1983. *The Managed Heart: The Commercialization of Human Feeling.* Berkeley: University of California Press.

Hooters. 2012. "About Hooters." Hooters.com. Retrieved December 10, 2014 (www.hooters.com/company/About.aspx).

Huebner, Lisa C. 2008. "It Is Part of the Job: Waitresses and Nurses Define Sexual Harassment." *Sociological Viewpoints* 24 (Fall): 75–90.

Jamieson, Dave. 2011. "Hooters Lawsuit Claims Rival Restaurant Stole 'Trade Secrets.'" HuffingtonPost.com, September 30. Last modified November 30, 2011. Retrieved December 10, 2014 (www.huffingtonpost.com/2011/09/30/hooters-lawsuit_n_988972.html).

Kang, Miliann. 2010. *The Managed Hand: Race, Gender, and the Body in Beauty Service Work.* Berkeley: University of California Press.

Kilgore v. Outback Steakhouse, 160 F.3d 294 (6th Cir. 1998).

Kuebelbeck, Amy. 1993. "Sexual Ornament or Invitation to Harassment at Hooters Bar?" *Los Angeles Times,* August 8. Retrieved December 10, 2014 (http://articles.latimes.com/1993-08-08/news/mn-21750_1_sexual-harassment-lawsuit).

LaPointe, Eleanor. 1992. "Relationships with Waitresses: Gendered Social Distance in Restaurant Hierarchies." *Qualitative Sociology* 15 (4): 377–93.

Loe, Meika. 1996. "Working for Men at the Intersection of Power, Gender, and Sexuality." *Sociological Inquiry* 66 (4): 399–421.

Lynn, Michael. 2009. "Determinants and Consequences of Female Attractiveness and Sexiness: Realistic Tests with Restaurant Waitresses." *Archives of Sexual Behavior* 38 (5): 737–45. Retrieved December 11, 2014 (www.chapter14.net/misc/MichaelLynn2009.pdf).

Mantell, Ruth. 2007. "The 10 Worst Jobs in America: Low Pay, No Benefits Put These Workers in a Tough Spot." *Wall Street Journal: MarketWatch,* November 1. Retrieved December 10, 2014 (www.marketwatch.com/story/the-10-worst-jobs-in-america).

Margalioth, Yoram. 2006. "The Case against Tipping." *University of Pennsylvania Journal of Labor and Employment Law* 9 (1): 117–46.

———. 2010. "The Social Norm of Tipping, Its Correlation with Inequality, and Differences in Tax Treatment across Countries." *Theoretical Inquiries in Law* 11 (2): 561–88.

McGinley, Ann C. 2006. "Harassment of Sex(y) Workers: Applying Title VII to Sexualized Industries." *Yale Journal of Law and Feminism* 18 (1): 65–108.

———. 2007. "Harassing 'Girls' at the Hard Rock: Masculinities in Sexualized Environments." *University of Illinois Law Review* 2007 (4): 1229–78.

Mears, Ashley. 2011. *Pricing Beauty: The Making of a Fashion Model.* Berkeley: University of California Press.

Mikin, Mark. 2012. "Hostess of the Week, 'Breastaurant' Edition." Esquire
.com, June 27. Retrieved December 10, 2014 (www.esquire.com/blogs/food
-for-men/breastaurant-chains-5999331#).

Newman, Katherine S. 2006. *Chutes and Ladders: Navigating the Low-Wage
Labor Market.* New York: Russell Sage Foundation.

NIH–APIS (National Institutes of Health—Alcohol Policy Information System).
2014. "Underage Drinking: Minimum Ages for On-Premises Servers
and Bartenders." January 1, 2014. Retrieved December 10, 2014 (http://
alcoholpolicy.niaaa.nih.gov/Minimum_Ages_for_On-Premises_Servers
_and_Bartenders.html).

OAG–NY (Office of the Attorney General of the State of New York). 2000.
Beyond People v. Cipriani: *The Hiring of Women in New York City's Elite
Restaurants: A Report to the People of the State of New York from the Office
of the Attorney General.* July 6, 2000. Retrieved January 16, 2015 (www
.ag.ny.gov/sites/default/files/pdfs/bureaus/civil_rights/HIRING%20OF
%20WOMEN%20BROCHURE.pdf).

Ogbonna, Emmanuel, and Lloyd C. Harris. 2002. "Institutionalization of Tipping as a Source of Managerial Control." *British Journal of Industrial Relations* 40 (4): 725–52.

Original Hooters. 2015. "Hooters History: The Beginning." OriginalHooters
.com. Retrieved January 15, 2015 (www.originalhooters.com/saga/the
-beginning/).

Owens, Ryan, and Hana Karar. 2009. "Business Booming at 'Breastaurants':
Cheap Food, Beer and Sexy Women." *ABC News,* March 5. Retrieved December 10, 2014 (http://abcnews.go.com/Business/Economy/story?id=7008002).

Paules, Greta Foff. 1991. *Dishing It Out: Power and Resistance among Waitresses in a New Jersey Restaurant.* Philadelphia: Temple University Press.

Payne, Jonathan. 2009. "Emotional Labour and Skill: A Reappraisal." *Gender,
Work and Organization* 16 (3): 348–67.

Pencavel, John H. 1977. "Work Effort, On-the-Job Screening, and Alternative
Methods of Remuneration." *Research in Labor Economics* 1: 225–58.

Rhee, Jeannie Sclafani. 1997. "Redressing for Success: The Liability of Hooters
Restaurant for Customer Harassment of Waitresses." *Harvard Women's
Law Journal* 20: 163–204.

Rhode, Deborah L. 2010. *The Beauty Bias: The Injustice of Appearance in Life
and Law.* New York: Oxford University Press.

ROC–NY (Restaurant Opportunities Center of New York). 2010. *Waiting on
Equality: The Role and Impact of Gender in the New York Restaurant
Industry.* July 7. Retrieved December 10, 2014 (http://rocunited.org/wp
-content/uploads/2010/07/reports_waiting-on-eq_role-of-gender-in-nyc
-rest-industry.pdf).

ROC–United (Restaurant Opportunity Centers United). 2012. *Tipped over the
Edge: Gender Inequity in the Restaurant Industry.* Retrieved December 10,
2014 (http://rocunited.org/wp-content/uploads/2012/02/ROC_GenderInequity
_F1-1.pdf).

———. 2014. *The Glass Floor: Sexual Harassment in the Restaurant Industry.*
Retrieved January 15, 2015 (http://rocunited.org/wp-content/uploads/2014

/10/REPORT_The-Glass-Floor-Sexual-Harassment-in-the-Restaurant
-Industry2.pdf).

Rowe, Elizabeth A. 2013. "Intellectual Property and Employee Selection."
Wake Forest Law Review 48 (1): 25–64.

Sanburn, Josh. 2012. "Hooters' Big Experiment: New Menu, New Décor and a
New Target Audience." Time.com, August 2. Retrieved December 10, 2014
(http://business.time.com/2012/08/02/hooters-big-experiment-new-menu
-new-décor-and-a-new-target-audience/).

Schneyer, Kenneth L. 1998. "Hooting: Public and Popular Discourse about Sex
Discrimination." *University of Michigan Journal of Law Reform* 31 (3):
551–636.

Segrave, Kerry. 1994. *The Sexual Harassment of Women in the Workplace,
1600 to 1993.* Jefferson, NC: McFarland.

———. 1998. *Tipping: An American Social History of Gratuities.* Jefferson,
NC: McFarland.

Seltzer, Richard, and Holona Leanne Ochs. 2010. *Gratuity: A Contextual
Understanding of Tipping Norms from the Perspective of Tipped Employees.* Lanham, MD: Lexington Books.

Sutton, David. 2007. "Tipping: An Anthropological Meditation." Pp. 191–204
in *The Restaurants Book: Ethnographies of Where We Eat,* edited by David
Beriss and David Sutton. Oxford: Berg.

Thompson, Steven R. 2011. "Bone Daddy's Latest 'Breastaurant' to Set Sights
on Houston Market." *Houston Business Journal,* December 16. Retrieved
December 10, 2014 (www.bizjournals.com/houston/print-edition/2011/12
/16/bone-daddys-latest-breastaurant-to.html).

Tibbals, Anne Chauntelle. 2007. "Doing Gender as Resistance: Waitresses and
Servers in Contemporary Table Service." *Journal of Contemporary Ethnography* 36 (6): 731–51.

US Bureau of the Census. 2012. *North American Industry Classification System.* "Definition—Sector 72: Accommodation and Food Services, 722511
Full Service Restaurants." Retrieved December 10, 2014 (www.census.gov
/cgi-bin/sssd/naics/naicsrch?code=722511&search=2012%20NAICS
%20Search).

Valverde, Miriam. 2013. "'Breastaurants' Tilted Kilt, Twin Peaks Coming
to Area." *Sun-Sentinel* (Fort Lauderdale, FL), February 7. Retrieved
December 10, 2014 (http://articles.sun-sentinel.com/2013-02-07/business
/fl-breastaurants-opening-20130206_1_twin-peaks-hooters-girls
-breastaurant).

Wang, Lu-in. 2014. "At the Tipping Point: Race and Gender Discrimination in
a Common Economic Transaction." *Virginia Journal of Social Policy and
the Law* 21 (1): 101–66.

Warhurst, Chris. 2012. Review of *Honey Money: The Power of Erotic Capital,*
by Catherine Hakim. *Work, Employment and Society* 26 (6): 1036–38. doi:
10.1177/0950017012468303.

Warhurst, Chris, and Dennis Nickson. 2009. "'Who's Got the Look?' Emotional, Aesthetic and Sexualized Labour in Interactive Services." *Gender,
Work and Organization* 16 (3): 385–403.

Warhurst, Chris, Diane van den Broek, Richard Hall, and Dennis Nickson. 2012. "Great Expectations: Gender, Looks, and Lookism at Work." *International Journal of Work Organisation and Emotion* 5 (1): 72–90.

Witz, Ann, Chris Warhurst, and Dennis Nickson. 2003. "The Labour of Aesthetics and the Aesthetics of Organization." *Organization* 10 (1): 33–54.

Wollan, Malia. 2010. "Suits Challenge Hooters on Wage-and-Hour Issues." *New York Times,* April 10. Retrieved December 10, 2014 (www.nytimes .com/2010/04/11/us/11sfhooters.html?pagewanted=all&_r=0).

Yalom, Marilyn. 1997. *A History of the Breast.* New York: Knopf.

Yuracko, Kimberly A. 2004. "Private Nurses and Playboy Bunnies: Explaining Permissible Sex Discrimination." *California Law Review* 92 (1): 147–214.

Zatz, Noah D. 1997. "Sex Work/Sex Act: Law, Labor, and Desire in Constructions of Prostitution." *Signs* 22 (2): 277–308.

Zelizer, Viviana A. 1994. *The Social Meaning of Money.* New York: Basic Books.

———. 2011. *Economic Lives: How Culture Shapes the Economy.* Princeton, NJ: Princeton University Press.

CHAPTER 10

The Invisible Consequences
of Aesthetic Labor in Upscale
Retail Stores

CHRISTINE L. WILLIAMS AND CATHERINE CONNELL

In many businesses employers choose workers on the basis of their attractiveness, deportment, style, and accent. Workers have to "look good and sound right" for the job. The importance of this aesthetic labor is especially evident in upscale retail stores, where the frontline workers often seem identical to the store advertisements and mannequins. For example, at Abercrombie & Fitch a well-toned and muscular young worker stands shirtless next to a huge poster that could be a photograph of his chest. Workers at J. Jill and Coldwater Creek look like the thirty-something suburban women in their catalogs while those at Williams-Sonoma appear to be the minions of Martha Stewart. Upscale retail establishments hire workers to match their brands in order to convince shoppers that they, too, can achieve the right look—and the popularity, admiration, and sophistication that go along with it—if only they buy the right products.

Although aesthetic labor is by its nature highly visible, the organizational processes that generate it are not. In this chapter we reveal the methods that employers use to hire people who match their corporate aesthetic. Drawing on interviews with workers in upscale retail stores, we show how prospective employees can be duped into taking these jobs. They experience the equivalent a bait and switch: flattered by the possibility of representing brands with which they identify, they accept employment conditions that are extremely exploitative and degrading. Not surprisingly, these jobs have extremely high turnover rates. But our goal is not simply to warn prospective job applicants away from this industry. Instead, we argue that aesthetic labor has profound consequences for social inequality. Hiring workers on the basis of their looks is an insidious form of institutionalized racial, gender, and class discrimination. "Looking good and sounding right" is typically a proxy for being white, middle-class, and conventionally gendered. Aesthetic labor also reinforces class inequality in an indirect way. Workers are selected for these jobs because of their middle-class backgrounds: they do not have to rely on their meager paychecks to support themselves. But these workers do not use their class privilege to demand upgrades to these jobs. Because they identify as consumers and not as workers, they promulgate an ideology that harms those who do rely on their retail jobs for a living. The increasing degradation of retail jobs is an invisible result of aesthetic labor.

AESTHETIC LABOR IN UPSCALE
RETAIL ESTABLISHMENTS

The retail industry is one of the largest parts of the service sector, yet it generates some of its worst jobs (Doussard 2013). With median wages in 2012 around $10.30 per hour,[1] most retail workers do not earn enough money to support themselves or their families. In addition to low wages, retail jobs offer only part-time schedules that vary from week to week. They offer no benefits, no autonomy, and very limited opportunities for promotion. Many people who take these jobs are desperate for work. But this is not the case for those who work in upscale retail stores. Employers at these stores weed out potential employees who rely on their jobs to support themselves. In hiring workers—those who look good and sound right—to perform aesthetic labor, retail stores are, in effect, looking for middle-class people who have other means of economic support.

The concept of *aesthetic labor* is similar to *emotional labor*, a concept that draws attention to how workers in a wide range of service occupations—from flight attendants and bill collectors to courtroom attorneys—are trained to modify their feelings in order to elicit the desired emotional responses from customers. It is also akin to *body labor*, a characteristic of jobs that require intimate physical contact with the bodies of other people, such as nail salon workers, sex workers, and hospital workers. All of these concepts—*aesthetic labor, emotional labor,* and *body labor*—focus on the embodiment of workers and emphasize how interactions between customers and service workers are structured in ways that reproduce social inequalities.

However, studies drawing on the concept of *aesthetic labor* are based largely on the work of Pierre Bourdieu (1984), unlike studies of emotional or body labor, which are mainly inspired by Arlie Hochschild (1983) and Carol Wolkowitz (2006). The expectation of workers hired to perform aesthetic labor is that they are not merely "acting" or performing a role in a specific employment context but rather are expressing deep-seated dispositions. In other words, employers seek workers who embody a particular *habitus*.

Bourdieu's (1984) concept of *habitus* refers to mannerisms that are acquired in childhood and that are difficult to alter later in life. According to Bourdieu, a person's class background is embedded in these mannerisms. Virtually every preference, gesture, and posture—even the way a person blows her nose (p. 466)—signifies class habitus. In hiring workers to perform aesthetic labor—those who look good and sound right— upscale retail stores search for individuals who embody social class privileges. In this regard, aesthetic labor is quite distinct from emotional labor and body labor, which are typically performed by workers who are marginalized (vis-à-vis their customers) along the axes of race, class, and gender. Upscale retail employers, in contrast, try to hire workers who match the social demographics of the stores' preferred customers.

Upscale retail stores may be paradigmatic of work settings requiring aesthetic labor, but they are by no means unique. It is probably the case that every interactive service job has an aesthetic component, that is, a set of normative expectations regarding appropriate appearance and demeanor. What distinguishes upscale retail jobs is the weight that managers in these stores place on hiring people with the "right look"—to the exclusion of almost all other qualifications.

The particular emphasis that upscale stores place on aesthetic labor may be a reflection of their location between the discounters and the luxury stores. Members of the middle class are highly invested in cultivating sophisticated tastes to enhance their status and, ultimately, their economic power (Bourdieu 1984). For a middle-class shopper, a discount store cannot convey distinction, but an upscale store can. Thus, the store's aesthetic (including the appearance of its labor force) may be most significant when company profits depend on attracting a demographic seeking higher status—precisely what customers who patronize upscale establishments expect to achieve (Schor 1998; Williams 2006).

However, upscale retail stores face a quandary: how do they attract middle-class people to work in these substandard jobs? To answer to this question, we conducted in-depth interviews with thirty retail workers employed in a wide range of retail stores in Texas. This chapter focuses on the experiences of the nineteen workers in the sample who worked in "high-end" stores, including Victoria's Secret, Banana Republic, Macy's, and Crate and Barrel. We call these stores "high-end" or "upscale" to differentiate them from "luxury" establishments like Nordstrom's and Saks Fifth Avenue; "midrange" stores that target the working middle class, like Sears and J. C. Penney; and mass discounters such as Costco, Target, Home Depot, and Best Buy. Respondents who worked in these other categories of stores described very different labor regimes. Although they are not the subject of this chapter, we occasionally refer to their experiences for illustrative and comparative purposes.

Respondents who are the focus of this chapter include sixteen women and three men whose ages range from nineteen to sixty (the larger sample consists of twenty-four women and six men whose ages range from nineteen to seventy-five). All but five of these respondents were part-time employees (or "associates") in upscale stores at the time of their interviews. The other five had previous part-time experience in upscale stores and still worked in the retail industry: two had moved to a discounter, two had become full-time employees, and one is now a franchise owner. Half of the respondents with experience at upscale stores are white; the others are Latina or Latino, African American, and Asian American. Interviews were conducted between 2006 and 2008.

Our interviews reveal that upscale retail stores use a variety of organizational strategies to procure their ideal workforce. These include (1) vetting creative talents, (2) hiring customers off the floor, (3) offering discounts instead of higher wages, and (4) prolonging interviews and manipulating schedules. Each of these strategies produces a labor force with the aesthetic qualities associated with the retail brand.

First, some upscale retail stores require applicants to perform creative tasks during the job interview. These are intended to reveal insights about an applicant's personality, style, and imagination. For example, prospective employees in our study were asked to design a marketing campaign for a paper clip or to pick a toy and role-play a sales encounter. As part of her interview at Central Market, an upscale grocery chain in Texas, Laura, one of our study participants, was required to take items from the store and artfully display them in a gift basket.

Once hired, however, many retail workers find they are given no opportunity to use their creative talents. Managers rarely ask retail workers to design a display or to use any of their creative talents on the job. When we inquired whether she had ever been asked to give any opinions about her job, Laura said: "No. We're asked if the Mentos by our register are selling. . . . Even if you have simple ideas about, you know, 'Hey, you should put another person on express [check-out] because we're getting slammed over here,' . . . no." Most decisions about store layout, merchandise display, and daily operations are made in corporate offices, far away from the sales floor.

Another barrier to creative expression is the well-documented requirement to follow a regimented sales script (Leidner 1993; Williams 2006). This feature of the job particularly annoyed Kelly, who worked at Abercrombie & Fitch. She related, "People who work the front room are supposed to say the tag line, which is always something lame and cheesy like 'Have you checked out our cool shorts?' When I first started, it was 'Have you heard how great our jeans fit?' because we were really pushing denim. Who really wants to say that? Nobody. I really hated saying the tag line. It's the most embarrassing thing."

Retail workers are not permitted to stray from highly regimented routines, so screening employees by design skill or marketing savvy seems pointless. However, by vetting creative talents, retailers are making sure that the workers they hire look good and sound right when they utter the tag line. In other words, they ensure that workers already possess the disposition, style, and aesthetic sensibilities that match those of the brand.

A second way that employers screen applicants is by seeking out and hiring people on the shopping floor. Managers literally go up to people while they are shopping and ask them if they want a job at the store. This technique is especially common in fashion retail, an area in which workers are required to wear the clothes that they sell. Here is Michelle's account of how she was hired at Express:

> I was actually shopping there one day, and they asked me if I wanted to work there, like off the wall, and they were starting a new store so, I think, asking a few people who came in. But I had been looking for sales experience, so I was like, oh my goodness. It was really cool. It just kinda fell in.
>
> *Why do you think they asked you?*
>
> I don't know! I mean I shop there a lot. I had some pants on from there, so maybe they thought, she buys here a lot. I don't know.
>
> *And you just accepted the job on the spot?*

Yeah! Well, I had to interview afterwards. They asked me if I wanted to work there, but they had to interview me a few days later because I didn't want to right then because I had to do something. But they pretty much were like, "You have a job."

In fashion retail, workers are often required to wear the store's clothing. At some stores, like Abercrombie & Fitch and Express, clothes only go up to size 10 or 12, so employers have to take into consideration an applicant's size; hiring shoppers is one way to ensure that workers will fit into the clothes. Abercrombie & Fitch (A&F) calls its frontline retail workers "models" instead of sales associates, emphasizing this important feature of employment.[2]

But hiring people on the sales floor does more than ensure that they are the right size. This practice also selects for workers who are already knowledgeable and, ideally, passionate about the brand. They do not need to be trained about the "lifestyles" associated with the merchandise; they already know the store's image from a consumer's perspective. Gloria, an assistant manager at Coldwater Creek, explained that all of her employees are hired on the floor precisely because the store's customers are "extremely loyal" and dedicated to the brand.

Some respondents described being flattered when they were asked to apply because they already deeply identified with the brand. The offer of a merchandise discount then sealed the deal for them. Retailers offer employee discounts that typically range from 10 to 30 percent. Some stores offer even higher discounts during the employee's first few weeks on the job. Michelle described the discounts at Express: "Our first purchase is 50 percent off up to $300; then 20 percent off for sixty days, and then 30 percent off after that. And then we have weekend sales when new merchandise comes in, and salespeople have the first option. And that is an additional 15 percent, so that would be 45 percent off sometimes on the weekends. When there's the box sales, they have huge boxes, and they put $5 and $6 things in these boxes for clearing out the fall stuff. We get the first pick of the boxes on the weekend."

The discount is a primary draw for many retail workers. Several of those we interviewed said they had applied to work at stores where they liked to shop in order to get the discount. Angela applied to work at Crate and Barrel because of the 30 percent discount. She had just moved into a new condo and used the discount to furnish it with items from the store. Vanessa also said that the discount motivated her to apply for a job at Victoria's Secret: "I wanted a job that sounded cool; that's why I went to work at Victoria's Secret. When someone asks you, 'Where do you work?' and I say, 'Victoria's Secret,' it's always a huge conversation starter. That and I knew that they had a really good discount. . . . I always loved Victoria's Secret, the little lotions and all that crap. . . . They give you free stuff every time they bring out a new product; they give it to you free to try—and a 30 percent discount."

Recruiting workers from the ranks of consumers and offering deep discounts in lieu of reasonable wages are strategies that upscale retail stores use to staff their stores with workers with middle-class backgrounds. Using these practices, retailers can find people to hire who do not "need" their paychecks to support themselves or their families. Michelle and her coworkers could not possibly afford to spend $300 on clothes if they depended on a job that paid $7 an hour. Angela and Vanessa both admitted that they spent their entire paychecks at the store (earning $7.25 an hour and $7.15 an hour, respectively).

To be sure, most (but not all) of these workers actually do "need" money, or else they would not seek employment. Several indicated that their incomes "helped" to pay bills, but none relied on their wages to pay the major expenses associated with their middle-class lifestyles (e.g., rent, food, college tuition). Everyone we interviewed who worked part-time at an upscale store received economic support from family members or a retirement income.[3] Without this subsidy, they could not embody the lifestyles that made them desirable employees.

Thus, when we claim that workers in these stores do not "need" their paychecks, we are referring to employers' preference to hire associates who are primarily driven by consumer desires, not by their labor interests (Besen 2006). Offering steep discounts is one way to identify workers whose principal motivation is the desire to be associated with a cool brand—not the conventional worker concerns of decent pay, working conditions, future job opportunities, or benefits. Indeed, when asked about the benefits available to workers at her store, Michelle only mentioned the discount.

A fourth way that retailers ensure the right aesthetic in their workers is by prolonging interviews and manipulating schedules. In upscale stores the application process can take weeks, a situation that eliminates from the job pool anyone who depends on a paycheck. Laura, who works at Central Market, described the waiting: "The application process was really long. It took me a month to actually start working. You do an interview, and then they get a hold of you, and then you have to go and do this group interview. You do a group interview with people, and they pick out the people they want. . . . I waited, and then they will call you. So another week goes by, and then you get a final interview. . . . And then you get a drug test. So that is a whole month of the interview process." Laura explained that because she had saved up some money from a previous job (and because she could rely on support from her parents), she was able to hold out during the time it took to be hired, but she suspected her fellow applicants were less fortunate: "I was very lucky that I had money in the bank and could have time to wait. My coworkers, I'm not sure. The people I got hired with and that I knew from the group interviews—there were only two people out of the ten or fifteen in the group interview that would get hired—when I talked to them, they found it frustrating, and I found it frustrating. But luckily I didn't find it frustrating financially." Among our respondents, such long waits were not uncommon in upscale stores. In contrast, those hired for low-end retail stores were often hired on the spot. Prolonged waits select for applicants who have alternative sources of financial support and weed out those who do not.

In addition to being subjected to long waits, retail workers rarely have control over their schedules once they are hired. In the retail industry today, virtually all employees are hired to work *part-time*—yet they have to be available at *any time*. Schedules vary from week to week, and the hours can range widely without notice (Lambert 2008). For example, Vanessa was hired to work twenty hours per week at Victoria's Secret, but her hours fluctuated between nine and thirty-two, and she was given only two days' notice of the next week's schedule. She said that this random scheduling made it difficult to plan activities outside of work, plus the variability in hours meant that her income fluctuated drastically from week to week. Only those who can rely on other sources of economic support can afford to take these jobs.

All of these organizational practices eliminate applicants who are seeking jobs for conventional reasons like wages and benefits and select those who are driven by their consumer interests and identification with the store brand. These "ideal" retail workers are class privileged and consumer driven, and they are likely to conform to the aesthetic that matches the retailer's brand image.

SOCIAL CONSEQUENCES OF AESTHETIC LABOR

The demand for aesthetic labor in upscale retail work has altered the labor process in ways that not only exacerbate but also obscure social inequality. First, as we have already hinted, by appealing to the interests of worker-consumers, aesthetic labor highlights the enjoyment associated with shopping and downplays the drawbacks of working at a substand-ard job. This situation has consequences for worker resistance and change in these jobs. Second, the demand for aesthetic labor justifies continued job segregation, holding workers and customers—and not employers—responsible for the sorting of workers on the basis of class, race, and gender. Third, aesthetic labor contributes to consumer fetishism. By hir-ing workers who embody their "brands," retail stores obscure the social relations of production and diminish the possibility for social change.

Consumer Pleasure

The increasing importance of aesthetic labor in retail employment emphasizes the pleasures associated with shopping. This factor is impor-tant for understanding why workers consent to work at these bad jobs. Much happiness and satisfaction are to be found through cultural goods—and also through fitting in with a congenial group that shares similar interests and sensibilities. Yasemin Besen (2006) found that these pleasures were especially important to well-to-do teenagers work-ing in suburban coffee shops, who consider these low-paying jobs an integral part of their social life. They identify deeply with the brand of coffee they sell—some even wear their uniforms outside of work—and claim they would never work for a brand that is not "cool."

Retail workers hired for their aesthetic labor also comment on this gratifying aspect of their jobs. For example, Rachel is a twenty-year-old who works for MAC cosmetics. She explained her determination to get this job:

> I was trying to get a job there since I was eighteen. . . . Over two years I kept applying and saw other people get hired before me. But over the course of that time, I became a frequent customer, and I got in real well with the assist-ant manager there and a few of the girls there. I would go in and have make-overs done on me every couple of weeks and spend several hundreds of dol-lars on makeup every month. So when the opening came up in November, . . . the manager said to me, "I know you're in here a lot, and I know you don't have any experience, but I'm going to go ahead and give you an interview. Bring a model in, and I'll have you do a make-over on her. We'll see what your skills are." So that was real persistence that got me there. I wouldn't have got it otherwise, I don't think.

Earning $13.50 an hour, Rachel is a relatively well-paid retail worker, but her hours are limited to twelve per week. (According to Rachel, the company defines *full time* as thirty hours per week and allows only one full-time worker per outlet.) Her enthusiasm for the job is entirely bound up with the product line she represents. She explains that MAC "is the only makeup I've worn since I was fourteen. . . . It's much different than any other cosmetic line. It's only sold at Saks, Nordstrom's, Dillard's, and MAC stores." She considers herself a budding makeup artist—not a retail worker—and hopes that this job will eventually lead to a freelance career working for the film industry.

Rachel's enthusiasm for her job is similar to the sentiment described by Deborah Leslie (2002) in her study of fashion retail and by David Wright (2005), who studied booksellers. The workers in these studies identified with the clothing fashions or the books that they sold. They did not see themselves primarily as retail *workers* but rather as knowledgeable *consumers*. They articulated little interest in their labor rights; indeed, Wright found that booksellers viewed their low wages as a sign of their higher moral principles such as their antimaterialism and devotion to a calling. Rather than demanding better working conditions from their employers, many of these individuals seek respect and recognition for their product expertise from fellow consumers.

This goal of achieving respect and recognition is partially what motivates Rebecca, a sixty-year-old transwoman retail worker who is in the process of gender transitioning. She works in the backroom accounting office at David's Bridal and explained why she likes her job:

> I really like interacting with people, especially on a subject I enjoy. There were a couple times [when] we were really shorthanded, and the customer didn't seem to mind me actually being in the area where they were trying on stuff. Of course, they'd go into the room where they actually change and everything, but they'd call me over to have me zip them up or help them trying different stuff like different jewelry, veils, tiaras, and stuff. The few I did help didn't seem to have a problem [with me] and seemed to enjoy my different ideas. A couple of them went ahead and bought stuff I recommended. I really enjoyed that.

Similar to Rachel's comments, Rebecca's account invokes the gendered satisfactions involved in aesthetic labor. She was especially pleased when brides followed her advice about accessories since their doing so provided recognition of her fashion expertise, which was important to her because she was in the process of gaining confidence in her new presentation of self.

However, there is a flip side to the gendered gratification associated with these jobs. Vanessa worked for several years at Victoria's Secret, attracted to the job because she loved the brand. She was interviewed right after she had moved from Victoria's Secret to Home Depot. She noted, "Working at Victoria's Secret always made me aware of body imperfections. Like I have small boobs. . . . There are three girls that worked at my store that had their boobs done while I worked there, [including the manager]. Also highlighted hair, Chanel makeup, stuff like that. . . . I used to walk into Victoria's Secret and be really conscious [of how I looked]. And [now] I walk into Home Depot not wearing any makeup, and I feel a lot better about myself." We see here how body image can be shaped by employment context, exacerbated in jobs demanding aesthetic labor. Vanessa's account also emphasizes the hidden (and uncompensated) effort involved in achieving the right look.

Vanessa was reluctant to take the job at Home Depot, even though she was hired at $10.25 per hour (versus the $7.15 per hour she had earned after receiving several raises at Victoria's Secret).[4] She explained that she did not experience the same pleasure being associated with the merchandise at Home Depot, nor did the store give her the same cachet in her personal life. She also had a low opinion of her fellow workers at Home Depot. When asked about the difference in the dress codes between the two stores, she said, "It was a very big eye-opener to see the kind of people Home Depot employs versus the kind of people Victoria's Secret employs. At Victoria's Secret, it's 'Ladies, please wear makeup.' At Home Depot, it's 'Ladies, please wear bras. Please don't wear any shorts so that your rear end hangs out.' . . . I guess if they didn't tell people [not] to, they would [dress that way]. They evidently had to say it to somebody." Vanessa didn't identify with either the merchandise or the employees at Home Depot. Like many we interviewed, she said her goal was to leave retail as soon as possible. She had no interest in upgrading the job; in fact, she was upgrading herself (through her education) in order to escape this job, which she considered beneath her.

Middle-class workers seem similar in this regard: they do not consider retail a viable career, nor do they contemplate the possibility of upgrading a job in order to make it a viable career. Although several said that they would like to earn more money, not everyone agreed that retail work was *worth* more than the minimum wage. For instance, Jeremy, who worked at the Finish Line, was asked, "Do you think there's anything that can be done to make the job better?" He said:

> I don't think so. The way it is is the way it is. From a worker point of view, if you don't already know how it is, you'll find out quick. And if it's not for you, then you'll move on.

Do you think retail work should be paid more?

I don't. Because most of the people in retail don't need the money.

Others said that they "understood" that their jobs could not provide higher wages and benefits because the company could not afford the expense, because they believed that such compensation should be available only to full-time workers, or because it would mean higher prices for consumers. Grace, a part-time employee at the Learning Express, where she earns $10 per hour, admitted that she has never asked for a raise because "it's a retail job, so it's not worth that much more."

One might expect these decommodified workers to demand better working conditions. Instead, we found that workers in these upscale stores consent to their conditions of employment because they do not consider themselves workers. Their consumerist orientation is the outcome of institutionalized labor processes in the retail industry, which has defined upscale retail jobs as suitable for people who love to shop and who "don't need the money." In a masterful sleight of hand, the retail industry has transformed bad jobs into enjoyable pastimes, enabling this large employment sector to escape social criticism and reform.

Job Segregation

There is a high degree of segregation in retail jobs—an almost perfect sorting of people on the basis of race, class, and gender. Job-level segregation is a feature of virtually all types of stores. A worker at Winn Dixie described her workplace as 100 percent gender segregated: men in Produce, women in Florist, only women cashiers. At Home Depot men sell hardware and plumbing; women work in Design and Gardening. Crate and Barrel and Victoria's Secret both have a gender division between the front of house (all women and gay men) and the back of house (all straight men). The Women's Intimates Department at Macy's is all women while the Women's Shoe Department is all men. And in most of the upscale stores that we studied, white employees are preferred for face-to-face interactions with customers.[5] The few individuals who do not match the demographic of their departments are extremely visible; customers and coworkers often hold them accountable for their deviance (West and Zimmerman 1987; Williams 2006).

Most sociologists understand job segregation to be a product of employer discrimination (Reskin, McBrier, and Kmec 1999). This point of view was shared by some workers in our larger study who are not class or race privileged and who worked for discount stores. For example, Luther, an African American man who worked as a security guard for a number of big-box retail stores, argued that discrimination was widespread in the retail industry. He maintained that anyone turned down for a job in a retail store should charge the employer with discrimination and, if necessary, file a complaint with the Labor Relations Board. According to Luther, everyone is qualified for a retail job because the job does not require any skills. Therefore, any store that posts a sign that says "Now hiring" must accept all applicants; otherwise, the employer is guilty of illegal employment discrimination (see also Avery and Crain 2007).

In contrast to the discrimination framework, those we interviewed who worked in upscale stores used the framework of aesthetics to understand the sorting of people into different jobs, a focus that shifts responsibility for job segregation from the employer to the worker. According to the logic of aesthetic labor, if an employer does not hire an applicant for one of these "unskilled" jobs, it is not due to illegal employment discrimination; the employer is simply and rationally looking for someone whose appearance matches the brand. Many worker-consumers buy into this logic, seeing this sorting as a legitimate business practice that benefits consumers. Since they primarily identify as consumers themselves, they appear untroubled by this employment practice.

For example, Jeremy explained that at the Finish Line, "all cashiers were women. . . . It's not like it was sexist or anything, but if they hired guys, it was to work the floor, and they usually just hired women for cashiers." Jeremy claimed that women are better cashiers because they can calm down irate customers, who are reluctant to "verbally abuse some high school girl . . . who doesn't know what's going on." He explained, "The sales floor was mixed, but it depended on the department. Like in Kids', there's more women. It's just that [kids] have a better rapport with women. When I worked Kids', [here's] a six-feet-tall guy looking at this little kid like, 'Hey, can I get you something?' And he'd just look up at me, scared." Retailers thus use physical embodiment to sort workers in ways that match consumer expectations. This process involves not only gender but also race. This belief was articulated by Michelle, a twenty-year-old white woman who works at the Express clothing store. When asked about the skills needed to work at the Express, she said:

> You have to definitely be able to talk to people, relaxed. I see people who are really shy working, really quiet, don't have good communication skills, can't

even say a sentence right, and I see that they are really lacking really bad. It kind of puts a bad name on Express. . . . Some of the African Americans don't speak as well, and that kind of sets them apart. Customers don't put as much trust in them when they can't speak well and they say, "You should get this"—a $60 pair of pants! Well, it doesn't make sense if you are not well spoken.

Michelle is here articulating the logic of aesthetic labor. According to this view, employees should be selected on the basis of style, sensibilities, and comportment—which are the cultural manifestations of social inequality. Bourdieu (1984) argues that individuals are conditioned by their particular location in a stratified society to think, act, and feel in certain ways. These dispositions seem like second nature and common sense once acquired, but the fact that they vary by social class is a clue that they are tied to social inequality. But Michelle does not think that she is expressing a social prejudice; she is merely making an aesthetic judgment. These workers do not "sound right" for Express; maybe they should work for Kmart. The consequence of her logic is to eliminate groups whose "styles" do not match the brand image—and thus to further entrench job segregation. Note that white consumers are implicated as the ultimate drivers of this practice. Michelle identifies with this consumer logic: as a white customer, she would not want to buy expensive pants from an African American salesclerk who does not sound right. From her point of view, the company is doing a disservice to itself by hiring workers who do not fit the brand.

The upscale stores in this study privilege whiteness, which is embedded in mainstream beauty standards. Workers who do not embody whiteness may be relegated to invisible jobs in the storeroom or, more likely, are not hired in the first place (Gruys 2012). For example, Sam is a thirty-one-year-old Latino who has worked off and on in the stockroom at Banana Republic for six years. When he first applied for the job, he imagined that his work would consist entirely of aesthetic labor. He said, "Basically, when I first started, I thought it was just a job where you stand and look pretty, just do nothing, help people around the store and tell them how to find what they need." But he was put in the stockroom instead. He explained, "I basically started as a stock associate. And I think part of the reason was because my English wasn't as good, although I thought it was. I think my English from El Paso versus Austin was so different, . . . and that's why I think they put me in the back at first and also because they needed someone to help keep it organized back there." The focus on aesthetic labor encourages workers to blame themselves and not their employers for discriminatory labor practices. In this way cultural style obscures the workings of power and domination (Bourdieu 1984). Instead of protesting illegal job discrimination, these workers censure themselves for not "fitting" the aesthetic requirements of the job.

Fetishism of Consumption

Aesthetic labor contributes a new twist on the *fetishism of commodities*, Marx's term to describe a social-psychological consequence of living in a money economy. Marx observed that in the movement from a subsistence economy to a market economy, useful goods and services were converted into commodities with specific exchange values attached. Marx thought that fetishism was the inevitable result of the commodity form: when capitalism puts a price on goods, it obscures the social relations of production. Buyers wrongly think that the exchange value or "price" that they pay for an object reflects the inherent value of the object, not the congealed labor that went into its production. This is what Marx means by *fetishism*: when *things*, and not people, are seen as the source of meaning and value (Osborne 2005; Wells 1998).

Under the aesthetic labor regime, labor itself is fetishized, adding another layer of obscurity to the social relations of production. The people who become upscale retail workers are part of what is purchased: they are hired to emblematize and convey to consumers the intended cultural meanings associated with the items in the store. From management's perspective, workers are ideally perceived as "brand representatives," chosen to personify the products on display; they are *not* supposed to look or sound like low-wage workers struggling to make a living. From the consumer's perspective, the workers naturally embody the brand and its meanings, reflecting the inherent value (and "coolness") of the products. Upscale retail stores depend on this mystification: consumers are not supposed to see the production of these workers or the labor processes that sort workers into particular jobs.

A second meaning of *fetishism* is derived from Freud (1927), who used the term to refer to the fixation of sexual desire on a particular part of the body, type of object, or kind of substance. The goal of many marketing campaigns is to convert commodities into sexual fetishes in order to cultivate consumer demand for them. Advertising, display, and design are used to attach particular meanings to objects so that they become must-have signifiers of consumers' identities.

Clearly, retail fetishism impacts consumers (Zukin 2005). Shoppers decide where to shop based on advertised images that are designed to incite desire and that obscure the social relations of production. Race, class, and gender divisions are used by marketers in crafting an image of their store and by managers selecting workers with the "right" appearance to staff the store. Shoppers who are privileged by their class and race buy into these distinctions—and reproduce them—when they decide to enter one store and not another; those lacking social privileges may get the message that they are not welcome in upscale stores at all (Williams 2006). As noted, shopping involves making distinctions such as appropriate or inappropriate, fashionable or tacky, or refined or banal, which, according to Bourdieu (1984), are culturally coded terms that reify economic inequalities. Those who shop at upscale stores may think that they are simply expressing their superior judgment and taste, but they are really announcing and legitimizing their place in a social hierarchy.

Retail fetishism impacts upscale retail workers as well. Many of our interviewees had been drawn to their employment because as consumers they closely identified with the brands. However, the fetishized images were quickly dispelled: after an initial flush of excitement, workers explained, the merchandise lost its luster. Some described becoming saturated and overwhelmed by their purchases. Vanessa at Victoria's Secret, for example, realized that there were only so many bras that she could possibly use, making her employee discount worthless to her. Kelly, who was originally very excited about working as a "model" for Abercrombie & Fitch, eventually became disillusioned by the brand:

> When people say, "Oh, you work at Abercrombie," I'm like, "Yeah, unfortunately."
>
> *Really?*
>
> I do not highly publicize or encourage other people to work at Abercrombie. I am probably the worst advertisement they have.
>
> *Are you cynical about it?*
>
> I've come to the point where I think this company is ridiculous. They make so much money. . . . They could afford to pay us at least $7 an hour! Like really, really. The company is very cheap. It is a cheap company. The quality of the clothing is awful. It is so bad. Like with sensors. When you put a sensor on a shirt, if you do not put it directly on the seam, it rips a hole. When you take that sensor off, it rips a hole in the shirt. Most of the time, I just fold the shirt up and put it in the bag.

After two years with the company, Kelly had grown accustomed to seeing new hires come in every week with great excitement, only to eventually develop the same cynicism she now feels. She made fun of one of her coworkers who still believed the myth: "He loves the job. He is all about Abercrombie. I'm like, 'Mario, this job is a joke.' He's like, 'No, it's not! It's my life!' No. You need to leave the company." Others became disillusioned by their working conditions, which rarely called upon their carefully cultivated middle-class sensibilities and instead subjected them to a high degree of surveillance, deadening routines, and typically despotic forms of managerial control.

Low-wage service workers today experience the "scientific management" techniques invented by Frederick Taylor in the nineteenth century to control the industrial proletariat. For instance, Peter, who has worked for nine years as the backroom manager at Barnes and Noble booksellers, said that many people apply to work in the store because they love books, only to be subjected to Taylorized labor practices: "There's a lot of turnover at Barnes and Noble, and I can understand that. Because really, it's not a good place to be. . . . A lot of people seem to apply there like, 'Oh, hey, it'd be fun to work at a bookstore; I love books!' but that's not what it's about." Part of Peter's job is to monitor the shelving rates of the associates, who face the corporate requirement to complete 9.73 shelves per hour—in his opinion a virtually impossible task. He claims that workers are actually penalized if they talk about books with customers: "Barnes and Noble takes out all of what used to be personal about the experience—taking the time to chit-chat it up, talk about what people are buying, like, 'Oh, hey, I love this book!' But now you don't have time to do that because you'll get a line [at your register] if you're talking. You're supposed to be busy selling things and talking about the membership card. . . . We have those secret shoppers that come around and are testing to make sure you say the magic words when you are ringing someone up." Peter maintains that as a result of the mismatch between workers' expectations and corporate procedures, only one of four people lasts through the first day on the job.

Thus, worker-consumers take bad jobs in order to get closer to the refined and sophisticated brands that they covet and enjoy, but once employed inside upscale stores, they encounter extreme Taylorism and working conditions no different than those at Wal-Mart or McDonald's. They are fooled by the same hypocrisy that fuels the fetishism of commodities. Upscale retailers claim to sell refined products made by expert craftspeople; instead, their stores are filled with items mass-produced in overseas sweatshops. Similarly, their stores are staffed with worker-consumers who "look good and sound right" yet are rarely allowed to express their highly cultivated tastes in fashion and design. Instead, worker-consumers are expected to quickly and uniformly shelve books, fold shirts, utter tag lines, sell membership cards, and operate cash registers—all under conditions of extreme surveillance.

The upscale retail workers we interviewed almost universally criticized the fetishism of the retail industry. Those who stayed in the industry, like Peter and Kelly, developed a cynical attitude toward consumerism generally. They are no longer the ideal worker-consumers coveted by the industry. Instead of identifying with the "coolness" of their store's brand, they have transitioned from "worker-consumer" to a more conventional "worker" status (as did those who moved to discount employers). Pay, regular hours, and benefits became more important to them than the employee discount. However, none of these workers expected to stay in retail employment. They either thought of their jobs as supplementing their true calling (such as motherhood in the case of Grace, who worked at the Learning Express, or art in Peter's case) or redefined their jobs as a temporary way-station until they finished their education or something better came along.

Although almost everyone we interviewed was critical of the fetishism they observed in upscale stores, no one protested this basic feature of the industry. Because consumer fetishism is ubiquitous, they conceded its inevitability, unable to imagine any alternative.

. . .

Aesthetic labor consists of the requirement that service workers "look good and sound right" for the job. In many upscale retail stores, the ideal aesthetic is middle-class, white, and conventionally gendered. Employees are selected on the basis of whether or not their comportment and demeanor match the national brand's image. Because the industry resolutely refuses to upgrade working conditions, employers seek other ways to find and attract workers who embody the right aesthetic qualities. Retailers with "cool" brands are successful at attracting workers because they appeal to their consumer interests.

The worker-consumers who staff these retail stores consent to work because they are highly identified with the brands they sell and because their jobs offer enticing employee discounts. However, they rarely last long in these jobs because of the degraded working conditions. But instead of protesting and fighting to upgrade the jobs—something that they could do since these "decommodified" workers do not depend on their jobs for their livelihoods—they distance themselves from retail work, dismissing it as an unrespectable form of employment. Retail employers profit from the resulting high turnover, especially if they can rely on a steady stream of replacement worker-consumers eager to be associated with their cool brand.

In addition to worker consent, highlighting the importance of aesthetics explains other features of the labor process in upscale retail employment. Aesthetic labor offers a justification for employment discrimination that blames the worker, not the employer, for sorting workers on the basis of gender, race, and class. Assigning nonwhite workers to the backroom renders their labor invisible while further privileging the whiteness embedded in conventional notions of attractiveness. Aesthetic labor also contributes to the fetishism of consumption. Hiring workers who embody the brand image adds to the mystification of commodities, attributing value and meaning to *things* while obscuring the unequal and unjust social relations that produce them.

Aesthetic labor is highly visible in upscale retail establishments. This chapter has revealed the invisible practices that result in workers who "look good and sound right" for their jobs and has shown how these practices contribute to the degraded conditions of retail employment. Under the guise of offering sophisticated and stylish products, the industry produces bad jobs with low pay, erratic hours, no autonomy, and no opportunities for career development. The aesthetic labor regime in upscale retail stores justifies discrimination on the basis of gender, race, and class. Furthermore, by selecting employees who put their consumer interests above their worker interests, the industry guarantees itself a docile labor force. High turnover is a cost that retailers willingly pay as long as their brand remains "cool," a judgment that guarantees them a steady stream of consumer-workers willing to provide them with cheap aesthetic labor.

These labor practices may be invisible, but they are not inevitable. In other countries retail work is not degraded labor (Andersson et al. 2011; Doussard 2013). Ironically, upgrading working conditions in this country could reduce the power of retailers to implement aesthetic labor regimes. Higher wages and better working conditions would attract and retain those who depend on their jobs for economic survival and would probably reduce the high turnover rates in the industry. Enforcing equal opportunity laws would result in a wider array of people hired for these jobs, making it harder for stores to articulate worker aesthetics with brand image. If workers no longer "matched" the store brands, this particular source of gender and racial stereotypes, job segregation, and the fetishism of consumption would be undermined—changes that could benefit society as a whole.

Customers in upscale stores have come to expect that the clerks where they shop will match the store brand. Our goal has been to reveal the invisible social organization that underlies this expectation and to debunk the mystification and reification upon which it relies. Aesthetic labor is premised on social inequality and commodity fetishism. Understanding its attractions as well as its dangers—for workers, consumers, and worker-consumers—is a critical first step toward improving the working conditions in low-wage retail employment.

NOTES

Revised version of Christine L. Williams and Catherine Connell, "Looking Good and Sounding Right: Aesthetic Labor and Social Inequality in the Retail Industry," *Work and Occupations* 37 (3) (August 2010): 349–77. Used with the permission of Sage Publications.

1. US Bureau of Labor Statistics, "Occupational Outlook Handbook: Retail Sales Workers," accessed October 20, 2014, www.bls.gov/ooh/sales /retail-sales-workers.htm. Our study was conducted when retail workers earned less than $10 per hour on average. (The US minimum wage was $5.85 per hour from 1997 to 2007; in 2009, it was raised to $7.25 per hour).

2. A&F may have been motivated to rename frontline job titles after a lawsuit charging it with discriminatory hiring practices (McBride 2005). The occupation of "model" may not be subject to equal employment law because, arguably, gender and race could be considered bona fide occupational qualifications for this job.

3. In contrast, the retail workers we interviewed who were employed at discount and luxury stores did rely on their wages to support themselves.

4. Vanessa left Victoria's Secret because of the scheduling issues mentioned earlier. Home Depot guaranteed her twenty hours in addition to raising her hourly pay. Her ambivalence about this new job is also tied to her changed status from "consumer-worker" to low-wage worker, a subject for another study.

5. Kjerstin Gruys (2012) argues that some upscale "plus size" clothing stores may prefer to hire African American women to match their customer demographic.

REFERENCES

Andersson, Thomas, Ali Kazemi, Stefan Tengblad, and Mikael Wickelgren. 2011. "Not the Inevitable Bleak House? The Positive Experiences of Workers and Managers in Retail Work in Sweden." Pp. 253–76 in *Retail Work,* edited by I. Grugulis and O. Bozkurt. Hampshire, England: Palgrave Macmillan.

Avery, Dianne, and Marion Crain. 2007. "Branded: Corporate Image, Sexual Stereotyping, and the New Face of Capitalism." *Duke Journal of Gender, Law, and Policy* 14 (1): 13–123.

Besen, Yasemin. 2006. "Exploitation or Fun? The Lived Experience of Teenage Employment in Suburban America." *Journal of Contemporary Ethnography* 35 (3): 319–40.

Bourdieu, Pierre. 1984. *Distinction: A Social Critique of the Judgment of Taste.* Translated by R. Nice. Cambridge, MA: Harvard University Press.

Doussard, Marc. 2013. *Degraded Work: The Struggle at the Bottom of the Labor Market.* Minneapolis: University of Minnesota Press.

Freud, Sigmund. 1927. "Fetishism." Pp. 147–57 in Vol. 21 of *The Complete Psychological Works of Sigmund Freud.* Translated by J. Strachey. London: Hogarth.

Gruys, Kjerstin. 2012. "Does This Make Me Look Fat? Aesthetic Labor and Fat Talk as Emotional Labor in a Women's Plus-Size Clothing Store." *Social Problems* 59: 481–500.

Hochschild, Arlie. 1983. *The Managed Heart: Commercialization of Human Feeling.* Berkeley: University of California Press.

Lambert, Susan. 2008. "Passing the Buck: Labor Flexibility Practices That Transfer Risk onto Hourly Workers." *Human Relations* 61: 1203–27.

Leidner, Robin. 1993. *Fast Food, Fast Talk: Service Work and the Routinization of Everyday Life.* Berkeley: University of California Press.

Leslie, Deborah. 2002. "Gender, Retail Employment and the Clothing Commodity Chain." *Gender, Place and Culture* 9 (1): 61–76.

McBride, Dwight A. 2005. *Why I Hate Abercrombie & Fitch: Essays on Race and Sexuality.* New York: New York University Press.

Osborne, Peter. 2005. *How to Read Marx.* New York: Norton.

Reskin, Barbara A., Debra B. McBrier, and Julie A. Kmec. 1999. "The Determinants and Consequences of Workplace Sex and Race Composition." *Annual Review of Sociology* 25: 335–61.

Schor, Juliet. 1998. *The Overspent American: Why We Want What We Don't Need.* New York: Harper Perennial.

Wells, David. 1998. *Consumerism and the Movement of Housewives into Wage Work.* Aldershot, England: Ashgate.

West, Candace, and Don Zimmerman. 1987. "Doing Gender." *Gender & Society* 1: 125–51.

Wolkowitz, Carol. 2006. *Bodies at Work.* London: Sage.

Williams, Christine L. 2006. *Inside Toyland: Working, Shopping, and Social Inequality.* Berkeley: University of California Press.

Wright, David. 2005. "Mediating Production and Consumption: Cultural Capital and Cultural Workers. *British Journal of Sociology* 56 (1): 105–21.

Zukin, Sharon. 2005. *Point of Purchase: How Shopping Changed American Culture.* New York: Routledge.

CHAPTER 11

From Invisible Work to Invisible Workers

The Impact of Service Employers' Speech Demands on the Working Class

CHRIS WARHURST

This chapter examines how, through aesthetic labor, the body again becomes visible in analysis of work but how aesthetic labor also creates a new invisibility for the working class in service jobs. This development marks a shift in the debate about work and invisibility triggered by Arlene Daniels (1987) from a focus on the labor process to a focus on the labor market, and it extends the debate about invisibility from gender to class. It also raises new issues about the role of ascribed skill in creating these invisibilities.

The concept of *invisible work* was Daniels's attempt to explain how and why women's work was marginalized and undervalued. The problem, she stated, was that women's work occurs in the shadows of the private realm and is therefore "invisible": unobserved and uncredited. The skills that are acquired and used to undertake this work, even when transferred into the public realm within the expanding service economy, remain unappreciated, Daniels claimed. She illustrated this point by drawing on Arlie Hochschild's (1983) research on female air-cabin crew. Here workers used emotion-management skills to manage their own and customers' feelings in order to affect a favorable service encounter on behalf of the employer. However, because these jobs were held by women, these skills were regarded as "natural," "contribut[ing] to the idea that their work was less skilled—or that this part of their work should get less reward," Daniels (1987: 410) noted.

The strength of Daniels's argument was that it offered a cogent criticism of contemporary accounts of work, challenging the "folk" understanding of work as a public and formally remunerated activity. Daniels developed a new understanding of private and public sphere labor processes and the marginalization of women's work within these labor processes, challenging this naturalness argument about the skills used in women's work.

In some respects it is a timeless argument. Much of women's work has remained invisible, even as more of it has been transferred from the private to the public sphere within an expanding service economy (see Wolkowitz and Warhurst 2010). Much of it is literally "back-of-house"—as cleaners exemplify. Cleaning work is usually undertaken by women and in the case of hotels is a vital task. Nevertheless, hotel cleaners' work is organized so that contact with guests is minimal. One hotel executive housekeeper explicitly referred to her cleaners' invisibility: "I liken my staff to the elves in Harry Potter. . . . [B]eds are made, work is done, but no one sees anyone[.] [T]he majority of the work is done behind the scenes[,] and staff are more or less invisible" (from Hunter-Powell 2005, cited in Dutton et al. 2008: 97). These women and their work are intended to be unseen. One outcome of this invisibility, as Daniels might have predicted, is that room cleaners, already poorly paid, receive the lowest total remuneration in hotels because, unlike front-of-house hotel staff such as (typically male) valets, they do not receive tips. Guests forget that they exist and are, moreover, encouraged to forget them.

It was also an argument of its time. Emotional labor became the dominant paradigm for researching service jobs throughout the 1990s and early 2000s, and the focus on it raised the profile of skills involved in jobs typically undertaken by women. Sharon Bolton (2004) has even argued that emotion work is "highly skilled," and Ian Hampson and Ann Junor (2010) have been successful in having the emotional-management skills of some female-dominated service jobs recognized and rewarded, providing a useful template for evaluating the skills involved in these jobs. Consequently, there is now a lively debate about the nature of the skills involved in service jobs and the preferred and actual monetary value of these skills (e.g., Lloyd and Payne 2009).

In addition, the analytical lens through which service jobs are studied has recently changed, with emotional labor complemented by aesthetic labor (e.g., Witz, Warhurst, and Nickson 2003). If emotional labor foregrounds sentiments, aesthetic labor foregrounds the somatic, with the management of workers' corporeality now argued to be a feature of the employment relationship. Aesthetic labor involves the strategic use of this corporeality by employers and how and why they intervene to control and transmute this corporeality. While employer awareness of the commercial benefits of workers' corporeality is not new (Nickson et al. 2001), there seems to be a new, or at least more explicit, emphasis on employee appearance and its discipline (Wolkowitz 2006).

It would be wrong to assume that employers simply want employees who are "good looking"; just as important are employees with the "right look." Different employee "looks" produce different styles of service as companies target different market segments. Producing these styles is now regarded as a "skill" for employers.[1] Cast as a skill, the nature and site of this skill's formation have come under scrutiny, and Pierre Bourdieu's ([1984] 1998) concept of *habitus* usefully highlights the socialized nature rather than the naturalness of this putative skill. As socialization varies according to class, it follows that some workers acquire and others lack these skills and that "symbolic violence" occurs for some workers, particularly those from the working class. Consequently, discrimination and exclusion follow, rendering these workers invisible in the labor market.

These three issues—the demands of interactive service work, the importance of both the labor process and the labor market as analytical foci, and the nature of skill—bound this chapter. Through an examination of worker speech as part of aesthetic labor, the chapter reveals how the body is again made visible in interactive services but how employers' speech demands discriminate and exclude some workers, creating a new invisibility.

THE BODY AT WORK: NOW YOU SEE IT, NOW YOU DON'T

The visibility of the body was once a key issue. As part of the Industrial Revolution, employers needed to physically take workers out of homes and fields and put them into the mines, mills, and new factories in order to exert greater control over the labor of these bodies (e.g., Thompson 1967). Once there, with "overseers" installed, those bodies could be made to work longer or harder in order to be more productive and so enable employers to be more competitive.

As work became longer or harder, the physical impact on workers' bodies became a concern. For example, in the U.S. steel mills of the early twentieth century, exhausting work, heat fumes, and danger were endemic. In one mill almost a quarter of immigrant workers were injured or killed each year (Brody 1960). In what are now termed the "advanced economies," the worst ravages of work have been ameliorated through preventive interventions driven by religious moralists, organized labor, and supportive governments. Consequently, the physical toll on workers' bodies was progressively mitigated in the twentieth century. Accidents and injuries still occur, of course, but headline cases such as the 2013 Rana Plaza garment factory collapse in Bangladesh that killed more than 1,100 workers tend to occur in the newly industrializing countries (NICs). These countries' approaches to health and safety echo those of the now-advanced economies during their industrial revolutions, as the appellation *newly industrializing* suggests.

In the mid-twentieth century, the employment structure also began to change in the advanced economies: the primary and secondary sectors with their mining and manufacturing jobs shrank, with jobs displaced through overseas relocation (to the NICs) and the tertiary sector with its service jobs expanded. In the advanced economies, service jobs now dominate employment. With this shift, the nature of work also changed, with less manual and more mental labor. Daniel Bell (1973) articulated this change in his use of the metaphor of the *game*. Before the Industrial Revolution, the game in agriculture was between man and nature; in the industrial age, the game in factories was between man and machine. In the services-led, so-called postindustrial age, the new game is between people, Bell claimed.

During the 1990s and early 2000s, the dominant paradigm for studying such work—and a reference point in Daniels's argument about invisible work—was Hochschild's (1983) concept of *emotional labor*. Drawing mainly on research on female air-cabin crew, Hochschild noted how flight attendants had to manage their own and customers' feelings in order to facilitate a favorable service encounter for the employer. In terms of such work being game-like, Hochschild suggests that employees engage in deep or surface acting to pull off more or less convincing performances. More recently, focusing on retail work, Marek Korczynski (2005) has even claimed that employees now "enchant" customers with their sales patter.

Any residual health and safety issues in these "interactive service" jobs are less obvious—psychological, not physical—as research on job stress and burnout among workers illustrates (e.g., Schaubroeck and Jones 2000). These injuries tend to be hidden: less visible and less immediate. Rather than a crucial factor of production, the body only seems to have retained an analytical importance as a site of consumption (e.g., Bauman 1998). Such neat dichotomies can be overplayed, of course. Service workers also suffer physical injuries; hotel room cleaners can suffer back injuries (Dutton et al. 2008), and call center workers can lose their voices (Jones 2011). Nevertheless, although the body has continued to labor, it has disappeared from or at least been downgraded in analyses of work (Slavishak 2010; Muñoz de Bustillo et al. 2011, respectively).

However, and contrary to Bauman's claim, the service economy does commodify the body in production, not just in consumption. This point was first made by C. Wright Mills (1951) in his classic, *White Collar*. As the twentieth century was unfolding and services were becoming more prevalent, a "personality market" was emerging as well, he observed, in which workers sold their attitudes and appearance on the labor market to employers. This "personality" was important, Mills argued twenty years before Bell, because the shift to an economy of services involved not just a transition from manual to mental labor but also a transition in work—"from skills with things to skills with people" (p. 182). However, at this time, with the management of customer service still embryonic, employers' actions were typically limited to the hiring of employees with appropriate appearances. Once they had been hired, employers left these employees to self-determine, develop, and mobilize their appearance in work. In other words, workers' appearances remained a labor-market, not a labor-process, issue for employers, and Mills quickly dropped analysis of appearance in further discussions of the personality market.

Thirty years later, Hochschild (1983) picked up on Mills's point, also arguing in *The Managed Heart* that workers' personalities were being bought and sold on the labor market. She also noticed, however, that employers were now trying to manage that personality in work. Workers' personalities were thus no longer only a labor market issue but also now a labor process issue. This new focus explains emotional labor. With employees now recognized as part of the product being offered, they are required to manage their own feelings as well as the feelings of customers in order to deliver the managerially prescribed service encounter. Interestingly, Hochschild has pointed out that women are overrepresented in jobs that demand emotional labor and even "specialise in emotional labour" (p. 20). This specialization occurs, she argues, because "women are more accomplished managers of feeling" (p. 11), with gender a "determinant" (p. 20) of the skill required to manage feelings.

A counterargument made by Daniels (1987) is that these skills only appear to be natural; they are in fact developed by women through socialization. In family, friendship, and workplace settings, women "are trained in these skills. . . . [By] watching out for hesitances, likes, and dislikes of others in the social setting and trying to accommodate them[,] . . . these behaviours become habitual" (p. 14). In other words, the capacity for emotional labor is not natural to women; rather, it is acquired through informal learning. As discussed next, what Daniels is describing is "habitus" without Bourdieu ([1984] 1998)—something that was not uncommon at the time of Daniels's writing (see, as another example, Willis 1977).

As with Mills before her, Hochschild initially flagged the appearance of workers as part of this personality. As her core definition highlights, emotional labor involves "the management of emotion to create publicly observable facial and bodily display" (p. 7). As she acknowledged, the body is used "to show feeling" (p. 247n2). Body language is the outward indicator of feeling; it is the bodily expression—the smile to indicate friendliness, for example. In referring to this display work, however, as Mills did before her, Hochschild did not pursue further analysis of worker appearance. In her case, however, the reason differs. Hochschild's explicit aim was to foreground emotion in work and emotion work as a feature of the employment relationship. What she wanted to emphasize was that, as part of their surplus generating strategies, employers required that emotional labor be "sold for a wage and therefore [have] exchange value" (p. 7).

BRINGING THE BODY BACK INTO
THE ANALYSIS OF (SERVICE) WORK

Once a key issue, the body was thus analytically retired in the study of work by the end of the twentieth century. To rectify this oversight, aesthetic labor explicitly attempts to make visible again the body at work. If emotional labor focused on the management of workers' feelings as a feature of the employment relationship, aesthetic labor focuses on the management of workers' corporeality. Aesthetic labor highlights how interactive service work is "embodied work," with employees' bodies being organizationally "made up" to embody the desired identity of the organization (Witz, Warhurst, and Nickson 2003). Significantly, its focus is the work on the bodies of service workers rather than service workers' work on others' bodies. This latter focus is exemplified by Carol Wolkowitz's (2006) "body work" and Miliann Kang's (2010) "body labor" with their examples of medical doctors and nail salon manicurists, respectively.

The existence of aesthetic labor in services is not new, but it has become a deliberate employer strategy in recent years (Nickson et al. 2001). It has four features: first, it occurs within the service encounter involving interaction between employee and customer; second, it involves the management of employee corporeality by both the employee and employer to, third, positively affect customer or client perceptions or senses (hence "aesthetic labor") of the organization; and fourth, it is a feature of the wage–effort bargain between employee and employer. Employees are hired because of the way they look and talk; once employed, workers are instructed in how to stand while working, what to wear and how to wear it, and even what words to say to customers. Such comportment, dress, and language are intended to create a favorable service encounter that employers anticipate will generate new and repeat customers.

As employers mobilize, develop, and commodify workers' embodied dispositions through processes of recruitment and selection, training, and monitoring, these dispositions are recast as "skills" that are geared toward producing a style of service encounter that appeals to the senses of the customer. Following corporate branding expert Wally Olins (1991), aesthetic labor helps organizations create organizational distinctiveness through this identity or "style," "making the organization appear unique" (p. 75), and thus it is a commercial tool for private sector organizations "to make greater profit out of what they do" (p. 53). As its shipyards have closed, Glasgow has sought to reinvent itself as a shopping and short-break holiday destination. In a survey of the city's retail and hospitality employers that I conducted with colleagues, 82 percent of employers had policies and codes to prescribe employee appearance in order to establish and maintain a corporate image. These polices included the obvious dress codes but extended to makeup and/ or grooming for male and female employees and hair length and style (Nickson, Warhurst, and Dutton 2005).

As employers recast the management of corporeality (and feelings, see Bolton 2004) as a "skill," conceptualization of *skill* has broadened to include personal capacities and attributes (Grugulis, Warhurst, and Keep 2004). For example, a study of one hundred human resources professionals in the United States responsible for making hiring decisions for frontline hospitality jobs revealed that "pride in appearance" and "good attitude" were the top two employer skill demands (Martin and Grove 2002). The former encapsulates aesthetic labor; the latter, emotional labor.

Resonating with the point made by Daniels about emotional labor, the "skills" involved in aesthetic labor might be more accurately characterized as "habitus." Pierre Bourdieu seeks to explain how the individual is socialized and how the social is individualized. For Bourdieu ([1984] 1998), the body is a form of physical capital. It is both biological and social, and through the latter it acquires symbolic value. Key to understanding physical capital is habitus. *Habitus* are embodied dispositions that result in ways of being in and seeing the world and that are expressed in speech, body language, and dress. Habitus are produced by "conditions of existence," conditioned through familial socialization and "internalized as a second nature," and they produce ways of being in the world (pp. 170, 53). Individuals gain mastery of practice without knowingly engaging it; such mastery simply becomes akin to techniques of the body. Although Bourdieu's focus was social reproduction—that is, class—habitus, or embodied dispositions, are utilized with aesthetic labor for organizational reproduction.

That gender is a feature of aesthetic labor is not a surprise, particularly in respect to the sexualization of service work (Warhurst and Nickson 2009), and as with research on emotional labor before it, some research on aesthetic labor is keen to make the link between it and feminized performativity (e.g., Pettinger 2005). However, the fact that aesthetic labor applies to female workers might simply reflect the fact that the occupations thus far typically studied by researchers of aesthetic labor, such as retail and hospitality, mainly employ women (e.g., Warhurst and Nickson 2007; Williams and Connell 2010).[2] Nevertheless, these industries are employing more men, particularly young men studying at college. In addition, there is now a sex balance among women and men undertaking vocational training for the retail and hospitality industries in the United Kingdom. As such, the embodiment of interactive service work envelops male and female workers (Walls 2008). Claims of *lookism*—or employment discrimination based on looks—are a useful proxy for this development. Findings from research on one of the few jurisdictions to have anti-lookism legislation, the state of Victoria, Australia, reveal, as expected, that most claims of lookism were made by female workers in interactive services. However, claims were also made by male workers in these services, and in recent years the proportion of men making claims of lookism has grown relative to that of women (Warhurst et al. 2011).

The point is that many employees of both sexes now have to look good and sound right as part of getting and doing work in interactive services, as research on jobs in retail, hospitality, and call centers illustrates (e.g., Bain 2001; Hall and van den Broek 2012; Poster 2007; Warhurst and Nickson 2001; Warhurst and Nickson 2007; Williams and Connell 2010).

WAR OF THE WORDS

With habitus, the social is inscribed onto the individual. Thus, while habitus is manifest individually, it is at the same time collective. It is also socially differentiated and differentiating, denoting a particular position, such as a class. Consequently, habitus vary according to class "because different conditions of existence produce different habitus" (Bourdieu [1984] 1998: 170). Habitus is both a "structuring structure" (akin to a sorting mechanism) and a "structured structure" (providing a fixed point of reference) (p. 170). Speech encompasses what we say and how we say it. Even using the same language, there are different ways to speak. How we speak is a feature of habitus. It is learned in childhood, affected primarily by familial socialization but also by education. It is literally embodied: speaking in different ways requires different bodily uses—jaw, lip, and throat movements (Honey 1989). Importantly, speech does not just create habitus; it is an indicator of it. Knowing what to say and how to say it establishes membership of a position. What we say and how we say it contribute to our identity and sort us into types of people. Speech helps constitute an "us" and a "them." It is the most obvious indicator of social class, according to Fox (2004): "Your accent and terminology reveal the class that you are born into and raised in. . . . And whatever you do accomplish, your position on the class scale will always be identifiable by your speech . . . unless you painstakingly train yourself to use the pronunciation and vocabulary of a different class" (p. 82). As Halsey (quoted in Honey 1989) noted, that speech brands the tongue of every child.

It was the Norman invasion of England in 1066 that shaped the linguistic landscape of Britain. With that invasion two languages collided, and two linguistic codes were created that distinguished users into socially superior and subordinate. Norman French was established as the "polite language" of the ruling class. Those speaking French "felt distinctly superior to . . . fellow-islanders, the Celts" (Gillingham 2009: 75). This power-loaded linguistic distinction remains. Some of the words used in U.K. English today appear interchangeable but have subtle social differences that can be traced back to this Francofication. A meeting can "start" (Old English) or "commence" (French), with the latter term carrying "a touch more cultural clout," according to Melvin Bragg (2003: 59). By the early Middle Ages, *Received Pronunciation* (RP, or Standard English) was indicative of the ruling class—the language spoken by the court, the landed gentry, their administrators, and the professors of the ancient universities—and "became a tool for snobs, and a useful ally for hierarchs," says Bragg (p. 234). The expansion of university education in the nineteenth century helped diffuse Standard English, and into the twentieth century it became the "educated accent." University-educated teachers then went to work in state (publicly funded) schools and tried to impose Standard English on all pupils, though with varying success, as residual class—and regional—accents demonstrate in the United Kingdom.

WORDS AT WORK

In scholarly work, references to aesthetic labor often take the shorthand form by mentioning employees' "looking good and sounding right," but the latter attribute has received less attention. This bias is not surprising. Since the Enlightenment, there has been a "visual hegemony in the Western sensorium," according to C.M. Gurney and F. Hines (1999: 5). Western society thinks visually rather than aurally and is dominated by the eye. Thus, with respect to aesthetic labor, employers' attempts to appeal to customers' visual senses are more usual, and most research on aesthetic labor tends to focus on employees' looks. Nevertheless, with aesthetic labor, Elizabeth Eustace (2012) believes that speech is becoming commodified, also being recast as a "skill" by employers to be deployed in the services encounter for commercial benefit. Fortunately, there is now an emerging body of research that explicitly examines the management of speech—for example, in call centers (e.g., Poster 2007).

Employers are aware that the spoken word can affect customer perceptions. Speech is the "verbal presentation" of the organization, explained one employer, and "can be pivotal to business success" (quoted in Ward 2000: 6). Along with dress and body language, employee speech projects an organization's identity and can create symbolic capital and profit for organizations. Consequently, organizations want employees with speech that appeals positively to customers (Schneider and Bowen 1995). Therefore, employers attempt to proscribe and prescribe employee speech. Workers' knowing what to say and how to say it—or being told by management what to say and how to say it—is assumed by employers to generate a positive service encounter. As one consultant commented in a report by the Institute of Personnel and Development:[3] "People in front-of-house positions, from telephonists to account managers[,] are therefore expected to speak, as well as dress, in a particular way" (quoted in Younge 1997: 5). As a focus group participant stated in research that I undertook with colleagues: "If their voice is right, they can sell the product; that's what the company is looking for." In a survey of fashion retail in Manchester that we conducted, more than 27 percent of employers cited voice and accent as very important or essential in work that involves interacting with customers (Nickson et al. 2012).

The linguistic demands made on employees in terms of what they say and how they say it are based on a hierarchy and a belief that some ways of speaking are better than others. In the same way that children are socially branded by their tongues, employee speech helps brand companies. The prescribed speech is believed by employers to be more appropriate to good customer service generally and can also help define and promote a particular type of service by companies.

A good example of the proscription and prescription of speech is provided by Peter Bain's (2001) research of call centers in the United States. It reveals that these U.S. companies, which serve the domestic market, prefer to locate in states where the workforce is perceived "not to have an accent" (p. 13). To create jobs, Birmingham, Alabama, was keen to attract call centers. Training was provided "cost free" to employers and focused on basic work discipline such as punctuality and attendance but also on "non-accent training." This speech training was regarded as particularly important because the local Alabama accent is perceived elsewhere in the United States as "dumb," so workers needed to tone down their local accents, according to Bain.

In other call center research, Deborah Cameron (2000) similarly notes that employers want to produce a style of service by regulating employee speech and push to ensure "the valorization of a speech style" (p. 328). Because she is working within the emotional labor paradigm, Cameron equates such style with expressiveness, caring, empathy, and sincerity and suggests that this style is popularly aligned with the speech of women. However, recent research examining speech as part of aesthetic labor highlights how both sexes are required to manage their speech to appeal to customers' aural senses and help support the identity or brand of the employer. One such example is Anil, a male call-center agent based in India who fields customer calls for U.S. firms. He too relates how his employer requires him to manage his speech in his customer interactions (Poster 2007). Employers prescribe speech and seek to ensure that these prescriptions are followed because, referring back to marketing-speak, what is said and how it is said are affecting, differentiating, and value adding.

This point about speech's helping to shape and project a style of service is important. Companies have different styles of service and want to match product-marketing strategies with their labor market hires. In her research on emotional labor, Hochschild (1983) noted how different emotion work evokes different styles of service. These included the "girl next door" and "sophisticated" styles. What is often overlooked is that, although Hochschild described a number of different service styles among the airlines she studied, all of these styles involve employer-demanded "middle class sociability" (p. 97). The same occurs with aesthetic labor. Different speech aligns with different styles of service, yet overall, employers prefer speech that evokes middle-classness.

In one of the Glasgow focus groups that I conducted with colleagues (Warhurst and Nickson 2015), a retail employee working at an upscale designer fashion retailer selling to affluent customers explained how there was a list of proscribed and prescribed words when talking to customers and describing outfits. "You weren't allowed to say 'nice' or 'lovely.' You had to say that's 'exquisite,' that's 'glamorous.' You have to say 'fabric' and not 'material' and it's 'luxurious,'" said her colleague. The first employee then explained, "There's a type of customer who would really like that language" (quoted in Warhurst and Nickson 2016). Linking back to Bragg's point about how words denote and enforce hierarchy, prescribing words such as *exquisite* and proscribing words such as the more prosaic *lovely* reflect the class bias buried in language: *exquisite* has Latin (Norman) origins, and *lovely* is Old English (Celtic), thus they respectively denote upper or middle class and working class.

BEING RENDERED INVISIBLE

This attempt to eradicate working-class speech is symptomatic of a wider development: a gentrification of service style is occurring, and it is linked to a broader gentrification of skill. The latter development creates a new invisibility as the working class becomes overlooked in the labor market for what are, using standard United Kingdom occupational classifications (e.g., SOC2010),[4] working-class jobs such as those in retail and hospitality.

As Bourdieu ([1984] 1998) explains, speech defines and assigns value. Those individuals with positional power seek to impose their style of speech. For Bourdieu, aesthetic sensibilities (or tastes) align with class position and interests, making distinctions between what is regarded as "the beautiful and the ugly, the distinguished and the vulgar" (p. 6). Bourdieu's analysis is not particularly novel. Basil Bernstein (2003) also noted that the working and middle classes have different linguistic codes, even when speaking the same language. Bernstein also noted that these codes are shaped by power relations and that what becomes the standard does so because of asymmetries of power.

For example, those university-educated teachers imposed Standard English on their pupils, as one of Eustace's (2012) hospitality workers explained—and hated—when she reflected on how her schoolteachers had tried to force her to drop her working-class Glaswegian accent because it was deemed "bad English" and in need of correction. At work the same demand occurs, with middle-class speech required. As another Glasgow hospitality employee explained, "You get waitresses [who] instead of saying 'potatoes,' they'll say 'tatties'" (quoted in Warhurst and Nickson 2016). In this case, the workers' slang was not acceptable. "It's the way you speak that's most important," said a retail employee. "It's all part of the sale," her colleague continued (quoted in Warhurst and Nickson 2016).

What Bourdieu adds is recognition that this power can be obscured by the normality of language and the unconscious incorporation of the disempowered into the code's reproduction (Hanks 2005). However, habitus do not just socially classify; what Bourdieu calls *symbolic violence* acts to produce and maintain social hierarchy and inequality, imposing one taste over another. This violence is not physical but rather social, with some people treated as inferior and denied access to resources as a consequence. It is subtle and internalized by individuals through everyday practices: "something you absorb like air" and so a "more effective, and (in some instances) more brutal means of oppression" (Bourdieu with Eagleton 1992: 115). Two processes underpin this violence. First, it is not obvious that it is being executed; as Bragg (2003) says about class, it is buried in language. Second, it is executed with individuals' complicity; it seems "natural."

This inferior treatment and denial of access to resources occur to the working class with aesthetic labor. Aesthetic labor is not simply about workers having good looks but about having the *right* look—and the right speech. The intensity of aesthetic labor can vary, depending upon the marketing strategy of companies (Hall and van den Broek 2012). Although having demonstration effects on other service organizations, showing them what might be done, aesthetic labor's more developed form occurs in organizations operating in upscale product markets—the style bars, cafes, restaurants, and designer retailers identified in the original Glasgow study. In these organizations employers seek employees who "fit" the organizational identity (Warhurst et al. 2000). Only those employees who have the right habitus—more specifically, "middle-classness"—are likely to be hired. For example, a new boutique hotel that opened in Glasgow advertised for waitstaff not in the local evening newspaper, as might have hitherto been expected for working-class jobs, but in the national *Sunday Times* with its middle-class readership (Nickson et al. 2001). Job applicants who telephoned the hotel were asked a number of questions about themselves; these were the usual casual questions about what they were doing at the moment, what work experience they had, and so on. It was, the personnel manager said, "a general chat." However, it was not just what the callers said but how they said it that mattered. "They had to have the correct tone and a nice voice, nice manner, well spoken," she explained (Nickson et al. 2001:180). In practice, the telephone chats enabled the hotel to screen out callers from the lower social classes. "We didn't want someone who spoke in a guttural manner," the manager said (p. 180). This eradication of working-class speech evokes the "verbal hygiene practices" of employers in the hospitality industry noted elsewhere by Eustace (2012).

With this gentrification of skill, being middle-class means having the right skills. Often this middle-classness is hired through the employment of university students. (Interestingly, after recruitment at the new Glasgow hotel, the typical waitstaff worker was in her twenties, well traveled, and a graduate [Nickson et al. 2001]). In this way, the middle class, and middle-class youth in particular, is now colonizing working-class jobs and displacing the working class from those jobs (see also Dutton et al. 2005; Hofman and Steijn 2003; and Williams and Connell 2010). Being working-class means having a skill deficit, and although these jobs are putatively working-class, employers justify not employing the working class in these retail and hospitality jobs because of this perceived deficit. For example, in the boom before the latest global economic downturn, employers in Glasgow, particularly those in the retail and hospitality industries, had recruitment difficulties, with thousands of unfilled jobs (Holland 2000). At the same time, the city had pockets of high unemployment among the working class, often in walk-to-work distance of these employers. In such situations members of the working class suffer symbolic violence; their habitus—recast as a skill set—are deemed inferior, rendering them invisible in the labor market. In policy parlance, they are "socially excluded."

. . .

With the shift from manufacturing to services and with changes in the health and safety impacts of work, the body slipped off the analytical radar. Of course the body was—and is—always present in labor; it just became invisible: it has a hidden presence. As analytical interest in services became dominated by Hochschild's concept of *emotional labor,* Daniels and others were articulating their concern about the rendering of women's work as invisible in the labor process. Yet even as Daniels, through Hochschild and emotional labor, was explaining how and why women's work was invisible in services in the public sphere, emotional labor was contributing to the analytical invisibility of the body in work.

The body's presence is analytically revealed again through aesthetic labor, which again foregrounds workers' corporeality. With aesthetic labor, the embodied work in services becomes salient. This embodied work, aesthetic labor also highlights, is necessary in workers both performing and getting service jobs. As such, aesthetic labor is both a labor process and a labor market issue. Workers without the right aesthetic appeal, as determined by employers, are excluded from these jobs, creating a new invisibility, this time in the labor market. With employers regarding middle-classness as a key feature of the skills required of aesthetic labor, it is the working class who are discriminated against and excluded. Indeed, following Bourdieu, working-classness suffers symbolic violence by being treated as inferior, with the working class being denied access to an important resource—jobs—and to the type of jobs that are, ironically, classified as working-class jobs. As the exposition of speech as part of aesthetic labor demonstrated, although members of the working class have speech, they are not heard in the labor market.

Thus, if the older—though still continuing—invisible *work* articulated by Daniels centered on gender, this new invisibility—of *workers*—centers on class. This shift is poignant. As the chapter's opening discussion indicated, Hochshild's concept of *emotional labor* was the dominant paradigm for studying service jobs for almost twenty years and contributed enormously to debate and research on gender and skill. Although there is some, though relatively less, debate and research on race and skill, the issue of class and skill is relatively ignored. It is interesting to note that the initial formulation of "intersectionality" included only gender and race in its attempt to explain labor market "sorting" and discrimination (Crenshaw 1989).[5] This importance still stands: race-centered speech can also create worker invisibility, as the example of Chicana lawyers in the United States highlights (García-López 2008). Nevertheless, although insightful, this analytical pairing of gender and race needs to be expanded to incorporate other disadvantaged groups (cf. Poster 2002).

There are three accounts of skill: that which resides with the person, that which relates to the job, and that which is socially constructed (Grugulis, Warhurst, and Keep 2004). The first two accounts rely on *achieved* skill—that is, formalized education and training leading to publicly accredited qualifications. The third account argues that skill and that what is classified as a skill are the outcome of a political process. If in the past (male) employees organized to have themselves classified as skilled, now it is employers who determine what is a skill (Warhurst, Tilly, and Gatta 2015): whatever employers in the Anglo-Saxon economies say is a skill is a skill (see Lafer 2004). In other words, U.S. and U.K. employers no longer equate skill with qualification. This shift has occurred with the rise of the service economy, the decline of trade unions, and a swing in the balance of power within the employment relationship in favor of capital. In service jobs, workers' productive value tends to be aligned with *ascribed,* rather than achieved, skills, with socialization rather than education the source of skill formation (Goldthorpe 2003; Nickson, Warhurst, and Dutton 2005)—or with what was once thought of as simply "personality " (Grugulis, Warhurst, and Keep 2004). What is also significant about employers' strategic use of aesthetic labor is how these ascribed skills are more readily associated with middle-classness.

Already having restricted access to achieved skill, the working class continues to lose out in the shift by employers to ascribed skills. Previously classified, hierarchicalized, and discriminated against by achieved skill, the working class continues to be classified, hierarchicalized, and discriminated against with ascribed skills. The danger is that some sections of the working class already at the bottom of the pile now become excluded from the labor market. Moreover, for the "unskilled" working class, exclusion from the labor market has become a personal problem, with the victims being blamed and becoming the point of remedial policy intervention. Policy makers worry that the working classes have a skills deficit. If, with ascribed skills, skill formation is no longer an outcome of education but, as Goldthorpe (2003) notes, of socialization, then responsibility for skills development lies with the family, and blame for workers being unskilled rests with bad parenting. Their children are economically disabled, Larry Elliott, economic editor of the *Guardian* says, because "working-class people are sort of seen as a problem. They drink too much, they smoke too much, they don't look after their kids properly, they're feckless, [and] they're work-shy" (quoted in Jones 2011: 86). Owen Jones ably counters such views, and any understanding of employability in the labor market requires a factoring in of both supply and demand in the labor market (Nickson et al. 2012). Nevertheless, there is a tendency ("probability" in the language of economists) for class attitudes and behaviors, including those related to work, to be transmitted from parents to children across all classes (Bourdieu [1984] 1998). What is different now is that responsibility for working-class employability is shifted onto the working-class individuals themselves and their personal behavior—it is they, not employers, who are seen as the problem.

The issue is what, if anything, could or should be done to address this problem—in short, whether intervention is needed. One position is that it is not needed because the market deals with the problem. Virginia Postrel (2003: 130) takes this approach in her *New York Times* bestseller *The Substance of Style*. Making reference to aesthetic labor, she argues that workers' appearance is a legitimate criterion of employment: "If a charming or intelligent person can have an edge in the job market, why not a handsome or stylish one?" she asks (p. 130). While employers and employees should have freedom of expression, employers should have the right to use employees' aesthetic appeal to create their desired organizational identity. Employees who fail to conform are disagreeable, unwilling to engage in give-and-take: "Forcing an employer to accept an unwanted [employee] style is . . . like forcing a newspaper to publish articles that disagree with its editorial viewpoint," Postrel says (p. 128). There is thus no need for regulatory intervention to prevent discrimination and exclusion on the basis of employee aesthetics.

Pro-interventionists would challenge this position and offer two alternatives (Warhurst, Tilly, and Gatta 2016). The first would be hard intervention through the law. Lookism, while seemingly widespread, is not a prohibited form of discrimination in the vast majority of countries (Rhode

2010). As noted earlier, one jurisdiction that does have an anti-lookism law is Victoria, Australia. As part of its Equal Opportunity Act 1995, which includes sex, race, and disability, among other areas, it is unlawful in Victoria to treat people unfairly or to discriminate against them because of their physical features. During the first ten years of the law's operation, lookism attracted 1,876 enquiries to the Victorian Equal Opportunity and Human Rights Commission, with its salience increasing by the end of this period, as measured by a rising number of enquiries about it to the commission from employees (Warhurst et al. 2011). Initially, immutable physical features such as disfigurement were the concern, but over time, mutable features such as dress have been included. Such laws currently center on employee looks. Even though application of the law has stretched to mutable features in Victoria, that it might stretch to include speech has yet to be tested, though speech is clearly emerging as a basis for discrimination by employers (Nickson et al. 2012).

The second would be soft intervention though training. Referring to the previously mentioned mismatch between employer recruitment difficulties and high unemployment among the working class in Glasgow, Nickson and colleagues (2003) contend that "a proportion of those jobs are likely to remain unfilled unless long-term unemployed people are equipped with aesthetic skills. Such jobs, such as hospitality, clearly demand employees to affect the appropriate role—required bodily dispositions, adopting 'masks for tasks' or simply 'surface acting,' and the unemployed should be aware of this need" (p. 11).

However, providing training to develop the aesthetic "skills" of unemployed members of the working class has been criticized by the tabloid press in the United Kingdom as an "Eliza Doolittle syndrome"—trying to make them something that they are not. Nevertheless, it should be remembered that it is flower-girl Eliza herself who seeks out this training in George Bernard Shaw's 1910 play *Pygmalion,* doing so in order to gain better employment and improve her life chances. By the end of the play, she has succeeded and, moreover, has literally found her voice—being able to challenge her overbearing linguist and voice coach Professor Henry Higgins (Shaw [1910] 2010). Similarly, the unemployed in Glasgow who participated in training to improve their voices and other self-presentation skills were encouraged to understand that it is acceptable to "speak in tongues"—i.e., use different speech when with their family and friends and when at work—so that they would feel comfortable with "code-switching," or alternating their style of speech to meet employers' aesthetic skill demands (cf. Rampton 1995).

Many such training programs also exist in the United States (Gatta 2014). While useful, they ultimately stop at encouraging marginalized groups of workers to code-switch to the dominant habitus. Warhurst and colleagues (2015) argue that policy makers need to do more: affirmative action is needed that preferentially places these groups into these programs; the training provided by the programs should also translate into achieved skills so that they might be better understood and valued by employers (cf. Hampson and Junor 2010). Without these interventions, the working class will continue to be invisible in the labor market, compounding the ongoing invisibility experienced by many women in the labor process. Doing so, of course, means that existing linguistic hegemony is maintained, but ultimately, members of the working class need to be able to make their own informed choices and have the resources to support those choices, as Eliza did, about developing their employability and, by extension, their life chances.

NOTES

1. This situation is more so in the liberal market economies, less so in the coordinated market economies, in which skill is more tightly coupled with qualification.

2. A similar point can be made for emotional labor; see Warhurst et al. (2011).

3. The forerunner of the CIPD (Chartered Institute of Personnel and Development) and the professional body in the United Kingdom for human resources professionals.

4. The United Kingdom's latest and internationally compatible Standard Occupational Classification; see www.ons.gov.uk/ons/guide-method/classifications /current-standard-classifications/soc2010/index.html.

5. The focus of this chapter is class. However, it is also clear that nationality might be added to the analysis as research reveals that some nationalities' speech is also suffering symbolic violence as services such as call centers globalize (see, for example, Poster 2007 and Nath 2011).

REFERENCES

Bain, Peter. 2001. "Some Sectoral and Locational Factors in the Development of Call Centres in the U.S.A. and the Netherlands." Occasional Paper 11, Department of Human Resource Management, University of Strathclyde, Glasgow, Scotland.

Bauman, Zygmunt. 1998. *Work, Consumerism, and the New Poor.* Buckingham, England: Open University Press.

Bell, Daniel. 1973. *The Coming of Post-Industrial Society.* New York: Basic Books.

Bernstein, Basil. 2003. *Class, Codes, and Control.* London: Routledge.

Bolton, Sharon. 2004. *Emotion Management in the Workplace.* London: Palgrave.

Bourdieu, Pierre. (1984) 1998. *Distinction.* Translated by Richard Nice. Reprint, London: Routledge.

Bourdieu, Pierre, with Terry Eagleton. 1992. "In Conversation: Doxa and Common Life." *New Left Review* 191: 111–22.

Bragg, Melvin. 2003. *The Adventure of English.* London: Sceptre.

Brody, David. 1960. *Steelworkers in America.* New York: Harper & Row.

Cameron, Deborah. 2000. "Styling the Worker: Gender and the Commodification of Language in the Globalized Service Economy." *Journal of Sociolinguistics* 4 (3): 323–47.

Crenshaw, Kimberlé. 1989. "Demarginalizing the Intersection of Race and Sex: A Black Feminist Critique of Antidiscrimination Doctrine." *University of Chicago Legal Forum* 140: 139–67.

Daniels, Arlene K. 1987. "Invisible Work." *Social Problems* 34 (5): 403–15.

Dutton, Eli, Chris Warhurst, Caroline Lloyd, Susan James, Johanna Commander, and Dennis Nickson. 2008. "Just Like the Elves in Harry Potter: Room Attendants in U.K. Hotels." Pp. 96–130 in *Low Wage Work in the U.K.,* edited by Caroline Lloyd, Geoff Mason, and Ken Mayhew. New York: Russell Sage Foundation.

Dutton, Eli, Chris Warhurst, Dennis Nickson, and Cliff Lockyer. 2005. "Lone Parents, the New Deal, and the Opportunities and Barriers to Retail Employment." *Policy Studies* 26 (1): 85–101.

Eustace, Elizabeth. 2012. "Speaking Allowed? Workplace Regulation of Regional Dialect." *Work, Employment, and Society* 26 (2): 331–48.

Fox, Kate. 2004. *Watching the English.* London: Hodder.

García-López, Gladys. 2008. "'Nunca Te Toman en Cuenta [They Never Take You into Account]': The Challenges of Inclusion and Strategies for Success of Chicana Attorneys." *Gender and Society* 22 (5): 590–612.

Gatta, Mary. 2014. *All I Want Is a Job!* Palo Alto, CA: Stanford University Press.

Gillingham, John. 2009. "The Beginnings of English Imperialism." Pp. 71–88 in *The North Atlantic Frontier of Medieval Europe,* edited by James Mudoon. Farnham, England: Ashgate.

Goldthorpe, John. 2003. *The Myth of Education-Based Meritocracy.* New Economy Series. London: Institute for Public Policy Research.

Grugulis, Irena, Chris Warhurst, and Ewart Keep. 2004. "What's Happening to 'Skill'?" Pp. 1–18 in *The Skills That Matter,* edited by Chris Warhurst, Irena Grugulis, and Ewart Keep. London: Palgrave.

Gurney, C.M., and F. Hines. 1999. "Rattle and Hum—Gendered Accounts of Noise as a Pollutant: An Aural Sociology of Work and Home." Paper presented at the British Sociological Association Conference, April 6–9, University of Glasgow, Scotland.

Hall, Richard, and Diane van den Broek. 2012. "Aestheticising Retail Workers: Orientations of Aesthetic Labour in Australian Fashion Retail." *Economic and Industrial Democracy* 33 (1): 85–102.

Hampson, Ian, and Ann Junor. 2010. "Putting the Process Back In: Rethinking Service Sector Skill." *Work, Employment, and Society* 24 (3): 526–45.

Hanks, William F. 2005. "Pierre Bourdieu and the Practices of Language." *Annual Review of Anthropology* 34: 67–83.

Hochschild, Arlie. 1983. *The Managed Heart.* Berkeley: University of California Press.

Hofman, W. H. A., and A. J. Steijn. 2003. "Students or Lower-Skilled Workers? 'Displacement' at the Bottom of the Labour Market.'" *Higher Education* 45 (2): 127–46.

Holland, C. 2000. "5500 Jobs That City Can't Fill." *Evening Times* (Glasgow, Scotland), January 24, pp. 1, 13.

Honey, John. 1989. *Does Accent Matter?* London: Faber and Faber.

Jones, Owen. 2011. *Chavs: The Demonization of the Working Class.* London: Verso.

Kang, Miliann. 2010. *The Managed Hand: Race, Gender, and the Body in Beauty Service Work.* Berkeley: University of California Press.

Korczynski, Marek. 2005. "The Point of Selling: Capitalism, Consumption, and Contradictions." *Organization* 12 (1): 69–88.

Lafer, Gordon. 2004. "What Is 'Skill'? Training for Discipline in the Low-Wage Labour Market." Pp. 109–27 in *The Skills That Matter,* edited by Chris Warhurst, Irena Grugulis, and Ewart Keep. London: Palgrave.

Lloyd, Caroline, and Jonathan Payne, 2009. "'Full of Sound and Fury, Signifying Nothing': Interrogating New Skill Concepts in Service Work—The View from Two U.K. Call Centres." *Work, Employment, and Society* 23 (4): 617–34.

Martin, Lynda, and Jim Grove. 2002. "Interview as a Selection Tool for Entry-Level Hospitality Employees." *Journal of Human Resources in Hospitality and Tourism* 1 (1): 41–44.

Mills, C. Wright. 1951. *White Collar.* New York: Oxford University Press.

Muñoz de Bustillo, Rafa, Enrique Fernández-Macías, Jose-Ignacio Antón, and Fernando Esteve. 2011. *Measuring More Than Money.* Cheltenham, England: Edward Elgar.

Nath, Vandana. 2011. "Aesthetic and Emotional Labour through Stigma: National Identity Management and Racial Abuse in Offshored Indian Call Centres." *Work, Employment, and Society* 25 (4): 709–25.

Nickson, Dennis, Chris Warhurst, Johanna Commander, Scott Hurrell, and Anne-Marie Cullen. 2012. "Soft Skills and Employability: Evidence from U.K. Retail." *Economic and Industrial Democracy* 33 (1): 56–84.

Nickson, Dennis, Chris Warhurst, Anne-Marie Cullen, and A. Watt. 2003. "Bringing in the Excluded? Aesthetic Labour, Skills, and Training in the New Economy." *Journal of Education and Work* 16 (2): 185–203.

Nickson, Dennis, Chris Warhurst, and Eli Dutton. 2005. "The Importance of Attitude and Appearance in the Service Encounter in Retail and Hospitality." *Managing Service Quality* 15 (2): 195–208.

Nickson, Dennis, Chris Warhurst, Anne Witz, and Anne-Marie Cullen. 2001. "The Importance of Being Aesthetic: Work, Employment, and Service Organization." Pp. 170–90 in *Customer Service: Empowerment and Entrapment,* edited by Andrew Sturdy, Irena Grugulis, and Hugh Wilmott. Basingstoke, England: Palgrave Macmillan.

Olins, Wally. 1991. *Corporate Identity.* London: Thames & Hudson.

Pettinger, Lynne. 2005. "Gendered Work Meets Gendered Goods: Selling and Service in Clothing Retail." *Gender, Work, and Organization* 12 (5): 460–78.

Poster, Winifred R. 2002. "Racialism, Sexuality, and Masculinity: Gendering 'Global Ethnography' of the Workplace." *Social Politics* (Spring): 126–58.

———. 2007. "Who's on the Line? Indian Call Center Agents Pose as Americans for U.S.-Outsourced Firms." *Industrial Relations* 46 (2): 271–304.

Postrel, Virginia. 2003. *The Substance of Style.* New York: HarperCollins.

Rampton, Ben. 1995. *Crossing: Language and Ethnicity among Adolescents.* London: Longman.

Rhode, Deborah L. 2010. *The Beauty Bias.* New York: Oxford University Press.

Schaubroeck, John, and James R. Jones. 2000. "Antecedents of Workplace Emotional Labor Dimensions and Moderators of Their Effects on Physical Symptoms." *Journal of Organizational Behavior* 21: 163–83.

Schneider, Benjamin, and David E. Bowen. 1995. *Winning the Service Game.* Watertown, MA: Harvard Business School Press.

Shaw, George Bernard. (1910) 2010. *Pygmalion.* Reprint, Camberwell, England: Penguin.

Slavishak, Ed. 2010. "'Made by the Work': A Century of Laboring Bodies in the United States." Pp. 147–63 in *The Body Reader,* edited by Lisa Jean Moore and Mary Kosut. New York: New York University Press.

Thompson, Edward Palmer. 1967. "Time, Work Discipline, and Industrial Capitalism." *Past and Present* 38: 55–97.

Walls, Stephen. 2008. "Are You Being Served? Gendered Aesthetics amongst Retail Workers." Doctoral thesis, Department of Sociology, University of Durham, Durham, England.

Ward, David. 2000. "Scousers Put the Accent on Success." *The Guardian,* September 22, p. 6.

Warhurst, Chris, and Dennis Nickson. 2001. *Looking Good, Sounding Right: Style Counselling and the Aesthetics of the New Economy.* London: Industrial Society.

———. 2007. "Employee Experience of Aesthetic Labour in Retail and Hospitality." *Work, Employment, and Society* 21 (1): 103–20.

———. 2009. "'Who's Got the Look?' Emotional, Aesthetic and Sexualized Labour in Interactive Services." *Gender, Work, and Organization* 16 (3): 385–404.

———. 2016. *Aesthetic Labour.* London: Sage.

Warhurst, Chris, Dennis Nickson, Anne Witz, and Anne-Marie Cullen. 2000. "Aesthetic Labour in Interactive Service Work: Some Case Study Evidence from the 'New' Glasgow." *Service Industries Journal* 20 (3): 1–18.

Warhurst, Chris, Chris Tilly, and Mary Gatta. 2016. "A New Social Construction of 'Skill.'" In *Oxford Handbook of Skills and Training*, edited by Chris Warhurst, K. Mayhew, D. Finegold, and J. Buchanan. Oxford, England: Oxford University Press.

Warhurst, Chris, Diane van den Broek, Richard Hall, and Dennis Nickson. 2011. "Heads, Hearts, and Now Bodies: Employee Looks and Lookism at Work." Pp. 122–40 in *The Future of Employment Relations—New Paradigms, New Developments*, edited by Adrian Wilkinson and Keith Townsend. Basingstoke, England: Palgrave Macmillan.

Williams, Christine, and Catherine Connell. 2010. "'Looking Good and Sounding Right': Aesthetic Labor and Social Inequality in the Retail Industry." *Work and Occupations* 37 (3): 349–77.

Willis, Paul. 1977. *Learning to Labour*. Westmead, England: Saxon House.

Witz, Anne, Chris Warhurst, and Dennis Nickson. 2003. "The Labour of Aesthetics and the Aesthetics of Organization." *Organization* 10 (1): 33–54.

Wolkowitz, Carol. 2006. *Bodies at Work*. London: Sage.

Wolkowitz, Carol, and Chris Warhurst. 2010. "Embodying Labour." Pp. 223–43 in *Working Life*, edited by Paul Thompson and Chris Smith. London: Palgrave.

Younge, Gary. 1997. "Ow to Talk Yerself out of a Job." *The Guardian*, January 2, p. 5.

PART FIVE

Branded and Consumed

CHAPTER 12

Self-Branding among Freelance Knowledge Workers

ADAM ARVIDSSON, ALESSANDRO GANDINI, AND
CAROLINA BANDINELLI

Self-branding has become a pervasive form of invisible labor in the information society. As what were once solid middle-class jobs are turned into freelance careers, knowledge workers are increasingly forced to sell themselves on the market. This process had already begun in the 1980s with upper-level managers as the new climate of flexibility and organizational restructuring drove managers to invest in reputation and brand as generalized assets that could be deployed and valorized when managers moved between organizations (Martin 2005). In the following decades, a combination of corporate restructuring, digital technologies that permitted more advanced means of outsourcing knowledge work, and a concomitant increase in the supply of skilled professionals—in particular, in the so-called creative industries—made self-branding a necessity for ever larger segments of the middle class (Arvidsson and Peitersen 2013). The shift toward the substitution of freelance careers for salaried employment is likely to intensify since advances in artificial intelligence and new digital technologies will permit the outsourcing of ever more advanced forms of knowledge work. IBM, for example, plans to reduce its salaried workforce by 70 percent by 2017 and at the same time increase its reliance on freelancers (Brynolfson and McAfee 2014; Peacock 2010). Indeed, to be able to sell oneself in a market is becoming something of a defining characteristic of contemporary selfhood (Gershon 2014).

Self-branding involves constructing a marketing proposition. This activity is a laborious process. As Alice Marwick (2013) has shown, urban freelancers invest a substantial number of hours and amount of energy tweeting, blogging, networking, and communicating on Facebook in order to create and maintain a viable brand. And this labor is largely invisible in the sense that it is not paid for, cannot be billed by freelancers, and generally is performed during time that is not accounted for: a *selfie* taken at the new trendy restaurant, a blog post written at night, a Facebook update made between time spent working on an Excel spreadsheet and on a Word document. The labor of self-branding is also invisible in the sense that this practice is rarely discussed or shared; it is simply something that one does as a matter of course, much like brushing one's teeth or working out at the gym. Self-branding is certainly a matter of working on the self, and as Arlie Hochschild (2012) describes in *The Outsourced Self*, it is work on the self that makes use of ready-made technologies and devices, from instruction manuals on self-branding to digital platforms like Facebook and Twitter that structure self-presentations in a certain way. It is, however, work on the self that is undertaken and directed by the *self* itself, and unlike the practices of corporate self-branding described in other chapters in this book (chapter 10, chapter 13), it does not directly follow templates imposed by an employer.

The fact that no one has dictated or is responsible for the conventions that govern self-branding does not mean that there are no conventions. As we will discuss, self-branding, even though supposedly a public presentation of the authentic values and qualities of an intimate self, tends to result in very standardized self-presentations. These standardized formats are related to the ways in which personal brands operate among freelance knowledge workers. Personal brands are not simply symbols or superficial packaging; nor are they merely a matter of distinct, and however authentic, personal identity. Rather, in the age of social media, personal brands have evolved into public entities, the values and contents of which are established in cooperation with others. The brand has become the means whereby the "self" can be rendered public, transparent, and measurable. As such, the brand can operate as an organizational device that gives direction and cohesion to social relations. In other words, the invisible labor of branding might—and this is a very hypothetical *might*—be in the process of being reappropriated by creative workers themselves as part of the construction of new forms of sociality.

In this chapter we draw on our ongoing research on freelance knowledge workers in London and Milan to discuss how such "public brands" operate within self-organized productive networks and how self-branding in its current usage points toward a different conception of value proper to such emerging networked models of organization.[1]

We suggest that since their origin as superficial symbols—perhaps the antithesis of ethics—brands, and in particular personal brands, are now becoming foundational devices for the realization of a new kind of ethics proper to the emerging modes of productive organization that knowledge workers promote.

KNOWLEDGE WORK AND CORPORATE CAPITAL

The category of *knowledge work* first emerged as part of the managerial revolution of the late nineteenth century. The emergence of large-scale state and industrial organizations created a demand for personnel skilled in the tasks of managing complex processes of productive cooperation. In its first incarnation, this "new class" was strongly tied to the bureaucratic ethos of the corporation. Up until World War II, the knowledge worker was conceived as a bureaucrat guided by the formal ethos of the bureaucratic office and devoted to the impersonal execution of a predefined job description. (In this sense the epitome of the prewar knowledge worker was Hannah Arendt's [1963] depiction of Adolf Eichmann blindly executing the evil of his job description *sine ira et studio*.)

While the notion of the new managerial stratum of knowledge workers as an amorphous mass, other-directed and devoid of an inner moral identity or sense of purpose, persisted in postwar American sociology, a different conception of knowledge work began to emerge from the managerial sciences. In the 1960s, this view was most clearly expressed in the revolutionary manifesto *The Human Side of Enterprise* (McGregor 1960). This vision emphasized the self-motivated nature of knowledge work and its resistance to imposed forms of bureaucratic command. Instead, Douglas McGregor proposed a "Theory Y," whereby efficient management of knowledge work was to be achieved by enabling individual motivations and organizational goals to coexist and not, as in the previous bureaucratic model, by letting the latter suppress the former. Peter Drucker (1967) made a similar point, suggesting that while manual work might be appropriately subjected to bureaucratic forms of management and measurement, knowledge work is by nature self-organizing and cannot be measured by similar standards. Most importantly, the knowledge worker cannot be supervised closely or in detail. She can only be helped, but she must direct herself (p. 4).

Since that time, managerial debates about knowledge work have centered on concepts like *teamwork, project management, postbureaucracy,* and *collaborative community.* A common theme has been that in a "knowledge economy," productive cooperation escapes the control of established corporate hierarchies and that what really creates value is the ability of knowledge workers to take charge of and organize their own forms of productive collaboration. At the same time, the tension between this self-organizing aspect of knowledge work—that is, knowledge workers' proclivity to form what Paul Adler and Charles Heckscher (2006) call a *collaborative community*—and the bureaucratic demands of corporate organizations was understood to be a constant source of individual frustration and a cause of organizational inefficiencies.

Outside of the workspace, the "new middle class" of knowledge workers was also viewed as proposing an alternative to the values and norms of industrial society. In the 1970s, sociologists and market researchers began identifying this class of "technocrats" (Touraine 1969), "knowledge workers" (Bell 1960), or "new cultural intermediaries" (Bourdieu 1979) both as carriers of new postmaterialist, individualized consumer needs centered around the concept of *lifestyle* and as the subjects behind a range of new social movements that politicized issues of sexuality, self-realization, and quality of life—what Ulrich Beck (1992) would later call "life politics."

In parallel with this mainstream articulation of an alternative within capitalism, a consumerist alternative composed of lifestyle experimentation and the championing of lifestyle-related political causes, the more radical and younger fringes of the knowledge working class began to experiment with autonomous modes of productive organization. In the 1980s and 1990s, hackers translated their inheritance of the 1970s subculture into new ways of organizing immaterial production, primarily of software (Turner 2010). In the burgeoning dance music scene, similar forms of productive organization were developed within the alternative entertainment sector that had sprung up in urban centers like London, Berlin, and New York (Reynolds 2012). These new models of productive organization would enter the mainstream during the dot-com boom of the 1990s as corporate actors threw cash at new media entrepreneurs with cultural origins in the urban undergrounds of the preceding decades, thus importing their modes of organization along with their cultural habitus first into the new media sector and later into the more mainstream corporate culture (Ross 2004). Indeed, the habitus of the new middle class of knowledge workers would be a driving inspiration for the "new spirit of capitalism" that had developed during the seventies, eighties, and nineties as a response to the struggles and contradictions that had become inherent in a declining industrial model. This new spirit placed an emphasis on creativity and self-realization as central to managerial thought (Boltanski and Chiapello 1999).

This cultural delinking of knowledge work from the values and organizational models of corporate capitalism was paralleled by a structural delinking of knowledge workers from their workplaces as corporate outsourcing and worker flexibility became key trends in the 1980s and 1990s. The extensive flexibility expected of the workforce resulted in a fragmented labor market and increasing levels of job precariousness with varying degrees of exploitation, and it undermined the established balance of work–life relations, particularly within the creative industries. With the outbreak of this crisis, a significant number of creative professionals found that their jobs had been outsourced or made redundant after budget cuts. Many were induced to switch to a freelance career in a competitive and individualized labor market.

In the creative industries, hiring freelancers has long been a cost-cutting option for employers. Although the overall cost of hiring staff on a temporary basis is generally higher in the short term, hiring freelancers represents an effective reduction of fixed costs for employment in the long run. Overall, freelancers offer the employer greater flexibility, a situation that meshes well with companies' increasing reliance on project-based management (Christopherson 2008).

But the precariousness of work situations and the development of a freelance economy do not result in only fragmentation. In our fieldwork in London and Milan, we have found that new ways of organizing knowledge work have emerged during the past decade. Whether based on physical coworking spaces supported by specific platforms like Elance that are dedicated to freelancers or based on more dispersed mediated networks of collaboration, such networked forms of organization are characterized by a diffused connectedness combined with a socialization of the process of value creation. By *diffused connectedness,* we mean that members of these networks might not interact with or know each other directly—that is, there are no, or low, levels of community—but the members might nevertheless seek out or contact each other for temporary collaborations or simply to exchange information or knowledge of job opportunities. One freelance worker might contact another to complement his skill base as required for a particular job or task, and this collaboration might remain temporary and evaporate once the task has been completed. This arrangement may be combined with the formation of formal organizational units that operate like firms. Participants of existing informal networks frequently unite in associations of freelancers in which various professionals assemble networks and skills of different kinds and gain a market position, branding themselves under a unique name. The peculiarity of such organizational arrangements consists in the establishment of organizational forms that may change from one project to another on the basis of specific requirements. Alternately, more permanent forms of cooperation—like coworking spaces—are organized formally or informally as full-service agencies in which incoming jobs are divided among members with diverse skills.

The point is that in these networked models of organization, freelance workers organize their own cooperative practices by drawing on what Marx called the "General Intellect" of their networks. The term *General Intellect* refers to the generalized knowledge and skills that are embedded in the productive environment. Marx ([1939] 1973) thought that this resource tended to become more important as a source of value and productivity as the economy grew more complex (p. 709). However, since the dynamic utilization of the General Intellect occurs in environments of diffused connectedness, productive cooperation poses the problem of how to generate the trust necessary to organize knowledge sharing when cooperating with strangers.

In day-to-day practice, these problems are solved through reputation systems. Freelancers choose to cooperate with and trust other freelancers on the basis of their reputations. Across informal networks, social media render public the image of the professional together with the visibility of his contacts and connections. This factor, in combination with referrals and recommendations, creates a situation in which reputation operates as a significant source of trust. Individuals whom one does not know can be selected on the basis of public knowledge and third-party endorsements. On digital platforms like Elance, where freelancers have public profiles and compete for publicly available jobs, reputation is quantified in various metrics on the basis of algorithms that calculate feedback and reviews to devise a score. Such reputation scores are important factors for the establishment of trust among strangers since interaction between freelancers and clients is mediated by the platform.

This scenario, combined with the prevalence of social media platforms, has rendered the activity of self-branding almost obligatory. As one freelancer whom we interviewed, a twenty-four-year-old male communication consultant in Milan, explained:

> Social media are fundamental, not simply for direct advantages. I don't generally get work directly from Facebook or LinkedIn, . . . but it's true that if I have to meet someone, I will look at the social networks. Maybe we are meeting because someone recommended you, or I met you somewhere, but social media are a portfolio and I want to know how you work. Through social media I look for information and I use them as a "shopping window" also on my side. If I have to work with you and I can't find you [on social media], I won't hire you.

Similarly, a thirty-seven-year-old male designer in London said: "If you want to be well known you need to write on blogs, write in magazines; these are good ways to establish yourself really fast. . . . I signed up for LinkedIn six years ago and then reactivated recently; I thought it was more corporate and stuff. . . . A lot of people contacted me from LinkedIn: 'Do I want this job? Do I want that job?'. . . People contacted me a lot from LinkedIn. You need to make yourself stand out in a way."

However, the combination of social media as a platform for organizing knowledge work and the development of new networked modes of organization has also changed the nature of personal brands. No longer primarily a packaging of the self, social media–based brands are now public representations and, to some extent, measures of an individual's ability to contribute positively to a group of peers.

THE EVOLUTION OF BRANDS

Self-branding became popular among knowledge workers with the onset of the new economy in the 1990s. Heralded by Tom Peters (1999) in his work *The Brand Called You,* self-branding was about signaling one's individual distinction within a knowledge economy marked by heightened competition, looser and more transitory forms of social relations—what Andreas Wittel (2001) calls "networked sociality"—and ever more generic skills. The consequence of skills becoming generic was in part due to an increased supply of university-educated knowledge workers. In part, it also resulted from the proliferation of computers and the Internet. New information and communication technologies rendered skills generic by incorporating them into software applications. For example, within the movie industry, shooting film and editing film were once skills that characterized distinct professions. Now these skills are both part of the generic profession of "filmmaker." Susan Christopherson (2008) illustrates this development well in her work on the Los Angeles film-making scene. She describes the replacement of older skilled craft workers by a new generation of flexible, generic workers who are the products of the enormous expansion of film and media education in the United States. In these programs, which have proliferated primarily in Los Angeles and New York, students learn a wide variety of production skills and are introduced to new technologies that cross conventional professional and craft boundaries. Christopherson explains, "They learn how to produce on 'shoestring' budgets and to work very rapidly and under severe time constraints. They learn how to work in efficient multi-functional production teams. When they graduate, they are hybrids, writer-directors, director-camera-operator-editors, who make up a flexible, independent contractor workforce" (p. 83).

The point is not that these individuals might be more or less talented than others in the field but that the nature of the talent now required for these jobs is somewhat different. Yes, it is still necessary to be skilled at operating a camera, but many people possess these skills. It is even more important to be skilled at learning new skills and adapting to new situations. Indeed, Christopherson's analysis shows how the value of television producers increases with their ability to acquire skills from the contexts in which they operate and, more generally with their cultivation of social skills, their ability to function as value-adding members of those contexts. Studies of other knowledge workers demonstrate similar results, in particular regarding the impact of social media. The value of these workers' labor becomes directly related to their ability to participate in inter-firm social flows of knowledge while the stock of knowledge and skills that they possess, their "human capital," is valued less. Indeed, in the introduction to their work on what they call "collaborative community" in knowledge-intensive organizations, Adler and Heckscher (2006) argue that it is not individual skills per se but rather the ability to draw on individual experience to make distinct contributions to common projects that has become the most valuable skill. A knowledge worker needs to be able to contribute to and demonstrate excellence in the utilization of common resources, in using and adding to the General Intellect that has become an ever more central feature of the knowledge economy.

The early literature on self-branding also reflects this emphasis on social skills. Tom Peters's work and the subsequent literature on personal branding suggested the construction of a list of personal "values" that marked one's distinct way of relating to others. Thus, the creation of a personal brand became an attempt to objectify the value of an individual's ability to function within a particular sphere, of one's ability to maneuver, contribute to, or valorize General Intellect; and the brand was a vehicle to convey that distinction in an efficient, "informational way" without deeper forms of interaction having to occur, without sociality being "rooted in a common and shared history" (Wittel 2001: 67).

In its first, 1.0, version, self-branding was a matter of *commodified reflexivity* (Wee and Brookes 2010) whereby the subject was encouraged to examine himself and to construct an objective list of traits that could be communicated to others so that his knowledge and trust could be conveyed without the need for prolonged forms of interaction. One successful self-branding manual describes the process:

> Step One: Identify the Areas Where Your Competences Matter
> Step Two: Examine Your Standards and Values
> Step Three: Define Your Style
>
> What is your responsiveness? Your tenacity? Your clear thinking? Your high energy? The thoughtfulness of your approach . . . ? Your willingness to take the lead—or be a team player or supportive resource?
> Think of the unique parts of your personality that make an impact on other people when you are at the top of your game. Do people consistently react to your positive attitude? Your humorous demeanor? Your straightforward approach? Your sense of calm? Your sincerity? Your sense of whimsy? Or your formal, no-nonsense personality? (McNally and Speak 2002: 63–67, as cited in Wee and Brooks 2010: 51)

The genealogy of these techniques of self-branding can be traced to the American self-help movement, with roots in Horatio Alger's philosophy and turn-of-the-century Protestantism and subsequently refined in the 1970s New Age environment. However, in contrast to its predecessors in the self-help movement, self-branding was to be undertaken without the support of transcendent values. Without belief in God, in the moral obligation to make the most of one's earthly existence, in the American Dream, or even in modernity as such, self-branding was undertaken exclusively in relation to a belief in one's own self and the sanctity of its success. This approach made cynicism an ever-present danger. Indeed, Tom Peters repeatedly railed against cynicism, often using *Dilbert* cartoons as a target of his ire: "We want (desperately) an anti-Dilbert character. I love Dilbert. He's right. He's funny. But I hate the cynicism, except as a wake-up call. It's my life, and I'll not spend it pushing paper in some crummy cubicle. And You?" (Peters 1999: 39, quoted in Lair, Sullivan, and Cheney 2005: 323).

The problem for Peters and his fellow self-branding gurus was that they did not have much to offer in lieu of cynicism. In a situation of more or less atomized individualism, the urge to make public one's qualities without embracing any collectively shared values approached the condition of "publicity without a public sphere," which, according to Paolo Virno (2004), inevitably favors cynicism as a structural condition of contemporary knowledge work. However, the problem of cynicism seems to have vanished in the settings that we have studied. Rather, the freelance workers whom we have studied are characterized by an almost unquestioning belief in the value of what they are doing, even if what they are doing is simply creating social media profiles of themselves.

Not only were our interviewees (with extremely few exceptions) wholeheartedly enthusiastic about self-branding practices and eager to talk at length about the strategies for and advantages of efficient networking, but their reported job satisfaction was also generally very high (on average 3.9 on a subjective scale of 1 to 5). These ratings were registered despite job conditions that, when viewed objectively, tended to approach Arne Kalleberg's (2011) definition of "bad jobs," those in which low economic compensation combines with lack of autonomy on the job and a prevalence of noneconomic, especially symbolic, rewards. Our previous studies of the Milan fashion scene had similar results: workers consistently reported high levels of job satisfaction despite job conditions marked by precariousness, low pay, long and variable working hours, and despotic office discipline (Arvidsson, Malossi, and Naro 2010). The explanation of this paradox might lie in the fact that for freelance knowledge workers, self-branding is also simultaneously a practice of articulating collective values.

The link between self-branding and the articulation of common values was most obvious in the London social enterprise sphere. Indeed, social entrepreneurs are constantly engaged in self-branding practices, but in order to be successful, they have to brand themselves as ethical beings. This means that they have to craft their identities as individuals who are keen to change the world for the better and who are devoted to the values of sustainability, social justice, and solidarity. In other words, they have to demonstrate that they belong to the realm of social entrepreneurs. Indeed, this milieu is characterized by a dynamic of inclusion that is based on one's ability to recognize and convey oneself as a social entrepreneur. As the CEO of an important London-based association supporting social entrepreneurship explained in a workshop, "A social entrepreneur is someone who thinks he is a social entrepreneur." This self-assessment procedure is quite open and inclusive. Indeed, the tag line of the Web site of Impact Hub Westminster (2014), one of the London branches of a major international network of coworking spaces for social innovation and entrepreneurship, reads, "Change the world. . . . You're invited." Still, to be able to actually "change the world" requires that the individual be able to constantly demonstrate what is supposed to be the correct attitude of a social entrepreneur and to be publicly recognized as one.

As Carolina Bandinelli and Adam Arvidsson (2013) point out, social entrepreneurs often follow a rather curious logic: in order to be able to "make a change"—that is, in order to implement a business that will have a positive social impact—they need to acquire visibility within their public; they need to make themselves known as people who have the ability to do so. Certainly, workshops with titles like "Brand Yourself a Changemaker" are quite popular. As Jon, a thirty-year-old aspiring social entrepreneur who was in the so-called idea-generating stage of his future business, claimed, "I need to contact important magazines in the field. I need to be interviewed by famous bloggers. I need to create a sort of partnership with the media. I need visibility. But I don't need it because of me, to fulfill my ego. I need it because if I become visible I will be able to have an impact and . . . help more people."

In Jon's case, the act of branding himself as someone who can have a positive impact on society precedes the concrete possibility of having such an impact. The brand predates the essence. However, the shallowness implied in such a process, the crude promotional mechanism, is somehow reterritorialized within an ethical dimension, for it is done in order to "help" more people, to have a deeper social "impact."

These examples indicate that these individuals' almost complete lack of cynicism about their self-branding can probably be explained to some extent by the brand's being perceived as a public device. That is, the value of your brand is not strictly related to your own inner qualities and to your ability to believe in them and live them in an authentic way. Rather, the brand is valued for what it is able to "give" to the public made up of peers. In this way, to construct a personal brand is to give and contribute, and to attract attention to one's personal brand is also about receiving recognition for one's ability to "give" and "contribute." As a forty-five-year-old female writer/consultant in London explained:

It was my blog that got me recognized, if you like. You know, as a freelancer you have to have something to offer; you have to be good enough, you know? There's a lot of people who aren't, and there's a lot of people who are. First of all you have to have something to offer that is at the right standard, of the right quality. And then you have to let people know that you've got it, that you're out there. So my blog was a very big thing; it got me noticed, but the thing that was the actual key was joining Twitter. . . . I think without Twitter it would have taken me longer and I'm not sure if it would have worked [to move to freelancing]. Twitter allowed me to get my blog out there; it allowed me to publicize my blog to exactly the client group who[m] I wanted to read it, who were in the position to give me work. So I used Twitter to market myself and I still use it as a professional tool. I don't use it as a kind of casual personal kind of game, or fun. I see it very much as part of my professional persona and I'm very conscious about what I tweet about. It enabled me to be part of conversations nationwide . . . without being in the same room, without going to meetings or having been in contact already.

In this view, self-branding on social media is about creating or conveying content that is useful for the "community" of peers and that gives a person a voice that enables her to experience herself as part of an ongoing conversation in a public sphere. As a thirty-four-year-old male arts consultant/writer in London told us:

In terms of my everyday kind of practice to promote myself or get new jobs, probably my most important tool is social media. . . . I have a Facebook page, mainly for my talks, but I don't use it that much. The main thing is Twitter [because] I found that institutions are quite active; museums and galleries are quite active and tend to engage with you. So whenever I do a talk, or [whenever] a piece I wrote is publicly available or if I [have] got something coming up I always tweet about it. I use [Twitter] purely professionally; I don't use it personally. . . . There's two ways of using it I think: one is to just promote yourself, which is one way; the other one is [to] kind of have a voice, and the voice is my voice. I like expressing my opinion on anything in the news concerning arts; it might be a big sale or an exhibition. I kind of like to be quite actively engaged with things that are happening. Although it's limited obviously, . . . it makes you feel like you're part of a conversation.

This public function of the personal brand means that curating an online presence is highly distinct from finding and emphasizing one's personal authentic qualities. In fact, managing a social media presence is understood as being quite the opposite of intimate self-seeking. As a twenty-seven-year-old male journalist in Milan explained, "On social media I can't write what I think. Now I care about what I write; these are tools that I use as a legitimation of my professionality. Both in terms of jobs and contacts [and] as an intermediary for new people, Twitter is a very useful tool. These are proofs of existence; they are shopping windows." Similarly, a forty-year-old female journalist/editorial consultant in Milan maintained: "Social media are a way to be visible, to get known by sharing content. I always say if you have time for just one thing, use Twitter and forget the rest. . . . [The site] has to be curated; you don't have to celebrate yourself extremely as [doing so] brings "unfollows," but it has to be done as it helps to get out of your nutshell and get known." Indeed, this imperative to share and contribute often takes the form of working for the community for free. A thirty-six-year-old female journalist and designer in Milan explained, "As for my experience, it has always happened [that I get noticed] only because they know me already for other things, through word of mouth. . . . But I would advise everyone to do something wonderful, for free, to begin with. That's the best investment." A forty-three-year-old female communication agent in Milan similarly related, "I worked a lot for free at the beginning; it's hard to demonstrate to an agency that you are capable of doing something unless you do it. Now there's the possibility to publish your work; this capacity you show . . . to all the people who may be interested, all at the same time; it's like publicly living your own portfolio." A thirty-five-year-old male arts consultant in London said, "I did some jobs for free [because] I think strategically it was a good idea to do. It was a strategic job. Generally speaking, though, I try [to do free work] as much as I possibly can. I tend to think about work in terms of how much time it can possibly take me [instead of] how much money [I am going to] make. It is obviously [a] strategic decision."

The consequences of the public nature of social media–based personal brands—the fruits of branding work: the recognition, job opportunities, and reputation that it brings—are understood to be just rewards for one's community contribution. A thirty-five-year-old female radio author/journalist in Milan told us, "[Social media,] if you use them well enough to create a diffused reputation, then they're useful. Make people laugh, comment, inform others. *If you deserve it, jobs will come because social networks are meritocratic* and bring out of anonymity those who do not deserve to be unknown" (italics added).

· · ·

The transformation of brands from devices for self-promotion to devices for the public appraisal of value and virtue is in part a consequence of a social media–based communications environment in which information about past actions remains permanently available and in which ratings and judgments are an intrinsic part. However, the transformation is also a consequence of the relations of production that characterize freelance knowledge work today. In an environment of generalized skills, value is contingent on the ability to make excellent use of generally available knowledge through the rapid and flexible formation of productive networks. In this context, the self-brand operates as a measure of an individual's capacity for cooperation, and this measure is, by definition, set by others. The invisible labor of self-branding has become a condition for professional visibility.

This public nature of personal brands also makes them potentially the conveyers of a new kind of ethics. Unlike modern ethical systems, these emerging ethics are not derived from transcendent values or metaphysical postulates. Rather, they are bottom-up ethics emerging from the continuous valuations and ratings of an individual's conduct and contributions. Such ratings, in turn, occur in relation to value horizons that are never spelled out but instead are contained within the privacy of subjective orientations. These are ethics that establish their values on the aggregation of affective investments rather than on deduction from established principles. And these ethics are by no means hostile to economic performance. Unlike the situation with modern ethics, there is no conflict between value and *values*. Rather, ethical conduct is understood as the key to economic performance. What we have is a curious new formation: an ethical economy (Arvidsson and Peitersen 2013) in which value and virtue seem to coincide.

It remains to be seen whether the ethical dimension of self-branding will lead to a proliferation of diverse value horizons or whether some common ground in terms of collective values might emerge. From our observations, it would seem that the second hypothesis has some validity. It would appear, in fact, that the public nature of brands, their constant susceptibility to the judgments of others, and the difficulty of the means by which they can be manipulated also turn them into tangible foundations for the emergence of collective values. These values can be spelled out and made explicit (if vague), as they are in the social enterprise sphere, in which having an impact remains an overall ideal and in which the value of brands is related to multidimensional estimates of virtuous conduct in relation to this ideal (which may encompass everything from actually landing a project that will have a real impact to not bringing nonorganic chicken to the Wednesday night potluck, as one of our informants did, with the resulting damage needing to be remedied through intense social media activity). These values can also be implicit and take the form of a vague, but nevertheless tangible, sense of the ever-watchful gaze of peers, as when creative freelancers feel that they constantly have to contribute to the milieu in which they operate in order to maintain a perception of their value. The emergence of such collective values helps explain the absence of cynicism in freelancer milieus since individual projects of professional self-realization remain anchored in the "social fact" of collective judgment. They might also point toward the possibility of a new conception of economic action: an ethical economy in which monetary value becomes tied to virtuous conduct. This situation is evident in the widespread ethos of "sharing" that characterizes these spheres, whereby freelancers deem it necessary to involve others in professional opportunities and to pass on contacts and jobs in order to remain employable themselves. It is also evident in emerging concepts of economic ethics, whereby the moderation of gain and avoidance of greed (in order to leave opportunities open for others) are identified as desirable values.

While the potential for an ethical economy can be discerned in the ways in which self-branding among freelance workers is framed at the level of discourse, it is much less developed at the level of practice. Freelance workers need to contribute to a milieu, and they need to cultivate their standing as virtuous members of that milieu in the eyes of others through their communications. In practice, however, the "sharing economy" often professed has a relatively minor impact. In our research on coworking spaces in Milan, we found that coworkers habitually share contacts and competences at the level of professional practice. This sharing amounts to helping each other with practical issues like fixing computer programs or assisting with social media campaigns. Other widespread practices include coworkers sharing advice about how to handle difficult clients and how to get paid or giving each other psychological support when dealing with the often problematic existential aspects of working as a freelancer in a precarious knowledge economy. However, such sharing stops short of affecting tangible economic realities. The cases in which freelancers have developed informal systems of mutual aid exist—a coworking space in Rome that we studied has developed an informal scheme for maternity leave in which members who are expecting children are paid a "wage" covered by the collective while the women are absent from work. But these cases are extremely rare. Coworkers themselves are aware of this discrepancy between the narrative about "sharing" on the one hand and the highly individualized practice of self-branding on the other, and they attribute it to a series of factors. On the one hand, there is recognition of the individual psychology of coworkers. Everybody is an individual; many have left what they understood to be the oppressive collectivism of corporate organizations to realize their own dreams. This deeply ingrained individualism is understood to be an obstacle that prevents the emergence of mutual aid and more practice-based forms of collective solidarity. Many cite a widespread disillusionment with politics and civic engagement. It is as if the idea of building a collective organization is a priori dismissed as something that belongs to an old world that has now lost almost all of its legitimacy. A final, more practical reason can be found in the nature of the labor market. The fact that coworking spaces consist of conglomerations of individual freelancers who are each pursuing an individual career creates fragmentation at the level of everyday practice that makes it difficult to inspire solidarity in the form of, for example, mutual aid.

However, the discrepancy between the potential for the existence of ethics at the level of discourse and the absence of their realization at the level of practice should not simply be taken as yet another sign of the hopeless condition of the modern precariat. If it is difficult for solidarity to develop out of a shared practice, it might instead develop from the necessity to communicate a reputation.

In fact, the condition of freelance knowledge workers exhibits a number of parallels to the ethics of early modern merchants as Max Weber ([1930] 2002) describes them in the first part of his work on the Protestant Ethic—concepts often neglected in modern readings of Weber but perhaps more relevant today. Weber argues that early capitalist entrepreneurs combined the pursuit of profit with the respect for collective values of moderation and the preservation of the opportunity of others. Then, as now, this ethical entrepreneurialism was implemented as the basis of free and fairly egalitarian competition. It was a system of ethics of the free market as Adam Smith described it (Arrighi 2007), before the arrival of large corporate monopolies and in which entrepreneurial activity was based on the use of common resources in the form of traditional, not-yet-subsumed relations of production. Perhaps new forms of solidarity can grow out of a new economic consciousness proper to the entrepreneurial economy of the commons that is emerging at the other end of neoliberalism.

NOTE

1. This chapter builds on a collective research project that we have been working on for several years. Within that project, each author has pursued individual fieldwork. Alessandro Gandini conducted eighty semistructured

interviews with freelance knowledge workers active in communication and design in London and Milan during 2012 and 2013 (Gandini 2014). As part of her ongoing PhD work, Carolina Bandinelli has conducted participant observation in coworking spaces for social entrepreneurs, or *changemakers,* to use their own term. Her fieldwork lasted eighteen months. Adam Arvidsson has drawn on his ongoing research on Italian coworking spaces for creative freelancers. To date, his material consists of twenty interviews and a survey with sixty-five respondents as well as his previous research on creative labor in the Milan fashion industry (Arvidsson, Malossi, and Naro 2010).

REFERENCES

Adler, Paul, and Charles Heckscher, eds. 2006. *The Firm as Collaborative Community: Reconstructing Trust in the Knowledge Economy.* Oxford: Oxford University Press.

Arendt, Hannah. 1963. *Eichmann in Jerusalem: A Report on the Banality of Evil.* New York: Viking.

Arrighi, Giovanni. 2007. *Adam Smith in Beijing.* London: Verso.

Arvidsson, Adam, Giannino Malossi, and Serpica Naro. 2010. "Passionate Work? Labor Conditions in the Milan Fashion Industry." *Journal for Cultural Research* 14 (3): 295–309.

Arvidsson, Adam, and Nicolai Peitersen. 2013. *The Ethical Economy: Rebuilding Value after the Crisis.* New York: Columbia University Press.

Bandinelli, Carolina, and Adam Arvidsson. 2013. "Brand Yourself a Changemaker!" *Journal of Macromarketing* 33 (1): 67–71.

Beck, Ulrich. 1992. *Risk Society.* London: Sage.

Bell, Daniel. 1960. *The End of Ideology: On the Exhaustion of Political Ideas in the Fifties.* Cambridge, MA: Harvard University Press.

Boltanski, Luc, and Eve Chiapello. 1999. *Le nouvel esprit du capitalisme.* Paris: Gallimard.

Bourdieu, Pierre. 1979. *La distinction: Critique sociale du jugement.* Paris: Gallimard.

Brynolfson, Erik, and Andrew McAfee. 2014. *The Second Machine Age: Work, Progress and Prosperity in the Time of Brilliant Technologies.* New York: Norton.

Christopherson, Susan. 2008. "Beyond the Self-Expressive Creative Worker: An Industry Perspective on Entertainment Media." *Theory, Culture and Society* 25: 73–95.

Drucker, Peter. 1967. *The Effective Executive.* New York: Harper & Row.

Gandini, Alessandro. 2014. "The Reputation Economy: Creative Labor and Freelance Networks." PhD dissertation, Department of Social and Political Sciences, University of Milan, Milan, Italy.

Gershon, Ilaria. 2014. "Selling Yourself in the United States." *POLAR: Political and Legal Anthropology Review* 37: 281–95.

Hochschild, Arlie Russell. 2012. *The Outsourced Self: What Happens When We Pay Others to Live Our Lives for Us.* New York: Macmillan.

Impact Hub Westminster. 2014. Retrieved February 14, 2015 (http://Westminster.impacthub.net).

Kalleberg, Arne. 2011. *Good Jobs, Bad Jobs: The Rise of Polarized and Precarious Employment Systems in the United States, 1970–2000*. New York: Russell Sage Foundation.

Lair, Daniel, Kate Sullivan, and George Cheney. 2005. "Marketization and the Recasting of the Professional Self: The Rhetoric and Ethics of Personal Branding." *Management Communication Quarterly* 18 (3): 307–43.

Martin, Bill. 2005. "Managers after the Era of Organizational Restructuring: Towards a Second Managerial Revolution?" *Work, Employment, and Society* 19 (4): 747–60.

Marwick, Alice. 2013. *Status Update: Celebrity, Publicity, and Branding in the Social Media Age*. New Haven, CT: Yale University Press.

Marx, Karl. (1939) 1973. *Grundrisse*. Reprint, London: Penguin.

McGregor, Douglas. 1960. *The Human Side of Enterprise*. New York: McGraw-Hill.

McNally, David, and Karl Speak. 2002. *Be Your Own Brand: A Breakthrough Formula for Standing Out from the Crowd*. San Francisco: Berret-Koehler.

Peacock, Louisa. 2010. "IBM Crowdsourcing Could See Employed Workforce Shrink by Three-Quarters." *Personnel Today*, April 23. Retrieved November 6, 2013 (www.personneltoday.com/hr/ibm-crowd-sourcing-could-see-employed-workforce-shrink-by-three-quarters).

Peters, Tom. 1999. *The Brand Called You: Fifty Ways to Transform Yourself from an "Employee" into a Brand That Shouts Distinction, Commitment, and Passion!* New York: Random House.

Reynolds, S. 2012. *Energy Flash: A Journey through Rave Music and Dance Culture*. London: Soft Skull Press.

Ross, Andrew. 2004. *No Collar: The Humane Workplace and Its Hidden Costs*. Philadelphia: Temple University Press.

Touraine, Alain. 1969. *La societé post-industrielle*. Paris: Denoël.

Turner, Fredric. 2010. *From Counterculture to Cyberculture: Stewart Brand, the Whole Earth Network, and the Rise of Digital Utopianism*. Chicago: University of Chicago Press.

Virno, Paolo. 2004. *A Grammar of the Multitude*. London: Verso.

Weber, Max. (1930) 2002. *The Protestant Ethic and the Spirit of Capitalism*. Reprint, London: Penguin.

Wee, Lionel, and Ann Brooks. 2010. "Personal Branding and the Commodification of Reflexivity." *Cultural Sociology* 4 (1): 45–62.

Wittel, Andreas. 2001. "Toward a Network Sociality." *Theory, Culture and Society* 18: 51–76.

CHAPTER 13

Consuming Work

MARION CRAIN

Why does it matter whether we conceptualize an activity as work or as something else—leisure, a volunteered effort, a training experience? In law it matters because the matrix of employment and labor laws applies only to "employees" performing "work." Protection against discrimination, guarantees of minimum wage and overtime pay, rights to organize and collectively bargain, and workplace health and safety laws, among others, extend only to employment relationships. But which activities are seen as work is even more fundamental in American society, in which employment is the ticket not only to financial security and independence but also to dignity, citizenship, and voice (Zatz and Boris 2014).

U.S. law categorizes as *work* activities that 1) are undertaken in expectation of compensation, 2) are controlled by the employer, and 3) primarily serve the employer's interests in ways that are essential to the core operations of the business. Activities that primarily further the individual's interests or are associated with individual agency, skill development, or pleasure are deemed not-work. The legal analysis is complicated by the typical employer's superior bargaining power over the individual worker and the background legal doctrine of employment at-will: employers may subtly or overtly condition initial or continued employment on the worker's compliance with a variety of policies. Workers may comply with policies that do nothing more than reinforce their preexisting preferences, or they may comply and be shaped by the experience of compliance—willingly or not. The classic dilemma, then, is how to distinguish between coercion and choice in a world of constraints.

This chapter explores how the law's emphasis on the compulsion/choice dichotomy in defining *work* creates opportunities for employers to transform commercial transactions that yield profits for the firm into consumption-centered, voluntary activities to which labor and employment law do not apply. Employers that are able to deploy a prestigious brand to reframe work as entailing consumption of the firm's brand (including the products, status, and experiences associated with it) can significantly reduce labor costs. The rise of the corporate brand and its relationship to status and identity in modern society attract youthful workers who place a higher value on affinity with the firm and its brand than they do on traditional compensation. Such an exchange may seem voluntary, but it has more subtle and insidious effects on identity and voice in a democratic society. When firms forge personnel policy around the brand by using it to recruit, retain, and compensate workers, they reap a more compliant workforce less likely to develop oppositional consciousness, assert workplace rights, or question the ways in which worker identity is marketized in service of the employer's business goals. Further, a citizenry conditioned to see life through a consumptive lens is more likely to approach political questions from a self-interested, individualistic perspective, making mobilization around other axes of identity challenging.

I offer two examples. The first involves consumption of branded products by employees who are paid to perform traditional services. Because workers are the physical manifestations of the brand for service and retail businesses, aesthetic labor is a critical part of value (and profit) creation. Many retailers require workers to represent the brand in ways that include purchasing and using the firm's products. Such workers model the firm's brand inside the store while simultaneously performing more traditional labor (processing sales, stocking inventory). In these contexts it is clear that the actors are workers at law, but the reframing of some of their activities as consumption makes it less clear that everything they do is work. The compulsory nature of this consumption is not visible to prospective customers and is typically embraced by the employees, willingly integrated into their identities and regarded as something other than work. Indeed, to the extent that the modeling duty is combined with employee purchasing discounts on fashionable products, the representation requirement may be reframed as an employee benefit.

The second illustration involves consumption of the firm's brand by persons specifically categorized not as employees but instead as something else: volunteers, interns, trainees, or students. These individuals are drawn to the firm by the promise of skills acquisition, experience, networking opportunities, and identification with a powerful brand that will confer future employment advantages through image enhancement (résumé value). In effect, they become consumers of the job and the firm's brand reputation. Examples include arrangements in which firms use student brand ambassadors on college campuses to forge lifestyle marketing campaigns in which the student publicly consumes the firm's product or service, hawking the product through friendship and social networks while the employment arrangement remains obscured; the deployment of volunteers to monitor virtual chat rooms and guide users through software communication systems, as at AOL; and the rise of unpaid or low-paid internships as an essential qualification for employment. Here it is not clear whether the individuals are workers, nor is it obvious that they are doing work.

Although individual workers often embrace these practices rather than resist them, the failure to conceptualize these activities as labor and these actors as workers harms workers as a class, reducing waged income and subtly shaping political consciousness by commercializing identity and marketizing voice. Ultimately, a more nuanced understanding of work that looks beyond the law's traditional compulsion/choice binary is essential to avoid these consequences. Critical to this understanding is an appreciation of the labor that is obscured by the illusion or appearance of consumption. This chapter describes consumptive labor and makes the case for understanding it as work.

DEFINING WORK AT LAW

All protective employment regulation contains a threshold definition of which persons are covered; typically, only "employees" and employment relationships are brought within the law's sweep (Zatz 2011). The most robust definitions of employment relationships in law are found in the federal wage and hour law, the Fair Labor Standards Act of 1938 (FLSA). The statutory text itself is quite unhelpful in defining an employment relationship: it defines an *employee* as "any individual employed by an employer" and defines *employ* as "to suffer or permit to work" (FLSA §§ 206, 207). The courts have been forced to augment this definition by using their own conceptions of what counts as work and which individuals appear to be employees as a matter of economic reality. In two early decisions, the Supreme Court shed light on what counts as work, explaining that *work* means "physical or mental exertion (whether burdensome or not) controlled or required by the employer and pursued necessarily and primarily for the benefit of the employer and his business" (*Tennessee Coal, Iron and Railroad Co. v. Muscoda Local No. 123* [1944]: 598), while one who labors "solely for his personal purpose or pleasure" does not *work* (*Walling v. Portland Terminal Co.* [1947]: 153).

The early legal definitions of *work* were developed against the backdrop of an industrial economy that featured a traditional divide between production and consumption. In this economy, exploitation of the labor process was the primary source of profits. Labor was thus the core driver of the economy, and most citizens constructed their identities around their work. By contrast, consumption was the purpose of production and the quintessential reward for labor that was typically arduous and immiserating (Smith 1985). This vision of employment as exploitation of the labor process was coupled with an assumption that the interests of business owners and workers were fundamentally antagonistic. Owners sought to extract more profit from production by making labor processes more efficient: mechanization, time and motion studies, and increased supervision disciplined labor (Braverman 1974; Montgomery 1979). Workers resisted the overt compulsion inherent in production by organizing unions.

Many challenging issues arose that blurred this oppositional rubric as the structure of work evolved, however. First, since an activity must be required by the employer in order to be considered compensable work, how should law treat activities performed "off the clock" in order to comply with the employer's productivity standards? Are they voluntary, or are they coerced by the at-will context in which they occur? Second, how should law distinguish between activities performed for the employer's benefit and those performed for the employee's personal benefit when the activity has elements of both? For example, many employers require employees to be "on call" when physically away from the workplace so they can be summoned on short notice via cell phone or pager. Should all of that time be compensable, even when the employee is able to perform activities that are predominantly for her own benefit while waiting to be called? Third, what about training time? Is it primarily for the employer's benefit, or is it primarily to the employee's advantage? A specific illustration of this latter dilemma is the unpaid internship undertaken for experiential purposes by the individual but potentially also a source of free labor for the firm. Results in these cases often turn on whether the training is of general value to the individual beyond that particular work context, whether the work is of significant benefit to the firm, and whether the individual understood and accepted the tasks as uncompensated.

Ultimately, the courts were left to determine whether the relationship comported with their intuitions of employment as a wage–labor bargain and whether it served the purposes of the FLSA to characterize the relationship as one involving employment. They developed various tests designed to ascertain who counts as an employee and what counts as work, but the results in particular cases remain unpredictable.

THE RISE OF THE CORPORATE BRAND AS LABOR POLICY

The industrial economy gave way to a service economy and subsequently shifted toward what some observers characterize as a consumption economy in which work plays a less fundamental role and consumers' desires are paramount (Bocock 1993; Schor 2000). The coercive dyadic rubric that had historically characterized employment no longer fit easily with a market conceptualized as a zone of freedom and choice in which consumers rather than the employer represented the nadir of power and sovereignty, "voting with their dollars" on which businesses succeeded and which failed (Korczynski and Ott 2004). Consumption replaced work as the measure of status.

Firms responded to the rise of the consumption economy with sophisticated marketing campaigns that influenced and reflected cultural trends and values. Corporate branding proved critical to these campaigns, allowing firms to distinguish their products and services in an increasingly crowded and competitive market (Aaker 1991; Ind 1997). Businesses spent billions constructing brands and marketing them to consumers. The corporate brand became the most valuable asset that many businesses possessed. The most successful brands created a relationship between the firm and its consumers, ensuring a sustained market characterized by customer loyalty that establishes a platform for brand extensions and growth into new product and service markets (e.g., Starbucks extended its coffee concept to ice cream sold in grocery stores; Apple extended its computer interface to the iPhone and iPad) (Ford 2005).

Promoting the corporate brand to consumers was only half the story for retail and service businesses, however, in which frontline workers serve as the primary point of contact with consumers: workers literally embody the brand and are an integral part of the customer's experience. Accordingly, many firms invest at least as much in internal marketing to employees—that is, selling the corporate brand inside the firm—as they do in external advertising campaigns directed at consumers. Internal branding programs include a coordinated hiring, training, and socialization program as well as a discipline-and-reward structure designed to imprint brand values (Mitchell 2002). Rules governing employees' appearance, dress, and job performance are essential components of such a program, making the branded product or service more tangible (Crain and Avery 2007). Such rules may be detailed and rigid or intentionally lax and quite subtle—but in every case they are carefully constructed to be consistent with the brand image. Southwest Airlines employees, for example, must demonstrate cheerfulness and humor while delivering "positively outrageous service," but individuality is encouraged; the regulation is accomplished through a rigorous selection process for "brand fit." Disney's employees must display a sense of happiness to effectively transport customers to fantasyland, something that Disney painstakingly conditions through a detailed hiring and socialization process that shapes workers to see themselves as "cast members" or "hosts," inculcating a sense of fun as part of the role (Crain 2010).

Effective internal branding thus channels worker behavior in particular directions so that decisions made by workers (within the imposed constraints) are perceived as freely chosen. The most successful companies strive for complete alignment between workers' identities and the corporate brand. Workers are selected for brand fit and aesthetic consistency with the brand's image (they are often chosen from the customer base) and are encouraged to recruit friends and contacts with similar class, racial, and ethnic characteristics. Workers are often attracted to positions as much or more by the social networks accompanying the brands as by the jobs themselves; strong communities within the firm (such as those at Starbucks, Apple, or Harley-Davidson) are powerful draws.

These brand communities are constructed around an iconic brand that is designed to appeal to human frailties, including basic needs for emotional security, reassurance of individual worth, and connection and roots (Holt 2004; Klein 1999). They address widely shared cultural anxieties; for example, Apple's brand offered the solution to the cultural contradiction between feelings of nonconformity and alienation on the one hand and the need for belonging on the other (Walker 2008). Starbucks leveraged the individual's longing for community and the intimacy associated with coffeehouses by providing the physical space for family-like social networks to form and integrating its branded coffee into that sphere. As Starbucks CEO Howard Schultz put it, "We are not . . . in the coffee business serving people. . . . [W]e are in the people business serving coffee" (quoted in Burmann and Zeplin 2005).

The brand frame yields significant loyalty that keeps consumers coming back to spend money on high-priced coffee even when money is tight. But the benefits of attracting a youthful, enthusiastic, and relatively class-privileged labor force willing to work for low wages are just as significant. In an ethnographic study of teen workers at a national coffee franchise, sociologist Yasemin Besen found that the mostly affluent teens were drawn to work by the sense of belonging and community. Relatively flat supervisory structures and supervisors who were peers or friends minimized any sense of subordination at work. Ads for employees do not emphasize pay, benefits, hours, or opportunities for advancement or experience; they solicit workers from Starbucks's youthful customer base, asking whether individuals "want a job with their coffee" (p. 334). Starbucks's labor policies thus effectively obscure the economic bargain, shifting workers' focus to the branded community by marketing the job as a product, "an enjoyable experience to be consumed" (p. 334). Starbucks reinforces the prospective workers' consumption patterns by offering discounts on the items sold—including coffee, mugs, food items, and stuffed animals. Teens see the opportunity to associate with a "cool" and prestigious brand through employment as "priceless," and they respond by actively transforming work that might objectively be characterized as oppressive because of the low wages, erratic scheduling, nonexistent benefits, and lack of opportunity for skill building or advancement into enjoyable leisure and social community experiences (p. 333).

TURNING CONSUMPTION INTO WORK

Some employers take this one step further, capitalizing on employees' brand affinity by requiring them to consume and model the items they sell. This marketing strategy is seen predominantly among fashion retailers that rely on store-based employees to convey an aesthetic consistent with the store's brand. Abercrombie & Fitch and Hollister are perhaps the best-known illustrations, but there are many others—Chico's, J. Jill, Polo Ralph Lauren, the Gap, Banana Republic, Victoria's Secret, Swarovski, and Foot Locker. In this business model, the customer's in-store experience is shaped by interactions with employees who portray and convey the brand's "personality"; these in-store experiences augment and even substitute for traditional advertising, reinforcing the "aspirational lifestyles" that are the hallmark of the brand and its core business driver, despite some legal risk associated with the policy of aesthetic consistency (*EEOC v. Abercrombie & Fitch Stores, Inc.* [2013]). To create the aesthetic, the employer mines new employees from its customer base, instructing its supervisors to solicit shoppers whose personal attributes best showcase the brand (Greenhouse 2003b). Once hired, the workers' bodies are used as the medium for conveying the brand promise. Workers are required to purchase and model branded clothing, footwear, and accessories in keeping with current fashions, including seasonal shifts, and to comply with grooming requirements that regulate hairstyle, facial hair, tattoos, makeup, jewelry, and fingernail length and color. They are barred from wearing clothing or accessories incompatible with the brand, including attire mandated by religious faith, such as the hijab. Those who fail to comply with the look policy are disciplined, scheduled for reduced hours, or discharged (*EEOC v. Abercrombie & Fitch Stores, Inc.* [2013]).

Like the Starbucks workers, most fashion retail employees embrace the brand, drawn to employment by the opportunity for product discounts and by the prestige or "cool factor" of the brand, the peer group, and the friendships made through the affiliation (Pettinger 2005; Quart 2003; Siegel 2001). The workforce displays the face of the brand, reflecting and idealizing the sociological characteristics of the target market—youthful, beautiful, class privileged, and ethnically or racially matched to the demographics of the store's customer base. But at the same time that workers reinforce the brand's association in the customer's mind with the kind of person who wears and uses the brand (the kind of person the customer longs to be)—fit, thin, beautiful, young, wealthy—the brand and its reputation are imprinted upon the workers (Harquail 2006). Employees whose identity, status, and social networks depend on their brand association are unlikely to assert workplace rights when doing so entails resisting the brand itself (Lindeman 2005).

Nevertheless, some workers have brought challenges alleging wage violations when the cost of the branded products suppresses wages below the minimum or when the firm's look policies effectively amount to a uniform requirement whose cost should be borne by the employer (*Bean v. Hugo Boss Retail, Inc.* [2015]; *Howard v. Gap, Inc.* [2007]; *Young v. Polo Retail* [2007]; Greenhouse 2003a).[1] Alternatively, they assert that the compulsory dress codes and look policies create a captive branded community from which the firms receive a double benefit— lower labor costs and increased sales—that amounts to an unfair business practice that undermines free competition and ties workers to their employment (*Spint et al. v. Swarovski North America, Ltd.* [2013]; *Young v. Polo Retail* [2007]). Retailers have defended themselves by arguing that employees chose the jobs because of their affinity for the brand and desire to own the branded apparel; substantial discounts on clothing (of between 30 percent and 65 percent [Merrick 2003]) were part of the inducement for the jobs. Thus, their clothing purchases were voluntary rather than compelled. In an ironic twist that seems to prove the employers' point, many of these cases have settled for a mix of cash and gift cards or clothing vouchers, indicating employees' continuing choice to wear the brand even as they challenged the dress code (Strasburg 2005).

BLURRING THE CONSUMER/WORKER LINE

Brand representatives are not confined to the physical boundaries of the stores. New categories of jobs further blur the line between worker and consumer. Firms use student brand ambassadors, sometimes called *brand evangelists,* to hawk brands to target markets on college campuses, capitalizing on students' social networks and inside knowledge of school traditions. Mass market retail clothiers (American Eagle Outfitters, the Gap, Victoria's Secret), tech firms (Google, Hewlett-Packard, Apple), beverage firms (Red Bull energy drinks, Coke, Mountain Dew), and sportswear (Nike) all utilize this form of marketing (Miller 2011; Schweitzer 2005). Marketing research suggests that teens, millennials, and Generation Yers are fanatical about the authenticity of marketing messages and therefore more likely to buy products based on recommendations from friends and peers whom they trust (Schweitzer 2005). Brand ambassadors are expected to spend between ten and fifteen hours per week "talking up" the brand to friends and peers; to be seen wearing, drinking, or eating the product; to coordinate events on behalf of the brand; and to use "guerrilla marketing techniques," including plastering bulletin boards, chalking sidewalks, sticking preprinted Post-it notes on computer screens, and even using erasable markers on cars

(Miller 2011; Schweitzer 2005). Their work is monitored through self-reports on online portals where students log numbers of fliers posted, list e-mail addresses collected, and provide other indicia of productivity. Software companies like Microsoft also monitor performance by tracking the number of student downloads of products by school (Singer 2011).

By fall 2011, approximately ten thousand college students were so employed on American campuses as the firms sought to attract a larger share of the estimated $36 billion that college students spend on clothing, computers, and other supplies during the academic year (Singer 2011). Although compensation arrangements vary, most appear to be structured as independent contractor arrangements or internships, neither of which are considered employment relationships regulated by the federal or state wage and hour laws. Students are paid by stipend on a per-project basis, receive "free" or discounted branded products, or are eligible to compete for prizes that function like bonuses, rewarding the highest producers. Many brand representatives receive either no pay or negligible pay, with firms instead touting the experiential value of the undertaking and its potential, as "the other internship" experience, to lead to a full-time job (see www.thecampusrep.com, which promises "great marketing experience," "useful references and credentials," and the opportunity to be hired by "the best companies in the country").

The immediate rewards for students appear to be affiliation with a brand that has cachet with peers and signals particular identity traits (such as Victoria's Secret, associated with sexual attractiveness) and the reputational value of the firm's name in garnering future employment (Miller 2011). Students who function in these roles often do not know how much they earn and do not care. They describe their incentives for performing the work as stemming from their "passion for the brand" and their interest in acquiring experience and affinity with the firm (Miller 2011).

HOW FIRMS BENEFIT

Of course, deploying workers' consumptive capacities to generate profits is not new terrain for American business. Historically, coal mining companies and textile mills reaped profits not only directly from workers' labor but also from their enforced consumption of company-owned housing and basic necessities at the company store in company towns. As a condition of continued employment, workers were required to patronize the company store, butcher shop, and saloon (Allen 1966). Monopolistic prices were higher at the company stores than elsewhere, and increases in wage rates could be offset simply by raising prices at the company store (Corbin 1981). Companies issued *scrip* in lieu of wages, a form of currency redeemable only at company-owned businesses (or in some independent stores, where they were discounted by between 10 and 25 percent) (Fagge 1996). The use of scrip dramatically reduced the real wages paid to workers, and store profits derived from sales to workers and their families sometimes outstripped the corporate profits earned from the mines or mills themselves (Corbin 1981).

Further, many companies have required employees to signal their loyalty to the firm by purchasing the firm's brand: "Work for Ford; drive a Ford" is a long-standing norm in the auto industry, for example. Discharges for disloyalty to the brand were reported when Ford employees purchased cars manufactured by competitors (*Paul Swanson*, 36 L.A. 305 [*Gochnauer*, Arb. 1961]). Discount programs were designed to facilitate worker purchases, and they turned out to be quite profitable for American automobile manufacturers; indeed, "Z-plan" and "X-plan" discounts are extended to friends and family on the rationale that beneficiaries function as "goodwill ambassadors" for the company. According to one estimate, the discounts in a single year accounted for additional sales demand sufficient to maintain two factories for that year (Blumenstein and Puchalsky 1998).

Though they can be conceptualized as existing along a spectrum that includes enforced consumption at the company store, company housing, and employee discount programs, modern branding programs are more insidious. First, they are invisible to onlookers. Branded employees function as human billboards for the firm, on and off the job. They perform an important advertising function that is even more valuable because the compulsory nature of their consumption relationship with the brand is hidden. Their branded attire signals to observers a prior act of consumption that is assumed to have been voluntary, chosen from among other options available. Further, the presumed act of voluntary consumption is performed by an employee chosen and groomed by the firm to represent its brand to consumers who hope to become that individual—to acquire, by purchasing the brand, the employee's habitus. And to the extent that brand purchases are mandatory, branding programs create a captive market of branded workers, conferring a significant competitive advantage in the market. They also potentially expand the workers' workday, marshaling a force of brand ambassadors who model the look by donning branded clothing each day, whether for work or play.

Second, branding programs facilitate managerial control that is all the more powerful because its influence is hidden from the workers themselves. Encouraged to see themselves as part of a community of insiders who are special and superior, even elite, workers who identify with the brand demonstrate strong commitment to advancing it—both inside and outside the workplace—and perform their jobs more effectively and have better morale than those who do not. They also require less rigorous management and oversight (Crain 2010).

Third, requiring employees to conform to look policies and to shop for, accessorize, and don branded clothing, footwear, and jewelry every time they come to work inevitably shapes the workers' identities. Employees are evaluated by supervisors and receive customer feedback on how effectively they operationalize the brand. They respond by further internalizing the brand, mirroring the social response to their branded personas (Harquail 2006). Of course, employees have long been required to adopt certain personas and to don particular uniforms, particularly in the service context. But the invisibility of the look policies—as contrasted with the visible nature of uniforms—brings different forces to bear. The expressive function of appearance and the invisibility of the compulsory character of look policies combine to produce an inauthentic message about who the worker is, merging the worker's persona into the brand. Moreover, look policies transcend workplace boundaries; unlike uniforms, a particular look that includes hairstyle, accessories, a way of carrying oneself, and a range of seasonally appropriate clothing, footwear, or jewelry choices cannot easily be shed at the end of the day.

In addition to producing loyal branded workers who are willing to "live the brand," using the brand to shape labor policy dramatically reduces labor costs. By substituting brand prestige for compensation and benefits, employers can deploy volunteers and interns to do work that they would otherwise have to pay employees to perform. In one highly publicized case, Internet service provider America Online (AOL) utilized a volunteer labor force of approximately fourteen thousand persons who managed and updated message boards, moderated chat rooms, updated content on forums, served as online tutors, and enforced AOL's terms of service for AOL's bulletin boards. The typical volunteer chat-room host, for example, worked scheduled shifts and submitted a report about each session to a paid supervisor. All volunteers submitted weekly reports listing hours worked and duties performed. In exchange,

AOL augmented their power to control the discussions in chat rooms and the content in forums, provided training in the use of its proprietary software, and furnished free AOL access, discounts at the AOL store, free antivirus software, and expanded space for Web pages. The value of the free AOL access shifted over time: initially, when AOL maintained an hourly pricing system and charged $3.95 per hour, the volunteers received two hours of access for every one hour worked; later, however, AOL shifted to flat-rate service, and the free account was worth about $20 per month (*Hallissey v. AOL, Inc.* [2006]). The volunteers eventually brought suit against AOL under the federal wage and hour law for nonpayment of wages; their collective action suit settled for $15 million in 2010 (Kirchner 2011). They testified that a sense of community, the desire to acquire skills, and the possibility of eventually obtaining employment with AOL had been the main motivating forces for their participation as "volunteers " (Postigo 2009).

Similarly, the Huffington Post relied heavily on unpaid writers to provide content. When Arianna Huffington sold the Huffington Post to AOL in 2011 for $315 million, social activist and blogger Jonathan Tasini brought a class-action suit on behalf of himself and other content providers, arguing that the Huffington Post had been unjustly enriched to the extent of $105 million through its practice of soliciting and deploying unpaid bloggers to provide content and by asking them to utilize social media to increase Web traffic to the Post. The Post responded that bloggers had been drawn to the Huffington Post platform by the opportunity to reach large numbers of people and the cachet of the Huffington Post name and that they had received both of those benefits as promised (Olivarez-Giles 2011; *Tasini v. AOL, Inc.* [2011]).

The Huffington Post's strategy of obtaining free content from high-profile writers through a combination of "charm and brand association" was widely hailed as a business strategy amounting to "a miracle for web publishing" that generated exceptional profit margins (Bell 2011). The judge hearing the case was skeptical of the bloggers' legal claims, however, suggesting that the bloggers had known they would not be paid when they submitted their work and indicating that because their work had been done out of "joy," it was difficult to conceptualize it as work (Vanderford 2012). Ultimately, the plaintiffs' efforts to cast themselves as consumers for purposes of alleging that the Post had engaged in deceptive business practices failed; in the court's view, they were neither employees nor consumers. The suit was dismissed in March 2012 (Bishop 2012).

The booming intern economy offers another example of how firms may substitute brand prestige for compensation, turning what might have been a job into an "experience." Students enthusiastically perform work in exchange for the promise of experience, résumé enhancement, and networking opportunities that they hope will facilitate entry into "real" jobs at some future date. It is no accident that the vast majority of internships are secured in sectors that are widely viewed as glamorous or prestigious occupations—such as theater, magazine publishing, journalism, and the creative arts, where part of what the interns consume is the entrée into the employer's prestigious occupation. Alternatively, internships in the government and nonprofit sectors confer the moral prestige of the organization and its mission; interns consume the organization's halo effect. Indeed, the ability to take an unpaid internship functions as a form of conspicuous consumption characteristic of the leisure or wealthy class (Veblen 1899) as the interns signal to others—and importantly, to prospective future employers—that they have the financial wherewithal to do so (even if the internship is ultimately funded by student loans).

Though the intern economy has been a fixture since the 1990s, the financial downturn provided it with a significant boost (Greenhouse 2010; Greenhouse 2012; Perlin 2011). By classifying interns as nonemployees, firms could avoid not only wage costs but also associated expenditures for fringe benefits. Litigation by interns disappointed that their internships had not led to real jobs or provided useful experience brought additional attention to the issue in the legal context. In 2011, interns on the movie *Black Swan* brought suit under the federal wage and hour law, alleging that the movie's producer, Fox Searchlight, had treated them like employees (requiring them to perform janitorial and secretarial work and to take and deliver coffee and lunch orders) but had failed to pay minimum wage (Greenhouse 2011; *Glatt v. Fox Searchlight Pictures, Inc.* [2013]). In 2012, Xuedan Wang, an intern at Hearst Corporation's *Harper's Bazaar* magazine, filed suit under both federal and state wage and hour laws, claiming that she had worked up to fifty-five hours per week for no pay performing jobs that regular employees would otherwise have performed, including helping with photo shoots and coordinating pickups and deliveries of samples furnished by fashion houses (Vanderford 2012; *Wang v. The Hearst Corp.* [2013]). The two cases reached opposite results in the lower courts and were certified for appeal by the Second Circuit Court of Appeals, which established a new legal test focusing on which party—the employer or the putative employee—is the "primary beneficiary" of the relationship (*Glatt v. Fox Searchlight Pictures, Inc.* [2d Cir. 2015]). This test harkens back to the law's original dichotomous notion of work as an activity pursued primarily for the benefit of the employer and its business, rather than for the individual.

LAW'S INEFFECTIVE FRAMES

The cases discussed above illustrate the two legal frames currently available to challenge what we might call the "soft coercion" imposed by employers who reframe work as consumption. The first frame focuses on the economic loss to workers: to what degree does compelled consumption deprive the worker of wages by reducing compensation to a level that falls below the minimum wage? This frame is available only to those workers who fit within a traditional employment relationship and thus qualify as "employees" covered by employment regulation. In these cases workers confront the argument that they have chosen to consume the branded apparel or products. Although workers cannot "choose" to work for less than the minimum wage, courts that have difficulty seeing consumption as work simply characterize the consumption as existing outside the wage–labor bargain. Thus, the time spent consuming the brand and the money dedicated to purchasing it are seen as acts of individual agency by the employee that primarily serve her own interests rather than those of the employer. Furthermore, such claims are not available at all to those whose status as an "employee" is contested, such as brand representatives and interns. In these cases, the worker's choice to consume the job itself—unremunerated—blocks his categorization as an employee for purposes of coverage under most protective legislation (*O'Connor v. Davis* [1997]).

The second frame focuses on economic loss to competitors as well as to workers: to what extent does the firm's compelled consumption policy create a captive branded market that confers an unfair advantage on the firm that deploys this strategy? These cases are typically litigated as unfair business practices cases, and the most appealing plaintiffs would be the firm's market competitors. Some workers have raised arguments regarding unfair advantage vis-à-vis competitors along with wage and hour claims, but it is difficult for courts to conceptualize the harm when the real parties in interest are not involved in the litigation. It is unlikely, however, that other firms in the same industry who also deploy look policies would seek to challenge them; the easier and less risky course is to emulate them. And even a court receptive to the argument—as was the court that oversaw settlement of the *Young v. Polo Retail* (2007) litigation, which settled for a mix of gift cards and cash—must still confront the employer's claim that its workforce willingly chose to purchase the branded products, an argument made all the more appealing by the fact that the workers were recruited on the sales floor from the consumer base.

Further, legal frames tend to focus on individual harm, ignoring the impact that obscuring work and workers has on workers as a class. Most obviously, substituting branded products or brand prestige for wages exerts a leveling-down effect on wages and labor standards across the industry, normalizing low wages and minimal fringe benefits. Though many aesthetic workers and brand representatives are class privileged (due in part to the selection bias created by hiring workers from the store's upscale customer base and preferring a class-privileged habitus [Williams and Connell 2010]), other mass market retailers such as Dillard's, J.C. Penney's, and Macy's employ workers who rely on those wages for subsistence. These firms conform their wages and benefits to those of the upscale retailers, even though their workers receive little brand prestige as a result of their association with the firm. This leveling-down (sometimes called the "Wal-Mart effect" in recognition of the phenomenon in low-wage, low-price retail sectors) impacts workers in the clothing retail sector as a class (Karjanen 2006).

More fundamentally, existing legal frames that turn on distinguishing compulsion from choice in the employment context do not respond at all to the effects on legal and political voice of labor policies that substitute brands for compensation. Compelled consumption policies require workers to marketize their identities to conform to the firm's brand as a condition of obtaining and retaining employment. When applied to shape appearance and self-presentation, these policies undermine the development of an authentic self, substituting in its place a literally branded identity. Dress, accessories, makeup, jewelry, and comportment are essential to how we form and enact our identities. By aligning the worker's identity almost completely with the firm's, the employer diminishes the psychological distance necessary for the development of independent agency. As Studs Terkel (1974) so eloquently put it, we become our jobs. Workers become more malleable, buying into a culture of submission and compliance in which compulsory consumption policies resonate with and reinforce their branded identities (Crain 2010; Williams and Connell 2010). Thus, the more powerful and prestigious the employer's brand and the more fully it is integrated with the firm's personnel policies, the more the compulsion is hidden. The labor is almost completely erased by the consumptive character of the jobs.

The youthful workers employed in aesthetic retail positions, campus brand representative jobs, and internships are particularly vulnerable to the brand's influence in identity formation because of their heightened concern about social conformity and peer acceptance. Moreover, their aspirations for work are powerfully influenced by their experience in early jobs. Employers shape workers' aspirations through job descriptions, hiring processes, and management policies that communicate expectations regarding the identity characteristics appropriate for workers in particular jobs (Schultz 1990; Williams and Connell 2010). Their on-the-job learning, then, encompasses more than skills: they absorb norms about what compensation is appropriate, what compliance is required, what level of control by the employer is acceptable, and what resistance will be tolerated.

The long-term effects of branding in personnel policy are subtle yet far reaching. The lack of psychological distance between the employee and the firm's brand diminishes the likelihood that branded workers will develop oppositional consciousness. They are less likely to organize a union, to file a lawsuit against the company, or to advocate for social and legal change (du Gay 1996; Webb 2006). Their identification with the brand ultimately erases their work and, along with it, their identity as workers. The political voice that workers might have had as a class has been erased. Indeed, the invisibility of consuming work becomes a politics of its own. Youthful workers come to see their choice of brand (and firm) as the remaining free space available to them, their route to participation in culture, society, and even the political world. Whether one approaches politics from a consumer frame or a class frame makes a world of difference, with implications for everything from jury duty to voting, but with particularly powerful implications for willingness to protest. When their jobs are constructed and experienced as hobbies rather than as real jobs, workers are able to "maintain a social fantasy that one floats above social class" (Bowers 2004; Williams and Connell 2010). No one is surprised or disturbed when the jobs do not yield a living wage. Thus, hiding the relations of production shields the industry and its practices from social and legal critique, reducing the possibilities for reform.

. . .

Consumption is a useful lens through which to examine the distinction between coercion and constraint because it is intuitively seen as the opposite of work—as work's reward, epitomizing choice and free will, the yin to work's yang. And consumers seem the quintessential non-employees, the third parties in the market triad of employer-worker-consumer. Thus, it is not surprising that work reframed as consumption and workers reconstructed as consumers exist outside the traditional wage–labor bargain that law recognizes as employment. But the law's narrow understanding of compulsion and choice misses the ways in which worker and firm interests in consuming work overlap and inter-sect, and it overlooks the implications that marketizing identity may have for the development of rights, consciousness, and political voice.

A firm with a powerful brand can hide work and erase workers by constructing the labor as consumption—whether of products and serv-ices (as in the case of retail workers subjected to compulsory consump-tion policies) or of a lifestyle or job itself (as in the case of campus brand representatives or interns). Because consumptive activities often (although not always) benefit workers as well as the firm, a more nuanced understanding of work that looks beyond the law's traditional compulsion/choice binary is necessary. In order to respond to the more fundamental effects of marketized identity on political voice and rights consciousness, the new frame should include consideration of what impact treating compelled consumptive activities as not-work has on workers as a class and on market competitors and what role it plays in shaping societal norms about work, identity, and voice.

NOTE

1. Even with significant clothing discounts, the amounts expended were not insignificant. A lead plaintiff in a wage lawsuit against Polo alleged that she spent more than $30,000 per year to purchase clothes to maintain a $22,000-per-year job (Cutler 2003).

REFERENCES

Aaker, David. 1991. *Managing Brand Equity: Capitalizing on the Value of a Brand.* New York: Free Press.

Allen, James B. 1966. *The Company Town in the American West.* Norman: University of Oklahoma Press.

Bean v. Hugo Boss Retail, Inc., No. 3:13-cv-05921 (N.D. Cal., Dec. 10, 2015).

Bell, Emily. 2011. "AOL + Huffington Post = Disaster?" *The Guardian,* Febru-ary 7. Retrieved November 11, 2014 (www.guardian.co.uk/commentisfree /cifamerica/2011/feb/07/huffington-post-aol).

Besen, Yasemin. 2006. "Exploitation or Fun? The Lived Experience of Teenage Employment in Suburban America." *Journal of Contemporary Ethnography* 35 (3): 319–40.

Bishop, Stewart. 2012. "NY Judge Axes HuffPo Bloggers' Pay Suit against AOL." *LAW 360*, March 30. Retrieved November 4, 2014 (www.law360 .com/articles/325292/).

Blumenstein, Rebecca, and Andrea Puchalsky. 1998. "The Real Reason People in Detroit Drive American Cars." *Wall Street Journal*, January 29, p. B1.

Bocock, Robert. 1993. *Consumption*. London: Routledge.

Bowers, Katherine. 2004. "The School of Cool." *Women's Wear Daily*, March 27, pp. 44, 187.

Braverman, Harry. 1974. *Labor and Monopoly Capital: The Degradation of Work in the Twentieth Century*. New York: Monthly Review Press.

Burmann, Christopher, and Sabrina Zeplin. 2005. "Building Brand Commitment: A Behavioural Approach to Internal Brand Management." *Journal of Brand Management* 12 (4): 279.

Corbin, David. 1981. *Life, Work, and Rebellion in the Coal Fields: The Southern West Virginia Miners, 1880–1922*. Urbana-Champaign: University of Illinois Press.

Crain, Marion. 2010. "Managing Identity: Buying into the Corporate Brand at Work." *Iowa Law Review* 95: 1179–1258.

Crain, Marion, and Dianne Avery. 2007. "Branded: Corporate Image, Sexual Stereotyping, and the New Face of Capitalism." *Duke Journal of Gender Law & Policy* 14: 13–124.

Cutler, Joyce E. 2003. "Three Retailers Sued for Requiring Employees to Wear Store's Clothes." *Daily Labor Report (Bureau of National Affairs)* 27: 8A.

du Gay, Paul. 1996. *Consumption and Identity at Work*. Thousand Oaks, CA: Sage.

EEOC v. Abercrombie & Fitch Stores, Inc., 731 F.3d 1106, 1109 (10th Cir. 2013).

Fagge, Roger. 1996. *Power, Culture and Conflict in the Coalfields, West Virginia and South Wales, 1900–1922*. Manchester, England: Manchester University Press.

Fair Labor Standards Act of 1938, ch. 676, 52 Stat. 1060, codified as amended at 20 U.S.C. §§ 201–219 (2011).

Ford, Kevin. 2005. *Brands Laid Bare: Using Market Research for Evidence-Based Brand Management*. Chichester, West Sussex, England: Wiley.

Glatt v. Fox Searchlight Pictures, Inc., 293 F.R.D. 516 (S.D.N.Y. 2013).

Glatt v. Fox Searchlight Pictures, Inc., 791 F.3d 376 (2d Cir. 2015).

Greenhouse, Steven. 2003a. "Chain in Accord on Workers' Required Clothes." *New York Times*, June 25, p. A16.

———. 2003b. "Going for the Look, but Risking Discrimination." *New York Times*, July 13. Retrieved on February 11, 2015 (www.nytimes.com /2003/07/13/us/going-for-the-look-but-risking-discrimination.html).

———. 2010. "Growth of Unpaid Internships May Be Illegal, Officials Say." *New York Times*, April 3, p. B1.

———. 2011. "Interns, Unpaid by a Studio, File Suit." *New York Times,* September 28, p. B3.

———. 2012. "Jobs Few, Grads Flock to Unpaid Internships." *New York Times,* May 6, pp. A1, A4.

Hallissey v. AOL, Inc., 99-CIV-3785, 2006 U.S. Dist. Lexis 12964 (S.D. N.Y. March 10, 2006).

Harquail, Celia V. 2006. "Employees as Inanimate Artifacts: Wearing the Brand." Pp. 161, 169 in *Artifacts and Organizations: Beyond Mere Symbolism,* edited by Anat Rafaeli and Michael G. Pratt. Mahwah, NJ: Erlbaum.

Holt, Douglas B. 2004. *How Brands Become Icons: The Principles of Cultural Branding.* Boston: Harvard Business School Press.

Howard v. Gap, Inc., No. C 06–06773 WHA, 2007 WL 1232050 (N.D. Cal. April 26, 2007).

Ind, Nicholas. 1997. *The Corporate Brand.* New York: New York University Press.

Karjanen, David. 2006. "The Wal-Mart Effect and the New Face of Capitalism: Labor Market and Community Impacts of the Megaretailer." Pp. 143–62 in *Wal-Mart: The Face of Twenty-First-Century Capitalism,* edited by Nelson Lichtenstein. New York: New Press.

Kirchner, Lauren. 2011. "AOL Settled with Unpaid Volunteers for $15 Million." *Columbia Journalism Review,* February 10. Retrieved November 6, 2014 (www.cjr.org/the_news_frontier/aol_settled_with_unpaid_volunt.php?page=all).

Klein, Naomi. 1999. *No Logo: Taking Aim at the Brand Bullies.* New York: Picador.

Korczynski, Marek, and Ursula Ott. 2004. "When Production and Consumption Meet: Cultural Contradictions and the Enchanting Myth of Customer Sovereignty." *Journal of Management Studies* 41 (4): 575–99.

Lindeman, Teresa F. 2005. "When Workers Wear Their Paycheck. " *Pittsburgh Post-Gazette,* June 12, p. C1.

Merrick, Amy. 2003. "Low-Wage Employees Challenge Dress Codes as Coercive and Costly." *Wall Street Journal,* Classroom ed., May.

Miller, Vanessa. 2011. "Student Ambassadors Push Brands on UI Campus Using Social Media." *Business 380,* November 10. Retrieved February 11, 2015 (web.archive.org/web/20111113160955/http://www.business380.com/2011/11/10/student-ambassadors-push-brands-on-ui-campus-using-social-media/).

Mitchell, Collin. 2002. "Selling the Brand Inside." *Harvard Business Review* 80 (1): 99–126.

Montgomery, David. 1979. *Workers' Control in America: Studies in the History of Work, Technology, and Labor Struggles.* Cambridge, UK: Cambridge University Press.

O'Connor v. Davis, 126 F.2d 112 (2d Cir. 1997).

Olivarez-Giles, Nathan. 2011. "Disgruntled Writer Sues Huffington Post and AOL for Piece of $315-Million Sale Price." *Los Angeles Times,* April 12. Retrieved November 7, 2014 (latimesblogs.latimes.com/technology/2011/04/huffington-post-writer-sues-the-huffington-post-aol.html).

Paul Swanson, 36 L.A . 305 (Gochnauer, Arb. 1961).

Perlin, Ross. 2011. *Intern Nation: How to Earn Nothing and Learn Little in the Brave New Economy.* London: Verso.

Pettinger, Lynne. 2005. "Friends, Relations and Colleagues: The Blurred Boundaries of the Workplace." *Sociological Review* 53 (2): 37–55.

Postigo, Hector. 2009. "America Online Volunteers: Lessons from an Early Co-production Community." *International Journal of Cultural Studies* 12 (5): 451–69.

Quart, Alissa. 2003. *Branded: The Buying and Selling of Teenagers.* Cambridge, MA: Perseus.

Schor, Juliet B. 2000. *Do Americans Shop Too Much?* Boston: Beacon Press.

Schultz, Vicki. 1990. "Telling Stories about Women and Work: Judicial Interpretations of Sex Segregation in the Workplace in Title VII Cases Raising the Lack of Interest Argument." *Harvard Law Review* 103: 1749–1843.

Schweitzer, Sarah. 2005. "Building a Buzz on Campus: Companies Enlist Students to Pitch Products to Their Peers." *Boston Globe,* October 24. Retrieved February 11, 2015 (www.highbeam.com/doc/1P2-7937131.html).

Siegel, David. 2001. *The Great Tween Buying Machine: Marketing to Today's Tweens.* Ithaca, NY: Paramount Marketing.

Singer, Natasha. 2011. "On Campus, It's One Big Commercial." *New York Times,* September 11, Sunday Business section, pp. 1, 4.

Smith, Adam. 1985. *An Inquiring into the Nature and Causes of the Wealth of Nations,* edited by Richard F. Teichgraeber. New York: Modern Library.

Spint et al. v. Swarovski North America, Ltd., No. 2:13-cv-03265 (C.D. Cal. Aug. 14, 2013).

Strasburg, Jenny. 2005. "Gap Close to Settling: Clothing Voucher Handout Proposed in Dress Code Suit." *San Francisco Chronicle,* January 28. Retrieved February 11, 2015 (www.sfgate.com/business/article/Gap-close-to-settling-Clothing-voucher-handout-2735163.php).

Tasini v. AOL, Inc., et al., 851 F.Supp.2d 734 (S.D.N.Y. 2011).

Tennessee Coal, Iron & Railroad Co. v. Muscoda Local No. 123, 321 U.S. 590, 598 (1944).

Terkel, Studs. 1974. *Working: People Talk about What They Do All Day and How They Feel about What They Do.* New York: Pantheon.

Vanderford, Richard. 2012. "Prospects Dim for $105M HuffPo Bloggers Pay Suit." *LAW360,* March 9. Retrieved November 7, 2014 (www.law360.com/articles/317668/).

Veblen, Thorstein. 1899. *The Theory of the Leisure Class: An Economic Study of Institutions.* New York: Macmillan.

Walker, Rob. 2008. *Buying In: The Secret Dialogue between What We Buy and Who We Are.* New York: Random House.

Walling v. Portland Terminal Co., 330 U.S. 148 (1947).

Wang v. The Hearst Corp., 293 F.R.D. 489 (S.D.N.Y. 2013).

Webb, Janette. 2006. *Organisations, Identities and the Self.* New York: Palgrave Macmillan.

Williams, Christine L., and Catherine Connell. 2010. "'Looking Good and Sounding Right': Aesthetic Labor and Social Inequality in the Retail Industry." *Work & Occupations* 37 (3): 349–77.

Young v. Polo Retail, LLC, 2007 U.S. Dist. LEXIS 27269 (N.D. Cal. Mar. 28, 2007).

Zatz, Noah D. 2011. "The Impossibility of Work Law." Pp. 234–55 in *The Idea of Labour Law,* edited by Guy Davidov and Brian Langille. New York: Oxford University Press.

Zatz, Noah D., and Eileen Boris. 2014. "Seeing Work, Envisioning Citizenship." *Employee Rights and Employment Policy Journal* 18: 95–109.

CHAPTER 14

Conclusion

WINIFRED R. POSTER, MARION CRAIN,
AND MIRIAM A. CHERRY

The foregoing chapters have explored how the following conditions structure labor as invisible even when it occurs within the context of formal paid employment: when work occurs in a technological platform that splits or masks workers' tasks, when the bodies doing the work are hidden through the physical organization of work time and space, when the work performed is seen as a voluntary or chosen activity, and when the work occurs within a social interaction that appears as leisure. Crossing the occupational hierarchy and spectrum from high to low, professional to manual, we have suggested a conceptualization of invisible labor designed to broaden our understanding of labor in the contemporary era.

By linking the microsetting of the workplace to broader regional and global environments, authors in this volume have situated the invisibility of labor in the systemic context of contemporary employment regimes. Our analysis proposes that what is hidden is neither necessarily the work itself nor the worker but rather the *management practices that are exploitative of the worker*. These management practices may serve to *hide the work from the worker, the workers from the consumer, or the work from the law*. Sometimes this action is accomplished through aesthetic labor and branding; sometimes it is done through technology, software, and digital platforms; sometimes it is accomplished through deception, whether of the worker or the consumer or both.

Furthermore, as Arlie Hochschild suggests in the foreword, what may also be invisible is the broader production system that undergirds the contemporary information technology, service, and consumer economies (e.g., all that goes on "behind the scenes"). Sometimes this invisibility is due to recent developments in the technological infrastructure of global business practice. In what Aneesh Aneesh (2009) calls "algocracy," many tasks previously done by supervisors or human resource professionals are now embedded within computer programs. Software code and algorithms perform "automatic management"—from the recruitment of employees to performance assessments and the distribution of incentives (Irani 2013). At other times, however, the submerging of production is a result of changing organizational models such as the rise of mega–retail establishments, which take production off the streets and into big-box stores. Alternatively, this submerging is a deliberate practice by firms and industries that seek to hide the nature of the labor process itself, including the location of the work; the conditions under which it is done; and the ethnicity, race, and nationality of the workers.

We turn, finally, to the future directions that this expanded inquiry might take and to its policy implications.

FUTURE DIRECTIONS

There are many forms of invisible labor that deserve attention; we make no attempt to catalog all of them here. Instead, we seek to gesture toward some of the possibilities. Much work has been done and remains to be done to capture fully the many forms that invisible labor might assume within the paid labor force.

One important and growing category of invisible labor is *care work*. Arlie Hochschild (2012) illuminates how care work has been turned into a market activity. Services for families, children, seniors, and selves are increasingly outsourced to a growing cadre of professionals and corporations. The most personal features of family life now "require the help of paid experts[:] . . . love coaches and wedding planners, birth surrogates and counselors, paid friends and mourners-for-hire" (p. 12). Ironically, this movement of tasks to the public sphere has made formerly unpaid and unrecognized labor "visible" and remunerable. Hochschild questions, however, the costs for families and society of this "commodification of intimate life" (p. 12).

Peggie Smith (2007, 2013) addresses a critical issue involving care work: the invisibility within the law regarding services for seniors. The senior population of the United States has grown at a staggering rate, from 4 percent to 13 percent over the last century. As Evelyn Glenn

(2010) noted in her book *Forced to Care*, the average length of time spent caring for elders in a typical family (eighteen years) now exceeds that of caring for children (seventeen years). The aging process often involves coping with a range of chronic health problems as well as social isolation. In turn, the number of positions for home health-care workers is increasing, and a majority of these workers are women of color. Smith (2007) reveals how this occupation is classified differently under the law (i.e., as a domestic service) than other types of jobs are, meaning that these workers qualify for fewer legal protections. Moreover, the state has begun recruiting family members for this role—so that they become *paid* caregivers for their own infirm kin—thus blurring "the boundaries between private and public, home and market, and family and work" (p. 1841).

Another significant area that deserves future study is sexual orientation and identity work. Queer employees invest a considerable amount of invisible labor into acting straight and downplaying their homosexuality (Giuffre, Dellinger, and Williams 2008; Williams, Giuffre, and Dellinger 2009). Currently, no federal law prevents an employer from firing an employee for being gay, and only approximately half of states offer gay employees any redress. Organizations have traditionally favored heterosexual identities in employee policies, programs, and benefits that often cover only nuclear families; events and rituals that celebrate heterosexual dating and marriage; and informal conversations and interactions that may stigmatize homosexuality. Consequently, even in gay-friendly workplaces, gay/lesbian/transsexual employees may feel pressured to alter how they look, act, and work.

Along these lines, Devon Carbado and Mitu Gulati (1999) developed the concept of *identity work* to expose the labor that minority employees are often forced to perform—outside the normal boundaries of their jobs—to counteract systems of racism, sexism, xenophobia, and heteronormativity. Identity work refers to the subtle performative activities that outsiders of a given workplace feel pressured to enact in order to emulate the behaviors of insiders. This effort amounts to a great deal of "extra" labor that subordinate groups of employees must do in order to fit in as they attempt to counter stereotypes in their everyday work routines.

For example, people of color may be encouraged to display subtle cues to show that they can act like whites: laughing alongside coworkers at racist humor, denying that they speak a foreign language associated with their background, participating in informal after-work activities, or lunching with whites rather than socializing with people of their own ethnicity. Such gestures serve as informal meaning systems that "signal that [the workers] are hardworking, collegial, team oriented, trustworthy" (Carbado and Gulati 1999: 1263). In these ways, minorities of many kinds (racial, gender, sexual orientation, and others) must work harder to demonstrate objective skills in their jobs *and, in addition,* to perform identity work to prove their subjective qualifications. Future studies on different groups of workers (for example, gays, lesbians, transgendered persons, and immigrants) will be helpful in elucidating the dynamics of contemporary invisible labor.

Finally, invisibility will be better understood through continued study of *globalized labor*. Despite appearances of "weightlessness" (Huws 1999), the information economy is predicated on the physical labor of hardware manufacturing—often done by women of color. To underscore this point, Lisa Nakamura (2014) reminds us that the labors behind our digital products are hidden both temporally and spatially. She has uncovered the surprising case of Native American women who were recruited to build microchips for Fairchild, a company instrumental in the building blocks of Silicon Valley: semiconductors. At "a pivotal moment of computing history" (p. 938) in the 1960s, this company relocated its factory to a Native American reservation, where it could take advantage of cheap land, the flexible labor of Native women, and exemptions from federal minimum-wage laws. As a provocative juxtaposition to this nearsourcing strategy, Fairchild was also one of the first companies to outsource its labor internationally.

Five decades later, the globalized electronics manufacturing industry in China is massive, fueled largely by contracts from the United States. Taiwanese outsourcer Foxconn, which makes iPhones and other products for Apple, is the tenth largest employer in the world, with 1.2 million workers (Chan, Pun, and Selden 2013; Qiu, Gregg, and Crawford 2014). In China its facilities sometimes hire hundreds of thousands of workers at a single site under conditions that have been called "military-style." Each year, approximately forty thousand workers break or lose a finger. Conditions of this labor were publicly quiet for many years. It was only when seventeen workers committed suicide on the premises of the manufacturing plants in 2010 that American consumers started to take notice of the workers who made their Apple devices.

These hidden forms of labor for the global economy are important points for future study. Aside from electronics, this includes the everyday work of construction, mineral extraction, farming, and garment production (Goria 2014). Rarely acknowledged, for instance, is the dirty work that occurs in the aftermath of these processes—the labor of "cleaning up after globalization" (Aguiar and Herod 2006) by international hotel cleaning staff, waste disposal employees, and recycling workers (Jackson 2013). These labors sustain the worldwide movement of goods, services, and finance. However, they are rarely seen by those who benefit from them (especially in the Global North)—until catastrophes occur, like fires and building collapses of garment factories in Bangladesh (Cherry and Poster, forthcoming) and chemical spills by multinational firms in Bhopal, India (Goria 2014).

IMPLICATIONS

The question remains why we should care about invisible labor at all. What is the significance of its invisibility? What should the policy response to it be? Our authors express a range of views.

Agency and Exploitation. Several authors point out that invisibility can have ambiguous implications because it raises provocative questions about free will and exploitation: To what degree is such labor consensual, and when does it become exploitative? If exploitation of a vulnerable population is part and parcel of the business model, as it may be, for example, in breastaurants or unpaid internships, should the policy response be to treat the invisible labor as we would any other labor and to regulate it accordingly? What if the workers themselves do not view themselves as exploited and eschew traditional forms of compensation for their labor?

Some of our authors suggest that we consider shifting the frame to focus on the injuries produced and reproduced in society and for workers as a class, even if these particular workers do not view themselves as harmed or exploited. Marion Crain (chapter 13) asks what impacts may be accomplished by reframing work not as leisure (from which employers profit surreptitiously) but as work that is freely chosen and beneficial to the individual. Does the erasure of work make the assertion of workplace rights or collective mobilization more difficult and thus harm workers as a class? If so, what regulatory moves might be most effective in reducing risk and harm at the institutional level? Christine Williams and Catherine Connell (chapter 10) suggest that the answer may not be as simple as treating the invisible labor as work and compensating workers for performing it.

Benefits of Invisibility. In some ways, of course, invisible labor can be an asset for workers, even leading to monetary payoffs. Employees can capitalize on invisible labor, if only indirectly: crowdworkers can reap a payoff from taking on online tasks; service workers can position themselves for modeling opportunities and earn higher tips by physically presenting themselves in certain ways; minority lawyers can attain promotions and partnerships by emulating white behaviors; interns can advance in the workplace by affiliating with prestigious brands.

There are nonmaterial payoffs as well. Workers can use their ability to be "unseen" as a strategy for autonomy, agency, and avoiding sanctions (Anteby and Chan 2013). Making oneself invisible on a temporary basis may help to balance work and family obligations. In this volume, Eileen Otis and Zheng Zhao (chapter 8) reveal the benefits of invisibility on the shop floor. Workers duck into corners (out of range of surveillance cameras) to hide their bodies and take breaks. Likewise, they control the visibility of the products they place in the store (withholding the new fruits and keeping the old ones on display) to save their own labor in restocking.

Social benefits, as well, can accrue from invisible labor. Adam Arvidsson and colleagues (chapter 12) find that through the work of self-branding on Internet employment Web sites, knowledge workers express a capacity for cooperation with one another (passing on contacts, sharing opportunities, and so on). These activities may have the potential to generate collective values for supportive coworking spaces online in the future.

Drawbacks of Invisibility. At the same time, our authors see a number of serious problems with invisible labor.

First, invisibility has *physical* effects on workers and their bodies. If workers are symbolically invisible, then no one sees their health or working conditions. The farmworkers Evan Stewart (chapter 7) describes routinely carry hundred-pound bags, risk exposure to toxic pesticides, and endure repeated falls out of the trees from which they pick fruit. In the ultimate irony, Otis and Zhao's service employees—who work stocking food on shelves—end up going hungry and underfed due to their low wages and chaotic schedules.

Second, invisibility also has *material* effects on wages and benefits. Employers are squeezing workers in the interests of lean production. This process is also lowering the standards for the wider industry as some forms of invisible labor normalize low pay and lack of benefits for a range of jobs (the so-called "Wal-Mart effect"). With interns, as Crain discusses, employers are shifting the costs of training, which were once integrated into the employment contract, onto employees. With retail workers, as Williams and Connell (chapter 10) illustrate, employers are substituting for actual wages what are essentially invisible rewards: discounts on the goods they sell. The ultimate example of a bad impact is layoffs. Automation, as Winifred R. Poster (chapter 5) discusses, can displace service workers altogether. A lingering question is what happens to the remaining employees: will these processes have an effect on the wages of nonautomated workers?

Third, invisibility may have *symbolic and psychic effects* that are personal and intimate for the employee. Many scholars document an increasing anxiety and fear among employees due to the lack of security in current labor regimes (Gregg 2011). There are cognitive costs, especially for employees, who lose an understanding of their role in the labor process and their connection to the work. With some types of virtual work, such as crowdsourcing and gamification, employees may be uninformed about how their labor contributions will be used or what the end result or product might be. Invisibility can be mentally draining. Our authors show how corporations are extracting the subjective, intangible features from workers—their emotional capacities to convey a brand, to relay sexuality, or to provide a mood through their language. This labor can be dehumanizing, in effect "creating a nonperson" (Goffman 1974; Star and Strauss 1999).

Fourth, invisibility feeds *legal disempowerment,* as alluded to earlier. Chapters by our legal scholars especially emphasize how the lack of recognition of a particular activity as work (for example, gamified labor) or a category of people as workers (for example, the disabled) prevents workers from seeking legal redress. Many of our authors call for changes in the legal system to facilitate rights-claiming. Furthermore, some invisible workers are caught between competing legal policies. Undocumented employees, as an example, experience mixed messages from *labor laws* that protect workers regardless of immigration status versus *immigration laws* that forbid them from working in the United States (Garcia 2012).

For victims of labor trafficking, in particular, these effects can spill over into many aspects of their lives (Owens et al. 2014). Not only do they face complications over their documentation status, but they live in fear of abuse and retaliation from their captors. Family members may have to maintain the silence and cover of their status as trafficking victims. Even after escaping these situations, victims report financial ruin due to wage theft by and debt to recruiters. They also face a lag time of years in receiving assistance from state agencies because of delays in temporary visas and a system unfamiliar with trafficking. Many have residual psychological problems, including anxiety, lack of ability to build trust, and posttraumatic stress disorder.

Fifth, invisibility clearly has implications for *worker mobilization*. Discussions of housework as work have recounted how invisible labor has disenfranchised and isolated women politically. Invisibility makes it difficult to imagine becoming an agent of one's own life. In turn, these barriers to individual agency cascade onto and inhibit group mobilization. As Williams and Connell show in chapter 10, invisible labor can channel resistance energies into self-loathing. Retail workers "censure themselves for not fitting the aesthetic requirements of the job . . . instead of protesting illegal job discrimination" (p. 207). Furthermore, invisibility has structural consequences for movement organizing. Stewart shows how a "persistent creation of public presence" (Miraftab 2012: 1219) has been a key factor of successes in prior immigrant labor movements (p. 132). Without this visibility, workers are unable to appeal for the popular support that is needed to leverage influence over employers and the state.

Finally, invisibility may *depress political voice within democracy*. If work is central to citizenship, then to be a fully participating citizen, one must perform visible work. Research shows that unemployed individuals do not fully exercise their political capacities relative to those who are employed. Further, when workers experience tyranny daily on the job, they come to accept or even exercise tyranny elsewhere. By contrast, workers who are union members are more likely to be politicized externally.

In sum, we do not mean to oversimplify the dynamics or implications of invisibility. Likewise, we do not offer invisibility as a stand-in for more complex dynamics of the labor process: stigmatization, disrespect, alienation, subadequate remuneration, underprotection by the law, disempowerment, and so on. In fact, our aim is to complicate the idea of invisibility and explore its synergies with these various forms of labor degradation.

Assessing the Trade-Offs. Invisibility has complicated implications for workers. Clearly, there are trade-offs as to what invisibility means in the labor process. The experiences of people of color in professional work are a case in point, as studies by Adia Harvey Wingfield (2012) and those with her colleague John Harvey Wingfield (2014) have so astutely shown. Hypervisibility can be simultaneously helpful and harmful for black male employees in predominantly white workplaces. On one hand, they experience far less tolerance for mistakes than their white counterparts do. On the other hand, hypervisibility also facilitates the receipt of social support from blacks at lower levels of the organization and outside the firm. Similarly, Rosabeth Kanter's (1993) classic study of women in male-dominated corporate settings found that hypervisibility often leads to experiences of tokenism, defining women as interlopers in the workplace and saddling them with the responsibility to represent their gender. Yet the opposite experience—of invisibility—can be problematic as well for women working as secretaries and corporate wives, undervalued and often poorly remunerated.

In short, as Susan Leigh Star and Anselm Strauss (1999) observe: "On the one hand, visibility can mean legitimacy, rescue from obscurity or other aspects of exploitation. On the other, visibility can create reification of work ... [and] opportunities for surveillance ... or come to increase group communication and process burdens" (pp. 9–10). Along these lines, some of our authors (like Miriam A. Cherry, chapter 4) argue that the impact of invisibility depends on how it is deployed through technology. Outcomes are dependent upon the "discretion, autonomy, and power over one's resources" with which visibility is structured (Star and Strauss 1999: 24). For Otis and Zhao, the lines between visibility and invisibility are porous, and workers move between spaces depending on their immediate needs and their interests in gaining control of the labor process.

This research prompts many questions: Under what conditions is visibility or invisibility problematic? For whom is the visibility or invisibility problematic—management, customers, and/or workers? Attention to the interactivity of these viewerships will be key in future studies. Indeed, our analysis would be much easier if invisibility applied to only one of these groups at a time. Many of the existing studies adopt this strategy, considering invisibility from one angle alone (for instance, in the way that aesthetic labor is unseen by management). Yet, as mentioned in the introduction, we argue that labor is very often invisible to many groups *simultaneously*. When it is invisible to managers, it is also invisible to workers, and vice versa. College students see being a brand ambassador as a voluntary and enjoyable leisure activity, as Marion Crain (chapter 13) illustrates, *and at the same time,* their roommate-consumers see their suggestions to shop at Victoria's Secret as originating from friends (rather than from a commercial actor engaged in advertising). In turn, it is easier for employers to subpay for those services and easier for brand ambassadors to be effective in marketing the brands.

Looking at invisibility through the prism of single sets of actors, therefore, would miss this complexity. For this reason, we encourage a view of invisibility as an interactive dynamic in which multiple viewpoints of labor feed off one another. Our analysis is richer for considering these multiple angles.

Finally, since the authors in this volume study work and workers in distinct places and geographic locales, we hope that future research will consider how these processes operate in varying occupations and national contexts.

Making Labor Visible: Why Visibility Matters. Our authors argue that despite the potential costs, we should strive to make invisible labor visible. For many, making work visible serves as a critical first step toward legal regulation, rights creation, or law reform.

Indeed, there are many promising examples of worker mobilization and regulatory changes to expose and recognize previously invisible forms of labor. For example, the Writers Guild of America gained credit for television and movie writers after two decades of organizing, permitting their names to be seen (literally) on the screen and providing them remuneration in the form of residuals (Fisk 2011). Aesthetic laborers in Australia have achieved gains through "anti-lookism" legislation that legally prohibits discrimination against "height, weight, size, or other bodily characteristics, including attributes such as hair length or colour" (Warhurst et al. 2012: 78). Crowdworkers have won a lawsuit in California requiring firms to recognize them as remunerable and state-protected "employees" rather than as exploitable "contract workers" (Cherry and Poster, forthcoming). And recent mobilizing by the Service Employees International Union (SEIU) has resulted in bargaining agreements at several universities for adjunct faculty, who teach at a fraction of the wages of regular faculty, without benefits or job security and often without acknowledgment in university official publications or on university Web sites.

It is inspiring that, at a time of unprecedented decline in unionization, many of the largest and most successful labor campaigns have been launched by people of color. These actions, in turn, have helped to expose the invisible labor of Latinos, African Americans, Asian Americans, and others. An example is Justice for Janitors, which unionized 90 percent of janitors, mostly Latino/a and female, in Los Angeles in the 1990s (Savage 2006). Continuing efforts have been waged by Mexican janitors and street vendors in Silicon Valley (Zlolniski 2006) and by

Latino gardeners in Los Angeles (Huerta and Morales 2014). Such campaigns often owe much of their success to mobilizing strategies based on deep connections and personal networks within Latino immigrant communities.

Likewise, the Workplace Project in New York has achieved some of the most extensive state-based labor protections for immigrant workers (Gordon 2009). Their combined strategies of collective action and legal advocacy have shed light on the dispersed sweatshops that are hidden among suburban sprawl and small businesses, rather than collected in a single factory site or retail establishment.

Through the Chicago Workplace Collaboration, African American workers in Illinois have agitated to uncover the concealed racial and gender discrimination in temporary staffing agencies (Evans 2016). Some employers rely on temp agencies as a way to "contract out" their discriminatory practices so they do not directly violate employment laws. Some make explicit requests to staffing firms for workers of a particular ethnicity or gender, or else use a set of code words (for example, *vanilla cupcakes* for whites, *number2s* for blacks, *number3s* for Latinos, or *heavy lifters* for men). Organizers sought to pass legislation requiring temp agencies to report the race and gender of applications, making employment processes more transparent and discrimination more easily recognized.

One of the most stunning examples of unmasking invisible labor is an exposé by the *New York Times* of abuses in nail salons in New York City (Nir 2015). This report shed light on a litany of hidden discriminations within interactive work that is otherwise highly visible: paying below minimum wage or not all; verbal and physical abuse by employers; health problems from dangerous exposure to toxic chemicals; and a blatant ethnic caste systems dividing Koreans, Chinese, Nepalese, Latina, and other women workers. Within one day of the release of the print edition of the article, the governor of New York established a task force to do salon-by-salon checks and promised to enforce penalties on firms that failed to pay back wages. Within six months, state legislation on nail salons was achieved (Gourarie 2015). Included among the measures was a requirement that employers post a worker "Bill of Rights," explaining in six languages that it is illegal to hire workers without paying them.

All of these cases illustrate how the invisibility of labor—whether concerning the worker, the work process, or mechanisms of discrimination—is being contested through collaborative efforts of workers, consumers, legal advocates, and state officials.

Even in the absence of legal action, there are pragmatic benefits to making work visible. Managers and firms might better support the labor tasks that employees are doing, making them more productive and efficient. Technology might be deployed to facilitate their work (Nardi and Engeström 1999). Understanding the nature of invisible labor might reveal weaknesses in current management strategies that are designed to respond to such work, helping to produce more effective management policies. And mobilizing and empowering workers—goals common to all our chapter authors—depend upon full worker consciousness not only of the benefits received through work but also of the losses sustained.

Ultimately, we hope that our exploration of invisible labor provokes further thought about what can be done to create and protect the public goods of a shared commons for all who work.

REFERENCES

Aguiar, Luis L.M., and Andrew Herod, eds. 2006. *The Dirty Work of Neoliberalism: Cleaners in the Global Economy*. Malden, MA: Blackwell.

Aneesh, Aneesh. 2009. "Global Labor: Algocratic Modes of Organization." *Sociological Theory* 27 (4): 347–70.

Anteby, Michel, and Curtis K. Chan. 2013. "Being Seen and Going Unnoticed: Working under Surveillance." Paper presented at the Annual Meeting of the American Sociological Association, August 13, New York.

Carbado, Devon W., and Mitu Gulati. 1999. "Working Identity." *Cornell Law Review* 85: 1259–1308.

Chan, Jenny, Ngai Pun, and Mark Selden. 2013. "The Politics of Global Production: Apple, Foxconn, and China's New Working Class." *Asia-Pacific Journal: Japan Focus* 11 (32): 1–10.

Cherry, Miriam A., and Winifred R. Poster. Forthcoming. "Crowdwork, Corporate Social Responsibility, and Fair Labor Practices." In *Research Handbook on Digital Transformations*, edited by Xavier F. Olleros and Majlinda Zhegu. Cheltenham, UK: Edward Elgar.

Evans, Will. 2016. "When Companies Hire Temp Workers by Race, Black Applicants Lose Out." *Reveal*, January 6, pp. 1–22 (www.revealnews.org).

Fisk, Catherine. 2011. "The Role of Private Intellectual Property Rights in Markets for Labor and Ideas: Screen Credit and the Writers Guild of America, 1938–2000." *Berkeley Journal of Employment and Labor* 32 (2): 215–68.

Garcia, Ruben J. 2012. *Marginal Workers: How Legal Fault Lines Divide Workers and Leave Them without Protection*. New York: New York University Press.

Giuffre, Patti, Kirsten Dellinger, and Christine L. Williams. 2008. "'No Retribution for Being Gay': Inequality in Gay-Friendly Workplaces." *Sociological Spectrum* 28: 254–77.

Glenn, Evelyn Nakano. 2010. *Forced to Care: Coercion and Caregiving in America*. Cambridge, MA: Harvard University Press.

Goffman, Erving. 1974. *Frame Analysis*. Cambridge, MA: Harvard University Press.

Gordon, Jennifer. 2009. *Suburban Sweatshops: The Fight for Immigrant Rights*. Cambridge, MA: Harvard University Press.

Goria, Corrine, ed. 2014. *Invisible Hands: Voices from the Global Economy*. San Francisco: McSweeney's.

Gourarie, Chava. 2015. "The Everyday Effects of *The New York Times*' Nail Salon Exposé." *Columbia Journalism Review*, December 2, pp. 1–11.

Gregg, Melissa. 2011. *Work's Intimacy*. Cambridge, England: Polity Press.

Hochschild, Arlie Russell. 2012. *The Outsourced Self: Intimate Life in Market Times*. New York: Macmillan.

Huerta, Alvaro, and Alfanso Morales. 2014. "Formation of a Latino Grass-roots Movement." *Azltan* 39 (2): 65–94.

Huws, Ursula. 1999. "Material World: The Myth of the 'Weightless Economy.'" *Socialist Register* 3 (2): 29–55.

Irani, Lilly. 2013. "The Cultural Work of Microwork." *New Media & Society* (November): 1–20.

Jackson, Steven J. 2013. "Rethinking Repair." Pp. 221–40 in *Media Technologies: Essays on Communication, Materiality and Society*, edited by Tarleton Gillespie, Pablo J. Boczkowski, and Kirsten A. Foot. Cambridge, MA: MIT Press.

Kanter, Rosabeth Moss. 1993. *Men and Women of the Corporation*. New York: Basic Books.

Miraftab, Faranak. 2012. "Emergent Transnational Spaces: Meat, Sweat and Global (Re)Production in the Heartland." *International Journal of Urban and Regional Research* 36 (6): 1204–22.

Nakamura, Lisa. 2014. "Indigenous Circuits: Navajo Women and the Racialization of Early Electronic Manufacture." *American Quarterly* 66 (4): 919–41.

Nardi, Bonnie A., and Yrjö Engeström. 1999. "A Web on the Wind: The Structure of Invisible Work." *Computer-Supported Cooperative Work* 8: 1–8.

Nir, Sarah Maslin. 2015. "The Price of Nice Nails." *New York Times*, May 10, pp. 1, 22–24.

Owens, Colleen, et al. 2014. *Understanding the Organization, Operation, and Victimization Process of Labor Trafficking in the United States*. Boston: Urban Institute, Northeastern University.

Qiu, Jack Linchuan, Melissa Gregg, and Kate Crawford. 2014. "Circuits of Labor: A Labor Theory of the iPhone Era." *Triple C: Capitalism, Communication, & Critique* 12 (2): 564–81.

Savage, Lydia. 2006. "Justice for Janitors: Scales of Organizing and Representing Workers." *Antipode* 38 (3): 645–66.

Smith, Peggie R. 2007. "Aging and Caring in the Home: Regulating Paid Domesticity in the Twenty-First Century." *Iowa Law Review* 92: 1835–1900.

———. 2013. "Who Will Care for the Elderly? The Future of Home Care." *Buffalo Law Review* 61: 323–43.

Star, Susan Leigh, and Anselm Strauss. 1999. "Layers of Silence, Arenas of Voice: The Ecology of Visible and Invisible Work." *Computer-Supported Cooperative Work* 8: 9–30.

Warhurst, Chris, Diane van den Broek, Richard Hall, and Dennis Nickson. 2012. "Great Expectations: Gender, Looks and Lookism at Work." *International Journal of Work Organisation and Emotion* 5 (1): 72–90.

Williams, Christine L., Patti Giuffre, and Kirsten Dellinger. 2009. "The Gay-Friendly Closet." *Sexuality Research & Social Policy* 6 (1): 29–45.

Wingfield, Adia Harvey. 2012. *No More Invisible Man: Race and Gender in Men's Work*. Philadelphia: Temple University Press.

Wingfield, Adia Harvey, and John Harvey Wingfield. 2014. "When Visibility Hurts and Helps: How Intersections of Race and Gender Shape Black Professional Men's Experiences with Tokenization." *Cultural Diversity and Ethnic Minority Psychology*, August 11, pp. 1–8.

Zlolniski, Christian. 2006. *Janitors, Street Vendors, and Activists: The Lives of Mexican Immigrants in Silicon Valley*. Berkeley: University of California Press.

About the Editors and Contributors

EDITORS

MARION CRAIN is Vice Provost, Wiley B. Rutledge Professor of Law, and Director of the Center for the Interdisciplinary Study of Work and Social Capital at Washington University in St. Louis. She also holds courtesy appointments with the Brown School of Social Work and the Program on Women, Gender, & Sexuality Studies. Before joining Washington University's faculty, she was the Paul Eaton Professor of Law at the University of North Carolina in Chapel Hill, where she directed the Center on Poverty, Work and Opportunity. Her scholarship examines the relationships among gender, work, and class status with a particular emphasis on collective action and labor relations. Her interdisciplinary publications include *Ending Poverty in America: How to Restore the American Dream* (with John Edwards and Arne L. Kalleberg, New Press, 2007) and *Working and Living in the Shadow of Economic Fragility* (with Michael Sherraden, Oxford University Press, 2014).

WINIFRED R. POSTER teaches at Washington University in St. Louis, with recent visiting positions at the University of Hyderabad, Linköping University, the University of Paderborn, the University of Toronto, and the University of California Irvine. Her interests are in digital globalization, feminist labor theory, and Indian outsourcing. For the past two decades, she has been following high-tech labor from the United States to India, both in earlier waves of computer manufacturing and software, and later waves of back-office work. Her research explores national identity management, reversals of work time to the night, and the uses of emotion to sell credit and debt. A forthcoming edited volume with Kiran Mirchandani, *Borders in Service: Enactments of Nationhood in Transnational Call Centers* (University of Toronto Press), documents the spread of this work beyond India to other regions of the Global South. Her latest research is on crowdsourcing, the labors of surveillance, the gendering of cybersecurity, and the automation of virtual receptionists.

MIRIAM A. CHERRY is Professor of Law at Saint Louis University School of Law. Her scholarship is interdisciplinary and focuses on the intersection of technology and globalization with business, contract, and employment law topics. In her recent work, Professor Cherry analyzes virtual work, crowdwork, the on-demand economy, and corporate social responsibility. Professor Cherry's articles will appear or have appeared in the *Northwestern Law Review, Minnesota Law Review, Washington Law Review, Illinois Law Review, Georgia Law Review, Alabama Law Review, Maryland Law Review,* and *Tulane Law Review,* among others. Professor Cherry attended Dartmouth College and Harvard Law School. After graduation from law school, Professor Cherry clerked for Justice Roderick Ireland, Chief Justice of the Supreme Judicial Court of Massachusetts, and then for Judge Gerald Heaney of the U.S. Court of Appeals for the Eighth Circuit. She is an elected member of the American Law Institute.

CONTRIBUTORS

ADAM ARVIDSSON teaches sociology at the State University of Milano, where he also directs the Center for Digital Ethnography (www.etnografiadigitale.it). Presently Adam works with the EU-funded project P2PValue, which analyzes forms of value creation in networks of peer production. He has published on the creative industries, new forms of freelance or precarious labor, and the political economy of information in general as well as the history of marketing and consumer culture. Overall, Adam's main research interest is the emergence of new forms of value creation in the information economy. Adam has written a number of scientific articles and is the author of *Brands: Meaning and Value in Media Culture* (Routledge, 2006) and *The Ethical Economy: Rebuilding Value after the Crisis* (with Nicolai Peitersen, Columbia University Press, 2013).

DIANNE AVERY is Professor Emerita at SUNY Buffalo Law School, The State University of New York. She received her BA from Duke University and a master of arts in teaching from Wesleyan University. A summa cum laude graduate of SUNY Buffalo Law School, she practiced law in Buffalo and taught at University at Buffalo as a lecturer before joining the law faculty. There, Professor Avery taught labor law, employment law, employment discrimination law, and sexual harassment law, and also served as Vice Dean for Academic Affairs. She was a Visiting Professor at Cornell Law School. Her scholarly publications have focused on labor law, labor history, employment discrimination law, women's rights, and gender stereotypes. As a member of the Labor Law Group, she coauthored three editions of the group's casebook, *Employment Discrimination Law: Cases and Materials on Equality in the Workplace.* Her current research is on sexualized labor in frontline service jobs.

CAROLINA BANDINELLI is a PhD candidate at the Centre for Cultural Studies, Goldsmiths College (London). Her thesis analyzes the discourses and practices of social entrepreneurship and innovation. In particular, it focuses on the forms of politics, ethics, and economy that produce and are produced by social entrepreneurial discourses. She is Associate Lecturer at Goldsmiths College and London College of Communication.

JOHN W. BUDD is Professor of Work and Organizations in the University of Minnesota's Carlson School of Management, where he holds the Industrial Relations Land Grant Chair and is the Director of the Center for Human Resources and Labor Studies. He is a graduate of Colgate University and earned a PhD in economics from Princeton University. Professor Budd is the author of *Employment with a Human Face: Balancing Efficiency, Equity, and Voice* (Cornell University Press, 2006); *Labor Relations: Striking a Balance* (McGraw-Hill/Irwin, 2012); *Invisible Hands, Invisible Objectives: Bringing Workplace Law and Public Policy into Focus* (with Stephen Befort, Stanford University Press, 2009); *The Thought of Work* (Cornell University Press, 2011); and numerous journal articles. Professor Budd has also been Director of Graduate Studies for the University of Minnesota's graduate programs in Human Resources and Industrial Relations.

CATHERINE CONNELL is an Assistant Professor of Sociology at Boston University. Her research and teaching address the intersections of gender, sexuality, and occupations/organizations. She is the author of *School's Out: Gay and Lesbian Teachers in the Classroom* (University of California Press, 2014). In a recent *Signs* article, she, with coauthor Ashley Mears, develops the concept of display work and discusses its implications for understanding gender and labor ("The Paradoxical Value of Deviant Cases: Toward a Gendered Theory of Display Work"). Her current research is focused on gender and sexuality ideology within the U.S. military in the post–Don't Ask, Don't Tell context.

ALESSANDRO GANDINI is a sociologist and a lecturer in the Media Department at Middlesex University, London. He is also a researcher at the Centre for Digital Ethnography, University of Milan. His research interests mainly concern the intersection of social media and work in the digital economy. His first book is *The Reputation Economy: Understanding Knowledge Work in a Digital Society* (Palgrave, 2016).

ARLIE HOCHSCHILD is Professor of Sociology Emerita at the University of California–Berkeley. Her nine books include *The Managed Heart: The Commercialization of Human Feeling, The Second Shift: Working Couples and the Revolution at Home, The Time Bind: When Home Becomes Work and Work Becomes Home, The Outsourced Self: Intimate Life In Market Times,* and *So How's the Family? And Other Essays.* Based on five years of fieldwork in southwest Louisiana, her newest book, *Strangers in Their Own Land* (New Press, 2016), explores what the Tea Party advocates she came to know "want to feel" about America and its political leaders. This she traces to a class conflict unacknowledged by the Right and located elsewhere by the Left. It evokes powerful feelings of lost identity and honor, she argues, and strong feelings about the imagined "proxy advocates" of each side in this war, the free market and government.

EILEEN OTIS is Associate Professor of Sociology at University of Oregon. She was a Postdoctoral Fellow at the Harvard University Fairbank Center and also held the position of Assistant Professor of Sociology at Stony Brook University. Her scholarship examines the gender and class dynamics of new labor practices within China's emergent urban service sector. Her book, titled *Markets and Bodies: Women, Service Work and the Making of Inequality in China* (Stanford University Press, 2011), examines gendered organizational processes that transform resource inequalities into interactive and relational hierarchies in China's consumer service workplaces. Professor Otis has also published in the *American Sociological Review, Politics and Society, Positions, American Behavioral Scientist,* and *Qualitative Sociology.* Her research has been recognized with awards from the Asia/Asian-American and the Sex and Gender sections of the American Sociological Association and from Sociologists for Women in Society.

ELIZABETH PENDO is Joseph J. Simeone Professor of Law at Saint Louis University School of Law and a member of the William C. Wefel Center for Employment Law and the Center for Health Law Studies. She teaches disability law, bioethics, and civil procedure. Her scholarly publications focus on disability law, policy, and experience in the health-care system and the workplace, with a particular interest in legal and social meanings of disability. Her current research is on disability disparities in health and health-care. For the past five years, Professor Pendo has served as the first Vice Dean at Saint Louis University School of Law. She is an elected member of the American Law Institute, and has received several awards for teaching, research, and leadership. She received her BA from UCLA and her JD from UC Berkeley School of Law. She practiced law in New York prior to entering academia.

RENÉE SKEETE is an advanced doctoral student in sociology at Georgia State University and a Fellow at the Oak Ridge Institute for Science and Education (ORISE). She is currently working in the Community Guide Branch at the Centers for Disease Control and Prevention (CDC) on systematic reviews of community-level public health interventions. Her scholarship explores social class and the ways housing and the built environment impact the quality of life, particularly for marginalized populations. Her interests include urban communities, public housing, housing policy, neighborhood transitions, social interaction in neighborhoods, and the black middle class.

EVAN STEWART is a doctoral candidate in sociology at the University of Minnesota. His research focuses on political culture across a range of institutional and community contexts, including public opinion on contentious policy issues, religious prejudice and symbolic boundaries, and the relationship between political judgment and secular identity formation. He is an Edelstein Fellow with the American Mosaic Project and an Interdisciplinary Doctoral Fellow with the Center for the Study of Political Psychology, and his dissertation research examines the political impact of the growing nonreligious population in the United States. He holds a BA in political theory from Michigan State University and an MA in sociology from the University of Minnesota.

CHRIS WARHURST is Professor and Director of the Institute for Employment Research (IER) at the University of Warwick in the United Kingdom. He is also a Trustee and Board Member of the Tavistock Institute in London and an Associate Research Fellow of the Centre on Skills, Knowledge and Organisational

Performance at the University of Oxford. Earlier he was Professor of Work and Organisational Studies at the University of Sydney and Founding Director of the Scottish Centre for Employment Research in Glasgow. His research focuses on job quality, skills, and aesthetic labor. As Director of IER, Chris Warhurst is motivated by wanting to see better scientific and policy understanding of work and employment. With colleagues, he has published a number of books, including *Workplaces of the Future* (1998); *The Skills That Matter* (2004); *Work Less, Live More?* (2008); and *Are Bad Jobs Inevitable?* (2012). He has been an expert adviser to the United Kingdom, Scottish, and Australian governments as well as to the Scottish Living Wage campaign and the OECD's Local Economic and Employment Development program. He is currently an adviser to Oxfam's Decent Work program.

CHRISTINE WILLIAMS is Professor of Sociology and the Elsie and Stanley E. (Skinny) Adams, Sr. Centennial Professor in Liberal Arts at the University of Texas at Austin. She writes on gender, race, and class inequality in the workplace. She has also studied sexuality, homophobia, and sexual harassment in a wide variety of workplace settings. Her most recent publications analyze gender inequality and diversity culture in the oil and gas industry. In her 2006 book, *Inside Toyland: Working, Shopping, and Social Inequality,* she exposes, through an examination of low-wage retail work, how the social inequalities of gender, race, and class are embedded within consumer culture. She has also written extensively about men and women in nontraditional (gender atypical) occupations, such as men in nursing and women in the U.S. Marine Corps. Dr. Williams edited the journal *Gender & Society* from 2003 to 2006. In 2014, she was awarded a lifetime achievement award from the American Sociological Association for her contributions to understanding women in society.

ADIA HARVEY WINGFIELD is Professor of Sociology at Washington University in St. Louis. She specializes in research that examines the ways intersections of race, gender, and class affect social processes at work. In particular, she is an expert on the workplace experiences of minority workers in predominantly white professional settings, and specifically on black male professionals in occupations where they are in the minority. Dr. Wingfield has lectured internationally on her research in this area, and her work has been published in numerous peer-reviewed journals, including *Social Problems, Gender & Society,* and *American Behavioral Scientist.* She is also a contributing writer for *The Atlantic.* Professor Wingfield is the author of several books, most recently *No More Invisible Man: Race and Gender in Men's Work* (Temple University Press, 2012), and has won multiple awards from sections of the American Sociological Association.

ZHENG ZHAO earned his PhD in sociology at Stony Brook University in 2011. Zheng's dissertation focused on labor, economic inequality, and market transition during China's Economic Reform since 1978. As part of his dissertation research, Zheng worked in a Wal-Mart store in Changchun, China, for four weeks in the summer of 2007. Zheng is currently based in Austin, Texas, where he works as a Senior Programmer Analyst at Pharmaceutical Product Development.

Index

Abercrombie & Fitch (A&F), 24, 197–98, 208–9, 263; salesworkers, 10
absent and disappeared workers: online, 10
Acker, Joan, 48, 51, 62
ADA. *See* Americans with Disabilities Act of 1990
ADAAA. *See* Americans with Disabilities Act Amendments Act of 2008
Adler, Paul, 242, 246
Adorno, Theodor, 134
advanced economies: dominance of service jobs, 217
aesthetic consistency: as fashion retail policy, 264
aesthetic labor, 6, 21–22; and body image, 203; and body labor, 194–95; concept of, 185; and consumer fetishism, 201, 207, 211; and creation of organization's image, 220; and emotional labor, 194–95; and employment discrimination, 211; and job segregation, 201; logic of, 205–6; and social inequality, 194; and management of workers' corporeality, 215–16; and invisibility of working class in service jobs, 214; as generated by organizational processes, 193; as part of value (and profit) creation, 258; reinforcing class inequality, 194; in retail work, 150; sexualized, 173–76; social consequences of, 200–212; of UK hospitality workers,

22; in upscale retail establishments, 193–200, 211; and visibility of body in work, 214, 228
aesthetic labor in services: as deliberate employer strategy, 220; requirements for workers, 210
aesthetics: as framework for job segregation, 205–6
aesthetic skills training: for the working class, 231–32
aesthetic workers: and class privilege, 272
Airus Media, 92, 94
algocracy, 280
Alice (virtual receptionist), 91–92, 92*fig.*
All-China Federation of Unions, 164–65, 165n2
Amazon.com, xiv, 19–20; hidden warehouse workers, 74–76, 81
America Online (AOL). *See* AOL.
American Farmer, The (Clark), 142*fig.*
American self-help movement: influence on self-branding, 247
Americans with Disabilities Act Amendments Act of 2008 (ADAAA): and broad definition of disability, 120
Americans with Disabilities Act of 1990 (ADA), 117, 127; employment provisions of, 115; recent amendments, 125–26; scope and purpose, 122; Title I, 119
Anderson, Elijah, 51